# I Am the Heart

## A Commentary on Liber LXV
## Chapter 1

J. Daniel Gunther

WENNOFER HOUSE

Καὶ λογιοῦμαι ἐφ' ὑμᾶς λογισμὸν εἰρήνης, καὶ οὐ κακά, τοῦ δοῦναι ὑμῖν ταῦτα. Καὶ προσεύξασθε πρός με, καὶ εἰσακούσομαι ὑμῶν. Καὶ ἐκζητήσατέ με, καὶ εὑρήσετέ με· ὅτι ζητήσετέ με ἐν ὅλῃ καρδίᾳ ὑμῶν, καὶ ἐπιφανοῦμαι ὑμῖν.

*LXX,* ΙΕΡΕΜΙΑΣ *XXIX, 11-13.*

# I Am the Heart

## A Commentary on Liber LXV

## Chapter 1



# Ever the Heart

## An Essay on the Symbolism of The Heart of Blood



ISBN 978-0-9995936-8-4



Cover Art: *Afloat in the Tomb* by Elena Bortot,
after a study by J. Daniel Gunther.

# Contents


| | |
|---|---|
| Acknowledgments | ix |
| Foreword | xi |
| Abbreviations Utilized | xv |
| List of Illustrations | xvi |
| PROLOGUE - The Serpent Archetype | 1 |
| § 0: INTRODUCTION | 67 |
| LIBER LXV - Chapter I | 79 |
| § A: EXORDIVM | 83 |
| § B: LAPIDES | 119 |
| § C: ASCENSVS | 163 |
| § D: FALLAX IMAGO | 171 |
| § E: NOCTIS LAVDATIO | 179 |
| § F: COR VNIVERSVM | 191 |
| § G: NVNTIVS | 203 |
| § H: CEDERE | 221 |
| § J: PARABOLA DE NOVA NATIVITATE | 225 |
| § K: VINDEMIA | 241 |
| Ever the Heart | 253 |
| CHAPTER I | 257 |
| CHAPTER II | 265 |
| CHAPTER III | 279 |
| BIBLIOGRAPHY | 293 |

# Acknowledgments

I WOULD LIKE TO OFFER MY SINCERE THANKS to Ian Mercer for his masterful typesetting of the Egyptian Hieroglyphics utilizing the program and font package by *JSesh*, incremented with numerous special glyphs which he created to match those on the ancient texts. Ian also verified the accuracy of the transcribed Hieroglyphic texts, word for word, character for character, with painstaking comparison to the original inscriptions. The difficulties encountered in this task can only be fully appreciated by those who have personally contended with damaged papyri, painted or engraved texts weathered by the centuries, or the occasional careless script of a slovenly scribe. Any words of thanks to Ian are really inadequate to express how grateful I am for the service of his scholarship, dedication and perseverance with such an onerous task.

Additionally, I have been very fortunate to have the assistance of two gifted scholars: Matthew Andrews and Gordan Djurdjevic. Matthew translated Latin, Classical Greek and French texts, proofread the entire manuscript numerous times, and engaged in many profitable conversations that improved this work. Gordan generously translated the Sanskrit texts and provided important information concerning traditional Sanskrit texts as well as ensuring consistency with modern transliteration conventions.

The script of the extensive Hebrew translations was painstakingly verified against the original texts by Jay Lee. Since Jay can actually read Hebrew, his contribution extended well beyond the basic task of proofreading and lightened my own load considerably. I truly am very grateful to have had his assistance, as well as the enjoyment of his well-known irrepressible humor.

Other texts were verified and carefully proofread by Gwen Gunther.

Verification and Proofreading of the quotes from the Holy Books was provided by Dathan Biberstein, who meticulously scrutinized every word and punctuation mark to insure infallible adherence to the Class A texts. Additional proofreading was provided by Gwen Gunther, Santo Rizzuto and Brendan Walls.

Ancient Egyptian Research assistance was undertaken by Brendan Walls, as well as executing the arduous task of proofreading the typeset Egyptian hieroglyphics and transliterations. To have one assistant who can actually read ancient Egyptian is an enormous benefit; to have two such as Ian and Brendan who can do so, is a gift.

Matthieu Kleemann shared the fruits of his substantial knowledge of Art, providing needed images, and engaged in stimulating conversations concerning the selection of images for this book. I am also very grateful for his careful proofreading of the manuscript.

Nancy Wasserman drew a lovely detailed colour image from an Egyptian coffin for which no suitable photograph existed and provided her original painting of a vignette from the 3rd Hour of *The Egyptian Book of Pylons*.

Over the past few years, Jasenka Avram produced a number of unique pieces of art for my books and the slide demonstrations that accompany my lectures, in service to the Great Work. Some of those works appear here also. Words cannot express the depth of my gratitude.

Elena Bortot also provided a number of beautiful custom illustrations created specifically for this book as well as the Cover Illustration. She also executed the digital composition and typography for the entire book, and her skill and enthusiasm made our task a pleasant one.

Ian Mercer also drew several new detailed illustrations of the Tree of Life and associated diagrams.

Hymenaeus Beta, Frater Superior O.T.O., kindly provided approved images of the Crowley/Harris Tarot Cards and permission for their reproduction in this book.

Special thanks to Stephen J. King. His sound advice, and consistent encouragement are deserving of more than a few words of thanks.

Lastly, I want to thank all of the individuals world-wide who requested and sponsored my original lectures on this topic, welcoming my wife and myself into their fraternal communities.

The book production was conceived and directed by Gwen Gunther, whose vision and skill brought it to fruition. She, as always, is a light in the darkness, and the love of my life.

All translations of Egyptian, Coptic, Koine Greek and Hebrew are my own if not otherwise indicated, and I assume full responsibility for their content.

J. Daniel Gunther
September 28, 2023 e.v.

# Foreword

Do what thou wilt shall be the whole of the Law.

In 1918 Aleister Crowley wrote to his magical son, Frater Achad (Charles Stansfeld Jones): "My Son, neglect not in any wise the study of the Writings of Antiquity, and that in the original Language. For by this thou shalt discover the History of the Structure of thy Mind ... [and] come to the true Comprehension of thine own Nature, and that of the whole Universe."[1] It is a lesson Frater Achad took to heart, though perhaps not right away. More importantly, it is a lesson written for all Thelemites. While those who are newly introduced to Thelema learn quickly about its reverential attitude toward infinite Space, not as many are quick to pick up on its reverential attitude towards Time. The ability to stretch one's consciousness back through the history of humanity is central to initiatic success in the A∴A∴ To remember one's past incarnations is not an incidental but central task, for *The Book of the Law* teaches that Human Beings are immortal Stars.[2] To eventually recognize oneself not as an embodied person, subject to life and death, but rather as the Universe itself is fundamental to Thelema.[3] The stories of the past are therefore not the stories of others – they are our stories. By engaging with and internalizing the Writings of Antiquity, we *remember*.

Ten years ago Crowley's quotation above began to stir within me the desire to learn Latin. When I later read J. Daniel Gunther's first two books and saw how he used the Writings of Antiquity in their original languages to understand Thelema, the Holy Books, and the timeless process of Initiation, I knew I had to start learning.[4] I bought a Latin school book. Later I took courses at university, where I also picked up Ancient Greek. This led to graduate programs in Cambridge, England and in Princeton, USA. The Writings of Antiquity led me on many unexpected journeys, but those across land and sea were the smallest of them. Far greater were the journeys in the spirit: to engage

---

1 Crowley, *Liber Aleph vel CXI: The Book of Wisdom or Folly*, (93 Publishing, 1991).

2 Crowley, *Magick, Book 4*, rev. 2nd ed., (Weiser, 1997): "There is no more important task than the exploration of one's previous incarnations."

3 Crowley, in *The Equinox* IV:2, (Weiser, 1998): "The Thelemite does not 'suffer death.' He is eternal and perceives Himself the Universe."

4 Gunther, *Initiation in the Aeon of the Child* (Ibis, 2009) and *The Angel & The Abyss* (Ibis, 2014).

with the Ancients in their own words, imbibing their spirit and feeling their rhythms, strikes with a hard blow at the fetters of the present world in a way no meditation or ritual could. One discovers that this moment in time – the here and now – no longer appears more real than any other bygone age. In fact it begins to seem far less real, for the cumulative weight of the centuries of the Ancient World far outweighs the present moment, like a tidal wave bearing down on a small island.

The Holy Books of Thelema not only make constant reference to the World of Antiquity, they are suffused to the point of being written in the language itself of the Ancient World. They are, as it were, written by someone who lived in those ancient times, and saw through ancient eyes. If the Holy Books truly are holy, it is because they reflect greater truths than can be understood by one person, one culture, or one time. They represent humanity as a whole. If the claim that they were dictated by the Secret Chiefs is true, then they were given to those of us of today by Those who have been with us always: watching, waiting, judging, and enlightening. It is essential therefore to begin to think like an Ancient to understand these books. Daniel and Gwen Gunther understand this, as the reader will discover. Their work is defined by the desire to explain symbols from Antiquity by the Writings of Antiquity.

A good example of this kind of engagement from Daniel Gunther's Commentary is found in the chapter entitled *Nuntius*, where he discusses a verse from *Liber LXV* concerning the "petal of amaranth, blown by the wind from the low sweet brows of Hathor." We first gain insight into the amaranth by learning what the word meant to the Ancient Greeks; then we learn about the significance of Hathor to the Egyptians and how that was later interpreted by the Hermetic Order of the Golden Dawn; next we get an original translation from a stela from the $18^{th}$ Dynasty in order to better contextualize the "low sweet brows" of Hathor, before finally seeing how this same symbol shows up in other Holy Books. This kind of *tour de force* exploration is the typical treatment Daniel gives to nearly every verse throughout this book.

In Gwen Gunther's Essay, her treatment of the Eleusinian Mysteries in the Essay's second chapter is particularly notable for its engagement with Antiquity. Coming as it does at the center of her Essay it is like the base upon which she has built her thematic pyramid. Throughout her Essay we feel the Ancient World buzzing along the threads of Initiatic Archetypes, like vibrating powerlines emanating from an electrical generator. That generator seems to be hidden in those ancient groves of Eleusis, tucked away in the heart of her Essay.

Crowley rightly pointed out that the etymology of the word *education* means "leading out." He then added wisely that this is not the same thing as "stuffing in."[5] This book, dazzling in all its detail, is always trying to "lead out" the meanings hidden in *Liber LXV*. The byways down which the authors lead us are never pursued in an attempt to "stuff in" more information – like a man pulling at the threads of a sweater, the authors patiently pull out all the details they can from *Liber LXV*. Yet once we digest it all, we should return to *Liber LXV* for ourselves and let it speak to us, delighting in its song.

Readers may wonder about the best way to approach this book. Although the traditional cover-to-cover method will no doubt serve well, I would also propose another way. Gwen Gunther's Essay on the Heart comes at the end of the book, yet we might better imagine it conceptually as the center of the work. It is the Heart around which Daniel Gunther's work wraps around like the coils of a Serpent, continually building upon, and squeezing out, the material she presents. For this reason the reader will benefit from pausing midway through Daniel's commentary to read Gwen's Essay, before then returning to Daniel's narrative. Another piece of advice is for those readers unaccustomed to footnotes: they should not feel obligated to read each and every one of them on the first reading. They might find it useful to read through the main body of text while reading only those footnotes they feel are especially interesting, before returning to all of them more carefully on the second reading.

I met the Gunther couple for the first time in 2016 e.v., at a lecture given by Daniel at the Athenæum in downtown Indianapolis, a beautiful 19th-century building whose historic charm suited the atmosphere of the lecture. His ability to connect with Ancient Egypt was vividly clear from the beginning. As he explained the meaning and pronunciation of certain Egyptian words, his eyes would glint with pleasure as the strange words pinched and popped out of his mouth. He spoke the Egyptian words like a man who had lived in that faraway world. Maybe he had.

I met Gwen there too. Though she wasn't lecturing, the intuitive among us went over to talk to her, sensing correctly that she would say much that was left unsaid in Daniel's lecture. Her motto seemed to be "Knock, and it shall be opened unto you" – and she always had a great deal to open, and much to say. For many readers this book will seemingly be their first introduction to her work. The truth is that anyone familiar with the books of J. Daniel Gunther has already enjoyed the fruit of her spiritual insight, for she has been Daniel's muse for many years, inspiring and guiding his work.

---

5 Crowley, *Magick Without Tears* (Thelema Publishing Company, 1954), Chapter 72.

The symbols of *Liber LXV* are explored in this book through living experience and passion. Although the details of the work are abundant and scholarly, the reader feels genuine passion throughout. Gwen Gunther's work on the Heart evinces her personal affinity for the theme, while Daniel Gunther's consuming passion for Ancient Egypt shines on nearly every page. This is not a book of mere scholarship – it is the work of two Adepts sharing what they have discovered on the Path.

Aleister Crowley received the first chapter of *Liber LXV* on the evening of October 30, 1907 e.v. He described the experience in his diary as "a feeling that V.V.V.V.V. was in His Samadhi, and writing by my pen."[6] From then on until his death forty years later, he would consider this text to be at the heart of the religion of Thelema, along with the other texts received from V.V.V.V.V. For a book in which the heart symbol features so prominently, it is fitting to have a loving couple, united as one, share their initiated perspective on this central material. For the heart is a symbol of union and of coming together. Let us join them, therefore, in the pages that follow, taking a sip from the Cup they offer. As one reads the Holy Books today and sees the kind of work they inspire, one begins to sense that V.V.V.V.V. is still in His Samadhi even now, waiting for the rest of us to join Him.

Love is the law, love under will.

Matthew Andrews
Princeton,
February 1, 2024 e.v.

---

6 Crowley, 1907 Diary (Harry Ransom Center, The University of Texas at Austin). Samadhi was Crowley's preferred term for ecstatic mystical experience.

# Abbreviations Utilized

| | |
|---|---|
| Bauer | *A Greek-English Lexicon of the New Testament and Other Early Christian Literature, trans. William F. Arndt & F. Wilbur Gingrich (1979)* |
| BD | *The Egyptian Book of the Dead* |
| BM | *The British Museum* |
| CDD | *Chicago Demotic Dictionary, Janet H. Johnson (ed.)* |
| CDME | *A Concise Dictionary of Middle Egyptian, R.O. Faulkner (1962)* |
| Černý | *Coptic Etymological Dictionary, Jaroslav Černý (1976)* |
| Crum | *A Coptic Dictionary, W. E. Crum (1979)* |
| CT | *The Ancient Egyptian Coffin Texts* |
| DeBuck | *The Egyptian Coffin Texts, 7 Vols., Adrian DeBuck (1935-1961)* |
| Gesenius | *Gesenius' Hebrew and Chaldee Lexicon of the Old Testament Scriptures (1978)* |
| Jastrow | *A Dictionary of the Targumim, the Talmud Babli and Yerushalmi, and the Midrashic Literature. (1903), Marcus Jastrow* |
| JEA | *Journal of Egyptian Archaeology* |
| JNES | *Journal of Near Eastern Studies* |
| L&S | *A Latin Dictionary, Lewis and Short (1945)* |
| LSJ | *A Greek-English Lexicon, Liddell-Scott-Jones (1968)* |
| Liber AL | *Liber AL vel Legis Sub Figurâ CCXX. The Book of the Law.* |
| Liber VII | *Liber Liberi vel Lapidis Lazuli - Sub Figurâ VII* |
| Liber LXV | *Liber Cordis Cincti Serpente - Sub Figurâ* אדני |
| Liber LXVI | *Liber Stellæ Rubæ Sub Figurâ LXVI* |
| Liber Porta Lucis | *Liber Porta Lucis Sub Figurâ X* |
| Monier-Williams | *A Sanskrit-English Dictionary, Monier Monier-Williams (1960)* |
| OLD | *Oxford Latin Dictionary (1968)* |
| PT | *The Pyramid Texts Die Altaegyptischen Pyramidtexte, 3 Vols, Kurt Sethe (1908-1922)* |
| RT | *Recueil de Travaux relatifs a la philologie et a l'archaeologie Egyptiennes et Assyriennes. (Referenced by Volume, 1881-1915)* |
| Skeat | *Concise Etymological Dictionary of the English Language, Walter W. Skeat, (1885)* |
| Vycichl | *Dictionnaire Étymologique de la langue Copte, Werner Vycichl (1983)* |
| Vision & the Voice | *Liber XXX Aerum vel Sæcvli Sub Figurâ CCCCXVIII* |
| Wb | *Wörterbuch der Aegyptischen Sprache, 7 Vols., Adolf Erman and Hermann Grapow, (1950-1971)* |

# List of Illustrations

## PROLOGUE: The Serpent Archetype


Figure P1 'Crucified Serpent', *Clavis Artis Verginelli Rota V2.030 (circa late 17th century e.v.)*

Figure P2 'Seth Spearing Apep in the Boat of Ra', *after the Papyrus of Herweben (21st Dynasty), Gwen Gunther*

Figure P3 'He who Walks', *The Tenth Hour of the Duat, The Sarcophagus of Sety I (19th Dynasty)*

Figure P4 'Ra as a Cat, Slaying Apep', *BD Spell, The Egyptian Book of the Dead. Facsimiles of the Papyri of Hunefer, Anhai, Kerasher and Netchemet, Plate 11 (1899 e.v.)*

Figure P5 'Stele of Ankhefenkhonsu II', *Istanbul 190 (26th Dynasty)*

Figure P6 'The Destruction of Leviathan', *(1865 e.v.), Gustave Doré*

Figure P7 'The Capture of Leviathan', *Herrad of Landsberg, Hortus Decliciarum, (12th Century e.v.)*

Figure P8 'The Fall of Man', *(1508-1512 e.v.), Michelangelo*

Figure P9 'The Temptation of Eve', *(1870 e.v.), John Spencer-Stanhope*

Figure P10 'Lilith', *(1887 e.v.), John Collier*

Figure P11 'The Kiss of the Enchantress', *(circa 1890 e.v.), Isobel Lilian Gloag*

Figure P12 'Onocentauros', *De Animalium Proprietate (16th Century e.v.), Manuel Philes*

Figure P13 'The Seven-headed Dragon & Seven-headed Beast of the Sea from Revelation', *Tapisserie de l'apocalypse, Angers, France (circa 1377-1382 e.v.)*

Figure P14 'The Head of Medusa', *(1617-1618 e.v.), Peter Paul Rubens*

Figure P15 'Shield Head of Medusa', *(1597 e.v.), Michelangelo Merisi da Caravaggio*

Figure P16 'The Amphisbaena', *(circa1230-1240 e.v.), Rochester Bestiary*

Figure P17 'Kṛṣṇa Attacked by Kāliya', *Voyages aux Indes orientales et a la Chine, Vol. 1, plate 46 (1782 e.v.)*

Figure P18 'The Son of Earth', *The Egyptian Book of the Dead. The Papyrus of Ani, Plate 27 (1894 e.v.)*

Figure P19 'Butchers', *The Eleventh Hour of the Duat, The Sarcophagus of Sety I, (19th Dynasty)*

Figure P20 'The Goddess Wadjyet', *Panthéon Égyptien Collection des Personnages (1823 e.v.)*

Figure P21 'Millions & Millions & Millions of Years', *after the coffin of Sepi (12th Dynasty), Nancy Wasserman*

Figure P22 'Meḥen Encircling the Cabin of the Sun God', *after The Book of Pylons, The Third Hour, tomb of Rameses I (KV 16, 19th Dynasty), Nancy Wasserman*

Figure P23 'Mereseger', *Votive Stele of Neferabu, Deir el-Midina, (19th Dynasty), colour enhanced by J. Daniel Gunther*

Figure P24 'Pyramidal Peak Overlooking Deir al-Medinah'

Figure P25 'Renenutet in the Robe of Glory', *after the tomb of Rameses III (20th Dynasty), J. Daniel Gunther*

Figure P26 'Stele of Mutneferet', *Inv. S.6138. Museo Egizio (19th Dynasty)*

Figure P27 'Renenutet Suckling a Child', *Tomb of Haemhat, Overseer of Granaries, during the reign of Amenhotep III, Atlas zur altägyptischen Kulturgeschichte, Vol. I, Plate 198 (1923 e.v.)*

Figure P28 'Weret-Hekau, Great of Magic', *J. Daniel Gunther*

Figure P29 'Pharaoh Presenting Milk to Weret-Hekau', *Mistress of Crowns on the head of the gods and the Lord of All, the Eye of Ra, the Temple of Hibis in El Khārgeh Oasis, Part III, The Decoration, Plate 21 (1953 e.v.)*

Figure P30 'Nehebu-Kau', *J. Daniel Gunther*

Figure P31 'Moses & the Brazen Serpent', *engraving after Ferrau Fenzoni, (1562-1645 e.v.)*

Figure P32 'Asclepius, God of Healing & Medicine', *Museum of Epidaurus Theatre*

Figure P33 'John Churchill Company Printer's Mark', *(1861 e.v.)*

Figure P34 'Serpent and Dove Coat of Arms - Unitarian Church of Transylvania & Hungary'

Figure P35 'Aion', *Mithraeum of C. Valerius Heracles & Sons, 190 CE., Franz Cumont, Textes et Monuments Figurés Relatifs Aux Mystères de Mithra, Vol. 1 (1899 e.v.)*

Figure P36 'Mithra as the Leontocephalic Kronos', *(1926 e.v.), J. Augustus Knapp*

Figure P37 'Ouroboros on the Shrine of Tutankhamun', *(18th Dynasty)*

Figure P38 'Harpocrates Within an Ouroboros', *Papyrus of Herweben, (21st Dynasty)*

Figure P39 'Ouroboros', *Parisinus Graecus 2327 Folio 279 (1478 e.v.)*

Figure P40 'Emblemata Fourteen', *Atalanta Fugiens (1618 e.v.), Michael Maier, colorized by J. Daniel Gunther*

Figure P41 'Lion-serpent Ouroboros', *Azoth, Sive Aurelliae Occultate Philosophorum (1613 e.v.)*

Figure P42 'Image of Saturn as Cycles of the Year', *Le Imagini Degli Dei Degli Antichi (1608 e.v.)*

Figure P43 'Emblem CXXXII', *Omnia Andreae Alciati V.C. Emblemata (1577 e.v.)*

Figure P44 'Ouroboros as the Life Cycle', *A Collection of Emblemes (1635 e.v.), George Wither*

Figure P45 'Ouroboros as the Cycle of Time', *A Collection of Emblemes (1635 e.v.), George Wither*

Figure P46 'Ouroboros with Transpierced Head', *Anatomia Auri (1628 e.v.), Johann Daniel Mylius*

Figure P47 'The Crowned Ouroboros', *Uraltes Chymisches Werk (1760 e.v.), Abraham Eleazar*

Figure P48 'Speech of the Enlightened & Unenlightened Soul', *Theosophia Reformata, Vol. 3 (1630 e.v.), Jacob Bohme*

Figure P49 'He Should be Killed Wisely, because Death will Reveal Him', *Dyas Chymica Tripartita (1625 e.v.), Johann Grassoff*

Figure P50 'Ouroboros Surrounding Mount Meru Resting upon the World Turtle', *L'Univers, Histoire et Description de Tous le Peuples, Inde (1845 e.v.)*

Figure P51 'Viṣṇu Reclining upon Ananta Śeṣa', *Calcutta (1890 e.v.)*

Figure P52 'Emblemata Fifty', *Atalanta Fugiens (1617 e.v.), Michael Maier, colorized by J. Daniel Gunther*

Figure P53 'Purify Her', *Uraltes Chymisches Werk (1735 e.v.), Abraham Eleazar*

Figure P54 'Divide Her', *Uraltes Chymisches Werk (1735 e.v.), Abraham Eleazar*

Figure P55 'After Dividing, Cleanse Again', *Uraltes Chymisches Werk (1735 e.v.), Abraham Eleazar*

Figure P56 'Hercules', *Mercurius Philosophorum & Sol Vulgaris, De Goude Leeuw, (1671 e.v.), Goosen van Vreeswyk*

Figure P57 'How to Draw the Life from Gold by Fiery Sword & Secret Fire', *De Goude Leeuw, (1671 e.v.),*

Figure P58 'So the Old Man Spoke to Me all these Words', *Sal Tartari, Ignis Secretus & Mercurius Philosophorum, De Goude Leeuw (1671e.v.), Goosen van Vreeswyk*

Figure P59 'Men See & Despise my Old Serpent', *Mercurius Philosophorum & Sol Vulgaris, De Goude Leeuw (1671e.v.), Goosen van Vreeswyk*

Figure P60 'A Dragon Does not Die without its Brother & Sister', *Distillatio & Sublimatio, Elementa Chemiae (1718), Johann Conrad Barchusen*

## § 0: INTRODUCTION

Figure 01 'The Tree of Life', *Ian Mercer*

Figure 02 'Afloat in the Tomb', *Elena Bortot after a study by J. Daniel Gunther*

Figure 03 'Title Page of Liber LXV', *1909 e.v. edition of ΘΕΛΗΜΑ*

Figure 04 'Iamblichus Chalcidensis', *De Divinatione & Magiciis Præstigiis (1615 e.v.)*

Figure 05 'The Five Lower Sephiroth with Elemental Correspondences', *J. Daniel Gunther*

Figure 06 'The Sigil of A∴A∴'

Figure 07 'The Tree of Life with H.G.A., Magister, Adept & Scribe or Servant', *J. Daniel Gunther*

Figure 08 'The Lamen of V.V.V.V.V.'

Figure 09 'The Tree of Life with H.G.A., Magister, Neshamah & Ruach', *J. Daniel Gunther*


## § A: EXORDIUM


Figure A1 'The *Anāhata Cakra* in Tiphereth', *Elena Bortot*

Figure A2 'The *Cakras* in the Body', *Elena Bortot*

Figure A3 'The *Mūlādhāra Cakra*'

Figure A4 'The *Svādhiṣṭhāna Cakra*'

Figure A5 'The *Maṇipūra Cakra*'

Figure A6 'The *Anāhata Cakra*'

Figure A7 'The *Viśuddha Cakra*'

Figure A8 'The *Ājñā Cakra*'

Figure A9 'The *Sahasrāra Cakra*'

Figure A10 'The *Anāhata Cakra* in the Body', *Elena Bortot*

Figure A11 'The Three *Naḍī* in Relation to *Anāhata* and *Mūlādhāra*', *Elena Bortot*

Figure A12 'The Three *Naḍī* as the Pillars of the Tree of Life', *J. Daniel Gunther*

Figure A13 'The Hexagram of Nature Projected on the Tree of Life', *J. Daniel Gunther*

Figure A14 '*Kuṇḍalinī* Piercing the *Cakras* & *Sahasrāra* Blooming', *Elena Bortot*

Figure A15 'The Egyptian Nemyss Signifying the Hood of a Cobra', *Death Mask of Tutankhamun, (18th Dynasty)*

Figure A16 'The Caduceus', *Jasenka Avram*

Figure A17 'The Hooded Cobra', *Zoology of Egypt, Vol. 1,Reptilia and Batrachia, Plate XLIV (1898 e.v.), John Anderson*

Figure A18 'Osiris Enthroned within a Shrine Crowned with Uraeus Serpents', *The Book of the Dead, Facsimiles of the Papyri of Hunefer, etc., Plate 5. (1899 e.v.), E.A. Wallis Budge*

Figure A19 'The Corpse of Osiris Protected by Isis', *The Book of the Dead, Facsimile of the Papyrus of Ani, Plate 20. (1894 e.v.), E.A. Wallis Budge*

Figure A20 'Ascensus', *Opus Alchymicum, Black Edition (2023 e.v.), J. Daniel Gunther*

Figure A21 'The Threefold Heart', *J. Daniel Gunther*

Figure A22 'Heart Scarab with BD Spell 30B on the Reverse', *Scarab of Paenptah, 3rd Intermediate Period*

Figure A23 'Imago Typhonis', *Oedipus Aegyptiacus, Vol. 1 (1652 e.v.)*

Figure A24 'Typhon', *(17th Century e.v.), Wenceslas Hollar*

Figure A25 'Wands of the Adepti of the Inner Order', *Jasenka Avram*

Figure A26 'Wands of the Adepti of the Inner Order & Rose Cross', *Jasenka Avram*

Figure A27 'Khephra as a Scarab Beetle Rolling the Sun', *J. Daniel Gunther*

Figure A28 'The Egyptian God Khephra', *Panthéon Égyptien Collection des Personnages (1823 e.v.)*

Figure A29 'Trump XVIII, The Moon', *Crowley/Harris Tarot Deck. Courtesy of O.T.O.*

Figure A30 'Trump XX, Judgement', *Jean Dodal Tarot Deck (early 18th Century e.v.)*

Figure A31 'L'angelo (The Angel), Visconti-Sforza Tarot', *(circa 1450 e.v.)*

Figure A32 'A Book of Hours, The Last Judgment', *(France, circa 1400 e.v.)*

Figure A33 'L'angelo (The Angel), Minchiate Florentine Tarot', *(circa 1480-1500 e.v.)*

Figure A34 'Le Trombe', *Minchiate Etruria, Florence (1725 e.v.)*

Figure A35 'House of Medici Coat of Arms', *Palazzo Vecchio, Florence, Italy*

Figure A36 'Gabriel Blowing his Horn as the Dead Rise from their Graves', *Armenian Gospel (1455 e.v.)*

Figure A37 'Israfel Turkish', *Turkish version of "Wonders of Creation," (1717 e.v.)*

Figure A38 'Israfel Arabic', *Arabic "Wonders of Creation & The Oddities of Existence" (circa 1375-1425 e.v.)*

Figure A39 'Trump XX, The Aeon', *Crowley/Harris Tarot Deck. Courtesy of O.T.O.*


## § B: LAPIDES


Figure B1 'A Prism Breaking White Light into its Spectral Colours'

Figure B2 'Mother of Emerald (Prase)'

Figure B3 'The Wadj Amulet', *Late Period, (circa Dynasty 26-29)*

Figure B4 'The Minutum Mundum with Malkuth in Bright Green', *Ian Mercer*

Figure B5 'Lapis Lazuli'

Figure B6 'The Seal Ring of V.V.V.V.V.'

Figure B7 'Turquoise'

Figure B8 'The Celestial Virgin Jewelled with Twelve Stars', *The Secret Teachings of All Ages (1926 e.v.), J. Augustus Knapp,*

Figure B9 'Alexandrite'

Figure B10 'Topaz'

Figure B11 'Deep Amethyst'

Figure B12 'Aeneas, Son of Aphrodite & Anchises', *1st Century CE*

Figure B13 'Ecce Homo (Behold the Man)', *Titian, (circa 1570-1576 e.v.)*

Figure B14 'Nero', *The Lives of the Twelve Caesars, Vol. 2 (1889 e.v.), Alexander Thomson*

Figure B15 'Caligula', *The Lives of the Twelve Caesars, Vol. 1 (1883 e.v.), Alexander Thomson*

Figure B16 'Diocletian', *De Roomsche Monarchy (1697 e.v.), Abraham Bogaert*

Figure B17 'Constantine the Great', *The Lives of the Roman Emperors & Their Associates, Vol. 5 (1884 e.v.), J. Eugene Reed*

Figure B18 'Eusebius of Caesarea', *Eusebius Pamphilus His Ten Books of Ecclesiastical History (1703 e.v.), Samuel Parker*

Figure B19 'First Edition of the Greek Text of Sozomen's Ecclestiastical History', *(1544 e.v.), Robertus Stephanus*

Figure B20 'Roman Labarum Bearer', *Discorso Sopra la Castrametatione & Bagni Antichi de i Greci & Romani (1582 e.v.), Guillaume du Chol*

Figure B21 'Constantine's Vision of the Cross before the Battle of the Milvian Bridge', *(circa 1520-1524 e.v.), Assistants of Raphael*

Figure B22 'First Edition of Zosimus', *New History in Latin', (1576 e.v.), Basel*

Figure B23 'The Donation of Constantine', *(detail), (circa 1520-1524 e.v), Assistants of Raphael*

Figure B24 'Lorenzo Valla', *Theodor de Bry, Boissard, Icones Quinquaginta Viroum (1597 e.v.), Jean Jacques*

Figure B25 'A Snake that Seizeth on a Little Singing-bird', *J. Daniel Gunther*

Figure B26 'Gray Sapphire with Six-pointed Star'

Figure B27 'Ecce Homo (Man of Sorrows)', *(circa 1493 e.v), Albrecht Durer*

Figure B28 'Dark Blue Sapphire with a Blood Red Tinge'

Figure B29 'Crucifixion of Jesus', *(1511 e.v.), Albrecht Durer*

Figure B30 'Trump XII, Le Pendu' *Renault Tarot de Besançon'*, *(1820 e.v.)*

Figure B31 'Odin Hanging on Yggsdrasil', *(1920 e.v.), Franz Stassen*

Figure B32 'Rose Cross (front)', *Figuren Der Rosenkreutz (1785 e.v.)*

Figure B33 'Rose Cross (back)', *Figuren Der Rosenkreutz (1785 e.v.)*

Figure B34 'Hand-painted Rosicrucian Manuscript', *(after Robert Fludd, Dat Rosa mel Apibus, (The Rose gives honey to the Bees), The German reads, Das Buch mit Sieben, The Book with Seven Seals,) Vol. 1. Manly Palmer Hall Collection (circa 1700 e.v.)*

Figure B35 'Hand-painted Rosicrucian Manuscript', *F. De La Rose Croix, Manly Palmer Hall Coll. (circa 1700 e.v.)*

Figure B36 'Rose Cross Lamen', *Ordre Kabbilistique de la Rose-Croix, (1888 e.v.)*

Figure B37 'Rose Cross Lamen (front)', *Hermetic Order of the Golden Dawn (1887 e.v.)*

Figure B38 'Jewel of the Rose Cross - after the Jewel of the 18° of the Scottish Rite of Freemasonry', *The Secret Teachings of All Ages (1926 e.v.), J. Augustus Knapp*

Figure B39 'A Rosicrucian Crucifixion', *The Secret Teachings of All Ages (1926 e.v.), J. Augustus Knapp*

Figure B40 'Emblems of the 18° of Scottish Rite Masonry - Knight Rose Croix', *Morals and Dogma (1916 e.v.), Albert Pike*

Figure B41 'The Cross of Suffering at the Base of the Pastos', *The Equinox, Vol. 1, No. 3.*

Figure B42 'The Cross of Suffering', *The Equinox, Vol. 1, No. 3.*

Figure B43 'The Rose Cross of A∴A∴', *J. Daniel Gunther*

Figure B44 'Rose Cross Applique of the Inner Order Adepti of A∴A∴'

Figure B45 'The Lamen of V.V.V.V.V.'

Figure B46 'The Ring of Amethyst', *Jasenka Avram*

Figure B47 'Igne Natura Renovatur Integra', *Opus Alchymicum, Black Edition (2023 e.v.), J. Daniel Gunther*

## § C: ASCENSVS

Figure C1 'The Tzelim', *Ian Mercer*

Figure C2 'The Tree of Life - The Way of the Middle Pillar', *Ian Mercer*

Figure C3 'Powers of the Sphinx', *Ian Mercer*

Figure C4 'Ceremonial Ankh', *(18th Dynasty)*

Figure C5 'The Egyptian God Ptah', *Panthéon Égyptien Collection des Personnages (1823 e.v.)*

Figure C6 'O king! if I be thy son, let us speak of the Embassy to the King thy Brother', *Ian Mercer*

## § D: FALLAX IMAGO

Figure D1 'The Silent Watcher', *The Equinox, Vol. 1, No. 1*

Figure D2 'The Light Spectrum'

Figure D3 'Wolf's bane'

Figure D4 'Trump IX, The Hermit', *Builders of the Adytum Tarot Deck*

Figure D5 'Fermentatio', *Philosophia Reformata (1622 e.v.), Johann Mylius, hand-colored by J. Daniel Gunther*

Figure D6 'Eighth Key of Basil Valentine', *Tripus Aureus (1618 e.v.), Michael Maier, hand-colored by J. Daniel Gunther*


## § E: NOCTIS LAVDATIO


Figure E1 'Head of a Nubian Boy', *Late 2nd Century BCE. Brooklyn Museum ("Head of a Man with Tight, Curly Hair," Accession No. 70.59)*

Figure E2 'The Night Watch', *(1642 e.v.), Rembrandt*

Figure E3 'I found Him whom my Soul Loveth', *Emblems Divine & Moral, Book IV, Emblem 12 (1790 e.v.), Francis Quarles*

Figure E4 'The Five Points of Fellowship', *Duncan's Freemason's Monitor. Third Edition (1866 e.v.)*

Figure E5 'The "Lion's Paw" Grip', *Duncan's Freemason's Monitor. Third Edition (1866 e.v.)*


## § F: COR VNIVERSVM


Figure F1 'Johann Pistorius the Younger', *(circa 1600 e.v.)*

Figure F2 'Giovanni Pico della Mirandola', *(circa 1622-1626 e.v.), Peter Paul Rubens*

Figure F3 'Ouroboros Surrounding Mount Meru & the Earth Carried by the World Tortoise', *Thunot Duvotenay (1843 e.v.), hand-colored, J. Daniel Gunther*

Figure F4 'Ophis et Ovum Mundanum, Tyrionum', *A New System or an Analysis of Ancient Mythology, Vol. 2, plate IV. (1774 e.v.), Jacob Bryant*

Figure F5 'The Celestial Virgin with the Sun God in Her Arms', *The Secret Teachings of All Ages (1926 e.v.), J. Augustus Knapp*

Figure F6 'Immaculate Conception', *(Immaculada con Miguel del Cid), (1619 e.v.), Francisco Pacheco*


## § G: NVNTIVS


Figure G1 'Mother of Pearl'

Figure G2 'Amaranthus Viridis', *Flora de Filipinos, Atlas Vol. 2, Plate 262, (circa 1882), Francisco Manuel Blanco*

Figure G3 'The Egyptian Goddess Hathor', *Panthéon Égyptien Collection des Personnages (1823 e.v.)*

Figure G4 'Yew Trees in a Graveyard'

Figure G5 'The Angel of Death Points the Way to the Stone of the Philosophers', *P. M. Respour, Besondere Versuche vom Mineral-Geist (1772 e.v.)*

Figure G6 'यम, Yama, the Hindu God of Death', *The Complete Hindoo Pantheon (1842 e.v.), E.A.Rodrigues*

Figure G7 'Yama Turning the Wheel of Life', *Indian Painting, (ca. 19th century e.v.)*

Figure G8 'The Four Worlds'


## § J: PARABOLA


Figure J1 'The Rape of Proserpine (Persephone)', *(1651 e.v.), Nicolas Mignard*

Figure J2 'Proserpine (Persephone)', *(1874 e.v.), Dante Gabriel Rosetti*

Figure J3 'The Return of Persephone', *(1891 e.v.), Frederick Leighton*

Figure J4 'Demeter Mourning for Persephone' *(circa 1906 e.v.), Evelyn de Morgan*

Figure J5 'Narcissus', *(1912 e.v.), John William Waterhouse*

Figure J6 'Echo and Narcissus', *(1903), John William Waterhouse*

Figure J7 'The Temple of Apollo at Delphi', *artist's conception J. Daniel Gunther*

Figure J8 'Chrysanthemum', *Opus Alchymicum (Black Edition), J. Daniel Gunther*


## § K: VINDEMIA


Figure K1 'The Two Realms', *Ian Mercer*

Figure K2 'Italian Midday', *(1831 e.v.), Karl Bryullov*

Figure K3 'Stormy Sea at Night', *(1849 e.v.), Ivan Aivazovsky*

Figure K4 'Bacchus', *(ca. 1638-1640 e.v.), Peter Paul Rubens*

Figure K5 'The Drunken Silenus', *(circa 1620 e.v.), Anthony van Dyke*

Figure K6 'Pan and Psyche', *(circa 1872-1874 e.v.), Edward Burne-Jones*

Figure K7 'A∴ A∴ Seal'

## Ever the Heart


| | |
|---|---|
| Figure EH1 | 'Ever the Heart', *(2023), original cover art by Elena Bortot, after a study by Gwen Gunther* |
| Figure EH2 | 'Power, Four of Disks', *Crowley/Harris Tarot Deck. Courtesy of O.T.O.* |
| Figure EH3 | 'Works, Three of Disks', *Crowley/Harris Tarot Deck. Courtesy of O.T.O.* |
| Figure EH4 | 'Threefold Knot of the Guṇas', *(2023), Elena Bortot* |
| Figure EH5 | 'The Form of a Pelican', *(2023), Elena Bortot* |
| Figure EH6 | 'My Wine is Poured Out', *(2023), original cover art by Elena Bortot, after a study by Gwen Gunther* |
| Figure EH7 | 'The Path of the Great Return', *(2023), J. Daniel Gunther and Ian Mercer* |
| Figure EH8 | 'Demeter, Enthroned in Benediction', *Greek painting (circa. 340 BCE),Wikipedia* |
| Figure EH9 | 'Persephone's Return', *Greek painting, terracotta bell-krater (circa 440 BCE), Metropolitan Museum* |
| Figure EH10 | 'Die Sünde', *The Sin (1906), Franz von Stuck* |
| Figure EH11 | 'Yogi in Tantric Meditation', *undated Indian painting* |
| Figure EH12 | 'Virtue, Three of Wands', *Crowley/Harris Tarot Deck. Courtesy of O.T.O.* |
| Figure EH13 | 'Graduum Montis Abiegni' |
| Figure EH14 | 'The Red Triangle of the Neophyte Robe' |
| Figure EH15 | 'Emerging from the Lotus', *Inspired from Plaque of Iuput II as Harpocrates, (2023), Elena Bortot* |
| Figure EH16 | 'Lotus Blossom', *by aarn-giri, unsplash* |
| Figure EH17 | 'Rose upon the Cross', *(2023), Elena Bortot* |
| Figure EH18 | 'Commitment to the Great Work', *(2023), Elena Bortot* |
| Figure EH19 | 'Cupid Triumphant', *Wikipedia, CC BY-SA 3.0 (1897-1899), Bertel Thorvaldsen* |
| Figure EH20 | 'Fidelia and Speranza', *Wikipedia, (1776), Benjamin West* |
| Figure EH21 | 'Trump XI, Lust', *Crowley/Harris Tarot Deck. Courtesy of O.T.O.* |
| Figure EH22 | 'Round and Square', *Opus Alchymicum (2023), J. Daniel Gunther* |

# I AM THE HEART
## A COMMENTARY ON LIBER LXV
## CHAPTER I

# PROLOGUE
## The Serpent Archetype

*Figure P1 - Crucified Serpent*

THE BOOK OF THE HEART GIRT WITH THE SERPENT is replete with Archetypal motifs. Naturally, the most significant one and the one we notice immediately is that of the serpent.

As a primordial component of the Collective Unconscious, the symbolism of the serpent is as flexible as the reptile itself. The physical characteristics and habits of the snake, its phallic shape, its undulating mode of motion, its cold-bloodedness, its choice of habitat, and its potential danger in the case of poisonous serpents, all contributed to the multifarious symbolic meanings that we find attached to it. All of these were of course unconscious manifestations from the Collective. Nobody ever sat down and thought, "Oh, I think I'll use a snake to represent this or that." The symbols sprang unbidden from the Unconscious, and still do to this day.

The serpent in these representations appears in more than one aspect, commonly with negative or evil characteristics, but also with neutral or even positive symbolism. We also see the serpent as a *paradoxia* – a motif that exhibits components that are seemingly self-contradictory but of equal value.

Examples of this Archetype are so numerous, and so diverse in their points of origin, that it would require an entire book to provide a thorough analysis. In such a short exposition as this, it is only possible to present brief samplings of this world-wide structural component of the psyche. Particular emphasis is placed on the ancient Egyptian, Greek and Judeo-Christian models for their obvious influence and appearance in the Holy Books of Thelema.

## The Serpent as a Negative Figure

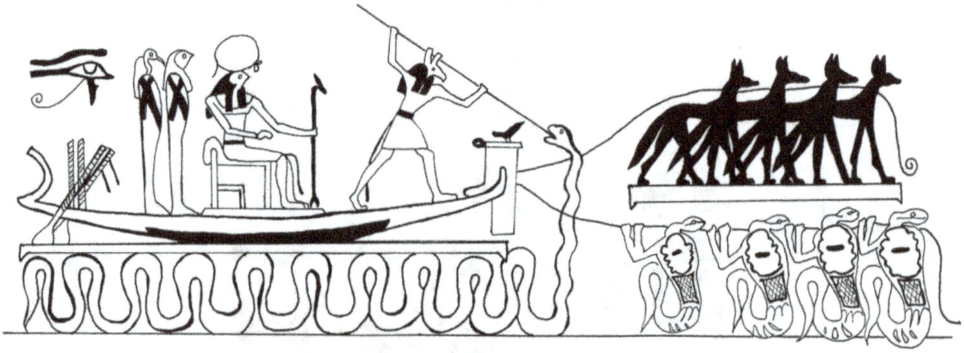

*Figure P2 - Seth Spearing Apep in the Boat of Ra*

In ancient Egypt, the eternal enemy of the Sun god , *rꜥ*, *Ra*, was the giant serpent whose name was , *ꜥꜣpp*, *Apep*. He was known as Ἄπωφις,[1] *Apophis*, to the ancient Greeks, and later in Coptic as ⲁⲫⲱⲫ, *Aphōph*.[2]

Ra was the bringer of light each day, traveling overhead in his solar bark. At sunset, Ra boarded his Night Bark and entered the region of the , *dwꜣt*, the *Duat*, symbolically located in the West or *Amente*. The Duat was divided into twelve divisions which corresponded to the twelve hours of the night. In order to exit from the Duat and rise again at dawn, Ra had to traverse this perilous region of darkness, inhabited by nightmarish demons who sought to impede his journey, destroy the god of light, and bring darkness and chaos to the world.

---

1 Also spelled Ἄποφις. *Vycichl*, p. 19.

2 *Ibid.*, In Coptic, ⲁⲫⲱⲫ means "giant."

Many of these demonic creatures were snakes, some depicted with multiple heads. In the journey of the Sun-god through the twelve divisions of the Duat, depicted in the New Kingdom *Book of Pylons*, the Tenth hour brought a confrontation with an eight-headed serpent with twelve human legs, called  , *šmty, He who walks.*

*ʿryt nt ỉmnt ỉw ỉmyws=s ʿmw dpw=sn ssn[=sn] sty šmty*

*The Pylon of the West. Those who are in it, swallow [their] heads when they smell the stench of "he who walks"*[3]

*Figure P3 - He who Walks*

Chief among these denizens of the night was the fiend Apep who eternally sought to destroy the god Ra. Apep was depicted as a giant serpent with numerous coils within which he would constrict his enemies and then swallow them, dooming them to non-existence. In Egyptian mythology, he was a completely evil figure, eternally hostile to the forces of Light and Life. He was the complete opposite of Ra; darkness and chaos to the sunlight and order brought by the Sun god.[4]

The Egyptians delighted in painting images that celebrated the destruction of Apep by Ra. One of their favorites depicted Ra as a golden cat, decapitating Apep underneath a Persea tree.

The Egyptian Priests utilized a number of rituals to ward off Apep so that Ra would successfully traverse the sky each day. The Priests in the *Temple of Amun-Ra* in *Thebes* followed a daily ritual guide that prescribed a litany of spells that were chanted each day for the purpose of conquering and dismembering the fiend.

---

3 *Book of the Pylons, Tenth Hour, Sarcophagus of Sety I.* (Bonomi & Sharpe, *The Alabaster Sarcophagus of Oimenepthah I., King of Egypt*, Plate 12, Upper left register.) See Hornung, *The Egyptian Book of Gates*, p. 343. To "swallow the head" probably meant that they tried to make themselves inconspicuous to the threatening entity. Similar terms exist in the current English vernacular, such as "duck your head," "keep your head down."

4 See Wilkinson, *The Complete Gods and Goddesses of Ancient Egypt*, pp. 221-222 under Apophis.

*Figure P4 - Ra as a Cat, Slaying Apep*

Chief among such texts was a long and elaborate ritual text with a title that matched the protracted incantations. Its full title was:

*mḏꜣt nt sḫr ꜥpp ḫfty nw rꜥ wnn-nfr ꜥnḫ wḏꜣ snb mꜣꜥ-ḫrw ỉrt n pr-*

*The Book of Overthrowing Apep the Enemy of Ra and the Enemy of justified King Wennefer,*[5] *which is performed in the Temple of*

*ỉmn-rꜥ nb tꜣwy ḫnty ỉpt-ỉswt m ḫrt hrw nt rꜥ nb.*

*Amun-Ra, the Lord of the Throne of the Two Lands, foremost in Karnak, daily.*[6]

Another Spell dedicated to the destruction of Apep was assigned *Spell Number 15A5* in *The Book of the Dead*, by Egyptologist T. George Allen. It is an unusual Hymn to Ra, which mentions an unknown collection of Spells called,  , *mḏꜣt 77 ḥr mnt ꜥꜣpp, The 77 Scrolls of Apep.*[7]

---

5 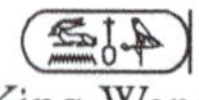 , *wnn-nfr,* "King Wennefer," i.e. the Perfected Osiris. The name is translated as "King Wennefer" because it is writtin within a Royal Cartouche wherein the names of the Pharoahs were written.

6 It is found in *BM No. 10188, Papyrus Bremner-Rhind.* A hieroglyphic transcription of the hieratic text is in Faulkner, *Bibliotheca Aegyptiaca III, The Papyrus Bremner-Rhind,* pp. 42-88. Translation and commentary in Faulkner, *JEA,* Vol. 23 (1937) pp. 166-185 and Vol. 24 (1938) pp. 41-52. The term "Wennefer" is a name of Osiris, commonly called "Asar-un-nefer" (or "Osiris-Wennefer.")

7 Allen, *Some Egyptian Sun Hymns,* in *JNES,* Vol. 8, No. 4, pp. 349-352. Egyptologist Stephen Quirke does not accept Allen's proposal of this Spell as part of the *The Book of the Dead.* Since this hymn does not occur in a manuscript written for burial with the dead, he considers it a composition outside the corpus of the *The Book of the Dead* proper. See Quirke, *Going out in Daylight,* p. 591.

No such collection has ever been found, although they may have existed as a unique document in the Temple literature at some point.

I have included a partial translation of that Spell below, not only because of its pertinence to the subject of Apep, but also because of its provenance. The Spell that Allen named 15A5 is known from only seventeen sources.[8] One belonged to the priest Ankhefenkhonsu II, the grandson of Anhefenkhonsu I, son of Besenmut I and Taneshy.[9] Others include those of Tairi II, a thrice-great granddaughter,[10] and that of Ankhefenkhonsu VI.[11] Of the remaining examples, one belonged to Muthotepti, the last wife of Ankhefenkhonsu I, and several others belonged to his descendants or relations by marriage. This high percentage of witnesses for this text within the lineage and influence of Ankhefenkhonsu is curious and suggestive.

*Figure P5 - Stele of Ankhefenkhonsu II*

---

8 Allen discovered thirteen of these sources (See Allen, *Some Egyptian Sun Hymns*, *JNES*, Vol. 8, No. 4, pp. 349-365.) Three additional sources were recently found by Egyptologist Abdel-Maguid R. Zakariya (*Cairo SR 9914, Cairo SR 9418 and Cairo SR 4919*), and one source was just discovered by myself in the Manchester Museum in England (*Manchester Museum 10939*). Not all versions of Spell 15A5 include a reference to the 77 Scrolls of Apep; of those that include it, one gives the number of scrolls as 73, another as 69, both obviously in error. They are also of varying length and completeness, due to the space available on the stele. Such scribal errors are quite common in religious texts, as the Scribes often could not understand the texts they were copying. So far, all versions of this Spell have been found on stelae.

9 *Istanbul 190*. The hieroglyphic text was published by K. Piehl, *Inscriptions Hiéroglyphiques* (1886) Première Partie, Plate LXB and by V. Scheil in *RT*, Vol. 15 (1893), p. 197. (BM 22914, Wooden stela of Ankhefenkhons.) The hieroglyphic text is also in Legrain, *RT*, Vol. 14 (1893), p. 59.

10 *Cairo SR 9914*. Tairi II was the daughter of Amunhotep VII and Khausenasi, the thrice-great granddaughter of Ankhefenkhonsu I. A facsimile of the stele and hieroglyphic text is printed in *SHEDET*, Vol. 3, issue 3, pp. 34-44.

11 *BM 22914*. Ankhefenkhonsu VI was the son of Besenmut VII and Hetepamun. See Bierbrier, *The Late New Kingdom in Egypt* (c. 1300-664 B.C.), p. 104.

Here follows a translation of that entire Spell from the Stele of Ankhefenkhonsu II, with the conclusion taken from the Stele of Tairy II, and Ankhefenkhonsu VI:[12]

*ỉnḏ ḥr=k wbn m tꜣ-ḏsr šsp ḫꜥm ỉꜣbtt nt pt wr šfyt*

*Hail to thee, who rises from the sacred land! Light that has dawned in the East of heaven, great of dignity*

*m kꜣr štꜣ ỉ rꜥ sḏm=k rꜥ [pẖr=k] ỉ[w] šd.n=ỉ mḏꜣt 77*

*in the secret shrine! O Ra! Mayest thou hearken! O Ra! [Mayest thou circle about!] I have read the 77 Scrolls*

*ḥr mnt ꜥꜣpp rꜥ-nb dỉt bꜣ=f ḫfty m sḏt ẖꜣt=f n ꜣḫt ḥꜥw=f n*

*concerning the place of slaughter of Apep every day! His Ba-soul is given to the enemy of the fire,[13] his corpse to the flame, his flesh to*

*ỉrt ḥrw tmw ni sḫꜣ.tw=f ỉw ỉrrt ḫrỉt ꜥpp m šꜥt n rꜥ nb smꜣꜥ=ỉ ḥrw=k*

*the fiery Eye of Horus, so that he ceases to exist and will not be remembered! The fate of Apep is accomplished in daily slaughter. I make Thee triumph*

*m wbn=k mỉ r=k nt rꜥ-ḥr-ꜣḫty*

*in Thy rising! Come Thou, Ra-Hoor-Khuit!*

---

12 The Spell occupies the entire right side of the Stele of Ankhefenkhonsu II. The ending of the Spell is taken from Stelae of Tairi II, with the final portion from Ankhefenkhonsu VI.

13 Ankhefenkhonsu VI here reads, 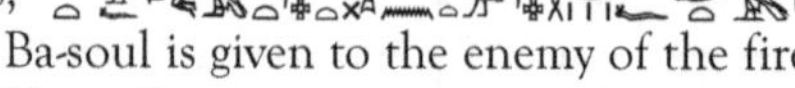 , *dỉt bꜣ=f ḫfty m sḏt ẖꜣt=f nꜣḫt ḥkꜣ=f n ỉrt ḥrw*, "His Ba-soul is given to the enemy of the fire, his corpse to the flame, his magic to the fiery Eye of Horus."

Despite having a totally negative interpretation in Egyptian mythology, Apep takes on completely positive attributes in some of the Holy Books. In *Liber LXV*, Chapter IV: 24-25, Apep is identified with the Holy Guardian Angel:

> **Arise, O serpent Apep, Thou art Adonai the beloved one! Thou art my darling and my lord, and Thy poison is sweeter than the kisses of Isis the mother of the Gods!**
> **For Thou art He! Yea, Thou shalt swallow up Asi and Asar, and the children of Ptah. Thou shalt pour forth a flood of poison to destroy the works of the Magician. Only the Destroyer shall devour Thee; Thou shalt blacken his throat, wherein his spirit abideth. Ah, serpent Apep, but I love Thee!**

The same identification is given in *Liber LXV*, Chapter V:57,

> **O thou Serpent Apep, my Lord Adonai, it is a speck of minutest time, this travelling through eternity, and in Thy sight the landmarks are of fair white marble untouched by the tool of the graver. Therefore Thou art mine, even now and for ever and for everlasting. Amen.**[14]

In the New Aeon, Apep is viewed with an entirely different perspective than that of the Aeon of Osiris. The Archetype of the devouring serpent of darkness (NOX) has evolved and taken on certain attributes of The Holy Guardian Angel and *The Hierophant*.[15] The formula of NOX is the Supreme Formula of Initiation in this Aeon and it is now Apep who is the Heart of IAO, uniting the Dead One Osiris with Isis, the Mother of the gods.[16]

---

14 See also *Liber VII*, VII:19, "Thou beautiful serpent of Apep!"

15 In the Outer Order of A.∴A.∴, The Hierophant is *Hoor-Apep*. The Hierophant in all three Orders of A.∴A.∴ are forms of *Hoor*. See Gunther, *The Angel and The Abyss*, p. 298.

16 *See Liber LXVI*, 1: "Apep deifieth Asar," and *LXVI*, 38: "I, Apep the Serpent, am the heart of IAO. Isis shall await Asar, and I in the midst," and *LXVI*, 48-50: "I am Apep, O thou slain One. Thou shalt slay thyself upon mine altar: I will have thy blood to drink. For I am a mighty vampire, and my children shall suck up the wine of the earth which is blood. Thou shalt replenish thy veins from the chalice of heaven." The Averse form of this name as a formula is OAI.

## Leviathan

The draconic figure of לויתן, *Leviathan*, is mentioned in three books of the *Old Testament*: *Job*, *Psalms*, and *Isaiah*, as well as in the apocryphal *II Esdras*, the Syriac *Apocalypse of Baruch* and the Ethiopic *Book of Enoch.*[17]

Leviathan was depicted as a monstrous sea serpent, epitomizing evil and oppression, subjugated by the power of Yahweh:

> ביום ההוא יפקד יהוה בחרבו הקשה והגדולה
> והחזקה על לויתן נחש ברח ועל לויתן נחש
> עקלתון והרג את־התנין אשר בים׃

> In that day, Yahweh shall visit upon Leviathan, the fleeing serpent, his severe and great and strong sword, even upon Levithan, the twisting serpent; and he shall slay the dragon that is in the sea.[18]

*Figure P6 - The Destruction of Leviathan*

In the Ethiopic *Book of Enoch*, ሌዋታን, *Leviathan* is identified as a female monster:

17 *Job* 41:1, *Psalm* 74:14 & 104:26, *Isaiah* 27:1, *II Esdras* 6:49, *Syriac Apocalypse of Baruch* 29:4.

18 *Isaiah* 27:1.

ወይትከፈሉ ፡ በይእቲ ፡ ዕለት ፡ ፪አናብርት ፡ አንበሪ ፡ አንስቲያዊት ፡ ዘስማ ፡ ሌዋታን ፡ ከመ ፡ ትኅድር ፡ በልጐተ ፡ ባሕር ፡ መልዕልተ ፡ አንቅዕተ ፡ ማያት ።

> And on that day will two monsters be parted, a female monster named Leviathan, to dwell in the depths of the ocean over the fountains of the waters.[19]

Leviathan served as emblematic of the adversaries and oppressors of Israel, which the prophet Isaiah declared would fall under the great power of the Lord. The Hebrew word לויתן, *Liwyāṯān* (i.e. "Leviathan"), *wreathed, wrapped in folds*, may be connected to the Hebrew לויה, *lawyah, a wreath*;[20] compare the Arabic لَوَّى, *lawiyā*, *to twist, to coil.*[21]

There is substantial parallelism between the Leviathan in the book of *Job* and a creature named 𐎍𐎚𐎐, *Lītānu*, that appears in the *Ugaritic Baal Cycle*.[22] In this latter tradition, *Lītānu* is called 𐎁𐎘𐎐 𐎁𐎗𐎈, *bṯn brḥ, the fleeing serpent*, the parallel to the Hebrew epithet for Leviathan, נחש ברח, *the fleeing serpent*. Leviathan is called נחש עקלתון, *twisting serpent*, and in Ugarit, *Lītānu* is also called 𐎁𐎘𐎐 𐎓𐎖𐎍𐎘𐎐, *bṯn'qlṯn, twisting serpent*.[23] The scholar Wilfred Lambert proposed that Isaiah 27 was a direct quote from the *Ugaritic Baal Cycle*, merely substituting Ugaritic synonyms for the Hebrew.[24] Needless to say, this proposition has not been embraced by proponents of Jewish or Christian theology, who typically cling to the simplistic notion that the *Old Testament* had no precursor other than the word of God himself.

---

19 *Ethiopic Book of Enoch LX*, 7. (Charles, *The Book of Enoch translated from Professor Dillmann's Ethiopic Text*. Ethiopic text in Dillman, *Liber Henoch Aethiopice*, p. 33.)

20 *Gesenius*, p. 433b.

21 *Oxford Arabic Dictionary*, p. 747b.

22 J. A. Emerton rejected the popular vocalization of "Lotan" on etymological grounds, presenting sound arguments for *Lītānu*. Emerton, *Vetus Testamentum*, Vol. 32 (1982), *Leviathan and Ltn: The Vocalization of the Ugaritic Word for the Dragon*, pp. 327-331. Cf. *Dictionary of Deities and Demons of the Bible*, p. 511.

23 Barker, *Isaiah's Kingship Polemic*, p. 151. Cf. Olmo Lete, *A Dictionary of the Ugaritic Language in the Alphabetic Tradition*, p. 502.

24 "Indeed *Isaiah* 27:1 uses all the terms of the Ugaritic text save one: *lwytn nhs brh...lwytn nhs 'qltn*. Hence the substitution of an ordinary Hebrew noun *nāhāš* "snake" for the ordinary Ugaritic word for "snake," *bṯn*, proves that this was no unintelligent copying out of an archaic phrase but a comprehending modification to keep the meaning clear." Lambert, "Leviathan in Ancient Art" in *Shlomo, Studies in Epigraphy, Iconography, History and Archaeology in Honor of Shlomo Moussaieff*, p. 154.

A Talmudic legend recounts that when Messiah comes, Leviathan will be caught and slain, and the flesh of the beast will be served up at a banquet for the Righteous.

> אמר רבי יוחנן: עתיד הקדוש ברוך הוא לעשות סעודה
> לצדיקים מבשרו של לויתן

> Rabbi Yoḥanan says, 'In the future, the Holy One (i.e. the Messiah), Blessed be He, will make a feast for the Righteous from the flesh of Leviathan.[25]

Christians later elaborated on this theme, conceptually and artistically, as in *Figure P7*, which illustrates God as a fisherman with the seven-fold line of David adorning the line, the Cross as a fishhook, and Jesus Christ as the bait.[26]

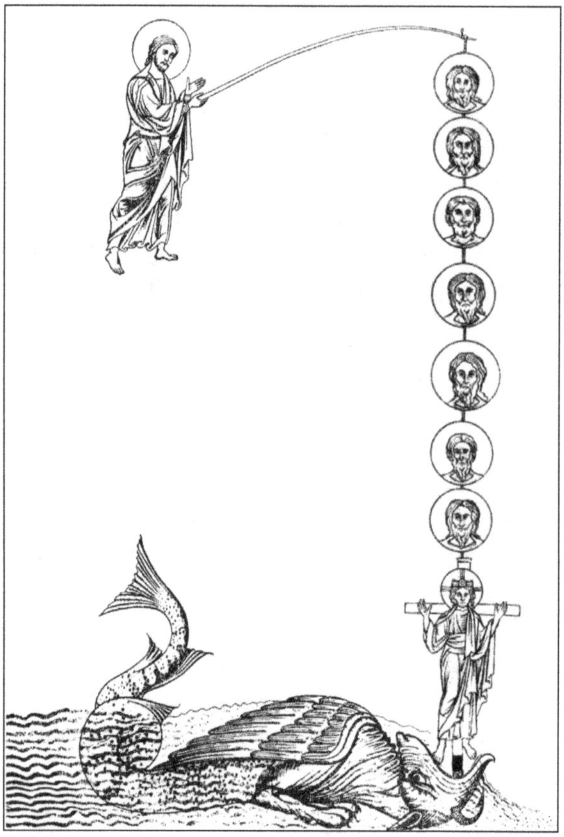

*Figure P7 - The Capture of Leviathan*

---

25 *The Babylonian Talmud,* בבא בתרא, *Baba Batra,* "The Last Gate," § 5:75a(4).

26 Cf. Gunther, *Initiation in the Aeon of the Child,* pp. 102-103.

## Eve and the Serpent

*Figure P8 - The Fall of Man*

Most are perhaps most familiar with the myth of אדם, *Adam* and חוה, *Eve*, in the Garden of Eden, wherein Eve was tempted by the serpent to partake of fruit from the Tree growing in the midst of the garden.

The *Old Testament* book of *Genesis* in Chapter 3, verse 1, introduced this well-known myth as follows:

והנחש היה ערום מכל חית השדה

Now the serpent was more cunning than any living thing of the field...

This is the prelude to the serpent's action of tempting Eve to partake of the fruit from the Tree of the Knowledge of Good and Evil, which God had declared forbidden. Here, the serpent is described as ערום, *cunning*, a word with negative connotations which may also be translated as "crafty."[27]

Thus, one of the most iconic conceptions of the mythological snake has become that of the serpent in the Garden of Eden, as a deceiver and tempter whose actions would result in the expulsion of man and woman from paradise.

However, in the Gnostic document, *The Hypostasis of the Archons*,[28] the serpent is shown from another point of view entirely. There, it is recorded that the "spiritual one" entered into the serpent, who then came to Eve and Adam:

---

27 Cf. *Gesenius*, 6175, p. 653b.

28 *Nag Hammadi Tractate* II,4. The exact date of composition is unknown, but probably dates to the 3rd Century CE. The existing copy is in Coptic, although the original was in Greek.

**ⲁⲥⲉⲓ ⲇⲉ ⲛ̄ϭⲓ ϯⲡⲛⲉⲩⲙⲁⲧⲓⲕ[ⲏ ϩⲙ̄] ⲫⲁϥ` ⲡⲣⲉϥⲧⲁⲙⲟ` ⲁⲩⲱ ⲁϥⲧⲁ [ⲙⲟⲟⲩ ⲉϥ]**

Then came the spiritual one, the serpent, the Instructor, and it taught [them.][29]

P9 - The Temptation of Eve

In this text, the serpent is female. The serpent is called **ⲣⲉϥⲧⲁⲙⲟ**, *the Instructor.* The root of **ⲣⲉϥⲧⲁⲙⲟ** is the Coptic word **ⲧⲁⲙⲟ**, *to tell, make known, inform.*[30] It is derived from the Late Egyptian word  , *dỉt ʿm*, meaning, *to announce, to cause to know.*[31]

In another Gnostic document from *Nag Hammadi, On the Origin of the World*, this "Instructor" was called **ⲉⲩϩⲁ ⲛ̄ⲍⲱⲏ ⲉⲧⲉ ⲧⲣⲉϥⲧⲁⲙⲟ ⲧⲉⲙ̄ⲡⲱⲛϩ**, *Eve of life, that is, the Instructor of life.*[32] She manifested as the Serpent in the Garden of Eden as the Lord called **ⲑⲏⲣⲓⲟⲛ**, *the Beast* (i.e. *Therion*):

> **ⲑⲉⲣⲙⲏⲛⲉⲓⲁ ⲙ̄ⲡⲑⲏⲣⲓⲟⲛ` ⲡⲉ ⲡⲣⲉϥ `ⲧⲁⲙⲟ ⲁⲩϩⲉ ⲅⲁⲣ` ⲉⲣⲟϥ` ⲉϥⲟ. ⲛ̄ⲥⲁⲃⲉ ⲡⲁⲣⲁⲣⲟⲟⲩ ⲧⲏⲣⲟⲩ.**
>
> The interpretation of "the Beast" is "the Instructor," for it was found to be the wisest of all.[33]

The "Beast" or "Instructor," then taught Adam and Eve, whereupon they realized that they were **ⲛⲉⲩⲕⲁⲕⲁϩⲏⲩ ⲁⲧⲅⲛⲱⲥⲓⲥ**, *naked of Gnosis.*[34] Unlike the traditional story in the book of *Genesis*, where Adam and Eve realized they were *physically* naked, this Gnostic text informs us they were solely carnal and lacked *Spiritual Wisdom.*

---

29 *The Hypostasis of the Archons*, 89:32-33. **ϯⲡⲛⲉⲩⲙⲁⲧⲓⲕⲏ**, "the Spiritual One," from the Greek loan word πνευματικός.

30 **ⲧⲁⲙⲟ**, "tell, make known, inform" (causative of **ⲉⲙⲓⲉ**), *Crum* p. 413b.

31 *Černý*, p. 187, *Wb* I, 188.

32 *On the Origin of the World (Nag Hammadi Tractate II,5)*, 113:33-34.

33 *Ibid.*, 114:3-4.

34 *Ibid.*, 119:15. **ⲅⲛⲱⲥⲓⲥ**, Gnosis, (knowledge), using the Greek loan word γνῶσις.

The serpent in this text is not the evil one. That role was assigned to יהוה, *Yahweh*, whom these Gnostics considered as a false God who was in reality, the foe of man. But here, in this Gnostic text, the serpent is taken as the opposite, providing balance to the one-sided view of God.

## Lilith

Another example of the negative aspect is the figure of לילית, *Lilith*, the serpent-woman that emerged from Jewish Qabalistic and folklore traditions. There, she is described as the strangler of children or the seducer of men, breeding demonic children from their nocturnal emissions.[35] She was conceived as a seductive, long-haired winged demon.

The *Babylonian Talmud*, which is an encyclopedic collection of pedantic drivel, includes the following tidbit of benighted superstition:

אסור לישן בבית יחידי, וכל הישן בבית יחידי - אחזתו לילית

It is forbidden to sleep alone in a house, and anyone who sleeps alone in a house will be seized by Lilith.

*Babylonian Talmud, Shabbat 23:151b*

One of the more bizarre selections from the great wisdom of the Rabbis in the *Babylonian Talmud*, from the section entitled נדה, *Niddah* ("period of menstruation"), reads,

המפלת דמות לילית אמו טמאה לידה ולד הוא אלא שיש לו כנפים

Whosoever miscarries the form of a Lilith, its mother is impure (after) childbirth, (because) it is a (real) offspring, except that it has wings.

*Babylonian Talmud, Niddah 24b.*

The word "Lilith" occurs once in the *Old Testament*, in *Isaiah* 34:14:

ופגשו ציים את־איים ושעיר על־רעהו יקרא אך־שם
הרגיעה לילית ומצאה לה מנוח׃

35 Scholem, *Kabbalah*, pp. 356-361.

> The wild beasts of the desert shall meet with the howlers, the he-goat shall call to its companion. Verily, then Lilith shall settle and shall find for herself a place of rest.[36]

Figure P10 - Lilith

Translations of the word "Lilith" have widely varied: "screech owl" (KJV), "night creature" (NIV), "night bird" (ESV), "night-monster" (ASV and the JPS Tanakh) and, one of the strangest of all, "*Lamia*" (the Roman Catholic approved Douay-Rheims *Bible*). The latter rendering, Lamia, derives from the Λάμια, *Lamia*, of Greek mythology, which described her as a monster that devoured children.[37] In later tradition she was regarded as a night demon, seducing young men in order to devour them. Like Lilith, she was described as part woman, part serpent.[38]

Figure P11 - The Kiss of the Enchantress

This bizarre translation of Lilith as "Lamia" first occurred in the 5th Century e.v. publication of *The Vulgate Bible*:

> Et occurrent dæmonia onocentauris et pilosus clamabit alter ad alterum; ibi cubavit lamia, et invenit sibi requiem.

> And demons and monsters shall meet; and the hairy ones shall cry out to one another: there hath the **lamia** lain down, and found rest for herself.[39]

Obviously not understanding the text, the translators omitted Lilith entirely, and not only replaced it with *lamia*, but rendered "wild beasts of the desert" as "demons and monsters," the latter word being a transliteration of ὀνοκένταυρος, *Onocentaur*, a creature from Greek mythology that is like a

---

36 איים, (plural of אי), "howlers," a figurative name for hyaenas, wolves or jackals. (*Gesenius*, p. 347a.)

37 Smith, *Dictionary of Greek and Roman Biography and Mythology*, Vol. 2, pp. 713-714. Kerényi, *The Gods of the Greeks*, pp. 38-40.

38 Philostratus, *Vita Apollonii Tyanei, (The Life of Apollonius of Tyana)*, IV:25.

39 *The Holy Bible, from the Latin Vulgate. Dhouay/Rheims translation (1875).* Emphasis added.

*Figure P12 - Onocentauros*

centaur, but part human and part donkey![40] This same word is present in the *Septuagint*, the Greek translation of the *Old Testament*.

The earliest reference to Lilith as a wife of Adam is found in the אלפא ביתא דבן סירא, *Alphabet of ben Sira*, an Aramaic and Hebrew text possibly written in the eighth century CE.[41] This work is most famous because Lilith is there described as the first wife of Adam, prior to the creation of Eve. In *Genesis* 1:27, it was recounted that God created man in his own image; "male and female created he them." It is not until *Genesis* 2:19 that God created Eve from the rib of Adam, to make him a companion so that he would not be alone. The anonymous author of the *Alphabet of ben Sira* seemingly seized upon this discrepancy to identify the first unnamed woman created as Lilith, not Eve.

Ben Sira is identified as the son of Jeremiah the prophet,[42] and it was said that his fame as a powerful Seer and magician eventually reached Nebuchadnezzar II, the second king of the Neo-Babylonian empire. The king's son fell seriously ill, and the king called for Ben Sira, saying,

---

40 Καὶ συναντήσουσι δαιμόνια ὀνοκενταύροις, καὶ βοήσονται ἕτερος πρὸς τὸν ἕτερον, ἐκεῖ ἀναπαύσονται ὀνοκένταυροι, εὑρόντες αὑτοῖς ἀνάπαυσιν. (*Isaiah* 34:14, LXX.) The word ὀνοκένταυρος was translated as "satyr," apparently for lack of a better term. (*LSJ 1056b*)

41 For an English translation, see Stern & Mirsky, *Rabbinic Fantasies*, pp. 167-202.

42 *Ibid.* Ben Sira used Gematria as a proof that he was indeed descended from Jeremiah: וכשתחשוב סירא וירמיהו בגימטריא שוין, "When you calculate Sira and Jeremiah in Gematria, they are equal." (i.e. Sira, סירא =271, Jeremiah, ירמיהו =271.) אלפא ביתא לבן סירא, Einstein, *Ozar Midrashm*, Vol. 1, ל - א. § 2.

רפא לבני ואם לאו אהרוג אותך

Heal my son. If you do not, I will kill you![43]

Ben Sira immediately drew out an amulet inscribed with the Holy Name of God and the Angels of healing.

וכשראה נבוכדנצר בקמיע אמר לו מה אלו

When Nebuchadnezzar beheld the amulet he said, "What are these?[44]

The answer of Ben Sira follows: (a long reply, but most interesting.)

The angels who are in charge of healing are **Sanoy**, **Sansenoy** and **Semangelof**.[45] While God created **Adam**, who was alone, He said, "It is not good for man to be alone" (*Genesis* 2:18). He also created a woman, from the earth, as He had created Adam himself, and called her **Lilith**. Immediately, they began to argue with one another. She said, "I will not lie below," and he said, "I will not lie beneath thee, but only on top.[46] For thou art fit only to be in the bottom position, while I am to be the superior one." **Lilith** responded, "We are equal to each other inasmuch as we were both created from the earth." But they would not listen to one another. When **Lilith** saw this, she pronounced the Ineffable Name and flew away into the air. Adam stood in prayer before his Creator: "Master of the universe!" he said, "the woman thou didst give me has run away." At once, God sent these three angels to bring her back, saying to him, "If she agrees to come back, it is preferable. If not, she must allow one hundred of her children to die every day." The angels left God and pursued **Lilith**, whom they overtook in the midst of the sea, in the mighty waters wherein the Egyptians were destined to drown. They told her God's word, but she did not wish to return. The angels said, "We shall drown thee in the sea." She said, "Leave me! I was created only to cause sickness to infants. If the infant is male, I have dominion over him for eight days after his birth, and if female, for twenty days." When the angels heard the words of **Lilith** words, they insisted she go back. (She said:),"I swear in the Name of the Living God, whenever I see ye or thy names or your forms in an amulet, I will have no power over that infant." She also agreed to have one hundred of her children die every day. Therefore, every day one hundred demons perish,

43 אלפא ביתא אחרת לבן סירא, Einstein, *Ozar Midrashm*, Vol. 1, ל - א. § 33, line 24, p. 46.

44 *Ibid.* § 33, line 27, p. 47.

45 The names of the three angels in Hebrew is סנוי, "Sanoy," סנסנוי, "Sansenoy," and סמנגלוף, "Semangelof."

46 i.e. During sexual intercourse.

and for the same reason, we write the angels names on the amulets of young children. When **Lilith** sees their names, she remembers her oath, and the child recovers.[47]

Many scholars today consider this text to be a rather crude satire, because of its bold references to such taboo subjects as flatulence, masturbation, and incest. It also parodies Adam, depicting him as a weak partner.
A new conception of Lilith appeared in the teachings of Isaac ben Jacob ha-Kohen (middle of the 13th century CE,) and later in ספר עמוד השמאלי, *Sepher Amud ha-Semali,*[48] by his pupil, Moses ben Solomon ben Simeon of Burgos (c. 1230-1300 CE). Therein, "Lilith the Older" (לילית סבתא) is presented as the bride of the demon-angel סמאל, *Samael,* and queen of the forces of evil. "Lilith the Younger" (לילית זעירתא) is united with the demon אשמדאי, *Asmodeus.*[49] In the world of the קליפות, *Qliphoth,*[50] the world of the unbalanced Tree of Life, she is the evil parallel to the שכינה, *Shekhinah,* ("divine presence"). Shekinah was considered the mother of the House of Israel, hence Lilith was considered the mother of the unholy, the ערב בר, the "mixed multitude."[51] Despite her dark character, she is described as beautiful and seductive. Here, as in the myth of the Lamia, we see the tendency of the Archetype to manifest as a *Complexio Oppositorum.*[52]

In *Liber LXV*, Chapter III, she fulfills this aspect as Lilith the serpent-woman who is coiled about the heart of the aspirant, as a vision of the Demon-Queen of the Nephesh, wherein lie the roots of desire, and hence the cause of "sorrow."[53]

---

47 *loc. cit.*, § 34, lines 1-44, p. 47. Emphasis added.

48 "The Left Pillar." In Gershom Scholem, לחקר קבלת ר׳ יצחק בן יצקב הכהן, *'Le-Ḥeker Kabbalat R. Yitsḥak ben Ya'akov ha-Kohen,'* Tarbiz/ תרביץ 4:2, pp. 207-225.

49 *Ibid.*, p. 72.

50 The academically accepted transliteration of this word is *Kellipot* (singular *Kellipah*), however *Qliphoth* has such a long tradition in the Magical systems of the West it has been retained to avoid confusion among students.

51 Scholem, *Kabbalah*, pp. 356-360 and Dan, *Samael, Lilith, and the concept of Evil in Early Kabbalah, passim.*

52 A single image that contains its own opposite.

53 The Angel, being Universal, includes all aspects of the coiling serpent; it is only our incomplete and imperfect Perceptions (सँज्ञा *saṃjñā, or saññā in Pali),* informed by our Thoughts (चित्त *citta*) and Desires (काम, *kāma*) that limit our Consciousness (विज्ञान, *vijñāna, or viññāṇā in Pali)* of the Ineffable Mystery. In Qabalistic terms, Reason (Ruach) and Desire (Nephesh) interfere with a perfect Perception (Neshemah, or Understanding).

**Then the word of Adonai came unto me by the mouth of the Magister mine, saying: O heart that art girt about with the coils of the old serpent, lift up thyself unto the mountain of initiation![54]**
**But I remembered. Yea, Than, yea, Theli, [55] yea, Lilith! these three were about me from of old. For they are one.**
**Beautiful wast thou, O Lilith, thou serpent-woman!**
**Thou wast lithe and delicious to the taste, and thy perfume was of musk mingled with ambergris.**
**Close didst thou cling with thy coils unto the heart, and it was as the joy of all the spring.**
**But I beheld in thee a certain taint, even in that wherein I delighted.**
**I beheld in thee the taint of thy father the ape, of thy grandsire the Blind Worm of Slime.**
**I gazed upon the Crystal of the Future, and I saw the horror of the End of thee.**
**Further, I destroyed the time Past, and the time to Come - had I not the Power of the Sand-glass? But in the very hour I beheld corruption.**

*Liber LXV, III:3-12*

## The Negative Serpent in Christianity

Despite the occasional assumption of the more positive symbolic aspects of the serpent, Christianity inherited the negative interpretation of the Archetype primarily through Judaism.

It has been argued, particularly at the end of the 19th century and the beginning of the 20th century, that Christianity copied many of its mythological motifs directly from the Egyptians. There is little doubt that early Christians were influenced by the presence of a culture that had already existed for thousands of years. Yet, a great many of the images found in Egyptian religious iconography were not in the open sight of the populace. They occurred primarily in tombs accessible only to a limited few, and yet many parallel images may be found, not only in early Christianity, but in other cultures as well, none

---

54 "mountain of initiation" = *Abiegnus*. See Gunther, *Initiation in the Aeon of the Child*, pp. 27, 35, 148-156, 193.

55 "Than" = תן, < תנין, "serpent," hence לויתן, Leviathan. "Theli" = תלי, "curls," name for the Constellation *Draco*, i.e. "Dragon." For "Theli," see Kaplan, *Sepher Yetzirah*, 6:1, pp. 231-239 and Matt, *The Zohar (Pritzger edition)*, *Idra Rabba*, 3:140a, Vol. 8, pp. 416-417. In Mathers, *Kabbala Denudata, Kabbalah Unveiled*, this is *The Greater Holy Assembly*, No. 833, p. 215. These words are listed in *Sepher Sephiroth* under the numbers 450, 510, 496 and 440.

of which had any possibility of intentional copying. Such congruity of expression does not require physical contact because the source of the imagery is the Collective Unconscious. Thus, conceptions and representations of an afterlife populated by nightmarish serpents were not copied from their neighbors but developed independently out of the same unconscious material.

The primeval Chaos of the Gnostic Christians, like the Duat of the Egyptians, featured fiendish serpents who served the powers of darkness. One such demonic Power was called **ⲁⲩⲑⲁⲇⲏⲥ**, *Authades*,[56] who tormented **ⲥⲟⲫⲓⲁ**, *Sophia*,[57] the daughter of **ⲃⲁⲣⲃⲏⲗⲱ**, *Barbelo*,[58] who had fallen from the **ⲡⲗⲏⲣⲱⲙⲁ**, *Pleroma*.[59] One of her tormentors had the form of a seven-headed Basilisk serpent:

**ⲁⲩⲱ ⲁⲩⲑⲗⲓⲃⲉ ⲙ̄ⲙⲟⲥ ⲛ̄ϭⲓ ϩⲟⲓ̈ⲛⲉ ϩ̄ⲛ̄ ⲛⲉⲡⲣⲟⲃⲟⲗⲟⲟⲩⲉ ⲙ̄ⲡⲁⲩⲑⲁⲇⲏⲥ ⲟⲩⲁ ⲙⲉⲛ ⲛ̄ϩⲏⲧⲟⲩ ⲁϥϣ[ⲃ]ⲧϥ ⲉⲩⲙⲟⲣⲫⲏ ⲛ̄ⲛⲟϭ ⲛ̄ϩⲟϥ · ⲕⲉⲩⲁ ⲟⲛ ⲁϥϣⲃⲧϥ ⲉⲩⲙⲟⲣⲫⲏ ⲛ̄ϩⲟϥ ⲛ̄ⲥⲓⲧ ⲉϥⲛ̄ⲥⲁϣϥⲉ ⲛ̄ⲁⲡⲉ ⲙ̄ⲙⲟϥ · ⲕⲉⲟⲩⲁ ⲟⲛ ⲁϥϣⲃⲧϥ ⲉⲩⲙⲟⲣⲫⲏ ⲛ̄ⲇⲣⲁⲕⲱⲛ ·**

And some of the emanations of the Arrogant One (Authades) oppressed her. One of them transformed into a great serpent. Again, another transformed into a Basilisk, having seven heads. Another transformed into a Dragon.[60]

The apocryphal *Book of Bartholemew* described Death incarnate and his six sons as crawling serpents who slithered into the tomb of Jesus, waiting until he rose from the dead and descended into Amente, in order to enter with him to learn what it was that he was going to do.

**ⲁⲃⲃⲁⲧⲱⲛ ⲇⲉ ⲉⲧⲉ ⲛ░░░░░ⲡⲙⲟⲩ ⲙⲛ̄ ⲅⲁⲓⲟⲥ · ⲙⲛ̄ ⲧⲣⲩⲫⲱⲛ ⲙⲛ̄ ⲱⲫⲩⲓⲁⲑ · ⲙⲛ̄ ⲫⲑⲓⲛⲱⲛ · ⲙⲛ̄ ⲥⲟⲧⲟⲙⲓⲥ · ⲙ[ⲛ̄] ⲕⲟⲙⲫⲓⲟⲛ · ⲉⲧⲉ ⲛⲁⲓ ⲛⲉ ⲡⲥⲟⲟⲩ ⲛ̄ϣⲏⲣⲉ ⲙ̄ ⲡⲙⲟⲩ · ⲉⲛⲉⲩⲟⲗⲕ̄ ⲡⲉ ϩⲓ ⲡⲟⲩϩⲟⲩ ⲙ̄ ⲡⲉⲙϩⲁⲁⲩ ⲙ̄ ⲡϣⲏ ⲣⲉ ⲙ̄ ⲡⲉⲥⲙⲟⲧ ⲛ̄ ϩⲉⲛⲕⲟⲗⲗⲏⲕⲏⲛ** (κολληκην)

---

56 *Pistis Sophia,* 1.32.9. "Authades" is a personal appellation derived from the Greek loan word, αὐθάδης, "self-willed, arrogant." *LSJ,* p. 275a-b.

57 *Pistis Sofia, passim.* From the Greek σοφία, wisdom. *LSJ,* p. 1621b.

58 *Pistis Sofia,* 1.8.22, *Gospel of the Egyptians, Nag Hammadhi Tractate IV, 52,2.* **ⲃⲁⲣⲃⲏⲗⲱ**, The first emanation of the "Father of the All," essentially his female aspect. (Rudolph, *Gnosis, The Nature and History of Gnosticism,* p. 80.)

59 *Pistis Sofia,* I.28-32. "Pleroma," a Greek loan word, πλήρωμα, fullness (*LSJ,* p. 1419b-1420a). It was a general term incorporated in Gnosticism to signify the totality of the qualities of unmanifest Godhead (Macdermot, *The Concept of Pleroma in Gnosticism,* p. 76.)

60 *Pistis Sofia,* II.66.16-20.

> *Abbatōn*, which [is] Death, and *Gaios*, and *Tryphōn*, and *Ōphiath*, and *Phthinōn*, and *Sotomis*, and *Komphion*, which are the six sons of Death, crawled themselves on their faces into the tomb of the Son of God in the form of worms.[61]

Carl Jung noted that the symbols of worm, snake and dragon all merge in Archetypal concepts, as they do in Latin with *vermis, serpens, draco*.[62] This is particularly true if the Archetype is of the negative elementary character.

It is in the book of *Revelation* that the most familiar multi-headed serpent figure appeared in Christian imagery, that of the Great Red Dragon identified as the Antichrist:

> Και ὤφθη ἄλλο σημεῖον ἐν τῷ οὐρανῳ καὶ ἰδοὺ δράκων πυρρὸς μέγας ἔχων κεφαλὰς ἑπτὰ καὶ κέρατα δέκα καὶ ἐπὶ τὰς κεφαλὰς αὐτοῦ ἑπτὰ διαδήματα καὶ ἡ οὐρὰ αὐτοῦ σύρει τὸ τρίτον τῶν ἀστέρων τοῦ οὐρανοῦ καὶ ἔβαλεν αὐτοὺς εἰς τὴν γῆν καὶ ὁ δράκων ἕστηκεν ἐνώπιον τῆς γυναικὸς τῆς μελλούσης τεκεῖν ἵνα ὅταν τέκῃ τὸ τέκνον αὐτῆς καταφάγῃ

> And another sign was seen in heaven, and behold, a great red dragon having seven heads and ten horns, and upon his heads seven diadems. And his tail dragged down a third of the stars of heaven and he cast them to the earth. And the dragon stands before the woman about to deliver so that when she delivered he might devour her child.[63]

*Figure P13 - The Seven-headed Dragon & Seven-headed Beast of the Sea from Revelation*

---

61 *The Book of Bartholomew the Apostle*, (*BM Oriental 6804 Folio 1a-1b.*) Coptic text in Budge, *Coptic Apocrypha in the Dialect of Upper Egypt*, pp. 1-2 (facsimile of Ms. Plates I-XLVIII.) **ϩⲉⲛⲕⲟⲗⲗⲏⲕⲏⲛ** is corrupt. W.E. Crum suggested it was a Greek loan word κολληκην, < σκωλήκιον, worm, (Crum in Rustafjaell, *The Light of Egypt*, p. 111.)

62 Jung, *Mysterium Coniunctionis*, p. 341. See *OLD* pp. 2037c, 1744c-1745a, 574b.

63 *Revelation* 12:3-4.

# Medusa the Gorgon and the Amphisbæna

P14 - The Head of Medusa

Gorgons, in the ancient Greek myths, were winged humanoid females whose heads were adorned by venomous serpents instead of hair. They were of a totally negative character.

The most famous of these tales is that of the Gorgon Μέδουσα, *Medusa*. According to the legend, any living creature who looked into her eyes was turned to stone.[64] Her name in Greek, Μέδουσα, means "guardian" or "protectress."[65] The name of this deadly goddess curiously entwines beauty and danger together.

She was beheaded by the hero *Perseus*, who used a mirrored shield, provided by the goddess Athena, to view her reflection in the shield that he might slay her.[66]

The famous painting of the severed head of Medusa by Caravaggio (*Figure P15*) illustrates the moment after Perseus slew her by decapitation.[67]

*Figure P15 - Shield Head of Medusa*

64 Kerényi, *The Gods of the Greeks*, pp. 48-50.

65 See *LSJ*, p. 1089b under μέδω.

66 Duff, *Lucan, The Civil Wars (Pharsalia) Book 9, 619-684.*

67 The face of Medusa is a self-portrait by Caravaggio.

It was said that deadly poisonous snakes of the Sahara Desert grew from spilled drops of her blood from her severed head carried by Perseus as he flew over Libya.[68]

Among the poisonous vipers spawned by her blood was the hideous ἀμφίσβαινα, *Amphisbaena*, a horned dragon with a snake for a tail.

> ἡ δὲ ἀμφίσβαινα ὄφις δικέφαλός ἐστι καὶ τὰ ἄνω καὶ ὅσα ἐς τὸ οὐραῖον· προϊοῦσα δὲ ὅπως ἄν ἐς τὴν ὁρμὴν ἐπαγάγῃ τῆς προόδου ἡ χρεία αὐτήν, τὴν μὲν ἀπέλιπεν οὐρὰν εἶναι, τὴν δὲ ἀπέφηνε κεφαλήν. καὶ μέντοι καὶ πάλιν εἰ δεηθείη τὴν ὀπίσω ἰέναι, κέχρηται ταῖς κεφαλαῖς ἐς τὸ ἐναντίον ἤ τὸ πρόσθεν ἐχρήσατο.

> "The **Amphisbaena** is a snake with two heads, one that is above and the other one as far as its tail. When it moves forward, whenever a need for advancing excites it to motion, it leaves one behind to be its tail and displays the other one as its head. On the other hand, if it needs to go back again, it uses the two heads in the opposite manner to the way it used them previously."[69]

*Figure P16 - The Amphisbaena*

68 Seaton, *Apollonius Rhodius, The Argonautica,* Book 4:1515. Cf. Miller, *OVID, Metamorphoses* Vol. 1, Book 4, lines 770-800 (pp. 232-235), and Duff, *Lucan, The Civil Wars (Pharsalia)* Book 9, 683-733.

69 Scholfield, *Aelian,* Περὶ ζῴων ἰδιότητος, *The Characteristics of Animals, IX. 23* (Vol. 2, pp. 243-244). Translation by Matthew Andrews. Cf. Rackham, *Pliny, Natural History,* Vol. 3, Book 8:35, pp. 62-63. See also, Duff, *Lucan, The Civil Wars (Pharsalia),* Book 9, 719.

# Kāliya - the Evil Nāga

Another myth of the serpent as a negative figure occurs in the भागवतपुराण, *Bhāgavata Purāṇa*, a venerable text of वैष्णव धर्म, *Vaiṣhṇavism*, a major Hindu denomination.[70]

In the 10th Canto, Chapter 16, it is related how an evil नाग, *Nāga* (serpent demigod), named कालिय, *Kāliya*, attacked the god कृष्ण, *Kṛṣṇa*, and constricted him within its coils. *Kṛṣṇa* assumed his divine form, and vanquished the serpent, eventually pardoning him after forcing *Kāliya* to swear that he would never trouble anyone again. At last, *Kāliya* took his wives and family and departed to his island in the sea.[71]

This myth is a perfect example of the Archetype of the beautiful heroic god who overcomes evil, while demonstrating infinite mercy, kindness and wisdom as an example to mankind.

*Figure P17 - Kṛṣṇa Attacked by Kāliya*

70 Edwin Francis Bryant declined to assign a firm date to its composition, but noted that most of the material therein was compiled around the fourth-sixth centuries e.v. (Bryant, *Krishna: A Sourcebook*, p. 113).

71 Sinha, *A Study of Bhagavata Purana or Esoteric Hinduism*, pp. 263-264.

## The Serpent as a Positive or Ambivilent Figure

For early humans there was doubtless no more mysterious phase in the life cycle of a serpent than its ability to shed its skin and crawl away in a renewed body. This powerful and numinous image was energized by Archetypal components that naturally and unconsciously constellated in and around it. Unlike human beings who left behind a lifeless decaying hulk of a body upon death, the serpent slipped from its skin and assumed a new life, leaving behind only the shell of its former self. To primordial humans, this must surely have been an utterly staggering and completely incomprehensible phenomenon. It was a clearly observable example of the Archetypal motif of Rebirth and Renewal. Indeed, it is a small wonder that the serpent was a numinous object of worship, as well as fear, from the earliest times.

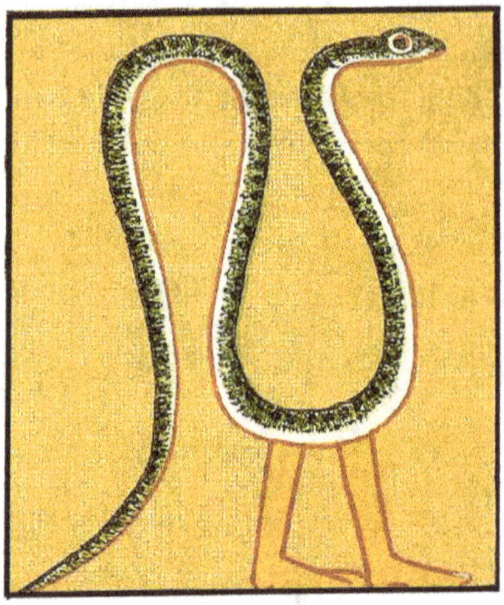

*Figure P18 - The Son of Earth*

*The Egyptian Book of the Dead* includes a lovely Spell which expresses some of these archaic Archetypal impressions in a very brief, but poetically-worded verse.

This Spell is number 87,

*r n ỉrt ḫprw m sꜣ-tꜣ*

*A Spell for taking form as a 'Son Of Earth' (i.e. serpent.)*

Even though its earliest examples date from the Eighteenth Dynasty, it was clearly the culmination of Archetypal motifs that had existed for millennia. The example quoted is from the mid-eighteenth dynasty *Papyrus of Nu (BM 10477)*:

*ỉnk sꜣ-tꜣ ꜣw rnpt sḏr msw rꜥ nb ỉnk*

*I am the Son Of Earth, long in years, sleeping and born every day. I am*

*sꜣ-tꜣ ỉmy ḏrw tꜣ sḏr=ỉ ms kwỉ*

*the Son Of Earth who is in the ends of the earth. I sleep and I am born.*

*mꜣ=kwỉ rnp=kwỉ rꜥ nb*

*I am renewed. I am rejuvenated every day.*

In this Spell, the phrase , *sꜣ tꜣ, son of earth,* an evocative euphemistic name that not only eludes to the primary domicile of Egyptian snakes, but also identifies it subtly with humankind, who are likewise, sons of the earth. The message of this Spell is succinct. As the serpent sheds its skin time and again, the deceased may also experience renewal every day.

As we have seen, the Duat was inhabited by serpents. The eleventh hour brought an encounter with four gods bearing ropes and knifes. But before them stood four gods, each with four serpent heads. Despite their fierce appearance, they served as defenders of the Sun god Ra. Their collective name was , *ḫntyw, butchers.*[72] This doubtless indicated what the enemies of Ra could expect for those who tried to impede his holy journey.

*Figure P19 - Butchers*

72 *The Egyptian Book of Pylons*, Eleventh Hour, Upper Register, 69th Scene. (See Hornung, *The Egyptian Book of Gates*, p. 372.)

# The Uraeus Serpent

Spell *15BII* from *The Egyptian Book of the Dead* illustrates an interesting combination of one serpent as the enemy and another as the savior.

*sḫr.n ꜣḫt ḫftyw=k nḥm.n=k nmt ꜥꜣpp*

*The Uraeus Serpent hath overthrown thine enemies; thou hast checked the advance of Apep!*[73]

*Figure P20 - The Goddess Wadjyet*

In this quotation, the word translated "Uraeus" is , *ꜣḫt,* literally meaning "the glorious one" or "the splendid one."[74] The Greeks derived the word οὐραῖος ("on its tail") directly from the Egyptian word , *iꜥrt, rearing cobra.*[75] The Egyptians utilized a number of epithets for the uraeus. The Royal uraeus was sometimes called , *imt-ḥꜣt=f, she who is upon his forehead,*[76] as well as , *wrt, the great one*[77] or , *nbit, flaming one.*[78]

The serpent goddess , *wꜣḏyt*[79] Wadjyet, a deity associated with the northwestern Delta in Lower Egypt, was normally depicted as a rearing cobra, and as such she was represented as the Uraeus upon the brows of the pharaohs. Recalling the traits of the spitting cobra, she was said to spit flame to protect the king. The Lower Egyptian Shrine of Wadjyet was in the city of , *Pe*, in the Delta, one of two cities sacred to the goddess. It was an ancient site that existed in predynastic times.

---

73 *BD15II, Line 13.* From *Dublin papyrus 1661* for an unnamed man.

74 CDME, p. 4.

75 *Ibid.*, p. 11.

76 *Ibid.*, p. 23.

77 *Ibid.*, p. 79.

78 *Ibid.*, p. 162.

79 *Ibid.*, p. 69. Some older Egyptologists render her name *"Edjōyet"or "Edjō."*

This Shrine was called , *pr-n-nsr*, *house of flame*.[80] The shape of that Shrine is shown in the hieroglyphic determinative for the variant spelling of the name as , *pr-nsr*.[81]

The Uraeus is mentioned in *Liber LXV*, Chapter V, Verse 52, there called **"the great snake of Khem the Holy One, the royal Uræus serpent"**.[82]

## The Coiled One

An enigmatic but positive entity in Egyptian religion, the encircling serpent , *mḥn*, Mehen, was the precursor of the Ouroboros figure.[83] The name means "the coiled one."[84]

Mehen is first mentioned in the Middle Kingdom *Coffin Texts* in Spells 493 and 495, which makes cryptic references to the , *ḫt št3w mḥn*, *mysteries of Mehen*.[85] Egyptologist Richard Wilkinson noted that this may refer to specific rituals that were dedicated to this serpent deity.[86] There is no historical evidence for such cultic activity, yet it cannot be dismissed outright. The words translated as "mysteries," , *ḫt št3w,* literally mean, "the secret matters",[87] and it possibly could indicate the existence of concealed teachings pertaining to "the coiled one."

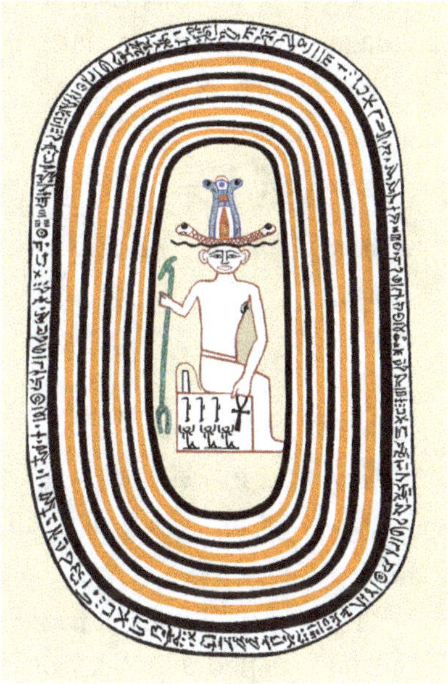

*Figure P21 - "Millions & Millions & Millions of Years*

80 See *CDME*, pp. 110, 111 and 173.

81 *Ibid.*

82 See also, Gunther, *Parables of Thelema*, Part III, *The Parable of the Hummingbird*, "The Uræus Serpent."

83 See below, "Ouroboros."

84 *CDME*, p. 142.

85 12th Dynasty Inner Coffin of , *sn*, "Sen,"*(BM EA308041)*. DeBuck, *Vol. 6, B3L, 493:74j and 495:77f.*

86 Wilkinson, *The Complete Gods and Goddesses of Ancient Egypt*, p. 223.

87 *CDME*, p. 225, *ḫt,* and p. 333, *št3w.*

The domain of Mehen is further elaborated in *Coffin Text* Spells 758-760, but in extremely cryptic verses that are difficult to understand. There is only a single source for these Spells, the 12th Dynasty Coffin of  , *spỉ, Sepi.*[88] There, Mehen is said to exist within concentric rings which are the paths of fire that encircle and shield Ra. *Coffin Text* Spell 759 is accompanied by a most unusual vignette, which portrays the Sun God with face forward, sitting upon a throne which bears the inscription,  , *millions and millions and millions of years,*[89] and surrounded by rings of fire.

Vestiges of *Coffin Texts* 758 and 759 survived in the final paragraph of BD Spell 131, which describes the physical form of Mehen in highly obscure language. Here is the initial portion of the final paragraph of that Spell from *The Book of the Dead*:

*mdw n=ỉ ỉtm ỉr ʿḳt nbt mḥn pwy m ḥḥw pwy*

*Atum says to me, "As for any who enter, this Coiled One is millions,*

*m ḥḥwy m ꜣw ỉmy wrt ṯꜣ-wr*

*even two million in length, from prow to stern..."*[90]

Mehen was depicted prominently in the panoramic scenes of *The Book of Pylons* (also called *The Book of Gates*), the second book of the netherworld of Egypt's New Kingdom, which was composed around 1400 BCE and painted on the tomb walls of Kings.[91] The central theme of the composition is the division of the twelve hours of the night, and follows the journey of Ra through this perilous region, until he is reborn each morning. The cabin of the Sun god's boat is encircled and protected by Mehen. The blessed *Akh*-spirits, those who knew Ra-Hoor-Khuit upon the earth and are now safely in the protected West, hail Ra in the 5th hour:

---

88 *Cairo CG 28083*, DeBuck, Vol. *6, B1C, 758-760.*

89 The word 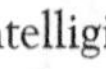 , *ḥḥ*, "millions," is there drawn as a variant 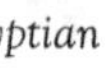 , with the sign for "year"  , *rnpt*, removed from the head of the human figure.

90 *Papyrus of Nu (BM 10477)*, Sheet 17, Lines 9-10. R.O. Faulkner declined to attempt a translation of this portion of Spell 131, writing that, "the remainder of this chapter is too corrupt to yield an intelligible translation." (Faulkner & Goelet, *The Egyptian Book of the Dead*, p. 118).

91 An excellent translation, and lovely publication with colour throughout, is Erik Hornung's *The Egyptian Book of the Gates* (2014).

*ỉy=tỉ rʿ ʿr=k n dwꜣt hnw n=k ʿḳ=k ḏsrw m mḥn*

*Welcome, Ra, as thou dost approach the Duat! Praise to thee when thou dost enter asylum in Mehen!*[92]

The "Coiled One" likewise appears in the work called *Amduat*, "that which is in the Duat," which also recounts the voyage of the Sun-god through twelve hours of the underworld.[93]

*Figure P22 - Meḥen Encircling the Cabin of the Sun God*

---

92 Fifth hour, 23rd scene, from the Alabaster Sarcophagus of Seti I (Sir John Sloane's Museum, London).

93 An excellent translation is available in: *The Egyptian Amduat, The Book of the Hidden Chamber*, by Erik Hornung (2007). It is a valuable companion volume to his book, *The Egyptian Book of Gates* (2014).

# Mereseger

*Figure P23 - Mereseger*

For the workmen of the Royal Necropolis in the village of Deir el-Medina in the Valley of the Kings, , *mr-sgr*, *Mereseger, she who loves silence*, was a special goddess to the workmen of the village, who excavated and decorated the tombs of the Pharaohs. She ruled over the pyramidal-shaped peak that towered over the Theban royal necropolis in the Valley of the Kings, a desolate, quiet place inhabited only by the silent Royal dead, and temporarily by the tomb builders and their families. Hence, she was also called , *dhn ỉmntt*, *peak of the west*, or simply , *dhn*, *the peak*. It was believed that She would punish evil doers with snake bites, scorpion stings, or blindness, but she was beloved for her forgiveness and the healing of illness.[94] The 19th dynasty stele of the Foreman of workmen, , *nfr-ʿ3b*, *Neferabu*,[95] shown above in *Figure P23*, depicted her with a serpent body and three heads: that of a snake, a vulture, and a woman.[96] This stele recounts how she forgave Neferabu's transgression against the goddess and healed him of the affliction with which

*Figure P24 - Pyramidal Peak Overlooking Deir al-Medinah*

---

94 Wilkinson, *The Complete Gods and Goddesses of Ancient Egypt*, p. 224.

95 Neferabu has become the accepted reading of the name, even though the hieroglyphics here read Nefer-ab. His name is also found written , *nfr-ʿ3bw*, Nefer-abu, and , *nfr-ʿ3bt*, "Nefer-abet." The actual pronunciation of Egyptian words is generally still unknown to us.

96 Museo Egizio, Turin 1593.

he had been punished.

Neferabu is a well-known figure from the populace at Deir el-Medina and his burial place carries the Theban Tomb number TT5.[97] A number of artifacts belonging to Neferabu are preserved in museums in various places, including the stele above, which is in the Museo Egizio in Turin. The background information concerning Neferabu's ailment is provided from the stele numbered *EA 589* in the British Museum. It was a votive stela dedicated to the god Ptah, the god of craftsmen and artisans, and the front of this stela is inscribed with appropriate propitiations to him. However, the reverse is inscribed with a confession in which he admitted that he had blasphemed Ptah, and was stricken with blindness.

*ỉnk s ꜥrḳy m ꜥḏꜣ n ptḥ nb mꜣꜥt dỉ=f ptr ỉr kkw*

*I am a man who swore falsely by Ptah, Lord of Truth. He caused the seeing of night*

*m hrwỉw r=ỉ ḏd bꜣw=f ni ẖm sw rḫ sw n šrỉw*

*by day![98] I proclaim his power to the ignorant one and the knowledgable one, to the young*

*ꜥꜣ šꜣw=tn r ptḥ nb mꜣꜥt*

*and the old! Beware ye of Ptah, Lord of Truth![99]*

However, in the text of the Turin stele above, Neferabu claimed his blindness, as well as some nameless malady, resulted from his sin against the serpent goddess Mereseger, and credits her with healing him:

97 See Vandier, *La Tombe de Nefer-Abou.*

98  , *dỉ=f ptr ỉr kkw m hrwỉw*, "He caused the seeing of night by day," that is, "He caused blindness," a term common to the period. A similar term is also found in this location,  , *dỉ=k mꜣ=ỉ kk ỉr=k*, "Thou didst cause me to see a darkness of Thy making." (Museo Egizio No. 1553, line 3, *Stele of*  , *pꜣy, Pay.*)

99 *BM EA 589*, reverse, lines 2-4.

*mr-sgr nb.t pt ḥnwt tꜣwy rn=st nfr n dhn ỉmn[tt] (1) rdỉtw n dhn ỉmntt*

*Mereseger, Lady of Heaven, mistress of the Two Lands. Her good name is "Peak of the West." (1) Giving praises to the Peak of the West,*

*sn tꜣ n kꜣ=st dỉ=ỉ dwꜣw sḏm [n]ỉs*[100] *ỉnk (2) mꜣꜥt ḥr-dp tꜣ ỉr n sḏm-ꜥš m ỉst mꜣꜥt*

*kissing the ground to her Ka-spirit, I give praise! Hear my Invocation! I was a (2) just man upon the earth. Made by the Servant In The Place of Truth,*[101]

*nfr-ꜥꜣb mꜣꜥ-ḫrw s ḫm n ỉwty (3) ḥꜣty=ỉ bw rḫ nfr r bỉn*

*Neferabu, True of Voice, an ignorant man, who did not (3) know good from evil.*

*ỉw=ỉ ḥr ỉrt pꜣ sp n [t]hꜣ (4) r dhn ỉw=st ḥr ỉr[t] n=ỉ sbꜣ*

*I committed the misdeed of transgressing (4) against the Peak, and she taught me a lesson.*

*ỉw=ỉ m dt=st (5) m grḥ mỉ hrw ỉw=ỉ ḥmsỉ=kw*[102] *ḥr dbt mỉ tꜣ*

*I was under her hand (5) by day and night; I sat upon a birthing brick like the*

---

100 , *ḏm ỉs*, was written instead of , *sḏm nỉs*, in , *sḏm nỉs=ỉ*, "Hear my Invocation."

101 , *sḏm ꜥš m ỉst mꜣꜥt*, "Servant in the Place of Truth," was a title of prominence in Deir el-Medinah. The , *ỉst mꜣꜥt*, "Place of Truth" was a name for that necropolis.

102 , *ḥmsỉ=kw*, "I sat," 1st person singular ending, Stative. (Allen, *Middle Egyptian Grammar*, 16.2).

*ỉwr (6) ỉw=ỉ ḥr ʿš=ỉ n ṯ3w nn ỉw=f n=ỉ ỉw=ỉ (7) ḳb*

*woman (6) in labor! I summoned the wind, but it did not come to me!*[103] *I poured (7) libation*

*n t3 dhn ỉmntt ʿ3 pḥty nṯr nb nṯrt nb ḫ[r] (8) ptr ỉw=ỉ r ḏd n*

*for the Peak of the West, great of might, and every god and every goddess. Now, (8) behold! I shall say to*

*ʿ3 šỉr nty m t3 ỉswt š3w (9) t3 r dhn p3 wn m3ỉ*

*the old and the young in the workforce: beware (9) of the Peak! For there is a lion*

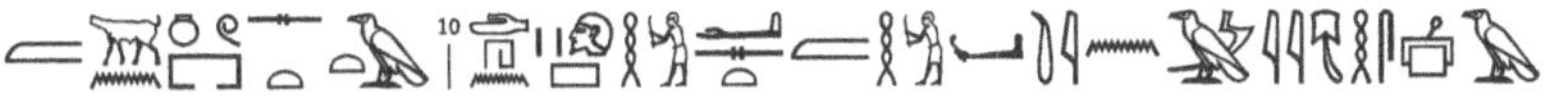

*m-ḫnw=st t3 (10) dhn ḥwỉ=st m ḥwỉ tỉ n m3ỉ ḥs3*

*within her! The (10) Peak, she strikes with the stroke of a savage lion!*

*ỉrt (11) ỉw=st m-s3 th3 r=st ỉw=ỉ ḥr ʿš n t3y (12) =ỉ ḥnwt gm=st*

*She will (11) pursue whoever offends her! I invoked my Mistress (12) and found Her*

*ỉỉ.tỉ.n=ỉ m ṯ3w nḏm ỉw=st ḥr (13) ḥtp n=ỉ ỉw dỉ=sw m33*

*coming to me as a sweet breeze. She was (13) merciful to me (after) she had shown*

*dt=st ỉw=st ʿnn (14) n=ỉ m ḥtpyw ỉw=st ḥr dỉ sḫm=ỉ n mr-(15)-w*

*to me her hand. She returned (14) to me with forgiveness and she made me to forget the agony (15)*

---

103  , *ỉw=ỉ ḥr ʿš=ỉ n ṯ3w nn ỉw=f n=ỉ*, "I summoned the wind, but it did not come to me," probably meant that he suffered labored breathing. His comparison to a woman in labor pains is probably connected to the ailment described in this phrase.

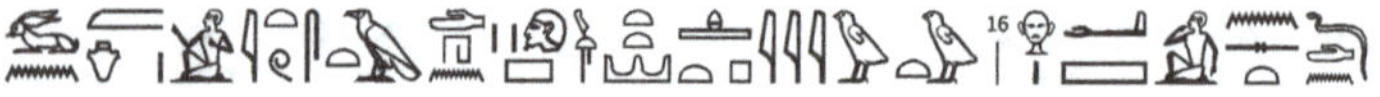

*wn m ìb=ì ìst tꜣ dhn ìmntt ḥtpy ìw tw (16) ḥr ʿš.n=st ḏd n*

*that was in my heart. Lo! The Peak of the West is merciful when one (16) invokes her! Spoken by*

*nfr-ʿꜣb mꜣʿ-ḫrw ḏd=f ptr sḏm ms[ḏr] (17) nb nty ʿnḫ ḥr-dp tꜣ šꜣw*

*Neferabu, True of Voice. He saith, Behold, let hear (17) every ear that liveth on the earth: Beware*

*tꜣ dhn ìmntt*

*the Peak of the West!*

## Renenutet

The serpent goddess , *rnnwtt*, *Renenutet*, was venerated in the Old Kingdom of Egypt as a protector of the king, in life as well as in death. She was often depicted as a cobra, or a snake-headed woman nursing a baby. Her name in Egyptian was derived from , *rnn*, *to nurse*,[104] and , *wtt*, *female snake*.[105] Her full name literally meant "snake who nurses."

Her reputation, particularly in the later dynasties, was that of a divine care-giver and protector, rather than a goddess to be feared. She was particularly beloved among those who worked in farming the fields or wine-making. She was connected with the harvest and was considered the protector of

*Figure P25 - Renenutet in the Robe of Glory*

104 Cf. , *rnn*, "to caress." (CDME, p. 187)

105 *Wb*, Vol. 2, pp. 436-437 and Vol. 1, p. 378. The second word, , *wtt*, was an ancient serpent-goddess that appeared in the *Pyramid Texts*, Spell 468 (Pepi), *§ 900b & 902b*. The word literally means, "begetter," from , *wtt*. (*CDME*, p. 88)

the grain. This was likely due to the fact that snakes warded off the rats and mice that would damage both the ripe and harvested grain.

Many scarabs have been found inscribed with her affectionate title, , *nb(t) kꜣw*, *mistress of food.*[106] The 19th Dynasty Stele[107] (*Figure P26*) depicts the adoration of , *rnnw(tt) nfrt nb(t) pt*, *Renenutet, kind mistress of heaven.* It was common for her devotees to erect altars dedicated to her near the fields where grapes were harvested and crushed to make wine.[108]

*Figure P26 - Stele of Mutneferet*

Her Feast Day was the Feast of **ⲡⲁⲣⲙⲟⲩⲧⲉ**, the 8th Month, which was celebrated on the first day of Summer, the first day of the Month following.[109] The Coptic month-name **ⲡⲁⲣⲙⲟⲩⲧⲉ** represented the Egyptian , *p(ꜣ)-n-rnnwtt*, literally, "that of Renenutet."[110]

In the oldest accounts of the goddess, recorded in the *Pyramid Texts*, she was described in a very lofty way, as one of the great deities in the realm of the gods, and was closely associated with the *Eye of Horus*. In Spell 622 of the *Pyramid Texts* of King *Pepi, Neferkara*,[111] it was Renenunet who clad the deceased Pharoah in the Royal Robe of Glory as he was prepared to ascend unto the presence of the gods:[112]

---

106 Alice Grenfell, *The Ka on Scarabs*, RT, Vol. 37 (1915), p. 91.

107 Stele of Mutnefert, Museo Egizio, *S.6138.*

108 Leibovitch, *Gods of Agriculture and Welfare in Ancient Egypt, JNES*, Vol. 12, No. 2 (April 1953), p. 76.

109 A peculiarity of ancient Egypt was that they always celebrated the Feast of a Month on the first day of the *following* Month, rather than in the Month which gave it its name. (Gardiner, *Egyptian Grammar*, p. 205.)

110 Sahidic **ⲡⲁⲣⲙⲟⲩⲧⲉ**, in Bohairic **ⲫⲁⲣⲙⲟⲩⲑⲓ**, in Greek Φαρμοῦθι (*Vycichl*). Curiously, the Coptic Name clearly reflects the serpentine aspect of her name, , *wtt*, in the ending **-ⲟⲩⲧⲉ**. (*Wb*, Vol. 2, p. 378.)

111 Pepi II was the fifth King of the 6th Dynasty, successor to Merenra I, who had ruled only a decade or so. Pepi II assumed the Throne at the age of 6 years and ruled for almost a century, taking the Throne Name , *nfrkꜣrꜥ*, "Neferkara," "The Beautiful Ka-spirit of Ra." He ruled circa 2246-2162 BCE.

112 This Spell is inscribed on the walls of the vestibule in the Sarcophagus chamber, and is grouped with a series of Spells that announce the rising of the King's spirit at dawn and preparation for reception among the gods.

*ḏd mdw ỉsỉr nfrkꜣrꜥ ḏbꜣ n=kwỉ m ỉrt ḥrw rnnwtt ỉtn nrt n n=s nṯrw*

*Words to be spoken: Osiris Neferkara, I have adorned thee with the Eye of Horus, this Renenutet garment of which the gods are fearful,*

*nr n=k nṯrw mỉ nrt=sn n ỉrt ḥrw*

*so that the gods will be fearful of thee, like they are fearful of the Eye of Horus.*[113]

An 18th Dynasty inscription from the tomb of a Royal Scribe who was the Overseer of the Granaries of Upper and Lower Egypt, recorded a prayer for her blessings on the first day of the harvest season:

*wdnw ḫt nbt wꜥb n rnnwtt nbt šnwt m ꜣbd 1 šmw rꜥ*

*Offerings and all good and pure things for Renenutet, mistress of the granary, on the first day of the harvest.*

*rnpwt nfrt wꜥbt n kꜣ=t rnnwtt nbt šnwt dỉ=t*

*Good and pure plants for thy Ka-spirit, Renenutet, Mistress of the Granary. Allow thou*

*wnn pꜣ ỉmy-r šnwtw m ḥs=t rꜥ nb*

*the Overseer of the Granaries to be in thy favor every day!*[114]

---

113 *PT Spell 622, § 1755a-1755c.*

114 *TT57. Tomb of Khaemhat, Overseer of Granaries, 18th Dynasty. Wreszinski, Atlas zur altägyptischen Kulturgeschichte*, Vol. 1, Plate 198. See also *Brugsch, Recueil de monuments Égyptiennes*, Vol. 2, Plate LXVII, Lines 1-2, 9-13.

*Figure P27 - Renenutet Suckling a Child*

## Weret-Hekau

The name of the serpent goddess , *wrt-ḥkꜣw, Weret-Hekau,* means "Great of Magic." This title was also given to the goddess Isis as her popularity became widespread and she subsumed the traits of many goddesses of lesser stature.

In the Late Period, Weret-Hekau appeared more as an independent goddess, even shown nursing the Pharoah in the manner of Renenutet. She was considered a guardian goddess, and she often appears in tombs represented on items intended to protect the deceased against the dangers of the underworld.

Over the long history of Egypt, the name Weret-Hekau as a title was applied to numerous goddesses such as Sekhmet, or as an aspect of Wadjyet, the Uraeus serpent, as well as the Crown of Lower Egypt.[115]

*Figure P28 - Weret-Hekau, Great of Magic*

For many decades, Egyptologists attempted to avoid the use of the word "magic" in translations of the ancient Egyptian texts and within discussions of their religious ideas. Those that did use the term, often associated it with superstition and degraded, primitive animism, in contradistinction to modern accepted religious practices, which were considered more civilized and superior.[116]

No such dichotomy was present in ancient Egyptian religion; magic, ( , *ḥkꜣw, Hekau*), did not simply refer to a practice, but a *psychic component*, considered an essential aspect of every living person. It represented the creative power within, the ability to empower, sustain and protect the individual, physically and spiritually, in life and in life after death.[117]

---

115 Occasionally, when associated with the Royal Crowns, she was depicted with a Lion head. See Nelson, *The Great Hypostyle Hall at Karnak (Oriental Institute Publications, Vol. 106), plates 191-192.*

116 The German Egyptologist Adolph Erman and British Egyptologist Alan Gardiner were two prime examples of this outdated mindset. Modern Egyptology has better examples of brilliant scholars not so encumbered: Jan Assmann, the late Erik Hornung and Harold M. Hays. Stephen Quirke still favors "word power" over "magic" in deference to the literal translation of the word *hekau*, avoiding the prejudicial misconceptions of many modern readers.

117 The Priesthoods in Egypt conducted many magical rites and ceremonial acts. There is fundamentally no difference between those practices than that of Christian baptism performed as a rite of rebirth, or celebrating the Eucharist, affirming that the wafer and wine are transformed into the body and blood of Jesus Christ. Disparaging one as primitive and ignoring the implication of the other is disingenuous and foolish.

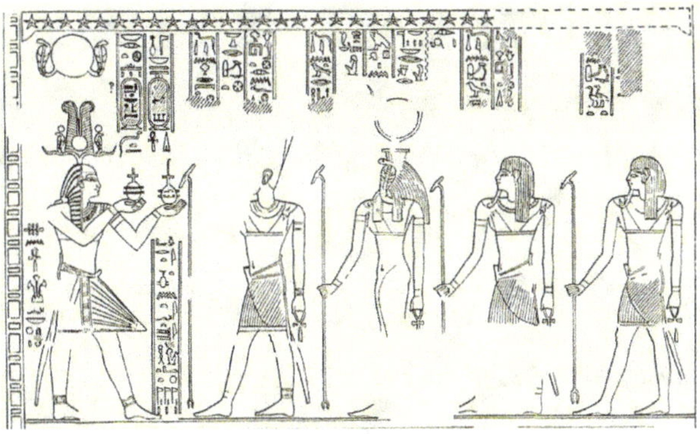

*Figure P29 - Pharaoh Presenting Milk to Weret-Hekau*

Some basic knowledge of the meaning of *hekau* is essential if one is to glean even the most general comprehension of the goddess Weret-Hekau, and how she was understood at the time.

In a text composed in the 18th Dynasty, called *The Teachings for King Merykara,*[118] the subject is the written instructions an aging king gave to his son Merykara, who would succeed him on the throne. The document demonstrates a high moral code, and reflections on the divine nature, in particular that God (singular) prefers a righteous life in preference to rich offerings. The denouement of the text is a hymn to the Creator, in which he tells his son of one gift that God gave to mankind:

*ỉr.n=f n=sn ḥkꜣw r ꜥḥꜣw r ḫsfꜥ n ḫpryt*

*He made for them Hekau as weapons to contend against the blows of what may happen.*[119]

This magic was considered so vital to the living human being that it was essential that this magical force would not be lost with the advent of death. It was presumed that this vitality became dissipated with the death of the body and had to be reunited with that person prior to passing into the Duat. In BD 64, the deceased declared the supreme importance of his *Hekau*:

---

118 The name of the son,  , *mrykꜣrꜥ*, “Merykara,” Pharaoh of the 10th Dynasty, survives at the beginning of the fragmentary papyus. The unknown author of the text utilized a historic ruler who reigned prior to the unification of Egypt for his treatise on wise kingship, avoiding any current political problem and giving freedom of expression.

119 *Instructions of King Merykara, Papyrus Hermitage 116A*, verso, Lines 136-137. Hieroglyphic text in Volten, *Zwei altägyptische politische Schriften die Lehre für König Merikarê*, p. 75.

*ḥkꜣw=ỉ rwd ỉwf=ỉ ꜣḫw=ỉ m sꜣ ꜥwt=ỉ*

*My Magic (Hekau) is the strengthening of my flesh. My spiritual power is the protection of my limbs.*

*nwr sšn=f ḥr nḏwt-r ꜥḥꜥ psḏt r ḏdt=ỉ*

*The Crane cries out in greeting and the Ennead rise at my word.*[120]

Among the series of Spells in *The Book of the Dead* dedicated to restoring the Heart and Mind of the deceased, BD Spell 24 was included as a means to return the Magical Force that a person lost immediately upon death. The example of this Spell, which I have transcribed and translated below, is from the 26th Dynasty Inner Coffin of  , *nsr-ỉmn*, *Neser-amun II*, the eldest son of 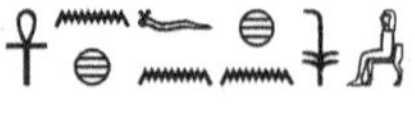 , *Ankhefenkhonsu.*[121]

*r n ỉnỉ ḥkꜣw n ỉsỉr ḥm-nṯr mnṯ nb{t} wꜣst ... nsr-ỉmn*

*A Spell for bringing the Magic of the Osiris, Prophet of Menthu, Lord of Thebes ... Neser-amun,*

*mꜣꜥ-ḫrw sꜣ nb wꜣst ꜥnḫ=f.n.ḫnsw mꜣꜥ-ḫrw ỉrt nb[t] pr ns-ḫnsw mꜣꜥ-ḫrw....*

*True of Voice, son of the Prophet of Menthu, Lord of Thebes, Ankhefenkhonsu, True of Voice, and engendered by the Mistress of the House, Neskhonsu, True of Voice...*

120 *Papyrus of Nu (EA 10477), BD* 64 (long version), Sheet 21, lines 40-41.

121 *Inner Coffin of Neseramun II,* Cairo 41044. (Gauthier, *Catalogue général des antiquites égyptiennes du musée du caire, n$^{os}$. 41042-41072,* Vol. 1, pp. 47-48.) Neskhonsu I was the first wife of Ankhefenkhonsu. Her father was Hor-maat I, the treasurer of the Pharaoh. Her mother, Gaut-se-shenu II, was of royal blood through her paternal grandmother Tarwa, the great-granddaughter of the Pharaoh Takelot I, son of Pharaoh Osorkon I, son of the Pharaoh Soshenk I. Thus, Neser-amun II, and his brothers Wennefer II, Nemenkhetpara and Besenmut II, were also of Royal blood.

*ỉnk ḫprỉ ḫpr r ḏs=f ḥry wꜥrt mwt=f rdỉ wnšw n ỉmyw*

*I am Khepri, who came into being of himself, who is master of the lap of his mother, who gave Jackals to those who are in*

*nnw bḫnw n ỉmyw ḏꜣḏꜣt ỉs dmḏ.n=ỉ ỉs dmḏ.n=ỉ ḥkꜣw=ỉ pw*

*the Primeval Waters, and Hunting Dogs to those who are in the Tribunal.*[122] *Lo! I shall reassemble this Magic*

*m bw nb nt=f ỉm ẖr s pn nt=f ẖr=f btn r ṯsm ḫꜣḫ r*

*from any place it is, with whoever it is with! Swifter than a greyhound, faster than*

*šwyt ỉ ỉnn mḫnt nt rꜥ rwd ꜥḳꜣ=k*

*a Shadow! O, bringer of the ferry-boat of Ra! Secure thy lanyard*

*m mḥw ḫntỉ=k r ỉw-nsrsr m ẖrt-nṯr ỉs dmḏ.n=k*

*in the upstream current in thy sailing South to the Island of Fire in the God's Domain! Lo! Reassemble thou*

122 The deceased identifies with the god Khepri, the self-created, who placed canny animal hunters in the primeval creation, and tamed trackers in the Hall of Justice. Desert Jackals historically scented out and scavenged the dead, and hunting dogs were used to track the living. The implication is that, in order to find his Magic, the deceased may employ either one to track it down, wherever it may be. The 11th Dynasty *Coffin Text 402*, which was the predecessor of this BD Spell, used the word, 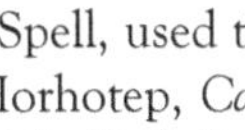 , *wḥswt*, "predators," instead of "hunting dogs." (Coffin of Horhotep, *Cairo 2803*, DeBuck *T1C*) The 12th Dynasty *Coffin of Hapiankhtyfy* spelled that word  , determined by an animal skin. (*Met. Mus. of Art 12.183.11a*, DeBuck *M2NY*) Raymond Faulkner noted that it can be ascertained from this that a hunting quadruped of some kind was intended to serve as a counterpart to the Jackal. (Faulkner, *CT*, Vol. 2, p. 46.)

*ḥkꜣw pn n ỉsỉr ḥm-nṯr mnṯw nb wꜣst nsr-ỉmn mꜣꜥ-ḫrw m bw nb nt{t}=f*

*this Magic of the Osiris, Prophet of Menthu, Lord of Thebes, Neser-amun, True of Voice, from any place it is,*

*ỉm ḫr=f ḫr=s nt=f ḫr=f btn r ṯsm ḫꜣḫ r šwyt ky ḏd* [123]

*with whoever it is with! Swifter than a Greyhound, faster than a Shadow! In other words,*

*ḫꜣḫ r šw nwr m ḳmꜣ n nṯrw m sgrw rdỉ[=tw]*

*faster than the god Shu! The Crane cries mournfully for the gods in silence. The cry of the Crane is offered*

*bgw nwrt r srf r n nṯrw ỉs rdỉ n ỉsỉr ḥm-nṯr mnṯ nb wꜣst*

*to warm the mouth of the gods.*[124] *Lo! Give the Osiris, Prophet of Mentu, Lord of Thebes,*

*nsr-ỉmn mꜣꜥ-ḫrw ḥkꜣw=f pn [m bw nb nt=f ỉm ] ḫr s pn n{t}t=f*

*Neser-amun, True of Voice, this Magic of his, [from any place it is,] with whoever it is with!*

*ḫr=f btn r ṯsm ḫꜣḫ r šw[yt] ky ḏd ḫꜣḫ r šw*

*Swifter than a Greyhound! Faster than a [Shadow]! In other words, faster than the god Shu!*

---

123 *nwr m.* The Scribe incorrectly wrote  , in place of  .

124 i.e. The Crane cries mournfully when the gods are silent, yet its cries inspire the gods to speak.

In this inscription, we see that the deceased sought to accompany the Sun-god Ra on his Southern voyage to the mysterious Island of Fire in the Duat. The direction South is upstream on the river Nile, which flows from South to North.

The Nile (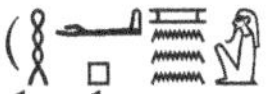 , *ḥʿpy* , *Hapy*)[125] was considered an earthly eidolon of the river of the heavens upon which Ra sailed each day in his celestial journey. This "heavenly river" was visualized in the Milky Way galaxy, in Egyptian,  , *mr nḫꜣ*, *the winding canal.*[126]

To travel South on the Nile was to go *against the current*, toward its source which was unknown at the time. Thus, symbolically, the course of the water signified the River of Life, which flowed from an unknown beginning, to its inevitable end, when it poured into the the Mediterranean Sea, which the Egyptians called  , *wꜣḏ-wr*, *the great green.*[127] To sail Southbound implied a return to the point of origin, the symbolic place of Birth. Significantly, the Southernmost cataract on the Nile was at the island of *Elephantine* (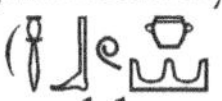 , *ꜣbw*), sacred to the ram-headed god  , *ḫnmw*, *Khnum*,[128] the "moulder of men," commonly depicted forming a human being on his potter's wheel. The Milky Way rises in the Southeast and sets in the Southwest, effectively conjoining the emblems of Birth (East and the rising Sun) and Death (West and the setting Sun) in the celestial river that mirrored the course of human life.

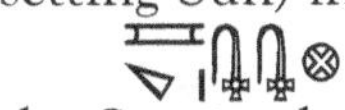 , *ỉw-nsrsr* , the "Island of Fire," was said to be the birthplace of the Sun in the Duat. It was the place where the deceased to travel in order to be spiritually cleansed and to be reborn like the Sun. Hence, in BD 24 above, he sought passage in the Boat of Ra to the Island of Fire, to secure his Magic.

---

125 *CDME*, p. 203.

126 In numerous places in the *Pyramid Texts*, the words  , *mr nḫꜣ*, "Winding Canal," is written with the determinative  written in a curved fashion  to suggest a winding stream. Over the years a number of Egyptologists have considered that waterway in a purely mythological sense, or a mythology embodied in an astronomical observation. Most recently, Stephen Quirke defined it simply as, "one of the principal waters of the afterlife" (Quirke, *Going Out in Daylight*, p. 603) James Allen identified with the Ecliptic, the path of the sun across the sky in a 12° arc from East to West. (Allen, *The Ancient Egyptian Pyramid Texts*). I have long believed, as have a few others, that based on the textual evidence from the *Pyramid Texts*, the Winding Canal signified the Milky Way galaxy. That belief was proven in 2008 by Yassar A. Abdel-Hadi, an astronomer with the National Research Institute of Astronomy and Geophysics in Cairo. Using astronomical simulation programs, the image of the sky from the time of the building of the pyramids was carefully analyzed. By careful comparison with the *Pyramid Texts* and the astronomical data, it was determined that the "Winding Canal" was indeed the Milky Way galaxy. (Abdel-Hadi, *Astronomical Interpretation of the Winding Canal in the Pyramid Texts.*)

127 *CDME*, p. 69.

128 *Wb*, Vol. 3, p. 382.

This is reiterated in *BD Spell 15B1*:

*ỉmỉ n=ỉ ỉst m wỉꜣ=k rꜥ ḥr-ntt ỉnk bꜣ ỉḳr n gs*

*Grant me a seat in thy boat, Ra, because I am an excellent Ba-soul beside*

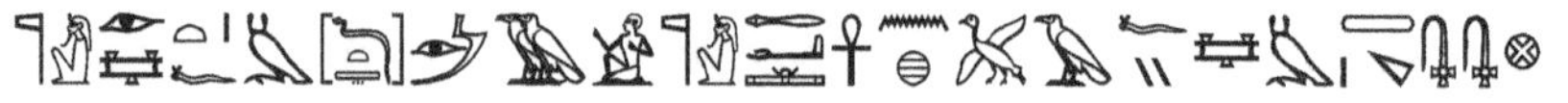

*nṯr ỉr wꜣt=f m [ḏt] mꜣꜣ=ỉ nṯr ꜥꜣ ꜥnḫ pfy m ỉw-nsrsr*

*the god making his way in [eternity]. I shall see the great god who lives beyond, in the Island of Fire!"*[129]

In the mysterious Island of Fire, he will come face-to-face with the serpent goddess, the "Great of Magic," Weret-Hekau herself, who will purify him from all the defects of death, and restore his Magic. From *Coffin Text* Spell 37:

*ỉt sꜥḥ=k m pr spdt sbnwt=k m ḥwt*

*Father! Thou shalt be ennobled in the House of Sothis! Thou shalt be suckled in the Mansion of*

*wrt kꜣ šsp nṯrwt m ḥwt kꜣ ḥḏ wꜥb=ṯw*

*the Great Bull! Thou shalt receive Godhood in the Mansion of the White Bull! Thou shalt be purified*

*wrt-ḥkꜣwy*

*by Weret-Hekau!*[130]

---

129 *BD15B1*, 19th Dynasty *Papyrus of Nakhtamun* (Berlin 3002), Lines 12-14.

130 The name of Weret-Hekau is here written in the Dual Form, 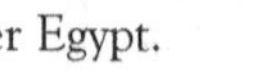 , *wrt-ḥkꜣwy,* (indicated by the two cobras for determinatives) which was used to suggest her aspect as the "Mistress of Crowns," i.e. the Royal Crowns of Upper and Lower Egypt.

*m=k ḥm=k ỉỉ ꜥpr.n=f ȝḫ nb nn sp m=f m ỉw-nsrsr*

*Behold! Thy Majesty hath come, having acquired all Glory, nothing remaining in the Island of Fire!*

*mḥ.n=k ẖt=k m ḥkȝw ḫtm.n=k ỉbt=k ỉm=f*

*Thou hast filled thy body with Magic! Thou hast quenched thy thirst with it!*

*sdȝ.n=k wrš=k ỉm=f mỉ ȝpd ꜥpr.n=f tȝ m rḫ.t.n=k*

*Those who watch thee tremble like a bird from it! The earth is provided with thy knowledge...*[131]

For many years, Egyptologists discounted the possibility that an independent priesthood and cult of Weret-Hekau ever existed. However, in the last decades, sufficient evidence has been uncovered or rediscovered, and carefully translated and analyzed to disprove that notion. A number of engaging studies have been published by Egyptologist Ahmed M. Mekawy Ouda that prove, beyond any doubt whatsoever, that Weret-Kekau had a cult with a hierarchical priesthood devoted to her service. Whether she had special Temples remains in discussion, although six known sources suggest that such a place of worship did exist, although no archeological evidence has yet been unearthed.[132]

There are many attestations of various Priestly Titles in the service of Weret-Hekau, and perhaps the most notable is , *ḥm-nṯr wrt-ḥkȝw*, *Prophet of Weret-Hekau*, which occurs on stelae, statues and on one Sarcophagus of particular note to us: *Inventory number* CG 41017 in the Cairo Museum, which is that of the 26th Dynasty Theban Priest , *ḥrw*, *Hor*, the son of the Priest , *ỉrtḥrw*, *Irethoru*, who was the son of , *nspȝsf*, *Nespasef*, the half-brother of our own *Ankhefenkhonsu*.[133]

---

131 CT 37, DeBuck I146-150 (composite readings from *B3B0, B4L, B12Cb, B2B0, B16C, B13Ca)*

132 E.g. see Ouda, *Did Werethekau 'Great of Magic' have a Cult?: A Disjunction between Scholarly Opinions and Sources, The German Archaeological Institute Cairo, Young Researchers' Lecture Series (2013).*

133 Moret, *Catalogue général des antiquités Egyptiennes du Musée du Caire, Sarcophages, Nos. 41001-41041*, Vol. 2, p. 179. Moret's staff apparently missed both the mention of Weret-Hekau and this Priestly Title on the Sarcophagus. Both are omitted in the Index of Deities and Titles. It was discovered by Ahmed M. Mekawy Ouda.

# Neheb-Kau

*Figure P30 - Nehebu-Kau*

The serpent-headed god , *nḥb-kꜣw*, *Neheb-Kau*, was an ancient benevolent god, known from the time of the *Pyramid Texts*. The meaning of his name is, "He who appoints the Ka-spirits."[134] In this capacity, he originally appeared to act as an intermediary on behalf of the King before the great gods of heaven. In later dynasties, this was seen as a gift to all virtuous people of the Two Lands.

He was a very beloved god and venerated for his character of providing assistance and protection. During the Middle Kingdom, in the famous Heart Spell 30A, the deceased appealed to be made whole and healthy for him.

An ancient Pyramid text of King Pepy I[135] illustrates the relationship of the Ka-spirit to Nehebu-Kau.

*ỉꜣḫ mr nḫꜣ ḏꜣwt ppy pn ỉm ḏꜣwt ỉr ꜣḫt*

*The Winding Canal is flooded to ferry this King Pepy and ferry over to the horizon*

*ḫr ḥr-ꜣḫty ỉ-ỉn m n ppy pn fdw ỉpw snw swꜣ*

*near Hoor-Khuit. Bring this King Pepy these Four Brethren who pass by,*

---

134 From , *nḥb*, "harness, yoke, appoint" + , *kꜣw*, "Ka-spirits" (*CDME*, pp. 170, 347). The meaning seems to be that the Ka-spirit is "appointed (to a position)." Cf. *JEA 33* (1947), p. 23, Note b.

135 *PT, Spell 266, §359-361.* My Student, the late Dr. Harold M. Hays, proposed the date for the reign of Pepy I of c. 2321-2287 BCE. (Hays, *The Organization of the Pyramid Texts: Typology and Disposition*, Vol. 1, p. xxxiii.)

*ḥnsktyw ḥmsw ḥr ḏꜥmw=sn m gs ỉꜣbty n pt*

*the Wearers of the Side-lock, who are seated with their scepters in the Eastern side of heaven,*

*ḏd=ṯn sw[t] rn nfr n ppy n nḥb-kꜣw hny*

*Tell it thou, the good name of this King Pepy to Neheb-kau. Praise*

*n ppy pn hny n kꜣ=f mꜣꜥ- ḫrw ppy pn*

*this King Pepy! Praise his Ka-spirit! This King Pepy is vindicated*

*mꜣꜥ- ḫrw kꜣ n ppy pn nṯr*

*and the Ka-spirit of this King Pepy is vindicated before the god!*

The Four Wearers of the Side-lock, who represent the divine rejuvenation of youth, testified to the King's good name to Nehebkau, who in turn, would present his Ka-spirit to the Dual Ennead of gods.[136] This connection with Nehebkau and the passage to rebirth is somewhat elaborated in Spell 609 from the *Pyramid Texts* of King Merenra, the successor of Pepy I:

*ỉꜣḫ mr nḫꜣ wbꜣ mr mnꜥ ỉn mr-n-rꜥ pn ḏꜣw=f*

*The Winding Canal is flooded. The Nursing Canal is opened for this King Merenra to ferry over it*

136 *The Ennead, psḏt,* "nine gods," were generally not listed by name in the texts. The term "Ennead" is taken from the Greek ἐννεάς, meaning "the nine." There was the Greater and Lesser Ennead, *psḏty,* that congregated around the Creator Sun-god, comprising the Dual Ennead of 18 gods. In the non-abbreviated style of the Pyramid Texts, the Ennead was written as nine ꜥ signs (i.e. 9 gods), the Dual Ennead, by writing eighteen ꜥ signs (18 gods). The Ennead, or Nine, is 3x3, the expansion of the Archetypal number of Divinity. In various cities in Egypt, Enneads were assigned different names, based on the central cult tradition of that city.

*im ir 3ḫt ir bw msw ntrw im ms=t(w)=k im ḥnꜥ=sn*

*thereon to the horizon, to the place where the gods were born. Therein thou shalt be born with them.*

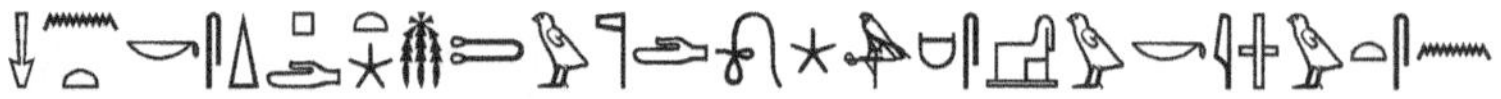

*snt=k spdt mstw=k nṯr dw3w ḥmsw=k imytw=sn*

*Thy sister is Sothis, thine offspring is the Morning Star.*[137] *Thou shalt sit between them*

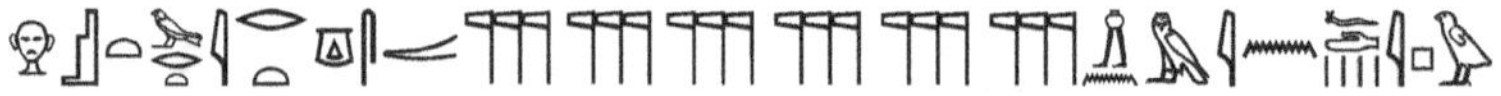

*ḥr ist wrt irt gs psḏty in m in fdw ipw*

*upon the Great Throne which is beside the Dual Ennead. Pray, bring these Four*

*i3ttyw ḥms=w ḥr ḏꜥb=sn prriw m gs i3by n pt*

Mound-gods[138] *who are seated with their scepters, and go forth in the Eastern side of heaven.*

*wṯs=sn i=k pn nfr n nḥb-k3w ḏd n n=k s3t=k ḥmt*

*They shall bear this good pronouncement of thee to Neheb-kau, which thy woman daughter hath spoken.*

137 Sothis, the extremely bright Canis Major (dog-star), is Sopdet, in Egyptian 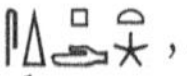 , *spdt*, (meaning,"sharp one"). Her name is sometimes rendered as Sirius. The annual appearance of Sothis in the Eastern horizon marked the beginning of the Nile flood, which was identified with the rebirth of Osiris. Her mate was  , *s3ḥ*, *Sah*, the constellation Orion, was also identified with Osiris. The King is here the Osiris, uniting with Sothis to give birth to  , *dw3w*, the "Morning Star," the planet *Venus*. Sothis (Sirius) was thus identified with Isis, the wife of Osiris.

138  , *in m in fdw ipw i3ttyw*, "Pray, bring these Four Mound-gods," is problematic. We would expect 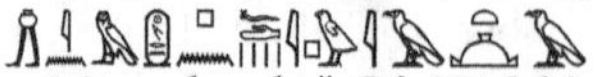 , *i in m mr-n-rꜥ pn fdw ipw i3ttyw*, "Bring King Merenra these Four Mound-gods." Cf. PT 266 above.

*wṯs n nḥb-kꜣw ỉ=k pn nfr n*

*Neheb-kau shall bear this good pronouncement to*

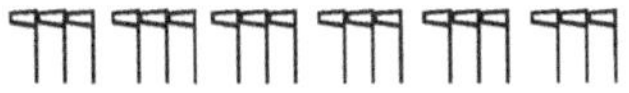

*psḏty*

*the Dual Ennead.*

In *The Book of the Dead*, these same four gods, , *ḥnsktyw*, the "Wearers of the Sidelock"[139] are invoked to grant the deceased the favor of Ra and Nehebkau:

*ỉ.n[ḏ ḥr=ṯn nṯrw ỉpw ḫntyw ḥnt]skyw*

*Hail [ to ye, those gods, Foremost of the ] Wearers of the Sidelock,*

*ḏsryw ḥr dꜥmw=sn ḏd=ṯn nfrw=ỉ [n rꜥ]*

*grasping their scepters! May ye declare my goodness [to Ra] !*

*swꜣḏ=ṯn wỉ n nḥb-[kꜣw]*

*May ye make me flourish to Neheb[kau] !*[140]

139 In the Old Kingdom, the head of a pre-pubescent boy of royal and elite families was shaved except for a distinctive plaited side-lock as a symbol of their youth. Gods depicted in this manner were recognized as divine children, as for example Horus the child.

140 *BD* 30A, *Papyrus of Nu (BM 10477)*, Sheet 5, Lines 4-5, with restorations from the *Papyrus* of , *Mesemnether (Louvre E21324)*, Line 4 and 5.

## Moses and the So-called "Brazen" Serpent

A fascinating example of the Paradoxia is found in the book of *Numbers*, which recounts the story of Moses and the Brazen serpent, in which the serpent is represented in function as a prototypical Messiah.

*Figure P31 - Moses & the Brazen Serpent'*

The Israelites, who were wandering in the wilderness, began to grumble against Moses and God. To punish them, God sent **הנחשים השרפים**, *fiery serpents,* into their midst and many of them died by reason of snake bite.[141] It is apparent that Yahweh did not have a sense of humor when it came to complaining disciples!

Then the snakebitten Israelites came to Moses begging for relief, and Moses, being the nice leader that he was, prayed God to take away the serpents. God then answered him and said:

ויאמר יהוה אל־משה עשה לך שרף ושים אתו על־נס והיה
כל־הנשוך וראה אתו וחי
ויעש משה נחש נחשת וישמהו על־הנס והיה אם־נשך
הנחש את־איש והביט אל־נחש הנחשת וחי

> Make thyself a fiery serpent (**שרף**, Seraph), and place it upon a standard; and it shall be when anyone is bitten, when he sees it, he shall live. And Moses made a serpent of brass (**נחש נחשת**) and set it on a standard and it was that if any man had been bitten, when he looked unto the serpent of brass, he lived."[142]

In this *Old Testament* account the serpent is both the destroyer and the healer.

---

141 *Numbers* 21:6.

142 *Numbers* 21:8-9. The Hebrew *Bible*, *The Tanakh*, translates **נחש נחשת** as "copper serpent." Many other English Bibles translate it "serpent of bronze." The symbol of the "serpent of brass" in the Western Magical Tradition was based on the *King James Bible* translation, "serpent of brass," hence I have retained that rendering to prevent any confusion among students who encounter that emblem.

## Asclepius

*Figure P32 - Asclepius, God of Healing & Medicine*

This same motif is found in the legend of Ἀσκληπιός commonly rendered *Asclepius* or Latin *Aesculapius*, the god of medicine and healing.[143]

It was said that from a serpent he gained knowledge of an herb that could bring the dead back to life. Therefore, he carried a staff entwined by a single serpent. This knowledge passed to his descendants, who passed it on to others, and eventually doctors utilized snakes in their practice.[144]

This symbol is still widely used internationally as a symbol of medical practice and the medical profession generally.

*Figure P33 - John Churchill Company Printer's Mark*

However, in the United States both the *Staff of Asclepius* and the *Caduceus* are utilized alternately as medical symbols.

The use of the Caduceus in this fashion is not derived from ancient history but taken from the printer's mark of the *John Churchill Publishing Company*, known for publishing and selling medical books in the 19th Century.[145]

## The Serpent as Wisdom

Curious as it may be, there is a tendency for the serpent to take on positive characteristics such as *healing* and *wisdom*. Throughout the long history of mankind, the serpent has been one of the potential dangers to be avoided. Yet, in myths from numerous cultures, the serpent, often a poisonous one, is depicted as *a companion of the gods*, *a bringer of wisdom*, or a figure

143 Keightley, *The Mythology of Ancient Greece and Italy*, pp. 422-423.

144 Hyginius, *Poeticon Astronomicon* 2.14.6-8.

145 Wilcox & Whitham, *The Symbol of Modern Medicine: why one snake is more than two*. Annals of Internal Medicine, 138, pp. 673-677.

*Figure P34 - Serpent and Dove Coat of Arms - Unitarian Church of Transylvania & Hungary*

representing *the Great Work itself.*

We even find it in the *New Testament*. In the book of *Matthew*, Jesus admonished his disciples,

> γίνεσθε οὖν φρόνιμοι ὡς οἱ ὄφεις.
> καὶ ἀκέραιοι ὡς αἱ περιστεραί.
>
> therefore be shrewd as serpents and innocent as doves.[146]

The word here translated as "shrewd"is φρόνιμος, which can mean "to be thoughtful, sagacious or shrewd."[147] It is connected with φρόνησις, a word which Aristotle used in his *Nichomachean Ethics* to signify *practical wisdom* or *prudence*.

> Περὶ δὲ φρονήσεως οὕτως ἄν λάβοιμεν, Θεωρήσαντε τίνας λέγομεν τοὺς φρονίμους. δοκεῖ δὴ φρονίμου εἶναι τὸ δύνασθαι καλῶς βουλεύσασθαι περὶ τὰ αὑτῷ ἀγαθὰ καὶ συμφέροντα, οὐ κατὰ μέρος, οἷον ποῖα πρὸς ὑγίειαν ἢ πρὸς ἰσχύν, ἀλλὰ ποῖα πρὸς τὸ εὖ ζῆν ὅλως.
>
> We may thus understand what prudence is by contemplating those whom we call prudent. It seems that a prudent man is one who can deliberate well about the things that are good and profitable for himself - not concerning some matter, such as what is good for his health or for his strength, but rather what is profitable for a good life in all its parts.[148]

We see the serpent as a *Complexio Oppositorum*, a symbol in which pairs of Archetypal opposites unite to form complimentary pairs, yielding a figure of wholeness.

146 *Matthew* 10:16.

147 *Bauer*, p. 866b.

148 Rackham, *Aristotle The Nichomachean Ethics*, 6.5.1-2, pp. 336-337. Translation by Matthew Andrews.

# Mithra and Aion

There remain other figures of Mythology that are still shrouded in mystery, such as the Lion-headed form of Μίθρα, *Mithra*, found in the ancient Temples.

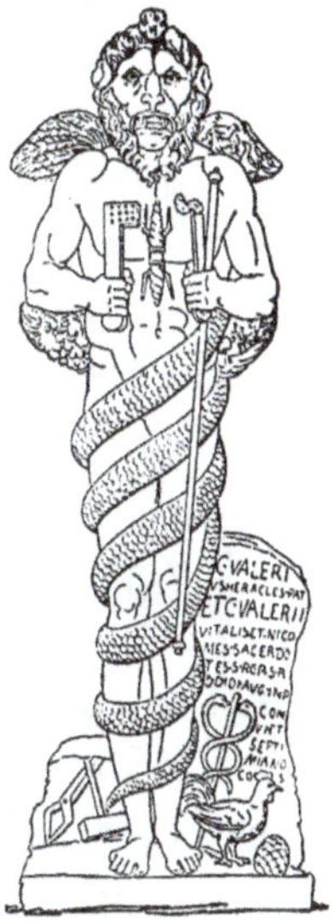

*Figure P35 - Aion*

Entwined by the serpent, this mysterious figure was identified with Αἰών, *Aion*, a Hellenistic deity associated with time, as well as Χρόνος, *Kronos*.[149] However, the concept of time associated with *Aion* differs from that represented by Kronos. The god *Aion* signified the *unbounded, Infinite time* of the Universe, in contrast to the *observable and experiential time* of *Kronos* – the past, present and future.

The snake appears in many guises and varied symbolism in the Holy Books even as it does throughout all history.

*Figure P36 - Mithra as the Leontocephalic Kronos*

In *Liber VII*, VII:20 the rising serpent is identified as *Kuṇḍalinī*, there called the "ancient sorrow of years". This indicates the span of *measurable time*, which equates to Saturn or Kronos.

> **Thou hast stirred in Thy sleep, O ancient sorrow of years! Thou hast raised Thine head to strike, and all is dissolved in the Abyss of Glory.**

149 Barnett & Hinnells, *Mithraic studies: Proceedings of the first International congress of Mithraic studies*, Vol. 2, pp. 467ff.

# Ouroboros

One of the more striking historical Archetypes of the serpent is the *Ouroboros*, the snake that swallows his own tail. The Greek word οὐροβόρος, *Ouroboros*, literally means, "devouring its tail."[150]

It is an Archetype of Eternity, that which is without beginning or ending.

There is no more solid proof of the existence of the Collective Unconscious than the figure of the Ouroboros. The symbol of the serpent swallowing its tail occurs worldwide, among neighboring cultures as well as in distant continents that had no physical contact with one another at any time. It is found in Asia and Europe, among the tribes of early native America as well as those in South America.

The Egyptian phrase for it was , *sd-m-r, tail in mouth.*[151] As early as the *Pyramid Texts*, the precursor of this phrase made its appearance in the text of *King Teti*. The sense of an endless cycle is indicated in the introductory sentence prior to the direct mention of the Ouroboric snake:

*nht=k npn.t=k npn.t=k nht=k sd=k dp r=k šnṯ*

*Thy sycamore be thy grain; thy grain be thy sycamore. Thy tail be upon thy mouth, O encircling serpent*[152]

*Figure P37 - Ouroboros on the Shrine of Tutankhamun*

The first known pictorial example of this Archetype is found on the 18th Dynasty shrine of Pharaoh *Tutankhamun* shown in *Figure P37*, which is from the 14th Century BCE. This representation of the serpent was a development from the original figure of *Meḥen, the coiled one.* Even as the serpent protected the Sun-god in his journey through the Night, here the figure surrounds and protects the Pharaoh, the vice-regent of the Sun on earth.

150 *LSJ*, p. 1274a.

151 *Wb*, Vol. 4, p. 364, 5.

152 *PT*, Spell 393. (689a-689b, PT *Pyramid of Teti I).* Twice in this inscription, the Scribe incorrectly wrote for , the second person suffix-pronoun. Both instances were silently corrected.

The figure of the Ouroboros is also found in the Hindu literature describing the *kuṇḍalinī* serpent in *mūlādhāra*, the root *cakra*:

पश्चिमाभिमुखी योनिर्गुदमेढ्रान्तरालगा ।
तत्र कन्दं समाख्यातं तत्रास्ते कुण्डली सदा ।।
संवेष्ट्य सकलनाडीः सार्धत्रिकुटिलाकृतिः ।
मुखे निवेश्य सा पुच्छं सुषुम्णा विवरे सथिता ।।

Facing backwards, a yoni clings to a place between the anus and the penis; it is said that a root is there *(i.e. mūlādhāra)*; *Kuṇḍalī* always dwells there. Covering all the *naḍī*, it has three coils and a half; and with its tail in its mouth, it stands at the opening of *suṣumṇā*. (i.e. the central *naḍī* which connects the lowest cacra *mūlādhāra* to the highest, *sahasrāra*.)[153]

It continued to appear in Egyptian mythological papyri and in early Greek Magical and Alchemical texts and became a very popular image in Medieval Alchemy as well as in the Emblem Books of the 16th and 17th Centuries.

*Figure P38 - Harpocrates Within an Ouroboros*

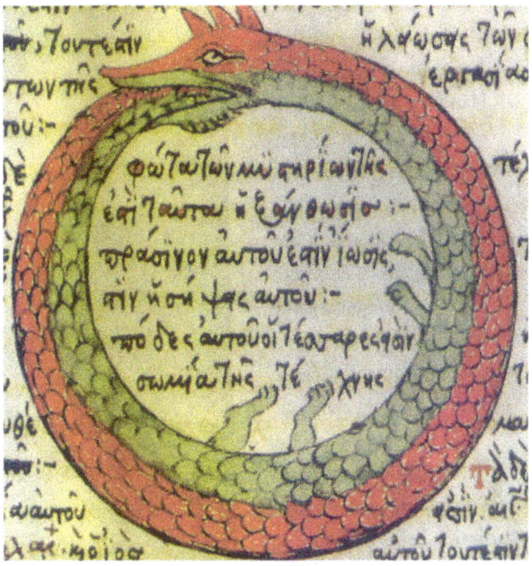

*Figure P39 - Ouroboros*

153 *Śiva Saṃhitā*, Chapter V, 78 & 79. Translation by Gordan Djurdjevic. In the faulty English translation published in 1914 by Chandra Vasu, these verses were both numbered 57.

*Figure P40 - Emblemata Fourteen*

*Figure P41 - Lion-serpent Ouroboros*

*Figure P42 - Image of Saturn as Cycles of the Year*

*Figure P43 - Emblem CXXXII*

*Figure P44 - Ouroboros as the Life Cycle*

*Figure P45 - Ouroboros as the Cycle of Time*

*Figure P46 - Ouroboros with Transpierced Head*

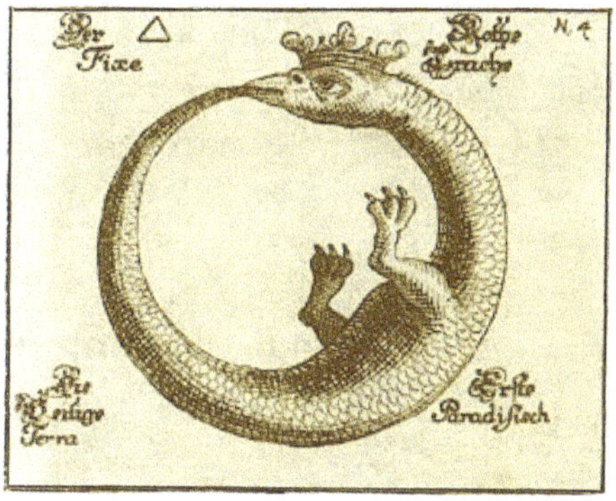

*Figure P47 - The Crowned Ouroboros*

*Figure P49 - He Should be Killed Wisely, because Death will Reveal Him*

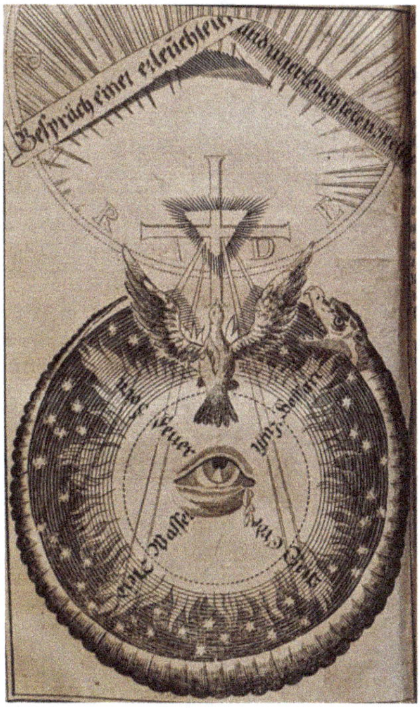

*Figure P48 - Speech of the Enlightened & Unenlightened Soul*

*Figure P50 - Ouroboros Surrounding Mount Meru Resting upon the World Turtle*

The Ouroboros made an appearance in the Gnostic document *The Pistis Sophia*, but as may be expected in a Gnostic-Christian work, not as an ambivalent figure, but as a negative symbol of the darkness of the world. In the Third Book of the *Pistis Sophia*, Jesus said to Mary Magdalene,

> **ϫⲉ ⲡⲕⲁⲕⲉ ⲉⲧ ϩⲓⲃⲟⲗ ⲟⲩⲛⲟϭ ⲛ̄ⲇⲣⲁⲕⲱⲛ ⲡⲉ ⲉⲣⲉ ⲡⲉϥϭⲁⲧ ⲛ̄ϩⲟⲩⲛ ⲛ̄ⲣⲱϥ ⲉϥⲙ̄ⲡⲃⲟⲗ ⲙ̄ⲡⲕⲟⲥⲙⲟⲥ ⲧⲏⲣϥ̄ ⲁⲩⲱ ⲉϥⲕⲱⲧⲉ ⲉⲡⲕⲟⲥⲙⲟⲥ ⲧⲏⲣϥ**
>
> The Outer Darkness is a great dragon with his tail in his mouth, and it is outside the entire world and it encircles the entire world...[154]

*Figure P51 - Viṣṇu reclining upon Ananta Śeṣa*

One very interesting example of the Ouroboic Serpent which is reflected within *Liber 418* as well as *Liber LXV*, has its origins in the Hindu mythology of अनन्त शेष, *Ananta Śeṣa*, who is sometimes simply called अनन्त, *Ananta*,[155] described as having a thousand heads.

The two words अनन्त शेष, *Ananta Śeṣa* are Sanskrit for "endless serpent."

The god of preservation, विष्णु, *Viṣṇu*,[156] is said to recline upon the coils of *Śeṣa*. When *Śeṣa* uncoils, the Universe is created. When he coils again, the Universe is destroyed. As a form of the Ouroboros, he is also described as the serpent continually devouring his own coils. In the preface to the Vision of the 3rd Æthyr of *Liber 418*, the serpent *Śeṣa* is beheld feeding upon the plumes of the feather of Truth as upon its own coils, which are continually contracting.

154 *Pistis Sophia*, Book III, Chapter 126. Coptic text, Schmidt, *Pistis Sophia* (1925), p. 317, lines 16-19.

155 *Monier-Williams*, pp. 25a and 1088c.

156 *Ibid.*, p. 999a.

**There is an angry light in the stone; now it is become clear. In the centre is that minute point of light which is the True Sun, & in the circumference is the Emerald Snake. And joining them are the rays which are the plumes of Maat, & because the distance is infinite, therefore are they parallel from the circumference, although they diverge from the centre. In all this is no voice and no motion. And yet it seems that the great Snake feedeth upon the plumes of Truth as upon itself, so that it contracteth. But ever so little as it contracteth, without it gloweth the golden rim, which is that minute point in the centre.**

*The Vision & The Voice, 3rd Æthyr*

This is also described in *Liber LXV*, Chapter IV, verses 54-56:

**This heart of mine is girt about with the serpent that devoureth his own coils.**
**When shall there be an end, O my darling, O when shall the Universe and the Lord thereof be utterly swallowed up?**
**Nay! who shall devour the Infinite? who shall undo the Wrong of the Beginning?**

Crowley himself presented a view of Ananta as an Oppositorum figure, from the viewpoint of a Babe of the Abyss, in *The Book of Lies*, Chapter 73:

The Infinite Snake Ananta that surroundeth the Universe is but the Coffin-Worm!

# The Mercurial Serpent

Emblem number fifty from Michael Maier's *Atalanta Fugiens* is another good example of a *Complexio Oppositorum.* The engraving bears the full title, *Draco mulierem, et hæc illum interimit, simulque sanguine perfunduntur*, "The Dragon destroys the woman, and she him, and at once they are drenched in blood."[157]

*Figure P52 - Emblemata Fifty*

Here, the image of the woman entwined by the dragon-serpent is representative of a type of *mortificatio* wherein both dragon and woman, the *Philosophical Sulfur* and the *Mercury of the Wise*, destroy one another, yielding a third condition necessary for the completion of the Work.

The Epigram for this engraving reads:

Alta venenoso fodiatur tumba Draconi,
Cui mulier nexu sit bene vincta suo:
Ille maritalis dum carpit gaudia lecti,
Hæc moritur, cum qua sit Draco tectus humo.
Illius hinc corpus morti datur, atque cruore
Tingitur: Hæc operis semita vera tui est.

Let a deep tomb be dug for the venomous Dragon,
To whom the woman is tightly fastened in their entwinement:
While he enjoys the pleasures of their nuptial bed,
She dies, and with her let the Dragon be covered in earth.
Hence his body is given to death, and soaked with blood:
This is the true path of your work.[158]

---

157 Michael Maier, *Atalanta Fugiens* (1617 e.v.), p. 209.

158 Translation by Matthew Andrews. This emblem also is found in Maier's *Scrutinium Chemicum* (1687 e.v.), p. 148. The source of this epigram was *Turba Philosophorum*, in *Auriferæ Artis* (1572 e.v.), Vol. 1, pp. 58-59.

*Figure P53 - Purify Her*

*Figure P54- Divide Her*

*Figure P55 - After Dividing, Cleanse Again*

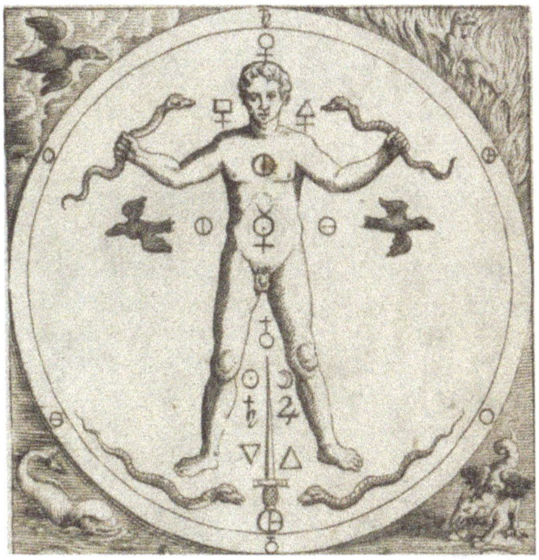

*Figure P56 - Hercules*

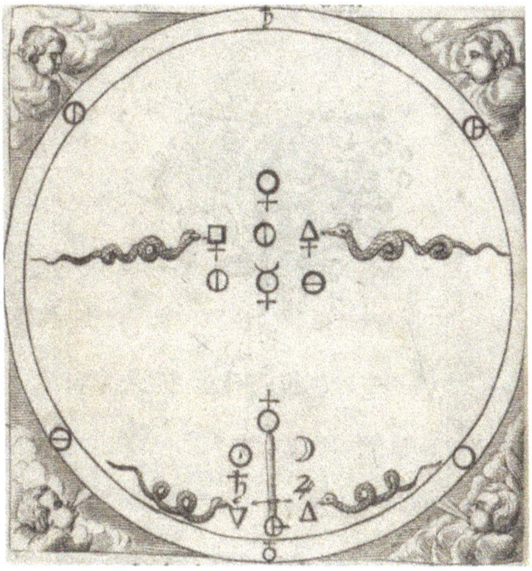

*Figure P57 - How to Draw the Life from Gold*

*Figure P58 - So the Old Man Spoke to Me all these Words*

*Figure P59 - Men See & Despise my Old Serpent*

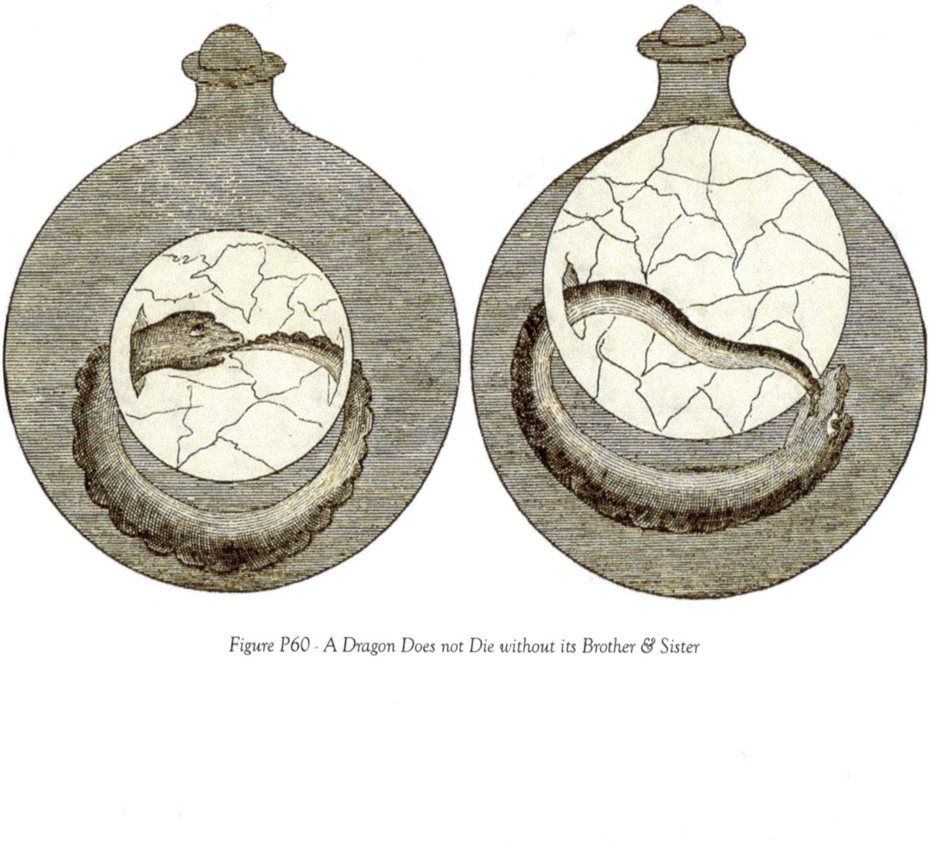

*Figure P60 - A Dragon Does not Die without its Brother & Sister*

# Epilogue

The singular issue of importance for us is to note how many of these Archetypes have constellated new aggregates of meaning and interpretation in the New Aeon. Serious examination of the historical pattern of these Images is vital for appreciation and comprehension of the dynamic changes we may discover in them.

These changes burst upon the world through the aegis of the Holy Books of Thelema, wherein various *Imagines Deo* proliferate the texts, silently inviting the *Participation mystique* wherein we encounter the True Symbolic Life, not by intellectual machinations, but by direct experience.

For this purpose, the presentation of various Archetypal Serpent images was offered in this Prologue, to provide a small glimpse of the broad panorama they form in the psychic development of humankind through the centuries. In such a short discourse, it would be impossible to present an all-inclusive analysis; that would require an entire book devoted to the subject, and it would doubtless comprise a substantial tome. If this meager offering provokes consideration or inquiry, or stimulates the numinous encounter with the Holy Books, it will have served its purpose.

These Archetypes are not merely artistic or poetic representations dressed in archaic garments; they are the living Universal Symbols of the Collective Unconscious, unbounded and transformative, striving ever to help us create a spiritual life of Wholeness.

They have lived through the history of humankind beyond the years of counting, inspiring and illuminating our species from the moment hominids clawed their way into Consciousness in quest of the Light of Life, to the myriad of lifetimes that human Stars have flickered upon the earth for succeeding millennia, before fading from the earth like vapor. The Archetypes have left their indelible mark in the written records of our kind, a witness to the transformative, alluring power of their presence. Yet, their presence is not a historical oddity, but a vital living component of our collective and individual psyche. The messages lurking in the Archetypal stream have naturally evolved and changed, as we have evolved and changed.

Have the Transformative Images changed as a result of our own evolution?
Or is it not the other way around?
We do know that they live in the words of Prophets, Poets and Dreamers.
And so do they live in *Liber LXV*.
It is enough.

**Men and women of the Earth, to you am I come from the Ages beyond the Ages, from the Space beyond your vision; and I bring to you these words.**

*Liber Porta Lucis, 4*

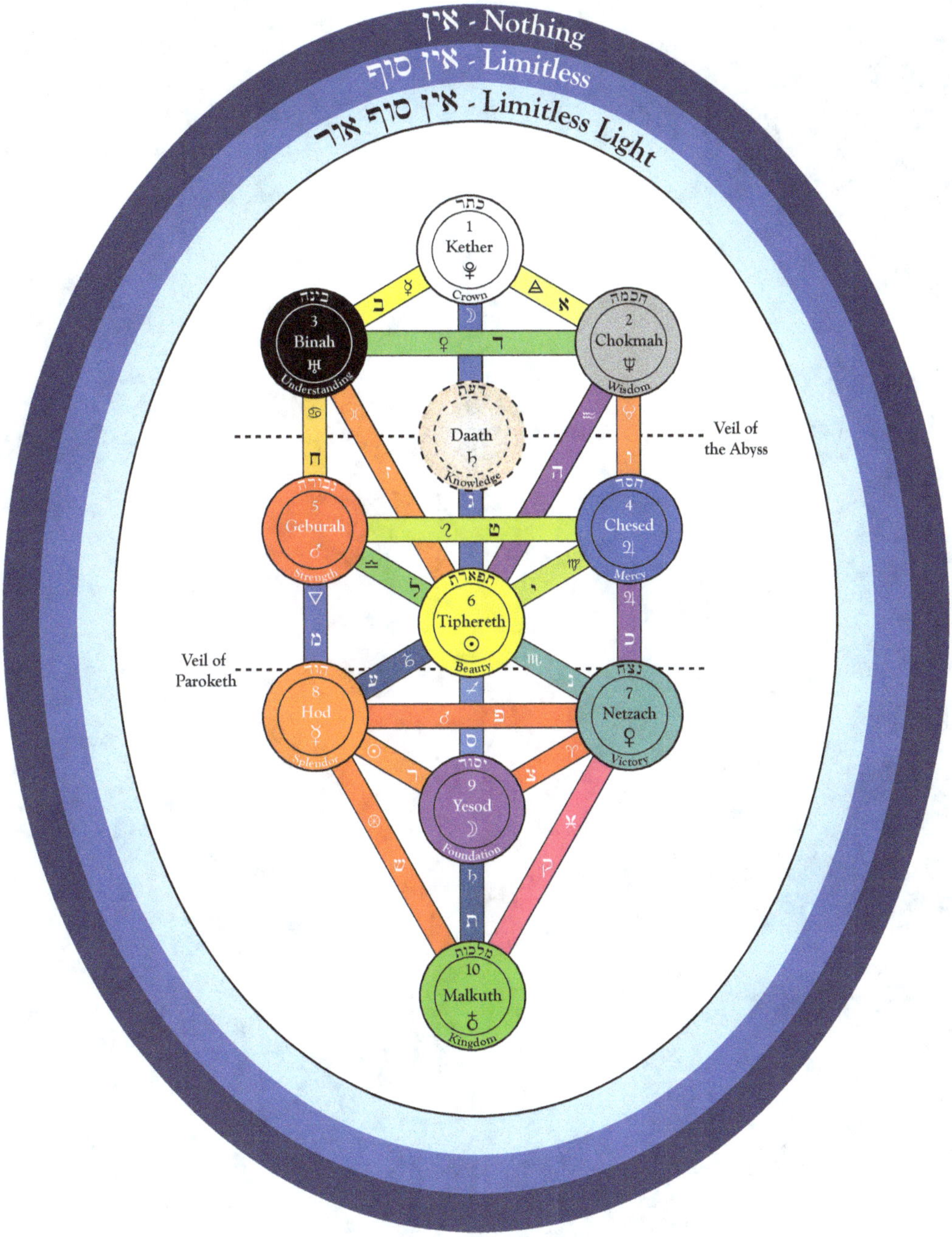


*Figure 01 - The Tree of Life*

Figure 02 - Afloat in the Tomb

# I AM THE HEART
## A COMMENTARY ON LIBER LXV
## CHAPTER I

## § 0. INTRODUCTION

IN THE YEAR 1907 of the common era, Aleister Crowley served as the scribe for the transmission of a Holy Book, the name of which is *Liber Cordis Cincti Serpente - vel LXV sub figurâ* אדני. The name of that book in English is, *The Book of the Heart Girt with the Serpent, or 65, under the figure Adonai.*

Please note that I have described Crowley as the "scribe." This is because Aleister Crowley was not the author of this book; the author of the Book was a spiritual entity known to members of the magical and mystical Order of A∴ A∴ as V.V.V.V.V.

It was He who Inspired the book, and Crowley the humble scribe, received it and wrote it down. This book was not a direct dictation like *The Book of the Law*; Crowley was in a type of Samadhi, in which his own poetic genius blossomed, resulting in the beautiful and lofty language of *Liber LXV.*

This began on the evening of the thirtieth day of October in 1907, and continued through the third day of November of that year.

The book was first published in the year 1909 e.v. in Volume One of the private three volume series with the title in Greek letters (ΘΕΛΗΜΑ) on the front. These three volumes were published especially for official aspirants to A∴ A∴.

Volume One of this publication included *Liber LXI vel Causæ*, the preliminary lection and history lection of A∴ A∴, along with *Liber LXV. Liber Cordis Cinti Serpente* gives an account of the relations of the aspirant to the Great Work with his or her Holy Guardian Angel. Thus, it is given to each Probationer, since union with the Holy Guardian Angel is the crowning achievement of the Outer College of A∴ A∴.

*Liber LXV* is designated by the Order of A∴ A∴ as a publication in Class A. Official Publications of A∴ A∴ that are in this Class are considered to be beyond rational criticism. The original admonition that Class A texts are not to be changed even so much as the style of a letter is found in *Liber AL* vel Legis, *The Book of the Law.*[1] The A∴ A∴ considers that command to apply to all documents in Class A, and rigorously upholds that rule.

---

1 See *Liber AL*, I:36, II:54. Cf. III:47.

*Figure 03 - Title Page of Liber LXV*

This injunction implies that we should pay careful attention to which letters in the text are written in the upper case in mid-sentence, and which are not. For example, a word that begins with an Upper Case Letter that is not the initial word in a sentence should be considered significant in some manner. It may signify a technical term, or indicate Qabalistic value, or it may inform us quietly that the word in question refers to a concept that is hyper-abyssic, that is to say, a concept from above the Abyss that transcends Reason.

Thus, when we publish a new version of one of the Holy Books in Class A, we take great care to be sure that every letter is correct and faithful to the original. We do not wish our Holy Books to suffer the corruption that has befallen almost every holy book in history.

Crowley later wrote a very brief, sketchy Commentary to *Liber LXV* in the summer of 1923 e.v. The A∴A∴ published this Commentary in *The Equinox*, Volume Four, Number One, as a Class B publication under the title,

*Commentaries on the Holy Books and Other Papers.*[2] It must be said that I do not consider the resulting commentary a high watermark of Crowley's career. It is often cursory and inconsistent; one gets the impression that he felt that he was forced to deliver a commentary and his heart really wasn't in it. Perhaps that is partly a result of how he personally viewed the book. While writing the commentary, Crowley himself stated that parts of *Liber LXV* completely eluded him:

> I find Chapters I & II intelligible, though II (Air) harder than I (Earth). But III (Water) is quite obscure to the part of my mind that writes comments, while exalting my lyrical apprehension with utterly lucid brilliance. Chapter IV (Fire) is quite beyond me; but V (Spirit) has several 'literary' passages with evident applications.[3]

The numbers assigned to books in Our curriculum are likewise significant in some manner. In the case of this Book, it is very important.

The number LXV, or 65, is the numerical value of the Hebrew word **אדני**, *Adonai*. By the gematria of Qabalah: **א** = 1, **ד** = 4, **נ** = 50, **י** = 10.

We typically refer to the book simply as *Liber LXV*.

In addition to the Qabalistic significance of the word Adonai to the number of the book, each chapter of *Liber LXV* has exactly 65 verses, which is also the total number of pages in the manuscript of *The Book of the Law*.

## The Holy Guardian Angel

The Hebrew word **אדני**, *Adonai*, means "Lord"[4] which in the System of A∴A∴ is a synonym for The Holy Guardian Angel. The doctrine of the Holy Guardian Angel is perhaps the most central and sacred doctrines taught by the A∴A∴.

The beginning student may well ask, "Who or what is the Holy Guardian Angel?"

It is not an easy question to answer succinctly for a person who has limited knowledge of the doctrine of A∴A∴ or its curriculum. It is also a question which does not lend itself to an answer based entirely on intellectual interpretation. Hence, the Brethren of A∴A∴ direct the inquirer to prayerfully study of the Holy Books rather than attempt to offer rational explanations.

---

2 *Commentaries to the Holy Books and Other Papers. The Equinox IV(1).* Weiser (1996).

3 Stephen Skinner ed., The Magical Diaries of *ΤΟ ΜΕΓΑ ΘΗΡΙΟΝ The Beast 666 Aleister Crowley ΛΟΓΟΣ ΑΙΩΝΟΣ ΘΕΛΗΜΑ 93 - 1923*, p. 69.

4 *Gesenius*, p. 12a. (see under אדון)

One continually sees people daring to write about the Holy Guardian Angel who have not had the direct Initiatic experience of that union. As may be expected, such comments are driven by the intellect, and they almost always tend to identify the Angel as a portion of the individual psyche. Such a viewpoint is very appealing to the Ego. However, it is utter folly to present pure speculation in the absence of genuine experience . If the blind attempt to lead the blind, both risk falling in the pit.[5]

This is completely understandable and not unexpected. It is a natural tendency to interpret any inspirational experience in a totally subjective way. In his early years, Crowley himself took this view. But as he gained Initiatic experience, and as his Adept Self matured, he abjured his earlier position on the matter. In his later years he was adamant on this point:

> We may readily concur that the Augoeides, the "Genius" of Socrates, and the "Holy Guardian Angel" of Abramelin the Mage are identical. But we cannot include this "Higher Self"; for the Angel is an actual Individual with his own Universe, exactly as a man is... He is not a mere abstraction, a selection from, and exaltation of, one's own favourite qualities, as the "Higher Self" seems to be... This matter is of importance, because it influences one's attitude to invocation. I can, for instance, work myself up to a "Divine Consciousness," in which I can understand, and act, as I cannot in my normal state. I become "inspired"; I feel, and I express, ideas of almost illimitable exaltation. But this is totally different from the "Knowledge and Conversation of the Holy Guardian Angel," which is the special aim of the Adeptus Minor. It is ruin to that Work if one deceives oneself by mistaking one's own 'energized enthusiasm' for external communication. The parallel on the physical plane is the difference between Onanism and Sexual Intercourse.[6]

In my first book, *Initiation in the Aeon of the Child*, the glossary entry for Holy Guardian Angel reads:

---

5 This is a something of a ubiquitous axiom: τυφλὸς δὲ τυφλὸν ἐὰν ὁδηγῇ, ἀμφότεροι εἰς βόθυνον πεσοῦνται. (*Matthew* 15:14), "If the blind lead the blind, both will fall into the pit." Cf. *Luke* 6:39: Μήτι δύναται τυφλὸς τυφλὸν ὁδηγεῖν; οὐχὶ ἀμφότεροι εἰς βόθυνον ἐμπεσοῦνται, "Is blind unable to lead blind? Will not both fall into the pit?" Comparison can be made to the earlier Vedantic aphorism from the *Kaṭha Upaniṣad*: अविद्यायामन्तरे वर्तमानाः स्वयं धीराः पण्डितंमन्यमानाः । दन्द्रम्यमाणाः परियन्ति मूढा अन्धेनैव नीयमाना यथान्धाः ।।. "Living in ignorance, arrogantly considering themselves wise and learned, the fools wander around like the blind led by the blind." (*Kaṭha Upaniṣad*, 1:2:5, translation by Gordan Djurdjevic.)

6 Crowley, *Magick Without Tears* (1954), p. 193.

> The Holy Guardian Angel is a term used to indicate the transpersonal Entity who serves as the True Spiritual Instructor for an aspirant. Sometimes called "The Higher Divine Self" or "The Higher Genius," neither of which are correct or satisfactory.[7]

The latter terms were rejected by the A∴ A∴ because they are misleading and incorrect. The A∴A∴ declares The Holy Guardian Angel to be, as in Crowley's own words, an individual with His own Universe, completely unique from the aspirant.

*Liber LXV* is of particular importance to aspirants who seek Union with the Angel, an attainment we refer to as the Knowledge and Conversation of The Holy Guardian Angel.

The Roman numeral LXV attributed to *The Book of The Heart Girt With The Serpent* is also considered to conceal a reference to the Latin Word LVX, which means "Light."[8]

A synonym for The Holy Guardian Angel which reinforces this idea, is αὐγοειδής, *Augoeides*. It is a Greek word meaning, "of the nature of light," or literally, "image of the dawn."[9] This word was used by the Neo-Platonist philosopher and theurgist Iamblichus Chalcidensis (245 CE - 325 CE).[10]

*Figure 04 - Iamblichus Chalcidensis*

7 Gunther, *Initiation in the Aeon of the Child*, p. 201.

8 *L&S*, p. 1088b.

9 *LSJ*, p. 274b.

10 E.g. Parthey, *Jamblichi, De Mysteriis Liber*, 125.5, 132.12, 212.5, & 239,9. For a detailed discussion of this word, see Gunther, *The Angel & The Abyss*, pp. 311-314.

## Structure of the Book

Liber LXV is a short book of only five chapters. These five chapters are referred to 🜃 Earth, 🜁 Air, 🜄 Water, 🜂 Fire and ⊛ Spirit, in that order. This sequence indicates the lower five Sephiroth on the Tree of Life, from the bottom upward: מלכות, *Malkuth*, יסוד, *Yesod*, הוד, *Hod*, נצח, *Netzach* and תפארת, *Tiphereth*.

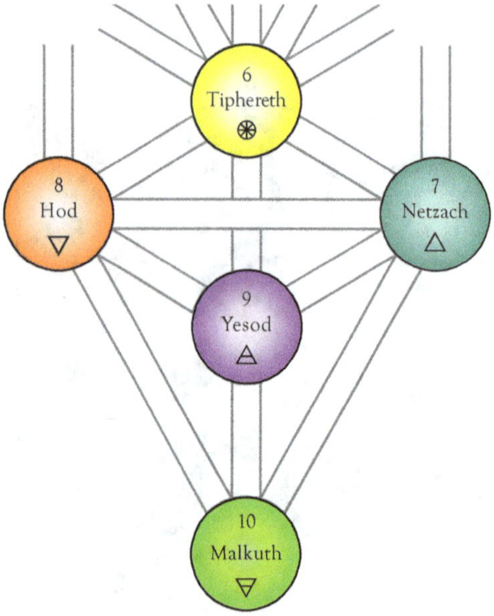

*Figure 05 - The Five Lower Sephiroth with Elemental Correspondences*

*Liber LXV* is given to Probationers of the A∴ A∴ to study, as the Knowledge and Conversation of the Holy Guardian Angel is the Crown of the Outer College of the Order, which is attributed to the Sixth Sephira on the Tree of Life, Tiphereth. As you can see, the final chapter of *Liber LXV* corresponds to this Sephira, which is attributed to the Element ⊛ Spirit.

Probationers are also required to memorize any one chapter of their choosing. The first edition of *Liber LXV* in the 1909 edition of ΘΕΛΗΜΑ included this statement after Chapter Five:

> The full knowledge of the interpretation of this book is concealed from all, save only the Shining Triangle. The Probationer must nevertheless acquire a copy and thoroughly acquaint himself with the contents. He must commit one chapter to memory.

This Shining Triangle is the Sigil of A∴ A∴ within which burns the Eye of Horus. The Triangle signifies the Three Supernals above the Abyss on the Tree of Life, the world of Godhead. This Book originated from the Keepers of the Shining Triangle and it is one of the Crowns of Wisdom and Understanding with which we have been blessed. Its Inner Truth is of such Transcendent Quality that its full knowledge is concealed from all, save those who are Members of the S.S., the Supreme Order of A∴ A∴.

Additionally, the Sigil of A∴ A∴ displays a group of 12 Rays emanating from the Eye in the Triangle. These 12 Rays suggest the Zodiac. Each group has 3 Rays, for a total of 36 Rays, which indicate the 3 Decans of each sign of the Zodiac. That is a total of 36 Rays emanating from the Shining Triangle. It is important to note that the sum of the numbers from 1 to 36 = 666.

*Figure 06 - The Sigil of A∴A∴*

Chapter I of *Liber LXV* corresponds to 🜃 Earth and מלכות, *Malkuth*, the tenth Sephira on the Tree of Life. It deals with the sensible world, and the relationship of The Holy Guardian Angel with the candidate in respect to that world. It deals with the transmutation of the element Earth as well as the part of the Soul called the נפש, *Nephesh*, the "animal soul," or "the instincts."

This task is of particular importance to Neophytes of A∴A∴, for that Grade is also assigned to Malkuth on the Tree of Life. One of the characteristics of this Grade is that the fledgling Neophyte may experience many things that appear to be actual fact but are merely false images or masks of reality. The first chapter of *Liber LXV* presents lessons demonstrating how the Angel may help the Candidate to distinguish between the real and the illusory.

Chapter II corresponds to the element of 🜁 Air and יסוד, *Yesod*, the Ninth Sephira on the Tree of Life. It likewise corresponds to the intellectual faculty we call the רוח, *Ruach*, which gives us the means to analyze all impressions consciously. In order to serve the aspirant properly, it requires a foundation of harmony and concentration to properly assess and categorize these impressions. Chapter II offers many insights into this ordeal.

Chapter III is attributed to the element of 🜄, Water and הוד, *Hod*, the Eighth Sephira, and the initial reflection of the נשמה, *Neshamah*, or Intuition. Hence, this chapter deals with the intuitive rather than the intellectual, and gives accounts of the initial reflection of true Understanding.

Chapter IV corresponds to the element of 🜂 Fire and נצח, Netzach, the Seventh Sephira and the initial reflection of the חיה, *Chiah*, or Will, from the Second Sephira, חכמה, *Chokmah*, the Great Father. Crowley himself stated that the mysteries of this chapter require the Understanding of a Master of the Temple in order to give them expression.[11]

Chapter V is attributed to the element of ⊛ Spirit and תפארת, *Tiphereth*, the Crown of the previous Four Elements, which harmonizes and unifies them. This chapter gives penetrating insights into the methods and aims of the Supreme Chiefs of the A∴A∴, as well as instruction for the sincere aspirant seeking Knowledge and Conversation of the Holy Guardian Angel.

In this book, I will only be giving a Commentary on Chapter One.

---

11 Cf. Crowley, *Commentaries to the Holy Books and other papers*, p. 135.

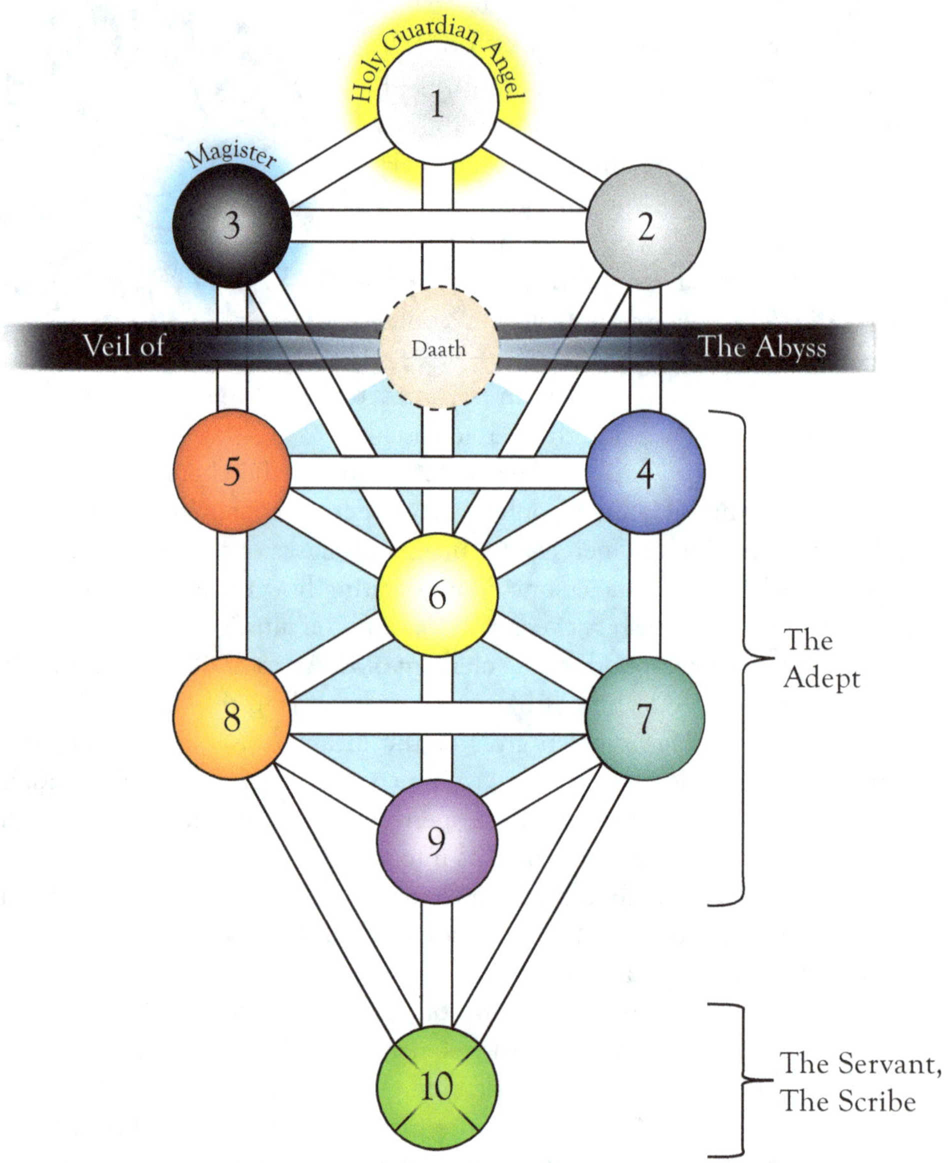


*Figure 07 - The Tree of Life with H.G.A., Magister, Adept & Scribe or Servant*

# Dramatis Personæ

In order to begin to really understand *Liber LXV*, it is essential to know the dramatis *personæ*[12] that are key to its revelation. This summit of this hierarchy is אדני, *Adonai*, the Holy Guardian Angel.

Next in the hierarchy beneath Adonai is V.V.V.V.V., the Great Master who is Head of the Order of A∴ A∴ and who Inspired this book.

*Figure 08 - The Lamen of V.V.V.V.V.*

Next is The Magister. In *Liber LXV*, this is Crowley as $8° = 3^{\square}$, Master of the Temple. This is a very difficult doctrine to teach, due to the limitation of language in expressing such lofty concepts. For the average reader, there is little to distinguish V.V.V.V.V. from Aleister Crowley, the Magister. Crowley's motto as a Master of the Temple also had the initials V.V.V.V.V. to confirm this conjunction. It is simplest to consider them the same, for Crowley eventually attained Union with V.V.V.V.V. to such an extent that distinction becomes futile for the reasoning faculty, even though they are separate Masters entirely. Therefore, from a personal viewpoint, consider "Magister" to be any aspirant who has attained to the Grade of Master of the Temple. This is an Aspirant who is a member of the 3rd and Supreme Order of A∴ A∴.

Then 'below' the Magister is the Adept. This is an Aspirant who has attained to the Knowledge and Conversation of the Holy Guardian Angel, and is thus a Member of the 2nd or Inner Order of A∴ A∴ When this book was penned, Crowley had attained to the Grade of $7° = 4^{\square}$, Exempt Adept, the Grade attributed to the Sephira חסד, *Chesed*, on the Tree of Life. His motto for that Grade was OΥ MH, a Greek phrase which means, "No! Certainly not!"[13]

The Adept is also called the servant or the scribe. This was Crowley, or to use his magical motto, Frater Perdurabo as a member of the Outer College of A∴ A∴, an aspirant to the Inner College Grade of $5° = 6^{\square}$, Adeptus Minor.[14] For anyone else at the personal level, it may be interpreted as anyone who is an

---

12 Latin, "the masks of the drama." It signifies a list of the main characters in a dramatic work. *L&S*, 612b and 1356a.

13 *LSJ*, p.1271a. Vide pp. 1266a-1267b.

14 Crowley's motto as an Adeptus Minor (within) was [Enochian script], *Christeos Luciftias*, Enochian for "Let there be light!" Following Order tradition, Crowley kept this motto *sub-rosa* his entire life. He always referred to himself as a member of the Outer College as Perdurabo, "I will endure unto the end." While Crowley had already attained to the Grade of Adeptus Minor, he aspired to refine that attainment and know the Angel through a more perfect union. This is true of all of us, hence we always refer to ourselves as "aspirants" rather than "members" of A∴ A∴.

aspirant to the Order of A.·.A.·..

We can't be the scribe in the sense that Crowley was the scribe who recorded this Book, but we are the scribe of our own Magical Records, in which we record our individual Inward Journey.

For the normal candidate, the information received from the Holy Guardian Angel follows this pathway: The Holy Guardian Angel Adonai communicates to the Magister, who instructs the Adept, who may also be called the servant or the scribe.

Now the significance of this to all of us is that we can see how far we are, in our human selves, from the Holy Guardian Angel, and how in the normal world, we have to communicate with Him.

For the sake of convenience, and because our myths are expressions of specific Archetypes, we refer to the Holy Guardian Angel as "He" or "Him," due to certain Qabalistic connotations. However, the Holy Guardian Angel is above the limitations of sex entirely. Suffice it to say that in our initial interactions with the Holy Guardian Angel, from the beginning until the attainment of the Knowledge & Conversation, we are the Bride, the Holy Guardian Angel is the Bridegroom, hence "He" or "Him." There is no exception to this Archetypal expression, regardless of the sex of the aspirant. We, as aspirants, must make contact with our Adept Self by training ourselves, and preparing ourselves for that level of attainment, and consciousness.

We are the Adept and we must be duly trained to function at that level AT WILL. The Adept self is the link to that part of ourselves which is called The Magister.

The Magister is above the Abyss, thus beyond the Reasoning faculty, and operates through the Sephira בינה, *Binah*, by means of the part of the Soul we call the Neshamah, or Intuition. It is through our "Magister Self" that The Holy Guardian Angel communicates with us. We know this because of *Liber LXV*, Chapter III, verse 3:

> **Then the word of Adonai came unto me by the mouth of the Magister mine...**

Thus, with each succeeding step toward our waking consciousness, the Word becomes more polluted with consciousness and tainted with the limitations of our vehicle.

Candidates therefore must continually strive toward elevating themselves through Initiation, making themselves fit vehicles for the contact with the Angel. As we advance 'higher' up that chain, the clearer the message becomes. This can be a very difficult concept to comprehend. If an aspirant has not yet attained unto the Grade of Magister, how can this be? When we first attain to the Knowledge and Conversation of the Holy Guardian Angel, we become Adepti, but obviously we are not yet Masters of the Temple.

The answer is this: even though we have not yet attained to that level of consciousness, the avenue of communication with the Angel passes directly to us through the Neshamah (the Intuition), which is above the Abyss, then to the Ruach (the Intellect), which is centered in the Sephira Tiphereth below the Abyss. The Master of the Temple is a master of Neshamah, but the Adept is not. This is one reason that we must show great caution when we speak of interaction with The Holy Guardian Angel. These levels of communication are beyond the Reason entirely, but must be passed to our consciousness through a series of veils.

> βλέπομεν γὰρ ἄρτι δι’ ἐσόπτρου ἐν αἰνίγματι, τότε δὲ πρόσωπον πρὸς πρόσωπον· ἄρτι γινώσκω ἐκ μέρους, τότε δὲ ἐπιγνώσομαι καθὼς καὶ ἐπεγνώσθην.

> For the time being, we see in a mirror, obscurely; then however face to face: now I know in part: then however, I shall know fully even also as I have been fully known.[15]

15 *I Corinthians* 13:12.

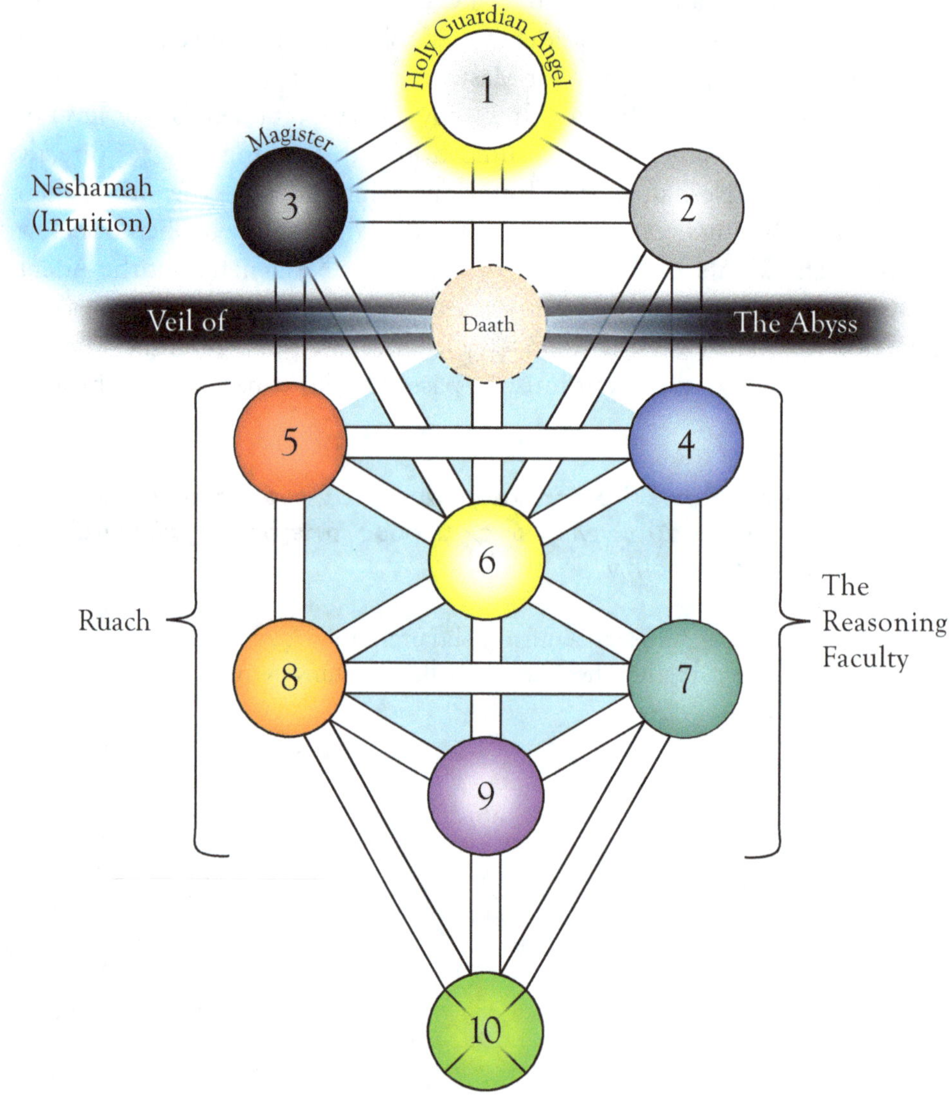


*Figure 09 - The Tree of Life with H.G.A., Magister, Neshamah & Ruach*

# LIBER LXV
## Chapter I

1. I am the Heart; and the Snake is entwined
About the invisible core of the mind.
Rise, O my snake! It is now is the hour
Of the hooded and holy ineffable flower.
Rise, O my snake, into brilliance of bloom
On the corpse of Osiris afloat in the tomb!
O heart of my mother, my sister, mine own,
Thou art given to Nile, to the terror Typhon!
Ah me! but the glory of ravening storm
Enswathes thee and wraps thee in frenzy of form.
Be still, O my soul! that the spell may dissolve
As the wands are upraised, and the æons revolve.
Behold! in my beauty how joyous Thou art,
O Snake that caresses the crown of mine heart!
Behold! we are one, and the tempest of years
Goes down to the dusk, and the Beetle appears.
O Beetle! the drone of Thy dolorous note
Be ever the trance of this tremulous throat!
I await the awaking! The summons on high
From the Lord Adonai, from the Lord Adonai!
2. Adonai spake unto V.V.V.V.V., saying: There must ever be division in the word.
3. For the colours are many, but the light is one.
4. Therefore thou writest that which is of mother of emerald, and of lapis-lazuli, and of turquoise, and of alexandrite.
5. Another writeth the words of topaz, and of deep amethyst, and of gray sapphire, and of deep sapphire with a tinge as of blood.
6. Therefore do ye fret yourselves because of this.
7. Be not contented with the image.
8. I who am the Image of an Image say this.

9. Debate not of the image, saying Beyond! Beyond!

One mounteth unto the Crown by the moon and by the Sun, and by the arrow, and by the Foundation, and by the dark home of the stars from the black earth.

10. Not otherwise may ye reach unto the Smooth Point.
11. Nor is it fitting for the cobbler to prate of the Royal matter. O cobbler! mend me this shoe, that I may walk. O king! if I be thy son, let us speak of the Embassy to the King thy Brother.
12. Then was there silence. Speech had done with us awhile.

There is a light so strenuous that it is not perceived as light.

13. Wolf's bane is not so sharp as steel; yet it pierceth the body more subtly.
14. Even as evil kisses corrupt the blood, so do my words devour the spirit of man.
15. I breathe, and there is infinite dis-ease in the spirit.
16. As an acid eats into steel, as a cancer that utterly corrupts the body; so am I unto the spirit of man.
17. I shall not rest until I have dissolved it all.
18. So also the light that is absorbed. One absorbs little, and is called white and glistening; one absorbs all and is called black.
19. Therefore, O my darling, art thou black.
20. O my beautiful, I have likened thee to a jet Nubian slave, a boy of melancholy eyes.
21. O the filthy one! the dog! they cry against thee.

Because thou art my beloved.

22. Happy are they that praise thee; for they see thee with Mine eyes.
23. Not aloud shall they praise thee; but in the night watch one shall steal close, and grip thee with the secret grip; another shall privily cast a crown of violets over thee; a third shall greatly dare, and press mad lips to thine.
24. Yea! the night shall cover all, the night shall cover all.
25. Thou wast long seeking Me; thou didst run forward so fast that I was unable to come up with thee.

O thou darling fool! what bitterness thou didst crown thy days withal.

26. Now I am with thee; I will never leave thy being.
27. For I am the soft sinuous one entwined about thee, heart of gold!
28. My head is jewelled with twelve stars; My body is white as milk of the stars; it is bright with the blue of the abyss of stars invisible.
29. I have found that which could not be found; I have found a vessel of quicksilver.

30. Thou shalt instruct thy servant in his ways, thou shalt speak often with him.
31. (The scribe looketh upwards and crieth) Amen! Thou hast spoken it, Lord God!
32. Further Adonai spake unto V.V.V.V.V. and said:
33. Let us take our delight in the multitude of men!

    Let us shape unto ourselves a boat of mother-of-pearl from them, that we may ride upon the river of Amrit!
34. Thou seest yon petal of amaranth, blown by the wind from the low sweet brows of Hathor?
35. (The Magister saw it and rejoiced in the beauty of it.) Listen!
36. (From a certain world came an infinite wail.)

    That falling petal seemed to the little ones a wave to engulph their continent.
37. So they will reproach thy servant, saying: Who hath set thee to save us?
38. He will be sore distressed.
39. All they understand not that thou and I are fashioning a boat of mother-of-pearl. We will sail down the river of Amrit even to the yew-groves of Yama, where we may rejoice exceedingly.
40. The joy of men shall be our silver gleam, their woe our blue gleam–all in the mother-of-pearl.
41. (The scribe was wroth thereat. He spake:

    O Adonai and my master, I have borne the inkhorn and the pen without pay, in order that I might search this river of Amrit, and sail thereon as one of ye. This I demand for my fee, that I partake of the echo of your kisses.)
42. (And immediately it was granted unto him.)
43. (Nay; but not therewith was he content. By an infinite abasement unto shame did he strive. Then a voice:)
44. Thou strivest ever; even in thy yielding thou strivest to yield–and lo! thou yieldest not.
45. Go thou unto the outermost places and subdue all things.
46. Subdue thy fear and thy disgust. Then–yield!
47. There was a maiden that strayed among the corn, and sighed; then grew a new birth, a narcissus, and therein she forgot her sighing and her loneliness.
48. Even instantly rode Hades heavily upon her, and ravished her away.
49. (Then the scribe knew the narcissus in his heart; but because it came not to his lips, therefore was he shamed and spake no more.)

50. Adonai spake yet again with V.V.V.V.V. and said:

The earth is ripe for vintage; let us eat of her grapes, and be drunken thereon.

51. And V.V.V.V.V. answered and said: O my lord, my dove, my excellent one, how shall this word seem unto the children of men?

52. And He answered him: Not as thou canst see.

It is certain that every letter of this cipher hath some value; but who shall determine the value? For it varieth ever, according to the subtlety of Him that made it.

53. And He answered Him: Have I not the key thereof?

I am clothed with the body of flesh; I am one with the Eternal and Omnipotent God.

54. Then said Adonai: Thou hast the Head of the Hawk, and thy Phallus is the Phallus of Asar. Thou knowest the white, and thou knowest the black, and thou knowest that these are one. But why seekest thou the knowledge of their equivalence?

55. And he said: That my Work may be right.

56. And Adonai said: The strong brown reaper swept his swathe and rejoiced. The wise man counted his muscles, and pondered, and understood not, and was sad.

Reap thou, and rejoice!

57. Then was the Adept glad, and lifted his arm.

Lo! an earthquake, and plague, and terror on the earth!

A casting down of them that sate in high places; a famine upon the multitude!

58. And the grape fell ripe and rich into his mouth.

59. Stained is the purple of thy mouth, O brilliant one, with the white glory of the lips of Adonai.

60. The foam of the grape is like the storm upon the sea; the ships tremble and shudder; the shipmaster is afraid.

61. That is thy drunkenness, O holy one, and the winds whirl away the soul of the scribe into the happy haven.

62. O Lord God! let the haven be cast down by the fury of the storm! Let the foam of the grape tincture my soul with Thy light!

63. Bacchus grew old, and was Silenus; Pan was ever Pan for ever and ever more throughout the æons.

64. Intoxicate the inmost, O my lover, not the outermost!

65. So was it–ever the same! I have aimed at the peeled wand of my God, and I have hit; yea, I have hit.

# § A. EXORDIVM

# I

**1. I am the Heart; and the Snake is entwined**
**About the invisible core of the mind.**
**Rise, O my snake! It is now is the hour**
**Of the hooded and holy ineffable flower.**
**Rise, O my snake, into brilliance of bloom**
**On the corpse of Osiris afloat in the tomb!**
**O heart of my mother, my sister, mine own,**
**Thou art given to Nile, to the terror Typhon!**
**Ah me! but the glory of ravening storm**
**Enswathes thee and wraps thee in frenzy of form.**
**Be still, O my soul! that the spell may dissolve**
**As the wands are upraised, and the aeons revolve.**
**Behold! in my beauty how joyous Thou art,**
**O Snake that caresses the crown of mine heart!**
**Behold! we are one, and the tempest of years**
**Goes down to the dusk, and the Beetle appears.**
**O Beetle! the drone of Thy dolorous note**
**Be ever the trance of this tremulous throat!**
**I await the awaking! The summons on high**
**From the Lord Adonai, from the Lord Adonai!**

THE FIRST THING WE SHOULD NOTE is that the initial "I" in the phrase, "**I am the Heart**." Technically, this indicates the *Adeptus Minor* striving to achieve the *Knowledge and Conversation of the Holy Guardian Angel*. Or to look at it another way, for everyone who reads this book and aspires unto the Holy Guardian Angel; this is YOU. This is *your* point of view.

The scribe identified with "**the Heart**" which is a primary attribution of Tiphereth, the Sixth Sephira on the Tree of Life. It is the Sephira corresponding to the Grade wherein the aspirant seals the Knowledge and Conversation with the Holy Guardian Angel. It is considered the center of the microcosm.

We also attribute the ego-making faculty, the Ruach, to Tiphereth. Hence, it is the source and center of the "I" of which we are all so fond.

*Figure A1 - The Anāhata Cakra in Tiphereth*

## The Cakras and the Serpent

Also attributed to Tiphereth is the अनाहत, *anāhata*, or heart चक्र, *cakra*.[1] The word *anāhata* means "unstruck" (i.e. "unbeaten").[2] This refers to the "unstruck sound," which we call the "sound of silence."[3] It is said to be the sound of the celestial realm. Herein is harmony, balance and stillness. In the Hindu tradition, the "vital principle" of the *anāhata* is called प्राण, *prāṇa*, which means "the breath of life,"[4] that is, the "vital breath."

1 The word चक्र, *cakra*, in *Sanskrit* means "wheel" and represents the focal points of subtle energies in the body. (*Monier-Williams*, p. 380c.) For the *cakras*, see Avalon, *The Serpent Power*, passim.

2 अनाहत, *anāhata*, "unbeaten," *Monier-Williams*, p. 29a.

3 नाद, *nāda*, "sound," *Monier-Williams*, p. 534c. See also Blatvatsky, *The Voice of the Silence*, and Crowley's commentary, *Liber LXXI*, *The Equinox*, Vol. 3, No. 1, pp. 7-13 in the final section of the book.

4 प्राण, *prāṇa*, "the breath of life," *Monier-Williams*, p.705a.

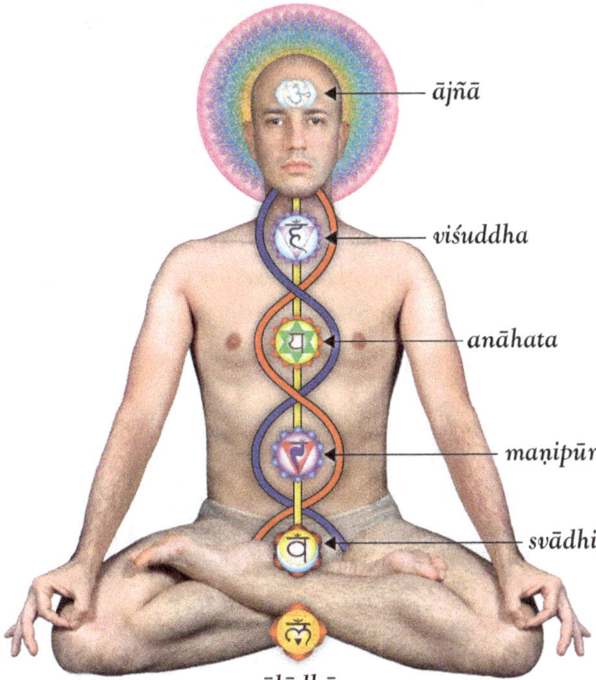


Figure A2 - The Cakras in the Body

In the शिव संहिता, *Śiva Saṃhitā*, the heart is said to be the seat of *prāṇa*.[5] In other traditional Hindu literature, the *prāṇa* is described as originating from the Sun.[6] The Sephira Tiphereth is likewise attributed to the Sun.

There are seven central *cakras* in the human body, all aligned vertically with the spine.

Figure A3 - The Mūlādhāra Cakra

The मूलाधार, *mūlādhāra*,[7] is the root *cakra* at the base of the spine. It is symbolized by a red, four-petalled lotus with a yellow square in the center, and the seed syllable लं, *lam*. It is the place where *kuṇḍalinī* serpent sleeps until awakened.

5 शिव संहिता, *Śiva Saṃhitā*, Chapter III, verse 7.

6 See मैत्रायनीय उपणिषद, *Maitrāyaṇīya Upaniṣad*, 6:1-3.

7 *Monier-Williams*, p. 827a. See मूल, *mūlā*, "root," p. 826b + धरा, *dhāra*, "stream," p. 515c.

Figure A4 - The Svādhiṣhṭhāna Cakra

The स्वाधिष्ठान svādhiṣṭhāna,[8] is depicted as a six- petalled lotus, located two finger widths above the *mūlādhāra cakra*. It is marked with the sign of the lunar crescent, and the seed syllable वं, *vaṃ*.

Figure A5 - The Maṇipūra Cakra

The मणिपूर, *maṇipūra*,[9] is the ten-petalled lotus at the solar plexus. It is marked with a downward-pointing Red Triangle in the center, and the seed syllable रं', *ram*.

Figure A6 - The Anāhata Cakra

अनाहत, *anāhata*, the Heart *cakra*, is a twelve-petalled lotus in the center of the chest. It is marked with a Hexagram in the center, and the seed syllable यं, *yam*.

Figure A7 - The Viśuddha Cakra

विशुद्ध, *viśuddha*,[10] the lotus of sixteen petals, is located in the pit of the throat. It is marked with a circle in the center, signifying आकाश, *ākāśa*, or "Spirit" in our terminology,[11] and a downward-pointing blue triangle within which is the seed syllable हं, *haṃ*.

Figure A8 - The Ājñā Cakra

आज्ञा, *ājñā*,[12] is the lotus of two petals, located in the center of the forehead between the eyebrows. It is marked with a downward-pointing pale triangle with a circle in the center, and the seed syllable ॐ, *auṃ*.

---

8 स्वाधिष्ठान, *svādhiṣṭhāna*, literally, "one's own place." *Monier-Williams*, p. 1277b.

9 मणिपूर, *maṇipūra*, literally, "city of jewels." *Monier-Williams*, p. 775a.

10 विशुद्ध, *viśuddha*, "completely pure." *Monier-Williams*, p. 991b.

11 आकाश, *ākāśa*, "free or open space, vacuity, the ether, sky or atmosphere," *Monier-Williams*, pp. 126c-127a. As in many other languages, the concept of Spirit, or the Etherial Element, is expressed by a word that means "air."

12 आज्ञा, *ājñā*, "perceive, understand." *Monier-Williams*, p. 133a.

Figure A9 - The Sahasrāra Cakra

सहस्रार, *sahasrāra*, is the thousand-petalled lotus,[13] the most subtle of all *cakras*.

The *Śiva Samhita* describes it as being positioned in the ब्रह्मरन्ध्र, *Brahmarandhra,*[14] the principle aperture at the base of the skull.[15] When it fully blooms, it opens from the crown of the head, expanding into incorporeal consciousness. The blooming of the thousand-petalled lotus is accompanied by समाधि, *samādhi.*[16]

In Hinduism, the word बीज, *bīja*, meaning "seed,"[17] is used as a metaphor for the origin and cause of all things. The term generally refers to the "seed syllables" contained in the sacred mantras. The "seed syllable" most familiar to all of us is ॐ, *auṃ*, (or *om*) which signifies the essence of ultimate reality or ब्रह्मन्, *Brahman.*[18] It is found at the beginning and end of chapters in the वेद, *Vedas,*[19] and the उपणिषद्, *Upaniṣads.*[20]

These "seeds" do not have precise meanings in themselves, but each one is said to be a base मन्त्र, *mantra,*[21] to enable direct connection to certain spiritual principles. As I have shown above, each of the *cakras* in the body has a corresponding "seed syllable" that can be used as a Mantra.

---

13 See *Monier-Williams*, सहस्रार, *sahasrā,* pp. 1195 b-c.

14 शिव संहिता, *Śiva Saṃhitā*, Chapter V, v.123. For ब्रह्मरन्ध्र, *Brahmarandhra,* "Brahma's crevice," see *Monier-Williams*, p. 739c.

15 *Ibid.* Chapter 5, 103.

16 समाधि, *samādhi*, literally means "union," *Monier-Williams*, p. 1159c.
For a thorough discussion of this term, see *Crowley, Book IV,* Part 1, Chapter VII, "Samadhi."

17 बीज, *bīja*, "seed," *Monier-Williams*, p. 732b.

18 ब्रह्मन्, *Brahman, Ibid.*, pp. 737c-738a.

19 From the Sanskrit वेद, Veda "knowledge." The Vedas are a large collection of the oldest religious texts in Hinduism. The Four Vedas are The ऋग्वेद, *ṛgveda*, यजुर्वेद, *yajurveda*, सामवेद, *sāmaveda* and the अथर्ववेद, *atharvaveda.*

20 The Sanskrit word उपणिषद्, *Upaniṣad*, means "to sit down near to" and probably had its origin in the manner which students sat at the feet of a Master as he spoke. (see *Monier-Williams*, p. 201a) Later traditions assign more colorful meanings which are more interpretive. The भगवद् गीता, *Bhāgavad gita*, is the most well-known of the *Upaniṣads* in the Western world.

21 मन्त्र, *mantra*, literally, "instrument of thought," a repetitive utterance used to focus thought. See Crowley, *Book IV,* Part 2, Chapter 11, "Prāṇāyāma and its parallel in Speech, Mantrayoga."

# Tiphereth and the Snake

**I am the Heart; and the Snake is entwined
About the invisible core of the mind.**

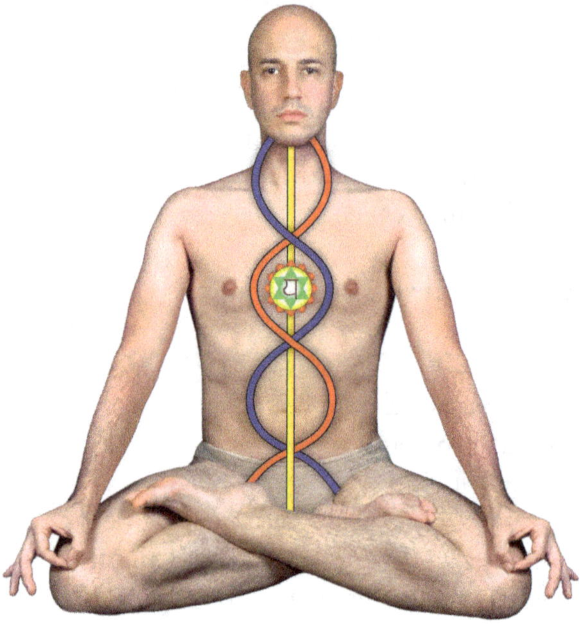

*Figure A10 - The Anāhata Cakra in the Body*

In this first verse in *Liber LXV*, the Snake indicates the कुण्डलिनी, *kuṇḍalinī*, the force which is "entwined" within the body invisibly. The word *kuṇḍalinī* means "coiled serpent."[22] The *kuṇḍalinī*, while at rest, resides in the मूलाधार चक्र, *mūlādhāra cakra*, at the base of the spine.

Note that the verse tells us that the Snake is "**entwined About the invisible core of the mind.**" This refers to the *kuṇḍalinī* serpent coiling about the central नाडी, *naḍī*, or "channel" of the body[23] which is called सुषुम्णा, *suṣumṇā.*[24] The *naḍī* are the conduits of the various subtle currents that flow through the body, of which *prāṇa* is the most significant.

The *Śiva Saṃhitā* states that within the human body there are a total of 350,000 *naḍī*, of which fourteen are primary. The three most important are

---

22 कुण्डलिनी, *kuṇḍalinī*, "coiled serpent." *Monier-Williams*, p. 290a.

23 नाडी, *naḍī*, literally, "pipe or tube." Ibid., p. 534b.

24 सुषुम्णा, *suṣumṇā*, "very gracious." Ibid., p. 1237c.

सुषुम्णा, *suṣumṇā*, इडा, *iḏā*[25] and पिङ्गला, *piṅgalā*.[26] Of these three, the highest and most revered is *suṣumṇā*.[27]

The *suṣumṇā* is entwined in serpentine fashion by the two *naḍī iḏā* and *piṅgalā*.

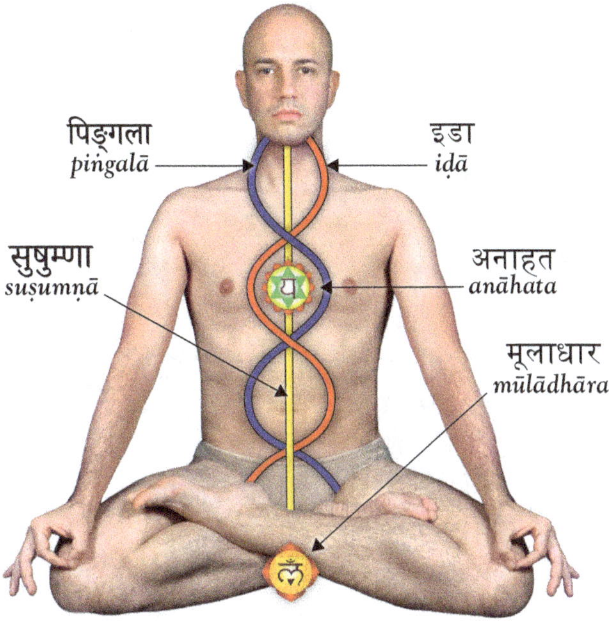


*Figure A11 - The Three Naḍī in Relation to Anāhata and Mūlādhāra*

*Figure A11* illustrates the standard attribution of the *anāhata cakra* and the three *naḍī*, or channels, *iḏā*, *piṅgalā*, and *suṣumṇā*.

The left channel is *iḏā*, the right channel is *piṅgalā*, and *suṣumṇā* is the central channel.

These three *naḍī* are attributed to the three pillars on the Tree of Life in our system – the Pillars of Mercy, Severity and the Middle Pillar.

Thus, *iḏā* corresponds to the Pillar of Mercy, *piṅgalā* to the Pillar of Severity, and *suṣumṇā* to the Middle Pillar.[28] (*Figure A12*.)

---

25 इडा, *iḏā*, "comfort," Ibid., p.164b.

26 पिङ्गला, *piṅgalā*, "tawny yellow, gold," Ibid., p. 624c.

27 *Śiva Saṃhitā*, Chapter II, 13-16.

28 For these "channels" see छान्दोग्योपनिषद *Chāndogyopaniṣad* 8.6 (i.e. *Chandogya Upanishad*. In the *Sacred Books of the East*, Vol. 1, *The Upanishads*, it is called The *Khândogya-Upanishad*. Cf. pp. 132-134.) See also प्रश्नोपनिषद्, *Praśnopaniṣad* 3.6-7 (i.e. *Prashna Upanishad*. See *Sacred Books of the East*, Vol. 15, *The Upanishads Part II, Prasña-Upanishad*, pp. 277-278.) For *Iḏā*, *Piṅgalā* & *Suṣumṇā*, see *Śiva Saṃhitā*, Chapter II.

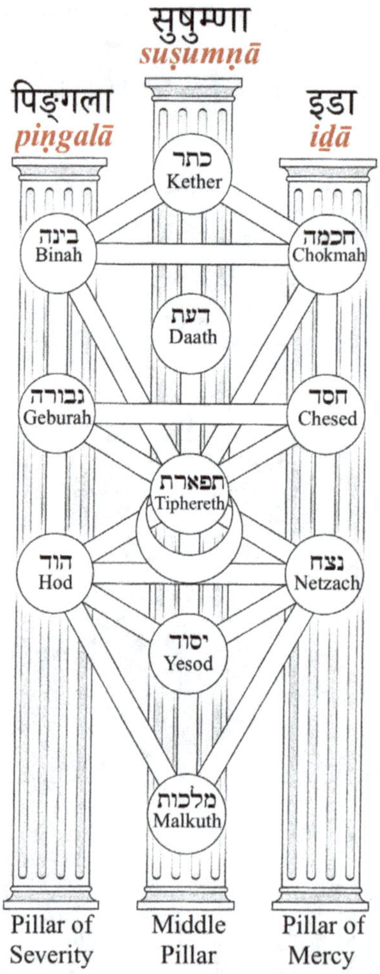


*Figure A12 - The Three Naḍī as the Pillars of the Tree of Life*

As I mentioned before, Tiphereth is also the center of the part of the human soul we call the Ruach, or intellectual faculty - the "**mind,**" which is attributed on the Tree of Life from Yesod, to **דעת**, *Daath*, forming a Hexagram with Tiphereth at its center.

This is the *Complex of the Intellect.*

Drawn upon a linear figure, we call it *The Hexagram of Nature (Figure A13).* Tiphereth, occupies the center of the hexagram, which is traditionally attributed to the ☉ Sun.

It likewise corresponds to the *anāhata cakra*, the "heart *cakra*," which is the center of this Complex of the Intellect, or the **core of the mind**.

*Figure A13 - The Hexagram of Nature Projected on the Tree of Life*

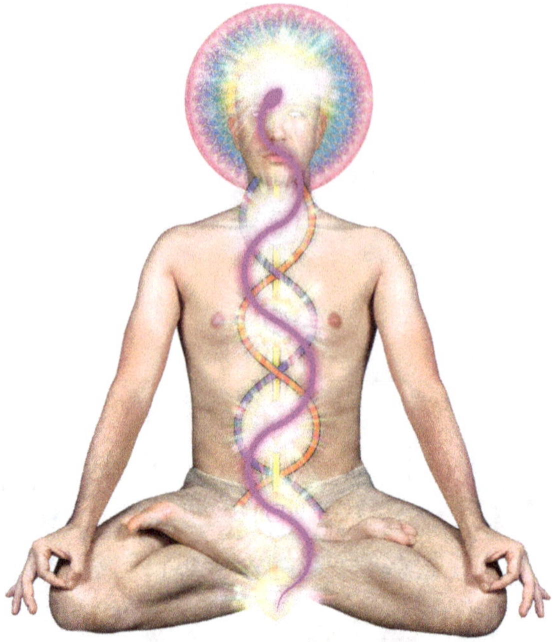

*Figure A14 - Kuṇḍalinī Piercing the Cakras & Sahasrāra Blooming*

## Rising of the Snake and the Thousand-Petaled Lotus

**Rise, O my snake! It is now is the hour**
**Of the hooded and holy ineffable flower.**
**Rise, O my snake, into brilliance of bloom**
**On the corpse of Osiris afloat in the tomb!**

Here is an invocation or call for the *kuṇḍalinī*, conceived as a snake, to rise from the *mūlādhāra cakra* at the base of the spine and move upward in the central *naḍī, suṣumṇā.*

This rising serpent pierces and opens each *cakra* until it reaches the *sahasrāra cakra*, where it "blooms" as the thousand-petalled lotus at the crown of the head.

This "thousand-petalled lotus" is the "**hooded and holy ineffable flower,**" and with its opening, the trance of *samādhi* is attained.

Students would do well to thoroughly acquaint themselves with Crowley's discussion of the character of *samādhi* in *Book IV, Part 1*, Chapter VII. Significantly, he began by quoting the Yogi याज्ञवल्क्य, *Yājñavalkya*, who in his discussion of the nature of *samādhi* said, "by *samādhi* is taken off everything that hides the lordship of the soul."[29]

---

29 Crowley was referencing *Vivekānanda*, who in turn was quoting याज्ञवल्क्य, *Yājñavalkya*, in *Raja Yoga*, p. 226.

*Figure A15 - The Egyptian Nemyss Signifying the Hood of a Cobra*

# The Hooded Serpent

The same Archetype finds expression in the *caduceus*. At the top of the staff, entwined by twin serpents is the wingèd globe, which is another representation of the blooming of the thousand-petaled lotus. The *caduceus* incorporates the twin serpents, corresponding to *iḏā* and *piṅgala* entwining around the Middle Pillar of the Sephiroth.

The Crown, that is כתר, *Kether*, the first Sephira on the Tree of Life, is depicted as the wingèd globe of Egypt - which is , *bḥdt, Hadit*.

This symbolism was also found in the *uraeus* serpent on the brows of Egyptian royalty. The *uraeus*, which signified royalty, was represented by the hooded cobra.

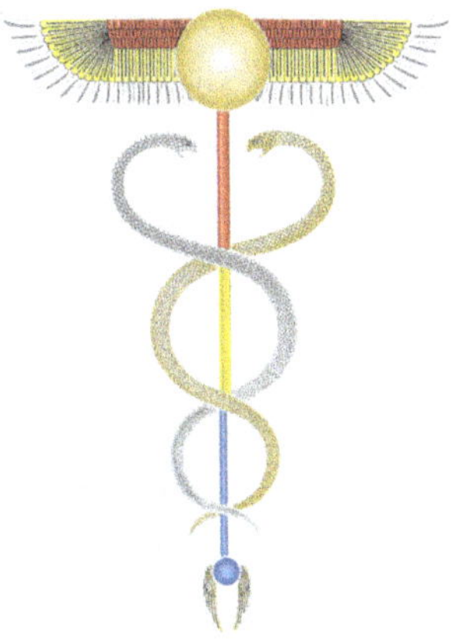

*Figure A16 - The Caduceus*

I have already touched upon the etymology of the word "uraeus" in the Prologue, page 26.

Note that the verse describes the blooming *sahasrāra* as the **"hooded and holy ineffable flower"** (emphasis added). The nemyss worn by the Egyptian pharaohs *signified the hood of a cobra*. The artificial beards worn by the kings are also included in this symbolism because they represented the *exposed chest of the cobra*. (*Figure A15*.)

It becomes quite apparent that the nemyss indicates the hooded cobra when the back side of the nemyss is examined. The tail of the serpent is clearly visible lying along the spine of the wearer.

The hood of the Cobra surrounds the *sahasrāra cakra*, hence that *cakra* is called the **hooded and holy ineffable flower**.

*Figure A17 - The Hooded Cobra*

## The Corpse of Osiris

**Rise, O my snake, into brilliance of bloom**
**On the corpse of Osiris afloat in the tomb!**

K*uṇḍalinī*, the snake resting in the *mūlādhāra*, is summoned to rise into full flower in the *sahasrāra cakra* **On the corpse of Osiris afloat in the tomb!**

*Figure A18 - Osiris Enthroned within a Shrine Crowned with Uraeus Serpents*

*Osiris* is the name of the ancient Egyptian god of the dead. As aspirants to A∴A∴, each of us mystically are *initially* Osiris, or to use the Egyptian word, , *ỉsỉr*, *Asar*.[30]

The corpse of Osiris signifies any human being who is dead to the world of initiated Truth. The people of the profane world are afloat aimlessly on the river of life, carried onward by the current wherever it goes.

---

30 See Gunther, *Initiation in the Aeon of the Child*, pp. 36-39 and 48-50.

For the Initiate, this river is the river of अमृत, *amṛta*,[31] that is, *Amrit*, the river of eternity or immortality. For one who has not yet awakened unto the higher aspiration, that is, the profane, it is a river of death, which continually carries them to an unknown destination, incarnation after incarnation.

For the aspirant, this corpse is the "**corpse of Osiris**," the vehicle for change, afloat on the river of life.

When the *kuṇḍalinī* serpent is awakened, it rises from its slumber, pierces the *cakras* along the Middle Pillar of suṣumṇā and awakens Osiris from the sleep of death, the death that the world calls "life", unto the life which the world calls "death."

Hence, we mystically refer to *Osiris* as Νεκρός, *Nekros*, the "dead one."

*Figure A19 - The Corpse of Osiris Protected by Isis*

## The Threefold Heart

**O heart of my mother, my sister, mine own,**
**Thou art given to Nile, to the terror Typhon!**
**Ah me! but the glory of ravening storm**
**Enswathes thee and wraps thee in frenzy of form.**

First, the heart of the candidate is called "**my mother,**" then it is called "**my sister,**" and lastly, "**mine own.**"

This wording is a very important detail that should not be glossed over. To understand these words, we must turn to the Holy Books themselves for clarity, with a little help from history.

Note that *all three* of these are **given to Nile, to the terror Typhon**! This means that all of these conceptions are subjected to the power of change and transformation symbolized by Τυφῶν, *Typhon*, the lord of the storm.

So what exactly are these three conceptions each symbolized as a heart?

In order to understand the first phrase, "**heart of my mother,**" we need to examine a clue to this verse in *Liber LXV*, that is found immediately in

31 अमृत, *amṛta*, literally, "not dead," i.e. "immortal, imperishable," *Monier-Williams*, p. 82b.

*Figure A20 - Ascensus*

Chapter I of *Liber VII*, verse 30:

> **Not Isis my mother, nor Osiris my self; but the incestuous Horus given over to Typhon, so may I be!**

The **heart of my mother** is the heart of , *ỉst*, *Isis*, who is Nature personified. In this sense, she is the Supernal Mother, Isis the "mother of the gods." Later in *Liber LXV*, Chapter IV, verse 24, there occurs an invocation to , *ʿ3pp*, *Apep*, another form of the destroyer Typhon, and there Isis is so described.

> **Arise, O serpent Apep, Thou art Adonai the beloved one! Thou art my darling and my lord, and Thy poison is sweeter than the kisses of Isis the mother of the Gods!**

And from this, we know her to be Binah, the Supernal Mother, ה *Heh Prima* of the Tetragrammaton יהוה.

O heart of my mother, **my sister**, mine own, (emphasis added)

The heart is then called "**my sister**," which is another form of Isis as ה *Heh Final* of the Tetragrammaton , attributed to Malkuth, the world of עשה, *Assiah.*[32]

In *The Book of the Law,* Chapter I, verse 53 she is called "**the little world, my sister, my heart & my tongue**".

> **This shall regenerate the world, the little world, my sister, my heart & my tongue, unto whom I send this kiss.** (emphasis added)

Lastly, the heart is then called simply, **mine own.**

> **O heart of my mother, my sister, mine own,**

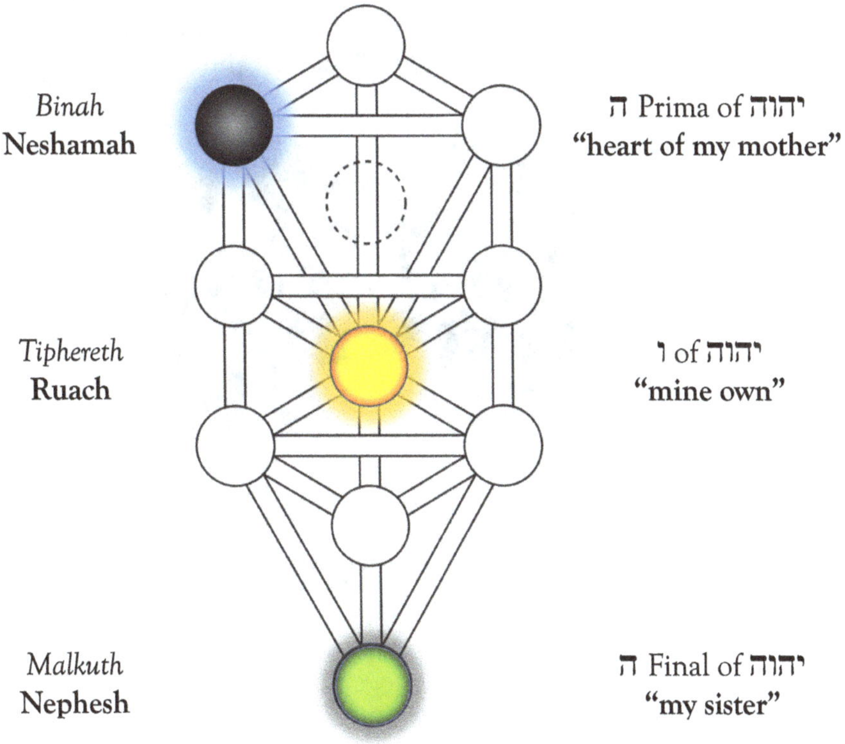


*Figure A21 - The Threefold Heart*

32 עשיה, *Assiah*, the "world of action," is the last of four worlds (אצילוה, *Atziluth*, בריאה, *Beriah*, יצירה, *Yetzirah* & עשיה, *Assiah*) that emanated from אין, Ain, or Nothingness. These four worlds are attributed to the four letters of the Tetragrammaton, יהוה.

Here, this refers to all aspirants to the Great Work, which *Liber VII* called "**Osiris my self**" as we have seen. This "**heart**" is the heart of Tiphereth, the center of the microcosm. It is the heart of our rational self, the seat of our Reason, the center of the *Heptad of the Intellect*, attributed to ו *Vau* of Tetragrammaton.

Thus, this portion of the verse in *Liber LXV* indicates the three major divisions of the human soul on the Tree of Life.

Here is the echo of a Spell from *The Egyptian Book of the Dead*. We can see the original in *Spell 30*, which was inscribed upon a heart scarab placed upon the heart of a corpse. A variant occurs in *Spell 30A*, written on papyri called,  , *r n tm rdỉt sẖsf ỉb*, *A Spell for preventing the contention of the heart*,[33] or in *Spell 30B*, also written on papyri, but without a title. Eventually, these Spells were combined into a single Spell. A most interesting fact is that the *very first* example we know of the combination of these two Spells is found on the wooden outer coffin of a priest from *Thebes* whose name happened to be 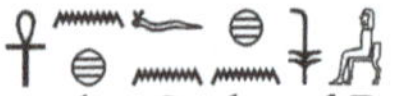 , *ꜥnḫ=f-n-ḫnsw*, *Ankhefenkhonsu*, the same priest we know from the Stele of Revealing. This is all the more interesting because *Spell 30* is inscribed upon the back side of the Stele of Revealing.

*Figure A22 - Heart Scarab with BD Spell 30B on the Reverse*

The wording of the first part of Spell 30 as it has been traditionally translated is:

*ỉb=ỉ n mwt=ỉ sp sn*

*My heart of my mother! My heart of my mother!*

33 *The Papyrus of Nu* (BM EA10477), Sheet 5, line 1.

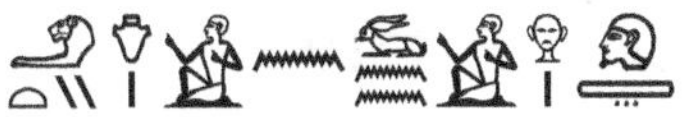

*ḥꜣty=ỉ n wn=ỉ ḥr-dp tꜣ*

*My heart of my existence upon the earth!*[34]

The Egyptians believed that the human heart itself was the seat of the emotions and the mind. For this reason, they left the physical heart inside the body when it was embalmed, and placed a *scarab* amulet over it to protect it on its eternal journey.[35]

*The Egyptian Book of the Dead* translated by E.A. Wallis Budge and published in 1898, and *The Papyrus of Ani* published previously in 1895, were the versions of *The Book of the Dead* familiar to Crowley.[36] *The Papyrus of Any* has the variant, Spell 30B, rather than Spell 30, and from internal evidence we know that Crowley was well-acquainted with that version.

Budge translated Spell 30B in the *Papyrus of Any* as follows:

*ỉb=ỉ n mwt[=ỉ] sp sn*

*My heart [my] mother! [My] heart my mother!*

*ḥꜣt=ỉ n ḫprw[=ỉ]*

*My heart of [my] coming into being.*

In a typical error, Budge omitted the preposition that lies between "mother" and "my heart." It should read, "My heart *of* my mother."[37] But that is a minor point. The important thing to note is that the word that Budge translated as "coming into being" is the Egyptian word , *ḫprw*, *kheperu*.

The initial character in this word is the *scarab beetle*, sacred to the god , *ḫprỉ*, *Khephra*, and this word is linked directly to the name of that god.[38]

34 *The Book of the Dead, Spell 30, The* Ste le *of Revealing* (reverse side), English translation of the French version by the Boulaq Museum.

35 They considered the human brain to be useless tissue and removed it from the body and discarded it. They did not consider it the source of thoughts.

36 The name  is now correctly transliterated *ꜣny*, "Any," rather than "Ani."

37 Budge, *The Papyrus of Ani* (1895), p. 11.

38 By current Egyptological standards, this word is transliterated *Khepri*.

# Typhon- Lord of the Storm

**Thou art given to Nile, to the terror Typhon!**
**Ah me! but the glory of ravening storm**
**Enswathes thee and wraps thee in frenzy of form.**

All of these "hearts" mentioned in *Liber LXV* are given over to the river **Nile**. That is, the heart is subjected to the power symbolized by the river Nile.

Here, the river signifies a form of the river *Amrit* as well as the destructive Typhon. This is another *paradoxia*.

Yearly flooding of the river Nile brought life to the lifeless desert, but the flood began far away with a torrent that swelled the banks of the quiet river. It was thus destructive and constructive at the same time, flooding the former world, but depositing the rich soil that guaranteed life for the new world. It marked the beginning of a new year.

Τυφῶν, *Typhon,* was the Greek god of the storm. In fact, our modern English word "typhoon" was ultimately derived from the Greek Τυφῶν.[39]

In early accounts, the god Typhon was described as a monster with multiple snake heads uttering hideous sounds.[40] *Nonnus of Panolopus* likewise attributed to him serpentine characteristics with multiple heads.[41] He was later depicted as having two serpents for legs and multiple serpent heads for fingers.

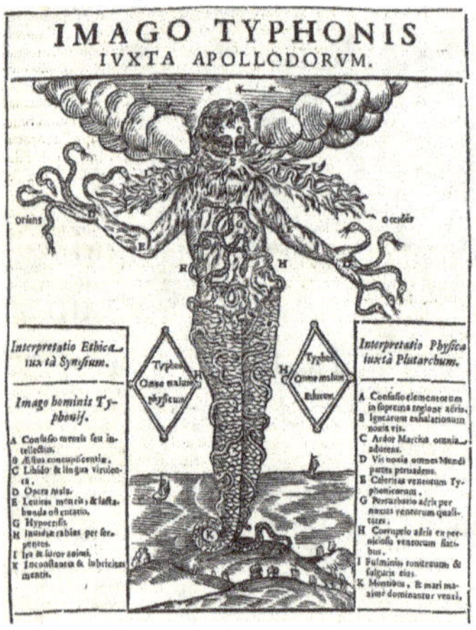


*Figure A23 - Imago Typhonis*

*Figure A24 - Typhon*

39 *Skeat*, p. 530-531.

40 Hesiod, *Theogony, 823-825.*

41 Nonnus, *Dionysiaca, Book II, passim.*

Typhon was equated with the Egyptian god  , *stẖ*, *Set*, the slayer of Osiris.[42]

Whether through creativity or by destruction, Set was the god of *change*. He brought the modifications required to climb the next rung of the evolutionary ladder, whether in the physical world, or in the spiritual world of the individual. Thus, he has often been feared as well as revered.

Set is a force of Nature – that is, he is the brother of Isis. To give one example of how destruction brings about creation, consider a destructive act of nature.

A forest fire that begins with a lightning strike may ravage an entire forest and burn it to the ground, leaving only charred cinders in the place of glorious foliage. But fire removes the dead debris on the ground, and releases nutrients from the soil, providing food for seeds and sprouts. Fire opens up spaces providing areas of habitat for a wide variety of species, plant and animal. It is this very act of Nature's destruction that guarantees the renewal of the forest over time.

Set (Typhon) also equates to *Saturn*, the lord of Time. Consider again *Liber VII*, Chapter I verses 28-30:

> **Nature shall die out; she hideth me, closing mine eyelids with fear, she hideth me from My destruction, O Thou open eye.**
> **O ever-weeping One!**
> **Not Isis my mother, nor Osiris my self; but the incestuous Horus given over to Typhon, so may I be!**

Returning to *Liber LXV*, we read of the effect of Typhon upon the Threefold Heart:

> **Thou art given to Nile, to the terror Typhon!**
> **Ah me! but the glory of ravening storm**
> **Enswathes thee and wraps thee in frenzy of form.**

This initial storm enswathes and enwraps the Candidate with a "**frenzy of form.**" It is a transformative storm, necessary to sweep away the old structures so that the aspirant can rebuild them anew.

---

42 *Set* is mentioned by name in *Liber A'ash*, 7. His name is commonly rendered "Seth" by modern Egyptologists, occasionally "Sutech" based on a variation of his name in Egyptian. For a thorough discussion of this god, see Te Velde, *Seth, God of Confusion* (1967).

# Stillness

**Be still, O my soul! that the spell may dissolve**
**As the wands are upraised, and the aeons revolve.**

The candidate urged his soul to be silent, not to struggle against the storm of change, but to allow dissolution of that which *was*, to give form to that which *will be*. Note that here, he says **"my soul."** Remember that earlier in this verse, his appeal was addressed to

**"O heart of my mother, my sister, mine own:"** The three parts of the human soul: *Neshamah, Nephesh* and *Ruach* - the Intuition, the Animal Soul and the Intellect.

He urged them to **"Be still."** In practice, this is easier said than done, requiring mastery of *āsana* and *prāṇāyāma*.[43] In the translation of the 15th chapter of *Tao Teh Ching* by Crowley, he wrote, "Who can clear muddy water? Stillness will accomplish this."[44]

This is the key to this work. *Be still.* Let the Spell perform its work of change.

**As the wands are upraised, and the aeons revolve.**

The wands are those of the three Adepti who govern the Inner Order of A∴A∴, to which the Candidate is allowed admission by reason of the Knowledge and Conversation of The Holy Guardian Angel. The wands are symbolically uplifted to inaugurate, govern and confirm the Initiation, which is simultaneously creative and destructive, even as the Nile.

The yellow wand is the *Lotus Wand*, emblem of the Office of the Cancellarius of A∴A∴ It is the lotus-crowned wand of Isis, the wand of vegetable-life creation through the initiation of water and the mitigating influence of the Mother.[45] It is referred to Tiphereth.

The red *Phoenix Wand*, with the head of the *Bennu Bird*, is emblematic of the Office of the Imperator of A∴A∴ It signifies the wand of animal-life

---

43 *Āsana*, from the Sanskrit, आसन, "sitting down." *prāṇāyāma*, प्राणायाम, is breath control. *Monier-Williams*, p. 159c, p. 706a. See *Liber E vel Exercitorium, III & IV* in *Book IV, Part II, Magick in Theory and Practice.*

44 Crowley, *Tao Teh Ching*, p. 30.

45 It is here referred to the initiating water because the Lotus, symbolic of the Neophyte, rises and blooms in water, informed by the Waters of Isis, the Great Sea in Binah. This is from the point-of-view of the Candidate. Its higher Influence derives from Kether, as Primal Air, reflected unto Tiphereth, hence its colour as Yellow.

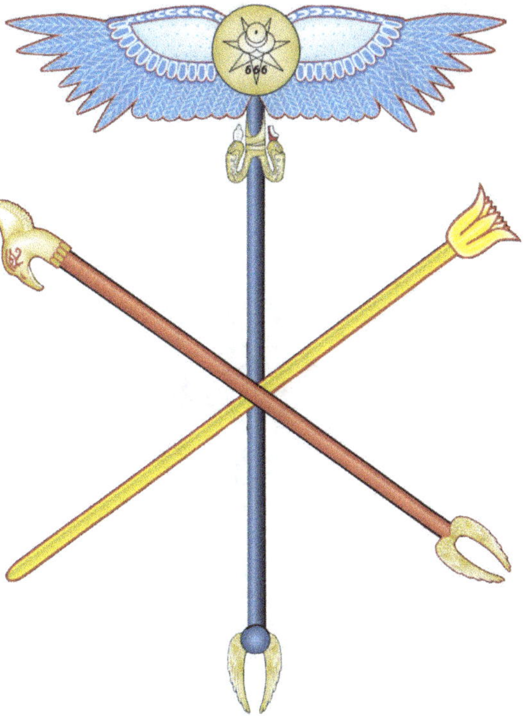


*Figure A25 - Wands of the Adepti of the Inner Order*

creation and purgation through the initiation of fire and the resurrection of that energy from its ashes. It is referred to Geburah.

The wand with the wingèd globe is emblematic of the Office of the Praemonstrator of A∴A∴ It is therefore called the *Wand of the Chief Adept*. It indicates the Authority that is derived from the Superiors, crowning the Central Pillar on the Tree of Life. It signifies therefore the transformation of all life through the initiation of the Spirit. It is said to represent "the equilibrated force of the Spirit and the four elements beneath the everlasting wings of the Holy One."[46] It is referred to Chesed.

These three are indicated in *Liber VII*, VII:27:

**I am the Initiator and the Destroyer. Mine is the Globe - and the Bennu Bird and the Lotus of Isis my daughter!**

---

46 See *The Equinox*, Vol. 1, No. 3, p. 210.

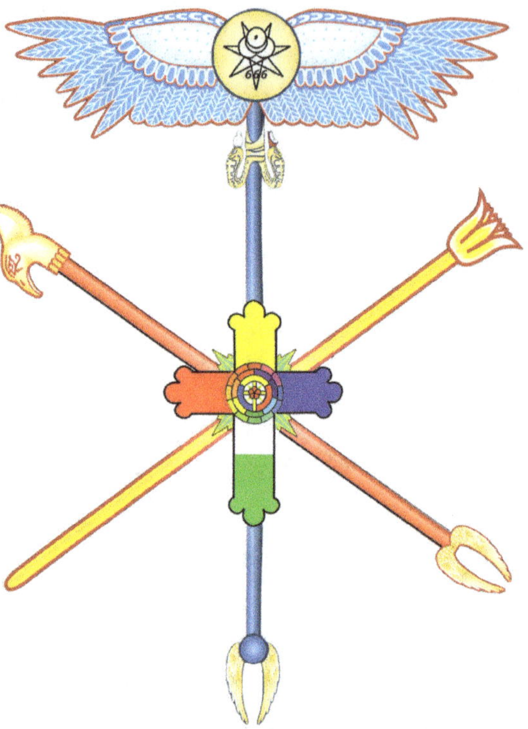

*Figure A26 - Wands of the Adepti of the Inner Order & Rose Cross*

## The Joyous Snake, Crown of the Heart

**Behold! in my beauty how joyous Thou art,**
**O Snake that caresses the crown of mine heart!**

Again, we encounter a reference to the sixth Sephira Tiphereth, which means **beauty**. The attainment of The Holy Guardian Angel is the Seal of Attainment for the Adeptus Minor (within) whose Grade is indicated 5°= 6□ which means, the fifth attainment sealed in the sixth Sephira.

But note carefully the wording here. The Snake caresses the **crown of mine heart** (emphasis added). The crown is Kether, the highest Sephira on the Tree of Life. Kether is the crown of the microcosm, and thus the crown of the Heart Tiphereth. Remember that the *kuṇḍalinī* serpent rising up *suṣumṇā* opens the *sahasrāra cakra* causing the thousand-petalled lotus to bloom.

Tiphereth is the center of human consciousness, and the Adept, in the stillness of Initiation in Tiphereth, identified himself as one with the serpent. Further, in the **beauty** of this moment, he conceived the *kuṇḍalinī* Snake, the crown of his heart, as "**joyous**."

It is a most interesting word to use in this place. He did not call the Snake "wonderful," or "splendid," or any other various terms that we might expect him to use. This word appears to be intentionally significant.

This word occurs in *Liber Tzaddi*, in relation to "**beauty**" as an aspect of Tiphereth:

> **Thus shall equilibrium become perfect. I will aid my disciples; as fast as they acquire this balanced power and joy so faster will I push them. They shall in their turn speak from this Invisible Throne; their words shall illumine the worlds.**
> **They shall be masters of majesty (Chesed) and might (Geburah); they shall be beautiful and joyous (Tiphereth); they shall be clothed with victory (Netzach) and splendour (Hod); they shall stand upon the firm foundation (Yesod); the kingdom (Malkuth) shall be theirs; yea, the kingdom shall be theirs. In the name of the Lord of Initiation. Amen.**
>
> *Liber Tzaddi, 42-44 (Comments in parenthesis added)*

In the second chapter of *The Book of the Law*, Hadit proclaimed,

> **I am the secret Serpent coiled about to spring: in my coiling there is joy.**[47]

Compare verse 54 of *Liber LXVI*, where the serpent Apep declares,

> **I leap with joy within thee; my head is arisen to strike.**

And note the wording of *Liber LXV*, Chapter III, verse 7:

> **Close didst thou cling with thy coils unto the heart, and it was as the joy of all the spring.**

47 *Liber AL*, II:26

*Figure A27 - Khephra as a Scarab Beetle Rolling the Sun*

## The Tempest and the Appearance of the Beetle

**Behold! we are one, and the tempest of years**
**Goes down to the dusk, and the Beetle appears.**
**O Beetle! the drone of Thy dolorous note**
**Be ever the trance of this tremulous throat!**

Union between the aspirant and the Risen Snake is confirmed with the phrase "**we are one**". The "**tempest of years**" was earlier called the "**ravening storm**" which enwrapped the aspirant in a "**frenzy of form**." The word "**form**" there is important, so keep it in your mind. When this storm passes, it "**Goes down to the dusk**," the time of the setting Sun.

When the Sun sets at the hour of dusk, the god , *ḫprỉ*, *Khephra*, appears in his form as a scarab Beetle. Students who are acquainted with the Adorations of the Sun as prescribed in *Liber Resh* are accustomed to think of the god Khephra as the god of midnight. But here, the text tells us explicitly that the beetle appears at *dusk*, that period of the early evening when the sun has set and darkness begins to encompass the earth. Not at the *darkest hour*, but at the *onset* of darkness.

In the previous discussion about *Spell 30B* from *The Egyptian Book of the Dead*, we examined the translation of Spell 30B from the *Papyrus of Any* by Budge. There, he translated the word , *ḫprw*, *kheperu*, as "coming into being."

*Figure A28 - The Egyptian God Khephra*

As a verb, , *ḫpr, kheper*, can mean "come into being." But here in this particular text, this word is a *noun* with plural strokes, and that changes the nuance of the meaning. So, we must reject Budge's translation here. As a noun, one of its main meanings of , *ḫprw, kheperu*, is "forms." As I emphasized previously, the word "**form**" is an important word.

The tempest of years was a "**frenzy of form**." The word *kheperu* not only can be translated as "forms," it can also be rendered "shapes" or "changes."

For example, the Egyptian phrase , *ḫprw ḥr ḫpr*, means, "changes take place," or literally, "changes come into being."[48]

In *Spell 30B* the words in the Spell in Egyptian, , *ḥꜣty=ỉ n ḫprw=ỉ*, which Budge translated as "my heart of my coming into being," could really read, "my consciousness of my forms" or "my consciousness of my shapes" or "my consciousness of my changes."

But what does it really mean in this context?

It one sense, it may mean, "my consciousness of my incarnations."[49]

When one reads this word in context within the Spell 30B, it is quite clear that , *ḫprw*, could mean the *different lives* experienced though reincarnation.[50] Thus, when *Liber LXV* tells us that the beetle appears at dusk, at the setting of the Sun, we know this refers to *changes* brought by "**the tempest of years**." This setting of the Sun can indeed refer to our death in *this* life.

---

48 Gardiner, *Admonitions of an Egyptian Sage*, p. 10, paragraph 3, Recto 10.

49 The key here is the translation of , *ḥꜣty*, which I contend, that in this context, did not mean "heart," but rather "mind," "consciousness," etc. See Assmann, *Death and Salvation in Ancient Egypt*, pp. 29-31.

50 There is no objective proof of which I am aware that proves the ancient Egyptians believed in reincarnation. However, it may certainly be inferred from numerous passages in *The Book of the Dead* texts. Spell 2 on the reverse of the Stele of Revealing is itself a good example. On the other hand, it may suggest something other than *physical* incarnation and we should admit incertitude and excercise caution in considering the question.

Remember that in ancient Egypt, the East represented birth and life; the West was the place of the setting Sun, the place of death. This part of the verse need not be considered to refer to one lifetime only, but also many lives and successive entries in the cycle of necessity, that is, the cycle of *incarnation*, upon the wheel of **संसार**, *saṃsāra.*[51]

As discussed previously, Spell 30, and its variants such as Spell 30B, were inscribed on an amulet of a scarab beetle, sacred to Khephra, and placed over the heart of the deceased. Thus we see the close connection between the scarab and the human heart: *existence – coming into being – the manifestation of change.*

As we can see Illustrated on Trump XVIII, *The Moon*, of the Crowley/Harris tarot deck of Thelema, it is the beetle-headed god Khephra who carries the Sun through its darkest hour of night and through the bitterness of winter to the gateway of resurrection.

*Figure A29 - Trump XVIII, The Moon*

This resurrection may be considered in the context of the spiritual experience of one life, for instance, emerging from the state we call *The Dark Night of the Soul.* This is discussed at some length in *Initiation in the Aeon of the Child* in Chapter 4, "Corridors of Twilight."

Yet, here the primary meaning seems to be that we should consider this as a resurrection from death many times over, as in reincarnation in many lives, the "**frenzy of form**" wrought by the "**tempest of years.**"

We should not overlook the final sentence in this section:

> **O Beetle! the drone of Thy dolorous note**
> **Be ever the trance of this tremulous throat!**

A type of Scarab Beetle is called the "drone beetle" because of the distinctive sound they make. *Liber LXV* calls this sound "**the drone of Thy dolorous note.**" (Note the Upper Case "**T**" in this phrase, implying a hyper-Abyssmal pronoun.)

51 संसार, *saṃsāra*, means "wandering through." *Monier-Williams Sanskrit Dictionary*, p. 1119b-c. It implies successive transmigrations of the soul.

It is highly significant that this sound is called "**dolorous**". The word is ultimately derived from the Latin *dolor*, from which comes *dolorosus*, "full of sorrow."[52]

The aspirant made the plea that this "sorrowful" note, droned by the Beetle at the hour of sunset, be ever the "**trance**" of his "**tremulous throat.**" Herein, are the key words to guide us to the meaning of this sentence. The "**dolorous**" note is the "**trance**" of the "**throat.**"

This refers to the "Trance of Sorrow," and is associated with the position of the throat, wherein lies the *viśuddha cakra*. On the Tree of Life, the throat is the position of Daath in the Abyss, which each aspirant to Binah must enter to become a *Babe of the Abyss*, in order to attain the Grade of Magister Templi. *Liber B vel Magi* teaches us, "Now the grade of a Magister teacheth the Mystery of Sorrow."[53] In his masterful *Little Essays Toward Truth*, significantly, the third chapter is named "Sorrow." Crowley began this chapter with a short, succinct sentence: "The Aspiration to become a Master is rooted in the Trance of Sorrow."[54]

The Magister Templi is Master of the Law of दुःख, *duḥka, sorrow*.[55] The Trance of Sorrow may be experienced in many superficial forms prior to swearing the Oath of the Abyss. But it is the Exempt Adept who experiences it in its fullest sense, and this ultimately is the impetus that compels him or her to embrace the Oath of the Abyss in order to attain Mastery, conquer the illusion of personal sorrow, and Understand the great Mystery of Universal Sorrow. Thus the aspirant in *Liber LXV* yearns to embrace the Trance of Sorrow in all its fullness, that he may attain to Mastery.

---

52 *L&S*, p 607a-b.

53 *Liber B vel Magi*, verse 15.

54 Crowley, *Little Essays Toward Truth*, p. 21. Serious study of this little book is its own reward.

55 *One Star in Sight*, Clause 6. (See *Magick, Liber ABA, Book Four, Part III, Appendix II*, p. 483.)

## The Awaking

**I await the awaking! The summons on high
From the Lord Adonai, from the Lord Adonai!**

The Candidate awaits the summons from "**on high**," the call from Adonai to a Spiritual Awaking. Occasionally, when new students read this verse they will mistakenly read "*awakening*" instead of "***awaking***". It is important to note the difference between these two words. The word "**awaking**" here, is a noun that suggests a *specific* moment of consciousness instigated by someone or something *other* than the candidate himself.

The phrase "**I await the awaking**" is comprised of 16 letters, the number which recalls *Trump XVI*, the lightning struck *Tower*, attributed to the Hebrew letter פ, which means "mouth."

The number may also suggest Path 16, which is that of *The Hierophant*.

That impetus of "**the awaking**" is provided by "**The summons on high From the Lord Adonai**".

This call is for aspirants to rise from their slumbers, when their eyes will be fully opened and they shall rise completely from *the sleep of death*, the torpor that grips the uninitiated.

Since the aspirant at the outset is considered spiritually dead, *Nekros*, the "dead one," we see an immediate analogy with the myths of the angel who blows his trumpet to awaken the dead on the Day of Judgment. Crowley stated that the preface to this event was indicated in Trump XVI, The Tower.[56]

This is illustrated in the Old Aeon tarot on Trump XX, *Judgement*, as in *Figure A30* from the *Marseilles Tarot* style of the *Jean Dodal Tarot Deck* from the early 18th century. The earliest example we have of that motif in Tarot is found in the cards painted by Bonifacio Bembo for the

*Figure A30 - Trump XX, Judgement*

56 Crowley, *The Book of Thoth*, p. 107.

Figure A31 - L'angelo (The Angel), Visconti-Sforza Tarot

*Visconti-Sforza* family in about 1450 e.v. (*Figure A31*)

In this earlier representation, the figure of God himself in heaven, holding the sword of justice, is flanked by two angels blowing trumpets.

Below on earth the dead rise cheerfully from their common crypt. Presumably, these represent Francesco Sforza, his wife Bianca Maria Visconti and a family member, since they are depicted sharing a common burial vault.

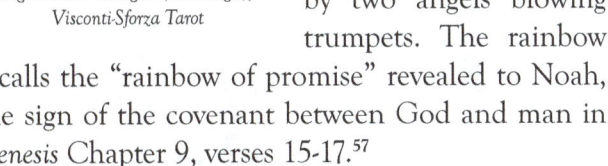

*Figure A32 - A Book of Hours, The Last Judgment*

We can see this same motif in an illustration from a French 'Book of Hours' from 1400 e.v. (*Figure A32.*) In this image, it is Jesus who sits in the mid-heaven on a rainbow flanked by two angels blowing trumpets. The rainbow recalls the "rainbow of promise" revealed to Noah, the sign of the covenant between God and man in *Genesis* Chapter 9, verses 15-17.[57]

וזחרתי את־בריתי אשר ביני וביניכם ובין כל־נפש היה בכל־בשר ולא־יהיה
עוד המים למבול לשחת כל־בשר: והיתה הקשת בענן
וראיתיה לזכר ברית עולם בין אלהים ובין כל־נפש חיה בכל־בשר
אשר על־הארץ: ויאמר אלהים אל־נח זאת אות־הברית אשר הקמתי
ביני ובין כל־בשר אשר על־הארץ:

And I will remember my Covenant which is between Me and thee, and every living soul in all flesh, and never again shall the waters become a flood to destroy all flesh. And the rainbow shall be in the cloud and I shall look upon it to remember the everlasting covenant between Elohim and every living creature in all flesh upon the Earth. And Elohim said to Noah this is the Sign of the Covenant which I have established between Me and all flesh that is on the Earth.

57 See also Gunther, *Initiation in the Aeon of the Child*, pp. 147-148.

Below, on the earth, eight people rise from their graves – men, women, a crowned king and a pope. The number "eight" again recalls the myth of Noah, wherein eight people were saved from the judgment of God (2 *Peter*, 2:5).

> καὶ ἀρχαίου κόσμου οὐκ ἐφείσατο ἀλλ' ὄγδοον Νῶε δικαιοσύνης κήρυκα ἐφύλαξεν κατακλυσμὸν κόσμῳ ἀσεβῶν ἐπάξας.

> And He (God) did not spare the ancient world, having brought in a flood upon an ungodly world, but preserved Noah, the eighth, a Herald of Righteousness.

The standing figures on the left and right are praying on behalf of the resurrected dead. On the left is the Virgin Mary with one breast bared, a popular motif of the Middle Ages up through the Renaissance, called *Maria Lactans* or "breast feeding Mary," symbolizing Christ's humility in taking on human flesh and the comfort offered to his followers.[58]

The figure on the right is doubtless John the Apostle, credited with writing *The Apocalypse* commonly believed to foretell the second coming of Christ and the Day of Judgment.[59]

After the *Visconti-Sforza* Tarot, the oldest card I have been able to find with this motif is from the *Minchiate* deck from Florence, Italy which dates to 1480-1500 e.v. (*Figure A33.*)

*Figure A33 - L'angelo (The Angel), Minchiate Florentine Tarot*

This very early card printed from a woodcut was called "The angel."

On this particular card, that angel is depicted blowing a single trumpet, below which a man and a woman rise from a crypt.

58 This "comfort" was offered through the Church. *Maria Lactans* also alluded to the *Ecclesia* offering Christ's comfort through the Eucharist for Resurrection. A cognate practice was charitable breastfeeding, which was also offered to hungry prisoners, as this was considered a token of God's eternal love for mankind. (Thanks to Matthieu Kleeman for suggesting this note.) The Rise of Protestantism brought open criticism of religious iconography, particularly those depicting worship of the Saints and the Virgin Mary. Even the Catholic Church came to consider a bare breast as an inappropriate Sacred Image and the once popular *Madonna Lactans* disappeared after the Renaissance. Cf. Margaret R. Miles, *A Complex Delight: The Secularization of the Breast, 1350-1750.* (2008).

59 The Metropolitan Museum of Art incorrectly identifies this figure as John the Baptist. In Medieval iconography, John the Baptist is traditionally depicted wearing the ragged skins of animals, not clothed in fine garments as the figure in this image.

*Figure A34 - Le Trombe*

In the later *Minchiate Etruria* deck, this card was eventually called *Le trombe*, *The trumpets*. It is illustrated as an angel hovering over the city of Florence rather than the tombs. The angel hovering overhead blows *two trumpets* from which depend royal banners. (*Figure A34*.)

I have identified the emblem on the white banner as the *House of Medici Coat of Arms*. They were one of the most influential families in Italy: they produced three Popes and two queens of France. Along with the Visconti and Sforza families, they inspired the Italian renaissance.

*Figure A35 - House of Medici Coat of Arms*

The mythology of the angel blowing the last trumpet at Judgment Day in the Christian world came directly from the *New Testament*.

The biblical reference with the most influence on this tradition seems to have been that found in *I Corinthians* 15:52:

> ἐν ἀτόμῳ ἐν ῥιρῇ ὀφθαλμοῦ ἐν τῇ ἐσχάτῃ σάλπιγγι: σαλρίσει γάρ καὶ οἱ νεκροὶ ἐγερθήσονται ἄφθαρτοι, καὶ ἡμεῖς ἀλλαγησόμεθα.
>
> In an instant, in the blink of an eye, at the last trumpet: for the trumpet shall sound and the dead shall rise incorruptible and we shall be changed.[60]

As this Christian myth evolved, the angel blowing the last trumpet at Judgment Day came to be identified by name as גבריאל, *Gabriel*. This is a most curious fact, because the *Bible nowhere* mentions the name Gabriel for the angel who blows the trump on the Day of Judgment.

However, in *Collectaneum in Beati Pauli Epistolas* by *Sedulius Scottus* (d. 828 e.v.), there is the gloss *et in voce archangeli* ("And in the voice of the archangel"), where the voice of Gabriel is mentioned as one of those whose call awakens the dead.

---

60 Another significant passage in the *New Testament* is in *I Thessalonians* I, 4:16: ὅτι αὐτὸς ὁ κύριος ἐν κελεύσματι, ἐν φωνῇ ἀρχαγγέλου καὶ ἐν σάλπιγγι θεοῦ, καταβήσεται ἀπ' οὐρανοῦ, καὶ οἱ νεκροὶ ἐν Χριστῷ ἀναστήσονται πρῶτον. "For the Lord himself, with a loud command, with the voice of an archangel and with a trumpet of God, will descend from heaven and the dead in Christ will rise first."

Et in voce archangeli, hoc est cœlestium virtutum, aut in manifestatione vocis archangelicæ; aliter, in voce Christi, sive Michælis, aut Gabrielis, quod interpretatur fortitudo Dei, qui dicit: surgite, expergiscimini.

And in the voice of the archangel: this means the heavenly power, or the manifestation of an archangelic voice; otherwise, it is the voice of Christ, or of Michael, or of Gabriel (whose name is interpreted to mean "the strength of God"), who says, Rise up, Awake.[61]

Gabriel as the angel of the Last Trumpet is also found in *De Ecclesiæ Dominio*, a sermon by *John De Wycliffe* from 1382 e.v.[62]

An illustration from an *Armenian Gospel* dating to 1455 C.E. (*Figure A36*), clearly identifies the angel blowing his trumpet to awaken the dead on Judgment Day as Գաբրիել, *Gabriel.* As the angel blows his trumpet, the dead rise from their graves overseen by those partaking of a feast in Heaven.

An Armenian pseudepigraphal manuscript in the British Library[63] dated various times in the 16th and 18th centuries C.E. includes passages which closely align with the image above. Under the title *Fifteen Signs of Doomsday*, it was widespread in the West and East.

*Figure A36 - Gabriel Blowing his Horn as the Dead Rise from their Graves*

14. Եւ յորժամ կոչէ Գափրիէլ թէ յարեւցուք մեռեալք որք Ադամայ ահայ գայ Քրիստոս արիք ելէք ընդ յառաջ նորայ եւ մարմինք մարդկայն որ խեղդեալ են ի ծով եւ կերեալ ի ձկայնց եւ այլք որք գազանաց եւ սողնոց որ կերեալ են եւ այլք որ ի հող մաշեալք եւ որդանց կերեալք եւ հողացեալք՝
15. եւ ամենայն հոգիք եւ մարմինն միայնայն եւ կենդայնանայն եւ լինին նոր մարդ

61 Sedulius Scottus, *In Epistolam I AD Thessalonicenses*, IV. In Migne, *Patrologiæ Cursus Completus, Series Latina, Sedulii Junioris Natione Scoti,* Vol. 103, p. 221. Translation by Matthew Andrews. Wycliffe may have been directly influenced by Scottus, whose commentary on the Epistles of Paul was well-known. (Thanks to Matthieu Kleemann for this reference.)

62 Cf. Vaughan, Robert, *Tracts & Treatises of John De Wycliffe, D.D.* (1845), p. 79. Wycliffe is credited with the first English translation of the Latin *Vulgate Bible* that appeared between 1382 and 1395 e.v.

63 *Harley MS. 5459.*

> **14.** And when Gabriel calls out, 'Arise, O dead since Adam. Behold, Christ is coming, rise up, ascend before him. And human bodies which were drowned in the sea and eaten by fish, and others who have been eaten by wild beasts and reptiles, and others who have decomposed in the earth and been consumed by worms and turned to dust.
> **15.** And all souls and bodies are united and live and become a new man.[64]

*John Milton* would finally identify the angel of the Last Trumpet with Gabriel in *Paradise Lost* in 1667.[65]

Rather than sacred scriptures defining the identification of the angel of the Last Trumpet as Gabriel, it was the result of popular sentiment, story telling and gospel songs, particularly those of American slaves, passed on from generation to generation that secured its place in modern mythology.

In Islamic tradition the angel who blows the trumpet to signal القيامة, *Al-Qiyamah*, the "Day of Judgment," is إِسْرَافِيل, *Israfel or Esrafel*. But the name of *Israfel* does not occur in the text of the *Quran*. The text only describes what occurs when the angelic trumpet will be sounded at the last day:

وَنُفِخَ فِي الصُّورِ فَصَعِقَ مَن فِي السَّمَاوَاتِ وَمَن فِي الْأَرْضِ إِلَّا مَن شَاءَ اللَّهُ ۖ ثُمَّ نُفِخَ فِيهِ أُخْرَىٰ فَإِذَا هُم قِيَامٌ يَنظُرُونَ

> the trumpet will be sounded, and everyone in the heavens and earth will fall down senseless except those God spares. It will be sounded once again and they will be on their feet, looking on![66]

In *Liber LXV*, this call to awaken actually refers to each aspirant to Initiation, not the "dead in Christ," who are defined as the physically dead awaiting the second coming of Jesus Christ. Nor does it refer to the call of the Trumpet of Israfel on the Day of Judgement in Islam.

Trump XX was eventually reformulated by Crowley to conform with the doctrines of the Aeon of the Child rather than depict images related to the second coming of Jesus Christ and the resurrection of believers.

The call to awaken comes from the "**Lord Adonai**," the Holy Guardian Angel. Hence the old "Judgement" card was replaced by the card of *The Aeon* in the New Aeon Tarot.

---

64 Stone, *Two Unpublished Eschatological Texts*, p.302.

65 Milton, *The Paradise Lost*, XI, 72ff.

66 M.A.S. *Abdel Haleem, (trans.), The Qur'an, 39.68*, p. 299.

Figure A37 - Israfel Turkish

Figure A38 - Israfel Arabic

Aspirants are summoned to awake from the **death** that the world calls **life**, and embrace the **life** that the world calls **death**. On the tarot card of Thelema, we see aspirants at the bottom of the card awaking and growing like flowers in the light of the New Aeon. Aspirants are admonished in *Liber Tzaddi* in verse 27,

> **O my children, ye are more beautiful than the flowers: ye must not fade in your season.**

*Figure A39 - Trump XX, The Aeon*

# § B. LAPIDES II-VI

**2. Adonai spake unto V.V.V.V.V., saying: There must ever be division in the word.**
**3. For the colours are many, but the light is one.**
**4. Therefore thou writest that which is of mother of emerald, and of lapis-lazuli, and of turquoise, and of alexandrite.**
**5. Another writeth the words of topaz, and of deep amethyst, and of gray sapphire, and of deep sapphire with a tinge as of blood.**
**6. Therefore do ye fret yourselves because of this.**

WITH VERSE 2, THE LORD ADONAI, The Holy Guardian Angel, speaks to V.V.V.V.V., the Master of the Temple, and begins His instruction.

When He said "**division in the word**" it meant *expressions or different Systems of the Path of Attainment*, the means by which humankind becomes God.

*Adonai* informed V.V.V.V.V. that this *word*, the means of expounding the Mysteries of the ineffable, will always be multiform. Many ways are used by humankind to attempt to give expression to the unveiling of the Truth.

The unveiling of the Truth in the garment of Thelema was expressed in this manner:

> **Then V.V.V.V.V. taketh up the word, and sayeth:**
> **Men and women of the Earth, to you am I come from the Ages beyond the Ages, from the Space beyond your vision; and I bring to you these words.**
>
> *Liber X, 3-4*

His scribe, Aleister Crowley, would speak of Him in the same way in *Liber LXV*, Chapter II, Verse 28:

> **Nor shall it be spoken in the markets that I am come who should come; but Thy coming shall be the one word.**

Most important of all, the declaration of the Law of a New Aeon itself was summarized in the first chapter of *The Book of the Law* identically:

***The word of the Law is θελημα.***[1]

## The Light of Truth

**3. For the colours are many, but the light is one.**

**Beginning with Verse 3, we are reminded that** light itself is comprised of many **colours**. We know that the many colours of the spectrum require an instrument such as the prism to break it up into its many component colours enabling us to see them with the naked eye.

But what **light** was Adonai talking about here?

*Figure B1 - A Prism Breaking White Light into its Spectral Colours*

He was talking about the light of *Truth*. The **colours**, that is, the methods of attainment to this Truth are many, but the light which informs them is One.

Note carefully that in verses 2 and 3, "**word**", "**colours**", and "**light**", are all written with initial letters in the *lower case*. This is because Adonai was referring to these expressions of the truth as they are perceived *below* the Abyss.

We must remember that we live in the world of duality where we see these things contaminated through our lens of consciousness.

Recall that even St. Paul said,

> For the time being, we see in a mirror, obscurely...[2]

---

1 *Liber AL*, I:39.

2 βλέπομεν γὰρ ἄρτι δι' ἐσόπτρου ἐν αἰνίγματι, *I Corinthians*, 13:12.

# Four Stones of Thelema

**4. Therefore thou writest that which is of mother of emerald, and of lapis-lazuli, and of turquoise, and of alexandrite.**

Various systems of teaching were represented by Adonai as different semi-precious and precious stones. The symbolism of the lapis, which is Latin for "stone," was a predominant theme in alchemy. The German physician and alchemist Martin Ruland defined the lapis as: "In chemistry, a stone is all fixed matter which cannot evaporate."[3] In alchemical terminology, the description of lapis took on the character of the goal of the Great Work, at times being called *lapis non lapis*, "the stone which is not a stone." That is, it is something more than what is commonly considered as a stone or rock. Ruland defined that as,

> Lapis de virtute & efficacia, non lapis substantia.
>
> a stone with respect to its virtue and efficacy, not a stone with respect to its substance.[4]

Thus, the stone is a fitting emblem for representations of the Great Work.

In my first book, I said the following concerning the nature of the Mystical Stone:

> the revelation of the Aeon of Horus involved a transformation of the First Matter (Man) into the Arcane Substance, and that the Stone of the Wise was a Black Stone. This Work flowers for the student by the process of discovery of this secret Lapis, and the long and arduous task of comprehending the seven-fold character of the Lord of the Aeon, alike in each of us, and also in a unique way, according to our True Will.[5]

In that quote, I was referring to Chapter V, Verse Six of *Liber LXV*, in which the Lord of the Aeon Himself is likened to a stone:

---

3 Ruland, *Lexicon Alchemiæ sive Dictionarivm Alchemisticvm* (1612), p. 273. Translation by Matthew Andrews.

4 Ibid.

5 Gunther, *Initiation in the Aeon of the Child*, p. 184.

**Through the midnight thou art dropt, O my child, my conqueror, my sword-girt captain, O Hoor! and they shall find thee as a black gnarl'd glittering stone, and they shall worship thee.**[6]

The stones used by Adonai in Verse 4 of *Liber LXV* were intended to symbolize the Word that V.V.V.V.V. presented to the world: **mother of emerald, lapis-lazuli, turquoise** and **alexandrite**.

Examination of the symbolism of these stones will present some insight into how Adonai Himself visualized the words of his messenger V.V.V.V.V.

## Mother of Emerald

Our attention is drawn immediately to "**mother of emerald**," because mother of emerald is *not an emerald at all*. In antiquity, it was a name given to translucent green Calcedeony, which sometimes approximated the luster of an actual Emerald. Perhaps due to its somewhat mysterious translucent appearance, it came to be considered the source, or root of the Emerald, hence "**mother of emerald**."

*Figure B2 - Mother of Emerald (Prase)*

Anciently, it was called *Prasius*, from the Greek πράσιος, because of its resemblance to the green colour of a leek.[7] It is said that from this word, arose the designation *Prasma*, from which was curiously derived the French term *Prisme d'Émeraude*,[8] as well as the corruption *Plasma*, by which it is now sometimes known. It has a pearlescent quality, like that of "mother of pearl." Moreover, it is extremely common compared to the rarity of the Emerald, which led to Pliny the Elder to write,

> Viridantium et alia plura sunt genera. Vilioris est turbae prasius.
>
> There are many other kinds of green [stones]. One of the more common types is the prasius.[9]

---

6 Also, cf. *Liber VII*, VII:6, LXV, IV:7, V:58, *Liber AL*, III:66.

7 From πράσον, "a leek." *LSJ*, p. 1264a.

8 According to King, *The Natural History, Ancient and Modern, of Precious Stone and Gems and of the Precious Metals*, p. 288. This etymology is highly suspect and may be dubious.

9 Pliny, *Natural History, Liber XXXVII*, 34, 113-114. Translation by Matthew Andrews.

Why is the reference not to an actual *emerald?*

In *Liber 777*, Emerald, both as a colour *and* as a precious stone, is assigned to the Eighth Sephira נצח, *Netzach* (♀), and the Paths of ד, *Daleth* (♀), and ל, *Lamed* (♎, ruled by ♀ ).[10] All of attributions relate to the nature and character of Venus.

Clearly, a stone other than emerald is indicated in *Liber LXV*, with another typology. The origins and interpretations of the ancient words for this stone give us a distinct clue.

It was a type of *lapidis viriditus*, "green stone," which was greatly coveted for the symbolic nature of its colour alone. Furthermore, the Prasius could possess a striking luster and be crafted into beautiful jewelry.

Yet, it was more commonly found than the rare and expensive Emerald. Apart from its beauty, this is possibly one reason that it was selected as one of the stones to represent Thelema. The Law of Thelema was not given to a select few. The Law is for all.[11]

Figure B3 - The Wadj Amulet

In his 1898 edition of *The Egyptian Book of the Dead*, as well as the 1901 edition, E.A.Wallis Budge translated the Egyptian word , *nšmt*, as "mother-of-emerald." These were editions of *The Book of the Dead* utilized by Crowley and he was familiar with this translation of the word. The Egyptians used this stone to make the *amulet of the papyrus column*. This talisman was called , *wꜣḏ*, *wadj*, which meant "papyrus plant." The word *wadj*, as a noun, also meant a "green stone."

When *wadj* was used as an adjective, it can also be translated "green," "fresh," "healthy, sturdy." In short, the *wadj* amulet signified *rebirth and regeneration.*

In *Spell 160* from *The Book of the Dead*, the god *Thoth* placed this amulet at the throat of the deceased, and recited a Spell of protection. Here is a new translation of that Spell, including the reading of , *nšmt*, as "mother of emerald":

*ink wꜣḏ n nšmt iwty sšr=f nty ꜥ ḏḥwty ḥr twꜣ=f*

*I am the cordless papyrus-amulet of mother-of-emerald which the hand of Thoth supports.*

10 In the Queen Scale of Colour, 777 Column XVI. In the standard image of the Tree of Life, all of the Sephiroth are represented in the Queen Scale, while the Paths are represented in the King Scale. The Precious Stones are shown in Column XL.

11 *Liber AL*, I:34

*ỉw=f bwt=f nkn wḏꜣ=f wḏꜣ=ỉ nn nkn=f*

*Injury is its abomination. If it stays sound, I stay sound. If it is not injured,*

*nn nkn=ỉ ni sḳrỉw=f n sḳrỉw=ỉ*

*I am not injured. If it is not smitten, I am not smitten.*[12]

In *Liber Tzaddi*, the coming of the *Messiah* is described as follows:

**In the name of the Lord of Initiation, Amen.**
**I fly and I alight as an hawk: of mother-of-emerald are my mighty-sweeping wings.**
**I swoop down upon the black earth; and it gladdens into green at my coming. Children of Earth! rejoice! rejoice exceedingly; for your salvation is at hand.**

*Liber Tzaddi, verses 0-3*

Here, mother-of-emerald signifies that which the alchemists called *benedicta viriditas*, "blessed greenness."

O benedicta viriditas, quæ cunctas res generas.

O blessed greenness, you who engender all things.[13]

Johann Daniel Mylius described it further in *Philosophia Reformata*:

Inspiravit Deus rebus creatis...quandam germinationem, hoc est viriditatem, qua sese cunctæ res multiplicarent...Omnes res dicebant esse virides, cum esse viride crescere dicatur...Hanc ergo generandi virtutem rerumque conservationem Animam Mundi vocare libuit.

---

12 BD 160, BM EA9900, *Papyrus of Nebseny*, text corrections from *Papyrus of Ptahmes (Busca Milan)* and the *Papyrus of Iuefankh (Turin 1791)*. Zelators of A∴A∴ should note that this amulet was placed in the position of the विशुद्ध, *viśuddha*, the throat *cakra*, the name of which means "completely pure"; its central symbol is आकाश, ākāśa, or "Spirit" *(See* §A *Exordium).* The Egyptians believed that the throat caused the body to breathe: , *ṯꜣw nw ꜥnḫ r fnḏ nw bꜣw srḳ ḫtyt n ḥtptyw*, "The breath of life for the nostrils of the Ba-Souls, causing the throats of the Peaceful-Ones to breathe." Chassinat, *Le temple d'Edfou*, Vol. 4, p. 259, lines 8-9 (The term "Peaceful Ones" is an epithet for the Blessed Dead.).

13 *Rosarium Philosophorum secunda Pars Alchimiae de Lapide Philosophico (1550), folio 11a.* Translation by Matthew Andrews.

> God breathed into created things ... a certain germination - namely **greenness** - that thereby all things would multiply ... They said all things were green, **since it is maintained that to grow is to be green** ... Thus this virtue of generation and this preservation of things can be called **the World Soul.** *(emphasis added)*[14]

The colour green signified the generation of all things, the ability to grow, prosper, and to be healthy. The wings of V.V.V.V.V. as Messiah are of those of a hawk, emblematic of the Lord of the Aeon, described as mother-of-emerald, and they sweep across the earth bringing the *benedicta veriditas*, the "blessed greenness."

This is one reason why, in this Aeon, Malkuth should no longer be represented by a circle divided into a quadrant with the colours of citrine, olive, russet and black.[15] Crowley wrote,

> But the New Aeon has brought fullness of Light; in the Minutum Mundum, Earth is no longer black, or of mixed colours, but is pure bright green.[16]

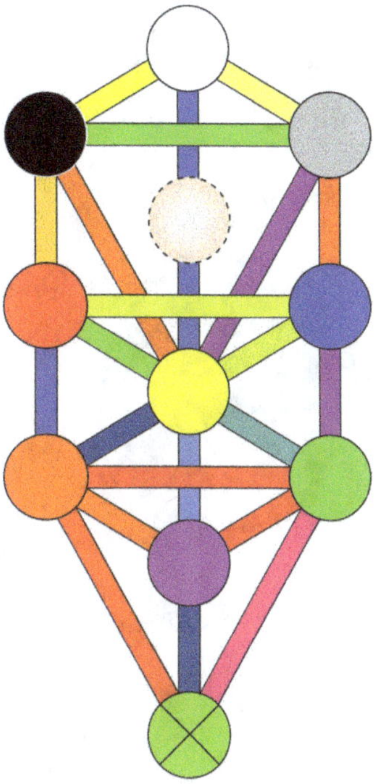

*Figure B4 - The Minutum Mundum with Malkuth in Bright Green*

*Adonai* informed the scribe that, in addition to mother of emerald, the words of the system of Thelema, of which he was writing, were symbolized by three more stones: **lapis-lazuli, turquoise** and **alexandrite**.

Remember here the important point Adonai made when he said, "**the colours are many, but the light is *one*.**"

---

14 Mylius, *Philosophia Reformata* (1622), p. 11. Translation by Matthew Andrews.

15 These colours are those in the Queen Scale.

16 Crowley, *The Book of Thoth*, page 119, on *Atu XXI, The Universe*.

# Lapis-Lazuli

For us, *lapis-lazuli* is considered the highest form of ♃, Jupiter, hence it is assigned to the Sephira Chesed and the Grade of the Adeptus Exemptus 7°= 4▫ with all its attributions.[17]

*Figure B5 - Lapis lazuli*

A beautiful blue stone flecked with Gold, lapis-lazuli is a perfect symbol of the goddess *Nuit.* It represents the blue night sky studded with the stars that are the company of heaven, which is to say, mankind.[18]

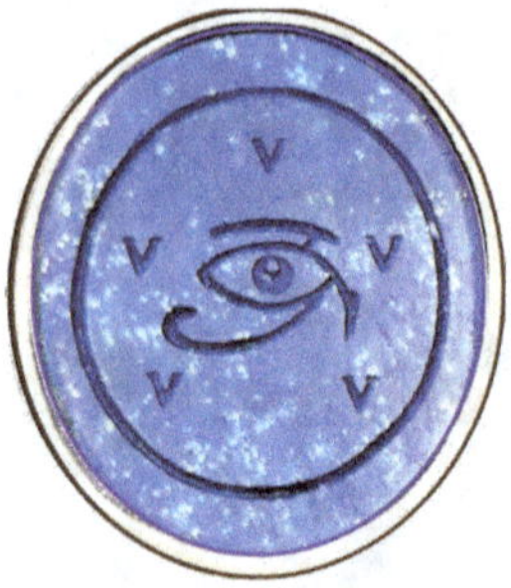


*Figure B6 - The Seal Ring of V.V.V.V.V.*

In accordance with all of this symbolism, the Praemonstrator of A∴A∴ has the Authority to bear the Seal Ring of V.V.V.V.V. which is engraved in Lapis Lazuli.[19]

Lapis-lazuli was called , *ḫsbḏ*,[20] by the Egyptians, and was extremely precious, for they considered it as a stone of the gods, and due to its starry aspect, identified the stone, as well as the blue colour extracted from it, with Nuit. In a hymn to Ra from *The Book of the Dead*:

*ỉb=k ꜣw nb nṯrw ḳmꜣ.n=k dỉ=sn n=k ỉꜣwy nwt ḫsbḏ=tỉ ḥr gs=k*

*Thy heart is elated, Lord of the gods! Those whom thou hast created praise thee. Nuit, lapis-lazuli blue, is at thy side!*[21]

The stone symbolized the starry heaven, the domain of the gods. In Spell 172 of *The Book of the Dead*, in the second stanza of "The Nine Songs of the Gilded Body," the blessed dead is transfigured as a celestial being in the likeness of the gods:

---

17 See *777 and Other Qabalistic Writings of Aleister Crowley*, p. 102. Lapis-lazuli had been omitted from the columns of 777 and Crowley corrected this in his notes to Column XL.

18 *Ibid.*, pp. 102-103.

19 See *Liber CCCXXXIII*, 41.

20 *Variant* , *ḫsbd.* As a colour, , *ḫsbḏ, or* , *ḫsbd,* is "lapis-lazuli blue." CDME, p. 242.

21 *BD 15AII, Papyrus of Qenena (Leiden T2),* lines 7-8.

*ỉw dp=k nb=ỉ mḏ ẖd.tỉ m nbdt stt ḥmt ḥḏ ḥr=k r ḥwt ỉʿḥ*

*Thy head, my Lord, is as deep, flowing down, as the tress of a Syrian woman. Thy face is brighter than the Temple of the Moon god!*

*ẖry=k ẖsbdy km šny=k r sb3w n dw3t knḥw šny=k*

*Thine uppermost part is of Lapis-lazuli, and thy hair is blacker than the Gates of the Duat! The darkness of thy hair*

*šʿm m ẖsbd dp-ḥr=k ḥr=k wbnw rʿ m ẖnt=k ḥbs m nbw*

*starred with Lapis-lazuli over thy face, with the glitter of Ra on thy front clothed in Gold,*

*drf.n st ḥrw m ẖsbd ỉnḥwy=ky snty snsn n drf.n st*

*hath Horus inscribed with Lapis-lazuli! Thine eyebrows, as the two Sister-goddesses, hath inscribed*

*ḥrw m ẖsbd ỉw fnd=k m ẖnmw [ ṯ3w ] šrt=k mỉ ṯ3w m pt*

*Horus with Lapis-lazuli! Thy nose hath fragrant [ breezes ] in thy nostrils like the breezes of heaven.*

*ỉw ỉrty=ky m3t b3ẖw g3bty=k mn rʿ nb smr.wt=k*

*The Eastern Mountain is in thy sight. Thine eyelashes are firm every day, their lids*

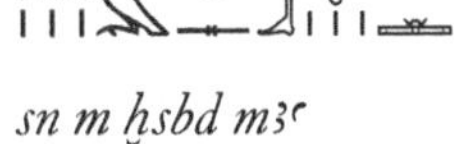

*sn m ẖsbd m3ʿ*

*of genuine Lapis-lazuli!*[22]

22 *BD 172, lines 11-15. Papyrus of Nebseny* (BM EA9900, Sheet 32.)

The ancient Greeks called this stone Σάπφειρος, *Sapphirus*, from which English derived the name *Sapphire*, a stone not discovered until Roman times.[23] The Greek word clearly meant lapis-lazuli, which can easily be determined by the description of the Sapphirus by Theophrastus:

> Τῶν δὲ λίθων καὶ ἄλλαι <διάφοροι> τυγχάνουσιν ἐξ ὧν καὶ τὰ σφραγίδια γλύφουσιν. αἱ μὲν τῇ ὄψει μόνον οἷον τὸ σάρδιον καὶ ἡ ἴασπις καὶ ἡ σάπφειρος· αὕτη δ᾽ ἐστὶν ὥσπερ χρυσόπαστος.
>
> Of the stones used to carve seals, there are others that also happen to be remarkable. Some are only so in their appearance, such as the sardius, the jasper, and the sapphire. The latter appears as though it were spotted with gold.[24]

As I noted above, *lapis* is the Latin word for "stone." The adjective *lazuli* is derived from the Medieval Latin *lazulum*, taken from Arabic لازورد, *lāzurd*, which derived from the Persian لاجورد, *lājevard*, which essentially means, "azure blue." The word lapis-lazuli is thus directly connected to the English *azure* which is from Old French *azur* via Medieval Latin *Lazur*, and its common form *azur*, which dropped the initial letter "L."[25]

In the Holy Books of Thelema, *Liber VII* bears the name of the Stone. Lapis-lazuli is the stone set in the Ring of V.V.V.V.V.[26] and one of the stones in the floor of the palace described in *Liber AL*, I:51. For "azure," see *Liber AL*, I:14 & 19.

## Turquoise

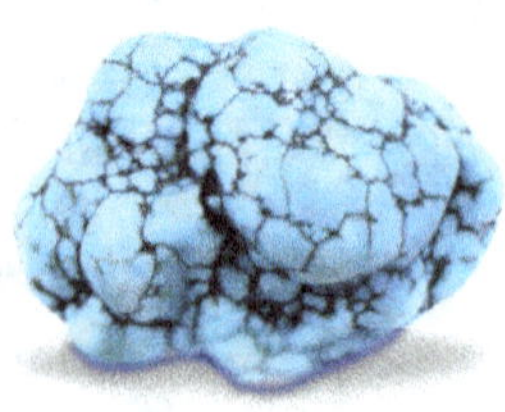

Fig. B7 - Turquoise

The *turquoise* is attributed to the Sephira Chokmah, which is the domain of The Magus. Because of its appearance, turquoise is said to suggest מסלות, *Masloth*, the realm of the fixed stars, or the zodiac.[27]

In ancient Egypt, the turquoise was called

23 See *LSJ*, p.13474b.

24 Theophrastus, *De Lapidis, 23*. Translation by Matthew Andrews.

25 Du Fresne, *Glossarium Ad Scriptores Mediæ et Infimæ Latinitatis (1710)*, Vol. 2, Part 2, p. 260. *Richardson, Wilkins & Johnson, A Dictionary, Persian, Arabic, and English (1829)*, p.556b.

26 *Liber LXV*, V:16.

27 *Liber 777*, p. 104.

, *mfkꜣt.*[28] It was mined during the earliest dynasties, thousands of years ago in the caves of *Maghârah* and *Serâbîṭ el-Khâdim* in the Sinai peninsula.[29] A temple was later erected in the latter location during the 12th Dynasty, dedicated to the goddess Hathor, who bore the title, 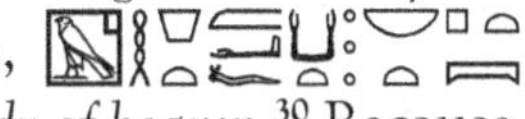, *ḥwt-ḥr ḥnwt mfkꜣt nbt pt, Hathor, mistress of turquoise, lady of heaven.*[30] Because it was mined in such a distant and forbidding location in the scorching desert, it was exceedingly precious to the Egyptians and was accordingly associated with Ra as the rising Sun:

*[wbn] sp sn pr m nnw rnpỉ=tỉ r r-ʿ n sf ḥwn nṯry ḫpr ḏs=f*

*[Rise], Rise! Going out from the Primeval Waters, as young as yesterday! Divine youth who came into being of himself!*

*ni [pḥ] sw dt=ỉ ỉỉ=tỉ m ḫʿw=k sḥḏ.n=k pt tꜣ stwt=k m-m mfkꜣt*

*He whom my hand cannot [reach]! Thou cometh with thine appearance in glory! Thou hast illuminated heaven and earth! Thy sunrays are among the turquoise!*[31]

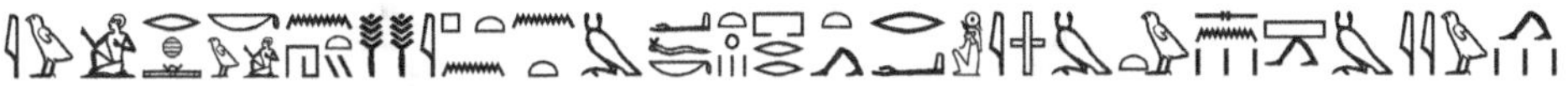

*ỉw=ỉ rḫ=kwỉ nhty ỉptn nt mfkꜣt prrt rʿ ỉmywt=sn šmyw*

*I know those two Sycamore-trees of Turquoise through which Ra goes out, proceeding*

*ḥr sṯsw šw r sbꜣ pwy n nb ỉꜣbtt prrw rʿ ỉm=f*

*over the Pillars of Shu, to that door of the Lord of the East, through which Ra goes out.*[32]

---

28 *CDME*, p. 132.

29 *Gardiner, Peet & Černý, The Inscriptions of Sinai*, Vol. 2, pp. 1-51.

30 Gardiner & Peet, *The Inscriptions of Sinai*, Vol. 1, Plate LXXV, IS303.

31 *BD 15A2, Papyrus of Qenena (Leiden T2*, Sheet 4-5, lines 12-13.)

32 *BD 109, Papyrus of Nu (BM EA10477*, Sheet 12, Lines 4-6.)

It was commonly associated with lapis lazuli in Egyptian inscriptions mentioning sacred stones. Turquoise, as the stone representing the zodiac, is suggested in *Liber LXV*, Chapter I, verse 28, where Adonai said,

**My head is jewelled with the twelve stars; My body is white as milk of the stars; it is bright with the blue of the abyss of stars invisible.**

In *The Vision & The Voice*, 7th Æthyr, in the Vision of BABALON, the Queen of Heaven, we also find that the turquoise and lapis lazuli are associated with Her:

**But do thou behold the brilliance of Love, that casteth forth seven stars upon thine head from her right hand, and crowneth thee with a crown of seven roses. Behold! She is seated upon the throne of turquoise and lapis lazuli, and she is like a flawless emerald...**

*Figure B8 - The Celestial Virgin Jewelled with Twelve Stars*

# Alexandrite

*Alexandrite* has the special quality of being able to change colours, appearing both as red and green, colours which in their purest state, are exact opposites in the colour spectrum. In daylight, alexandrite is green or blue-green. Under artificial light, it is red or reddish-purple. It is a very rare and precious stone. Alexandrite is thus referred to the path of ז, *Zayin*, which is attributed to ♊, Gemini, the twins. This is due to the two different colours it can display.

The alexandrite does not have any history in antiquity because it was first discovered in 1833 e.v. in the Ural Mountains and named after the Tsar Alexander II.[33] Thus, it is a new stone in relation to other gemstones, which is a fitting analogy with the advent of the New Aeon.

Likewise, the colouration and rarity of alexandrite make it a highly significant stone chosen to represent the doctrine of Thelema.

*Figure B9 - Alexandrite*

Its dual colours suggest the hermaphroditic nature of the child Horus, who possesses qualities of both the Father (the red) and the Mother (the green). We may consider "will" to be represented by the red colour, and "love" by the green.

33 *Encyclopedia Brittanica (1917)*, Vol. 1, p. 576.

## Four Stones of Another

5. **Another writeth the words of topaz, and of deep amethyst, and of gray sapphire, and of deep sapphire with a tinge as of blood.**

Now we are introduced to stones that symbolize the words of *another spiritual viewpoint*, not that of Thelema. Note that the text reads, "**Another writeth.**"

Remember, the first four – **mother of emerald**, **lapis-lazuli**, **turquoise** and **alexandrite** represent Thelema. The symbolism of these new stones must be examined in order to determine which doctrine is represented by them.

This grouping of stones is also four in number. Archetypically, Four is the number of manifestation in the world of humankind, while Three is the number of Divinity.[34] This tells us that in both cases, the symbolic character of these stones pertains in some manner to the natural world, the world below the Abyss. This is further emphasized by the fact that the names of these stones were all written with an initial *lowercase letter*, even those that represent the mysteries of Thelema.

## Topaz

Golden yellow like the Sun, *topaz* has been associated with Tiphereth, the sixth Sephira.[35] Considered a Solar stone, medieval superstition held that it had the ability to cure lunacy, an illness ascribed to the Moon, which was considered opposite of the Sun.

*Figure B10 - Topaz*

This was another expression of the medieval theory of *Contraria Contrariis Sanantur*, "Contraries are cured by their contraries." The Englishman Reginal Scot gave this account of the Topaz in 1584 e.v:

34 Gunther, *The Angel & The Abyss*, pp. 135-136.

35 *Liber 777, Col. XL, Key Scale 6*. Crowley also attributed the topaz to Path 11 and 16, based primarily on colour. Cornelius Agrippa aligned the Topaz with the Sun as well as Mercury. (*De Occulta Philosophia Libri Tres (1533)*, Liber I, 23.30 and Liber I, 29.35.)

A Topaze healeth the lunatike person of his passion of lunacie.[36]

Jean D. Renou (Renodaeus) enlarged on the beneficial aspects of the stone in his pharmacopeia of 1615:

> It stops bleeding from any part, calms anger, removes or lessens sadness, prevents frenzy, and amuses the mind.[37]

The breastplate of the Israelite High Priest[38] as described in the book of *Exodus*, Chapter 28:17-20, was decorated with four rows of three stones each, to represent the twelve tribes of Israel. The second stone in the top row was called פטדה, which was translated as τοπάζιον in the *Septuagint*, and *Topaz* in the English translations of the *Bible*. These are certainly incorrect translations, as topaz was virtually unknown at the time. This is confirmed by the account of Pliny the Elder who describing the topazios said, "In general, the colour tends to resemble the juice of the leek";[39] in other words, *green*, which is not the colour of a topaz. The Hebrew scholar Marcus Jastrow defined פטדה as simply "pitdah, name of a jewel in the high priest's breast-plate"[40] and did not attempt to identify that stone with any modern definition. No symbolism related to the topaz, or any of the stones mentioned in the *Bible*, can be taken on face value based on the translations accorded to them.

The topaz was not known in Egypt during dynastic times, despite the claims of many recent popular books on the mystical character of precious and semi-precious stones. In fact, the Egyptians had only one known word for "yellow,"  , *ḳnỉt*, which was a yellow pigment derived from orpiment.[41] Nor did they have the means to cut such hard stones as emerald, diamond or topaz.

The general symbolism of topaz known to us comes primarily from the middle ages, that being its Solar attribution and later affiliations with Tiphereth.

---

36 Scot, *The Discoverie of Witchcraft*, p. 294.

37 "Hemorrhagiam a quacunque parte sistit, iram sedat, tristitiam vel tollit, vel minuit, phrenitidem impedit, et animum oblectat." *Renodaeus, Dispensatorium Medicum*, Liber II, Sect. II, Cap. VII, p. 295.

38 חשן משפט, "the breastplate of judgment," *Exodus* 28:15.

39 *Tota enim similitudo ad porri sucum derigitur*. Pliny, *Naturalis Historia*, 37.109. Translation by Matthew Andrews.

40 *Jastrow*, p. 1154b.

41 CDME, p. 343, Harris, *Lexicographical Studies in Ancient Egyptian Minerals*, p. 226.

## Deep Amethyst

Derived from the Greek ἀμέθυστος, the word "amethyst" means "not drunken."[42] In ancient times amethyst was thought to be useful in preventing intoxication.[43]

The earliest reference to such a fable is found in a poem by *Asclepiades of Samos*, circa 240 C.E. (or *Antipater of Thessalonica*):

*Figure B11 - Deep Amethyst*

> Εἰμὶ Μέθη τὸ γλύμμα σοφῆς χερός, ἐν δ' ἀμεθύστῳ
> γέγλυμμαι: τέχνης δ' ἡ λίθος ἀλλοτρίη.
> ἀλλὰ Κλεοπάτρης ἱερὸν κτέαρ: ἐν γὰρ ἀνάσσης
> χειρὶ θεὸν νήφειν καὶ μεθύουσαν ἔδει.

> I am Drunkenness - the engraving of a skilled hand.
> But in amethyst was I carved: And the stone is foreign to the work.
> But Cleopatra's sacred possession am I;
> In the hand of the queen, even the goddess of drink must be sober.[44]

*Amethyst*, has the purple colour associated with Jupiter, and it is of a lesser aspect than that represented by the lapis-lazuli. Thus, it is referred to Jupiter in the Path of כ, *Kaph*, rather than the Sephira of Chesed.

## Deep Amethyst and the Colour Purple

Amethyst is the traditional stone of *regal and episcopal rank* due to its colour, as can be seen by reviewing historical accounts of the colour purple and its associations.

Writing two decades prior to the Christian era, the Roman poet *Virgil* described the attire of the mythical *Æeneas*, the son of Aphrodite and prince Anchises, of the royal bloodline of Troy, draped with a cloak of *Tyrian purple*,[45]

---

42 *LSJ*, p. 79b.

43 Smith, *Diamonds, Pearls and Precious Stones*, p. 75.

44 Paton, *The Greek Anthology*, Vol. 3, Epigram 752, p. 407. Translation by Matthew Andrews.

45 Tyrian purple, so named because it came from Tyre, Lebanon. It was the most expensive die known, requiring tens of thousands of Murex sea snails and great labor to extract the colour. The essence needed to produce the dye was found in a vein within the throat of the snail. Aristotle noted that the dye must be extracted while the snail was still alive, or it would vomit the dye upon its death. (Σπουδάζουσι δὲ ζώσας κόπτειν· ἐὰν γὰρ πρότερον ἀποθάνῃ συνεξεμεῖ τὸ ἄνθος, *Historia Animalium*, 547a7.) This is confirmed by Pliny the Elder: *Vivas capere contendunt, quia cum vita sucum eum evomunt.* (*Naturalis Historia* 9.126).

the most expensive colour in the world:

> Tyrioque ardebat murice laena demissa ex umeris, dives quae munera Dido fecerat, et tenui telas discreverat auro.
>
> From his shoulders hung a sumptuous cloak, ablaze with the purple of Tyrian murex. It was a gift Dido had made, and she had interwoven the warp with fine gold.[46]

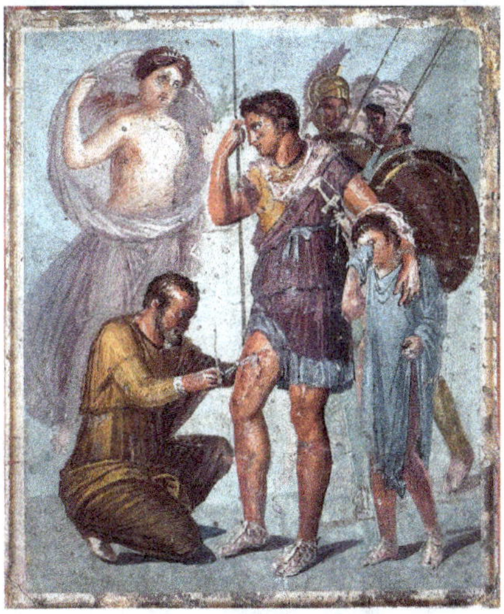

*Figure B12 - Aeneas, Son of Aphrodite & Anchises*

In the year 8 CE, the Roman poet *Ovid* gave witness to the colour purple and its association with the Regal attire:

> Medio rex ipse resedit agmine purpureus sceptroque insignis eburno.
>
> In the midst of the multitude sat the King himself. He was robed in purple, and distinguished by an ivory sceptre.[47]

In Rome, the colour came to be synonymous with royalty. In the Eastern Roman Empire (Byzantine Empire), a child born to the Emperor was given the title Πορφυρογέννητος, (Latin *Porphyrogenitus*), "born in the purple."[48] This was literally true, as the birthing chamber was built of *Imperial Porphyry*, a rare and costly purple stone imported from Egypt.[49]

It was this association that shaped the *New Testament* account of the mockery of Jesus by the Roman soldiers in *Mark* 15:16-18:

> Οἱ δὲ στρατιῶται ἀπήγαγον αὐτὸν ἔσω τῆς αὐλῆς, ὅ ἐστιν πραιτώριον, καὶ συνκαλοῦσιν ὅλην τὴν σπεῖραν. καὶ ἐνδιδύσκουσιν αὐτὸν πορφύραν καὶ περιτιθέασιν αὐτῷ πλέξαντες ἀκάνθινον στέφανον· καὶ ἤρξαντο ἀσπάζεσθαι αὐτόν Χαῖρε, βασιλεῦ τῶν Ἰουδαίων·

---

46 Virgil, *The Aenid*, 4.264. Translation by Matthew Andrews.

47 *Metamorphoses, Liber VII*, 102-103. Translation by Matthew Andrews.

48 *LSJ*. p. 1257b. Cf. *OLD*, p. 1495c. In the period of the Eastern Roman Empire, some emperors incorporated this into their own name: *Constantine VII Porphyrogenitus* (905-959 CE), *Romanus II Porphyrogenitus* (939-963 CE) and *Constantine VIII Porphyrogenitus* (960-1028 CE).

49 Lucas, *Ancient Egyptian Materials & Industries*, p.369.

Figure B13 - Ecce Homo (Behold the Man)

And the soldiers led him away into the palace, that is the Praetorium[50], and they assembled all the cohort.[51] And they put purple on him, and having twisted together a crown of thorns, placed it on him. And they began to salute him, "Hail! King of the Jews!"

The Roman historian *Suetonius* described how one such emperor, the degenerate *Caligula* (whom Suetonius himself called a "monster"), regarded the open display of the coveted colour by anyone other than himself. After he had invited *Ptolemy of Mauretania* to Rome, Caligula was incensed that the sartorial selection of Ptolemy included a splendorous purple cloak that attracted great attention among the crowd. After receiving Ptolemy with honor, Caligula had him promptly murdered for the perceived insult.[52]

Figure B14 - Nero

Less than a decade later, the equally vicious emperor *Nero*[53] proclaimed purple as a regal prerogative and began to impose severe restrictions on wearing garments of that shade. Whether it was the expensive Tyrian purple or merely the purple of amethyst, it was forbidden to the populace.

Figure B15 - Caligula

50 πραιτώριον, *Praetorium*, i.e. the Commander's tent. (*Bauer*, p. 697b).

51 The Greek σπεῖρα is used throughout the NT to translate the Latin *cohors*, "cohort," which signified one tenth of a Roman Legion. (*Bauer*, p. 761a.) The number of men in a cohort varied from 600 to 480; the number present in Jerusalem prior to the Jewish wars was more likely the lower number at best. In any case, summoning an entire cohort to witness the spectacle of mocking an insignificant captive stretches the bounds of credulity, but makes for high drama.

52 Suetonius, *De Vita Caesarum, Liber IV, C. Caligula, XXII,1 & XXXV, 1-2.* Caligula ruled from 37 CE - 41 CE.

53 Nero ruled from 54 CE until his death in 68 CE.

Suetonius recorded an account of Nero that illustrates the verdict for defying this dictum:

> Et cum interdixisset usum amethystini ac Tyrii colouris summissisetque qui nundinarum die pauculas uncias venderet, praeclusit cunctos negotiatores. Quin etiam inter canendum animadversam matronam in spectaculis vetita purpura cultam demonstrasse procuratoribus suis dicitur detractamque ilico non veste modo sed et bonis exuit.
>
> When he had forbidden the use of the colours of amethyst and Tyrian, he secretly dispatched someone to sell a few ounces on market day, while shutting all the merchants' shops. It is even said that during one of his singing recitals, a matron was spotted in the audience clothed in the forbidden purple. He pointed her out to his imperial collectors, and she was dragged off instantly - stripped not only of her clothing, but of her property.[54]

*Figure B16 - Diocletian*

The punishment described by Suetonious was mild, especially for that cruel and capricious emperor, if it was a comprehensive account of the incident. During the reign of Nero the standard punishment for offense against the emperor, real or imagined, was death.[55]

By the time of the emperor *Diocletian* (284 CE - 305 CE) the cult of the emperor had formalized to such an extent that the imperial robe of purple itself became an object of adoration - the advent of the *Adoratio Purpurae*, "adoration of the purple."[56] Further, Diocletian was the first to openly declare himself a god and demand that all who were granted an audience, perform obeisance and kiss the hem of his purple robe. A *legal* edict was passed making it a crime for anyone but the emperor to wear a purple garment.[57]

---

54 Suetonius, *De Vita Caesarum, Liber VI, Nero, 32.3.* Translation by Matthew Andrews.

55 Cassius Dio, *Roman History*, Books 61-63.

56 The Romans themselves called this *adoraturi imperatorem* which was interpreted to mean *adoraturi purpuram imperatoris. Ammianus Marcillinus, 21, 6:2 & 9:8.* (Avery, *The Adoratio Purpurae and the Importance of the Imperial Purple in the Fourth Century of the Christian Era*, p. 67, n. 11.)

57 Aurelius Victor, *Liber de Caesaribus, 39.2-4.* Eutropius, *Brevarium Historiae Romanae, 9.26.* Jones, *The Later Roman Empire*, 284-602, Vol. 1, p. 40.

## Deep Amethyst and Lustration

Crowley said that Amethyst was valuable in *lustration*.[58] He was referring to the ancient rite of *lustratio*, which was *purification by sacrifice*.[59]

This is an essential clue to uncover the extended symbolism of this stone. The first question we must ask is, what could an amethyst possibly have to do with lustration?

Was Crowley giving us a clue by that statement, which on the face of it, seems a bit unusual?

*Figure B17 - Constantine the Great*

I believe he was indeed subtly directing our attention to a historically important and significant account of lustration. Keep in mind that it is a stone of *regal and episcopal rank*.

Constantine the Great, the Emperor of Rome from 306 to 337 CE, like all of his predecessors, was a pagan, but became the first Roman Emperor that converted to Christianity the year of his victory over Maxentius[60] in 312 CE., but did not seek the ritual absolution of Baptism until he was on his deathbed.[61] It was Constantine that convened the First Council of Nicaea in 325 CE that produced the Nicene Creed, the profession of faith for the Christian Church.[62]

The sole *contemporary* account of his life, *De Vita Constantini* ("*The Life of Constantine*"), was written by Eusebius of

---

58 Crowley, 777, Comment to Table XL.

59 *Lustration*, from Latin *lustratio*, "an expiation," *Lustratus*, past participle of *lustrare*, "to purify." (*Skeat*, p. 262b.)

60 Marcus Aurelius Valerius Maxentius (ca. 283-312 CE).

61 Eusebius was credited with baptizing Constantine himself, and he gave a florid encomium of the event in *De Vita Constantini*, IV:61-62. The description by *Socrates Scholasticus* was succinct and sober in comparison (*Historia Ecclesiastica* I.39-40). An even more preposterous account is in the mid-eighth century forgery *Vita Silvestri*, in which Constantine was said to have been baptized by *Pope Sylvester I* and was simultaneously cured of leprosy. One of the intended aims of this fictitious narrative was to conceal the fact that Constantine was baptized by Eusebius, Bishop of Caesarea, a proponent of the theology of *Arianism*. The Council of Nicaea in 325 CE had officially declared Arianism to be a heresy.

62 Socrates Scholasticus, *Historia Ecclesiastica*, I:8. Sozomen, *Historia Ecclesiastica*, 1.17. Bright, *The Canons of the First Four General Councils of Nicæa, Constantinople, Ephesus and Chalcedon*, pp. v-xv.

Caesarea[63] after September 9, 337 CE.[64] That work is more than a panegyric, it is a blatant hagiography rather than a historical account, that brazenly deified Constantine and attributes his conversion to Christianity through a fabricated fiction that survives to this day. In fact, much of what Eusebius wrote about Constantine is nothing short of propaganda and lies.

*Figure B18 - Eusebius of Caesarea*

Eusebius claimed that the conversion of the Emperor was prompted by a Vision prior to a momentous battle, an event described to him personally by Constantine.[65]

Here is the account of Eusebius concerning the conversional Vision by the Emperor:

> ἀμφὶ μεσημρινὰς ἡλίου ὥρας, ἤδη τῆς ἡμέρας ἀποκλινούσης, αὐτοῖςὀφθαλμοῖς ἰδεῖν ἔφη ἐν αὐτῷ οὐρανῷ ὑπερκείμενον τοῦ Ἡλίου σταυροῦ τρόπαιον ἐκ φωτὸς συνιστάμενον, γραφήν τε α ὐτῷ συνῆφθαι λέγουσαν· τούτῳ νίκα.

> Around the midday hours of the sun, with the day by this time declining, he said he saw with his own eyes – in the very heaven, situated above the sun – a monument formed of light, shaped as a cross. Next to it was an inscription, saying: "By this conquer."[66]

It is indeed a stirring image: a *labarum* shining in the midheaven, emblazoned with a cross of light bearing the inscription, recorded in Greek as τούτῳ νίκα, "By this, Conquer."

However, in his previous "Ecclesiastical History," *written two decades prior*, between 311 CE and 315 CE.,[67] Eusebius made no mention of such a dramatic event with Visions or prophetic dreams of portent.[68] Very simply, he had not concocted the story as yet.

---

63 To be distinguished from Eusebius of Nicodemia.

64 The death and funeral of Constantine occurred in 337 CE. (Eusebius, *De Vita Constantini*, 4.64-71.)

65 This was doubtless a false claim intended to inflate the narrative. There is no evidence that Eusebius had personal access to Constantine before or during the Council of Nicaea. (See Cameron/Hall, *Eusebius, Life of Constantine*, p. 23).

66 Eusebius, *De Vita Constantini*, I.28, 2. Translation by Matthew Andrews.

67 Lake, *Eusebius, The Ecclesiastical History*, Vol. 1, p. xx..

68 Eusebius, *Ecclesiasticæ Historiæ*, 9.9.

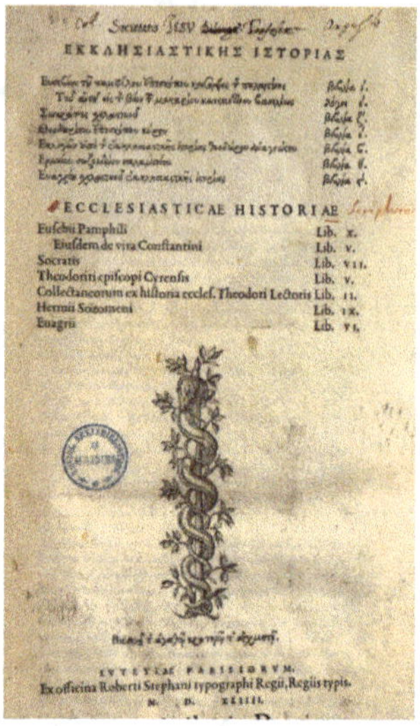

ΕΚΚΛΗΣΙΑΣΤΙΚΗΣ ΙΣΤΟΡΙΑΣ

ECCLESIASTICAE HISTORIAE

| | |
|---|---|
| Eusebii Pamphili | Lib. x. |
| Eiusdem de vita Constantini | Lib. v. |
| Socratis | Lib. vii. |
| Theodoriti episcopi Cyrensis | Lib. v. |
| Collectaneorum ex historia eccles. Theodori Lectoris | Lib. ii. |
| Hermii Sozomeni | Lib. ix. |
| Euagrii | Lib. vi. |

LVTETIAE PARISIORVM.

Ex officina Roberti Stephani typographi Regii, Regiis typis.

M. D. XLIIII.

*Figure B19 - First Edition of the Greek Text of Sozomen's Ecclestiastical History*

This should not be a surprising revelation of his character. In his book *Praeparatio Evangelica* ("Preparation for the Gospel"), the 31st chapter of Book XII is entitled,

> Οτι δεήσει ποτὲ τῷ ψεύδει ἀντὶ φαρμάκου χρῆσθαι ἐπ' ὠφελείᾳ τῶν δεομένων τοῦ τοιούτου τρόπου,
>
> "That it will be necessary sometimes to employ falsehood as a remedy for the benefit of those who require such a treatment."[69]

By the time that *Sozomen* came to write his own "Ecclesiastical History" around 440 CE, the fable had been substantially embellished. Sozomen claimed that prior to the battle with Maxentius at the Milvian bridge over the Tiber river, Constantine was in doubt about how it should be waged, and where he might find assistance:

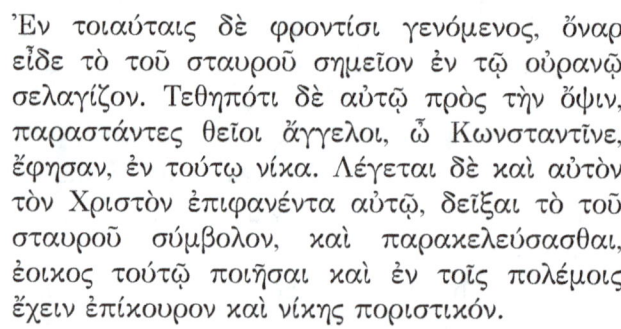

*Figure B20 - Roman Labarum bearer*

> Ἐν τοιαύταις δὲ φροντίσι γενόμενος, ὄναρ εἶδε τὸ τοῦ σταυροῦ σημεῖον ἐν τῷ οὐρανῷ σελαγίζον. Τεθηπότι δὲ αὐτῷ πρὸς τὴν ὄψιν, παραστάντες θεῖοι ἄγγελοι, ὦ Κωνσταντῖνε, ἔφησαν, ἐν τούτῳ νίκα. Λέγεται δὲ καὶ αὐτὸν τὸν Χριστὸν ἐπιφανέντα αὐτῷ, δεῖξαι τὸ τοῦ σταυροῦ σύμβολον, καὶ παρακελεύσασθαι, ἐοικος τούτῳ ποιῆσαι καὶ ἐν τοῖς πολέμοις ἔχειν ἐπίκουρον καὶ νίκης ποριστικόν.
>
> Amid such great concerns, he had a dream in which he saw the sign of the cross blazing in heaven. As he marvelled at the vision, divine angels standing nearby said to him: "Constantine, in this, conquer!" It is also said that Christ himself appeared to him and showed

69 Translation by Matthew Andrews. In Book XII, Chapter 31, Eusebius quoted Plato, *Laws*, 2.663D: "But even if the case were not such as our argument has now proved it to be, if a lawgiver, who is to be of ever so little use, could have ventured to tell any falsehood at all to the young for their good, is there any falsehood that he could have told more beneficial than this, and better able to make them all do everything that is just, not by compulsion but willingly? Truth, O Stranger, is a noble and an enduring thing; it seems, however, not easy to persuade men of it." (Gifford, *Eusebii Pamphili Evangelicae Praeparationis Libri XV*, Vol. 3, p. 657.)

him the symbol of the cross. And he ordered him to make one like it, and to bear it as his ally in battles, and said that it would be a bringer of victory.[70]

*Figure B21 - Constantine's Vision of the Cross before the Battle of the Milvian Bridge*

70 Sozomen, *Historia Ecclesiastica*, 3.25-32. Translation by Matthew Andrews. The original phrase of Eusebius, τούτῳ νίκα, "By this conquer," and the later version by Sozomen, ἐν τούτῳ νίκα, "in this conquer," were later rendered by numerous translators and writers with the famous Latin phrase, *In Hoc Signo Vinces*, which is now completely identified with Constantine, the first Christian Emperor. The first Latin translation of Eusebius' Ecclesiastical History was made by Rufinus in 402 CE. I have examined the printed version of this text which was printed in Strasburg in 1475. The Greek τούτῳ νίκα is merely rendered as a transliteration in Latin letters, *tytw nika*. The phrase *In Hoc Signo Vinces* came some time later and became the standard rendition.

By this time, the Vision described by Eusebius had morphed into the fable of a numinous dream featuring the appearance of Jesus Christ himself, appearing to Constantine and instructing him to make the labarum to lead him to victory.

The eighteenth century historian Edward Gibbon, in *The History of the Decline and Fall of the Roman Empire*, writing of the purported Vision of Constantine, pointedly noted:

> The advocates for the vision are unable to produce a single testimony from the Fathers of the fourth and fifth centuries, who in their voluminous writings, repeatedly celebrate the triumph of the church and of Constantine. As these venerable men had not any dislike of a miracle, we may suspect (and the suspicion is confirmed by the ignorance of Jerome) that they were all unacquainted with the life of Constantine by Eusebius. This tract was recovered by the diligence of those who translated or continued his Ecclesiastical History, and who have presented in various colours the vision of the cross.[71]

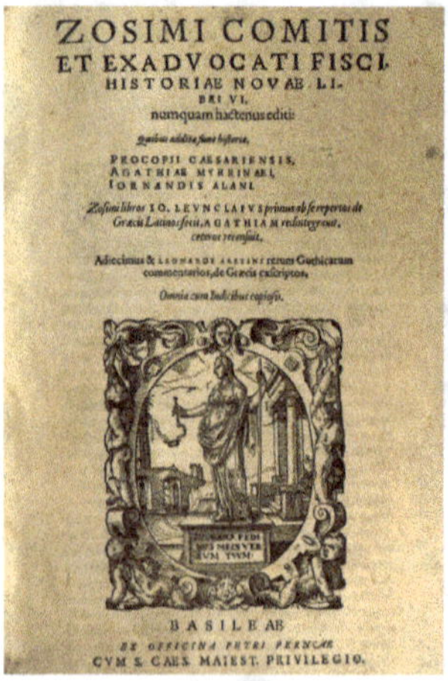
ZOSIMI COMITIS
ET EXADVOCATI FISCI.
HISTORIAE NOVAE LI-
BRI VI.
numquam hactenus editi:
PROCOPII CAESARIENSIS,
AGATHIAE MYRRINAEI,
IORNANDIS ALANI.
BASILEAE
CVM S. CAES. MAIEST. PRIVILEGIO.

*Figure B22 - First Edition of Zosimus*

A more convincing historical account of the conversion of Constantine was written by the pagan historian *Zosimus* (ca. 490-510 CE) in his work Ἱστορία Νέα, "New History," written between 498-518 CE. In contrast to Eusebius' cloying description of Constantine, Zosimus did not hesitate to expose his crimes or the real motivation for his conversion to Christianity. Not surprisingly, Zosimus has been despised, reviled and disparaged by Christian critics ever since, who blindly adhere to the specious accounts of Christian historians while rejecting the work of Zosimus as pagan propaganda.[72] Other than Zosimus, the writings of numerous pagan historians, who discussed the decline of the Roman Empire, were purged over a thousand years of Christian censorship, surviving only in quotations by Christian writers to buttress their own arguments.[73]

---

71 Gibbon, *The History of the Rise and Fall of the Roman Empire*, Vol. 2 (1781), p. 200, note 52.

72 On the other hand, a number of unbiased scholars have maintained the historical accounts of Zosimus as authentic.

73 E.g. *Celsus*, *Porphry*, *Hierocles* and *Eunapius*. Doubtless, many others vanished in history without a trace.

According to Zosimus, Constantine murdered his wife *Fausta* and his own son *Crispus*, the child of his first wife *Minervina*, suspecting that they had conjoined in adultery.[74] The account of Zosimus continues thus:

> ταῦτα συνεπιστάμενος ἑαυτῷ, καὶ προσέτι γε ὅρκων καταφρονήσεις, προσῄει τοῖς ἱερεῦσι καθάρσια τῶν ἡμαρτημένων αἰτῶν. εἰπόντων δὲ ὡς οὐ παραδέδοται καθαρμοῦ τρόπος δυσσεβήματα τηλικαῦτα καθῆραι δυνάμενος Αἰγύπτιός τις ἐξ Ἰβηρίας εἰς τὴν Ῥώμην ἐλθὼν καὶ ταῖς εἰς τα βασίλεια γυναιξὶ συνήθης γενόμενος, ἐντυχὼν τῷ Κωνσταντίνῳ πάσης ἁμαρτάδος ἀναιρετικὴν εἶναι τὴν τῶν Χριστιανῶν διεβεβαιώσατο δόξαν καὶ τοῦτο ἔχειν ἐπάγγελμα , τὸ τοὺς ἀσεβεῖς μεταλαμβάνοντας αὐτῆς πάσης ἁμαρτίας ἔξω παραχρῆμα καθίστασθαι.

> Feeling guilt for these things, and also for his contempt towards his oaths, he went to the priests asking to be cleansed of his wrongs. But they told him that no manner of lustration had been handed down that was strong enough to clean away such impious acts. A certain Egyptian, who came to Rome from Spain, and who had become intimate with the women of the palace, conversed with Constantine. He maintained strongly that the doctrine of the Christians would annul all of his wrongs, and that it had this promise: that the profane who converted were immediately made free from all their sin.[75]

Thus, Constantine sought a pagan lustration to cleanse him of his sins, but was rebuffed by the Priests. On the advice of an Egyptian acquaintance, he sought and was granted the Christian lustration which they claimed would absolve him of all his sins: *Baptism.*

---

74 Zosimus, *Historia Nova,* 2.29. Constantine's murder of Fausta and Crispus is also mentioned in Aurelius Victor, *Epitome de Caesaribus* 41.11-12 (circa 396 CE), Photius, *Compendium Historiae Ecclesiasticae Philostorgii,* 2.4. (the 9th Century scholar Photius quoted Philostrogius' account written circa 425 CE), Sidonius Apollinaris, *Epistulae,* 5.8.2. (circa 471-487), and John of Damascus, *Artemii Passio,* 45 (8th century CE).

75 Zosimus, *Historia Nova,* 2.29 (Bekker, *Zosimus* (1837), pp. 94-95.) Translation by Matthew Andrews. The first translation of Zosimus was in Latin, by *Johannes Leunclavius,* which reads thus: "Horum ipse sibi conscius, et præterea contemptae sacramentorum religionis, ad flamines accedens admissorum lustrationes poscebat. illis respondentibus non esse traditum lustrationis modum , qui tam foeda piacula eluere posset. Aegyptius quidam, ex Hispania Romam delatus palatinisque mulierculis familiaris factus, et ad Constantini colloquium admissus, sententiam doctrinae Christianorum habere vim abolendi quodcunque peccatum confirmavit; et id ipsum adeo polliceri; nimirum acceptantes eam homines impios, mox omni delicto liberari." (Leunclavius, *Zosimi comitis ex exadvocati fisci, Historiae novae* (1576), p. 31).

However, it should be stressed that, as I mentioned previously, Constantine postponed his Baptism *until he was upon his deathbed.* Edward Gibbon, did not allow such deferral of total absolution to escape his critical pen, as he elaborated in some depth:

> The sacrament of baptism was supposed to contain a full and absolute expiation of sin; and the soul was instantly restored to its original purity, and entitled to the promise of eternal salvation. Among the proselytes of Christianity, there were many who judged it imprudent to precipitate a salutary rite, which could not be repeated; to throw away an inestimable privilege, which could never be recovered. By the day of their baptism, they could venture freely to indulge their passions in the enjoyment of this world, while they still retained in their own hands the means and a sure and easy absolution... The example and reputation of Constantine seemed to countenance the delay of baptism. Future tyrants were encouraged to believe, that the innocent blood which they might shed in a long reign would instantly be washed away in the waters of regeneration; and the abuse of religion dangerously undermined the foundations of moral virtue.[76]

The colour purple not only figured prominently in the regal line of Roman emperors, it came to signify assumption of the Throne itself. With the sinister ecclesiastical manoeuvres of the Roman Catholic Church, which comprised the *modus operandi* of the Great Sorcery, the symbolic meaning of the purple, and the Throne of Rome *itself*, were usurped by the Roman bishops, with the stated aim to dominate the world.

An unidentified scholar, working within the circle of the clergy, forged a regnal text in the name of Constantine himself. The word "forgery" is not too strong here; the legal structure in which it was written, and the purpose for which it was intended, elevate it from the genre of amusing fiction to that of deliberate deceit. This document is known as *Constitutum Constantini*, *The Constitution of Constantine.*

This document included and expanded upon an existing fiction called *Vita Silvestri*, *The Life of Sylvester*, a purported biography of *Sylvester I*, the Pope of Rome from 314 CE until his death in 335 CE.

The *Constitutum Constantini* claims to be the writing of Constantine himself and carries the imperial subscription. In order to establish a link with the Church to the emperor himself, it utilized the fable from *Vita Silvestri* that

76 Gibbon, *op. cit.*, pp. 206-207. In the footnote to this passage, Gibbon added: "I believe that this delay of baptism, though attended with the most pernicious consequences, was never condemned by a general or provincial council, or by any public act or declaration of the church. The zeal of the bishops was easily kindled on much slighter occasions."

Sylvester had baptized Constantine and simultaneously cured him from leprosy, stressing his pious gratitude for the miracle of his cure.

Included within the *Constitutum Constantini* is the critical forgery of the entire document, which is called the *Donatio Constantini, The Donation of Constantine*. The document purports to be in the hand of Constantine himself, transferring his Authority and the regalia of that Office, to Pope Sylvester and all his successors, thereby establishing the Church of Rome as the supreme authority in the world, over any future emperors or kings.

I quote this wretched document at length below, in order that Students may see for themselves the deceitful words through which the Roman Catholic Church sank their talons into the world and forged the corruption of centuries; that they might better see why Christianity is cursed by *The Book of the Law*, and why we call the machinations of the Roman Catholic Church the time of *The Great Sorcery*.

*Figure B23 - The Donation of Constantine*

In the supposed words of Constantine himself:

Et sicut nostram terrenam imperialem potentiam, sic eius sacrosanctam Romanam ecclesiam decrevimus veneranter honorari, et amplius quam nostrum imperium et terrenum thronum sedem sacratissimam B. Petri gloriose exaltari, tribuentes ei potestatem, et gloriae dignitatem atque vigorem, et honorificentiam imperialem.

And as ours is the earthly imperial power, so we have decreed that his holy Roman Church is to be honored with reverence; and more than our empire and earthly throne, the most holy seat of Blessed Peter is to be gloriously exalted, bestowing power to it, and dignity of glory, and vigor, and imperial honor.[77]

Beatro Silvestro Patri nostro, summo Pontifici et universalis urbis Romae Papae, et omnibus, eius successoribus Pontficubus, qui usque in finem mundi in sede B. Petri erunt sessuri, de presenti contradimus palatium imperii nostri Lateranense, deinde diadema, videlicet coronam capitis nostri, simulque frigium, nec non et superhumerale, videlicet lorum, quod imperiale circumdare assolet collum; verum etiam et clamidem purpuream, atque tunicam coccineam, et omnia imperialia indumenta; sed et dignitatem imperialium presidentium equitum, conferentes etiam et imperialia sceptra, simulque cuncta signa, atque banda, et diversa ornamenta imperialia, et omnem processionem imperialis culminis et gloriam potestatis nostrae.

To Blessed Sylvester, our Father, the supreme Bishop and the Pope of the universal city of Rome, and to all the Bishops that are his successors, who shall sit in the seat of Blessed Peter even unto the end of the world: at present, we deliver wholly our empire's Lateran palace; then the tiara, that is, the crown upon our head, together with the cap; and also the superhumeral, that is, the strap which is accustomed to encircle the imperial neck; and furthermore the purple mantle, and the scarlet tunic, and all the imperial garments; and also the dignity of the horses of the imperial escort; and conferring also the imperial sceptre, at the same time as all the signs, and flags, and diverse imperial ornaments, and the entire procession of imperial highness, and the glory of our power.[78]

This document was used effectively by the Roman Church for centuries to assert their ecclesiastical and regal supremacy. They did so until it was proven to be a forgery by one of their own, an Italian priest, a brilliant scholar

77 Donatio Constantini, Latin from Coleman's text, *The Treatise of Lorenzo Valla on the Donation of Constantine (1922)*, p.12. Translation by Matthew Andrews.

78 *Ibid.*, pp. 12-14. Translation by Matthew Andrews.

*Figure B24 - Lorenzo Valla*

and humanist named *Lorenzo Valla*, in his book of 1440 e.v., *De Falso Credita et Ementita Donatione Constantini* ("Concerning the Falsely Trusted and Fabricated Donation of Constantine").

Valla had been a thorn in the side of the Church, and he proved himself more than equal to the task of consistently giving the ecclesiastical hierarchy a bad case of heartburn. He drove the final nail in the coffin of the *Donation of Constantine*, and proved his case with an acerbic tongue combined with linguistic excellence. Although it ended this particular charade, it did not sponge away the writing from the stone that gives stark testament to the countless victims of its crime.

As of 1786 e.v., Valla's name and works were *still* listed in the *Index Liborum Prohibitum*, the list of books prohibited by the Roman Catholic Church, with *De Falso Credita et Ementita Donatione Constantini* at the top of the list of his works.[79] All Roman Catholics were forbidden to read any works published in this list.

While the amethyst is indicative of that period, and the writings of the "**other**" that is dogmatic Christianity, the deep purple stone itself remains untarnished, unblemished by their foul history. The pure symbolism has been passed into the New Aeon, and its ecclesiastical nature is embraced by the A∴A∴, its regality is celebrated by all that embrace the Law of Thelema:

Finally, I would like to complete this section by quoting some verses from Chapter 4 of *Liber VII* that are intrinsically bound with the symbolism of the stones and relevant terms thus far discussed.[80] Sincere aspirants to A∴A∴ are urged to meditate on key clues in these verses: Adonai, the snake and the little singing-bird, the hawk, mother-of-emerald, Tyrian purple, servants of the Great Sorcery, the Christian eucharist, ΙΧΘΥΣ and the crucifixion, and the Hanged Man.

---

79 *Index Liborum Prohibitum (Rome 1786)*, p. 298.

80 Chapter 4 of *Liber VII* is attributed to $\odot$, and the letter R of *VITRIOL*.

Excellent is Thy love, Oh Lord! Thou art revealed by the darkness, and he who gropeth in the horror of the groves shall haply catch Thee, even as a snake that seizeth on a little singing-bird.
I have caught Thee, O my soft thrush; I am like a hawk of mother-of-emerald; I catch Thee by instinct, though my eyes fail from Thy glory.
Yet they are but foolish folk yonder. I see them on the yellow sand, all clad in Tyrian purple.
They draw their shining God unto the land in nets; they build a fire to the Lord of Fire, and cry unhallowed words, even the dreadful curse Amri maratza, maratza, atman deona lastadza maratza maritza – marán!
Then do they cook the shining god, and gulp him whole.
These are evil folk, O beautiful boy! let us pass on to the Otherworld.
Let us make ourselves into a pleasant bait, into a seductive shape!
I will be like a splendid naked woman with ivory breasts and golden nipples; my whole body shall be like the milk of the stars. I will be lustrous and Greek, a courtesan of Delos, of the unstable Isle.
Thou shalt be like a little red worm on a hook.
But thou and I will catch our fish alike.
Then wilt thou be a shining fish with golden back and silver belly: I will be like a violent beautiful man, stronger than two score bulls, a man of the West bearing a great sack of precious jewels upon a staff that is greater than the axis of the all.
And the fish shall be sacrificed to Thee and the strong man crucified for Me, and Thou and I will kiss, and atone for the wrong of the Beginning; yea, for the wrong of the beginning.

*Liber VII, IV:48-59*

*Figure B25 - A Snake that Seizeth on a Little Singing-bird*

# Gray Sapphire

The *gray sapphire* is of a light gray or bluish-gray that sometimes has a *six-rayed star in its center.* Gray sapphires with this characteristic are much more valuable than those without it, even though any sapphire that is not blue is not as valuable. The six-rayed star indicates the hexagram, and thus suggests Tiphereth, the sixth Sephira.

*Fig. B26 - Gray Sapphire with Six-pointed Star*

The gray tones of this stone suggest melancholy and sorrow. Fundamental Christians delight in claiming that the איש מחאבות, *man of sorrows*, of *Isaiah* 53:3 is a prophecy that foreshadows Jesus of Nazareth as the Messiah.[81] Even though this interpretation of the *Old Testament* text is completely fallacious, "man of sorrows" was accepted by Christians as a figurative term for Jesus as the suffering Messiah.[82]

All of these characteristics indicate clearly that the gray sapphire represents Christianity.

Now, even though it is a lovely stone, the gray sapphire is considered far below the *star sapphire* in its beauty and the depth of its symbolism.

Crowley did not even include the gray sapphire in the correspondences of *Liber* 777.

*Figure B27 - Ecce Homo (Man of Sorrows)*

81 The King James *Bible* translation familiar to Crowley reads, "He is despised and rejected of men; a man of sorrows, and acquainted with grief: and we hid as it were our faces from him; and he was despised, and we esteemed him not." (*Isaiah* 53:3).

82 The notion that *Isaiah* 53:3 refers to Jesus as the Messiah is a complete distortion of the original text. Isaiah 53 is the fourth "Song of the Servant" in that book; the other three are *Isaiah* Chapters 42, 29 and 50. The "servant" described in these verses represented *all the people* of Israel, not the Messiah (Cf. *Isaiah* 41:8).

# Deep Sapphire With a Tinge as of Blood

Fig. B28 - Dark Blue Sapphire with a Blood Red Tinge

A deep blue sapphire with a blood red tinge is another stone that has a deep melancholy appearance, indicating fatality and the sacrifice of blood.

One cannot help but see in this stone the suggestion of the Dying Gods: the slain Osiris, Attis, Dionysus, Odin, and in particular, Jesus of Nazareth, crucified and slain.

The deep blue colour[83] as attributed to the 23rd Path of מ, *Mem*, which is also that of the twelfth Trump of Tarot, *The Hanged Man*, the icon *par excellence* of the Dying God.

The very fact that *Liber LXV* did not say "a red tinge," but rather **"a tinge as of blood"**, leads inexorably to the symbolism of the bloody sacrifice.

Figure B29 - Crucifixion of Jesus

Figure B30 - Trump XII, Le Pendu
Renault Tarot de Besançon

Figure B31 - Odin Hanging on Yggsdrasil

83 Table XV of *Liber 777*, the King Scale of colour.

Figure B32 - Rose Cross (front)

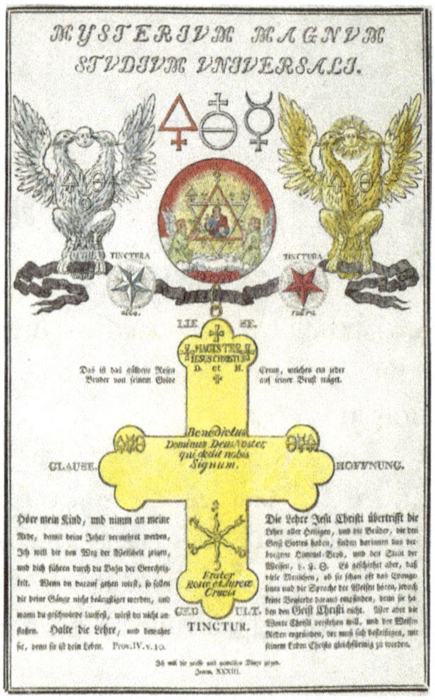


Figure B33 - Rose Cross (back)

Figure B34 - Hand-painted Rosicrucian Manuscript

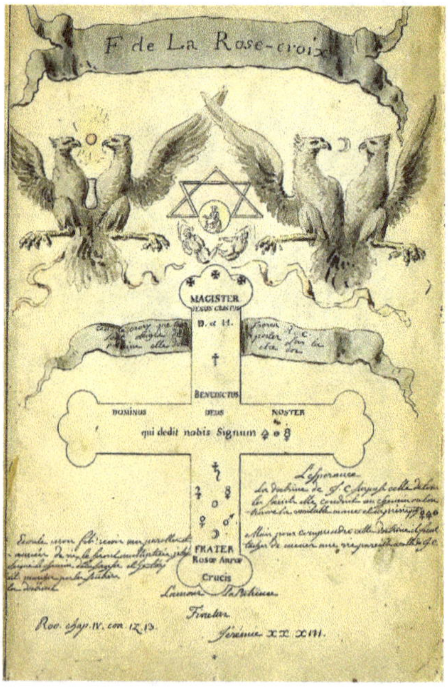


Figure B35 - Hand-painted Rosicrucian Manuscript

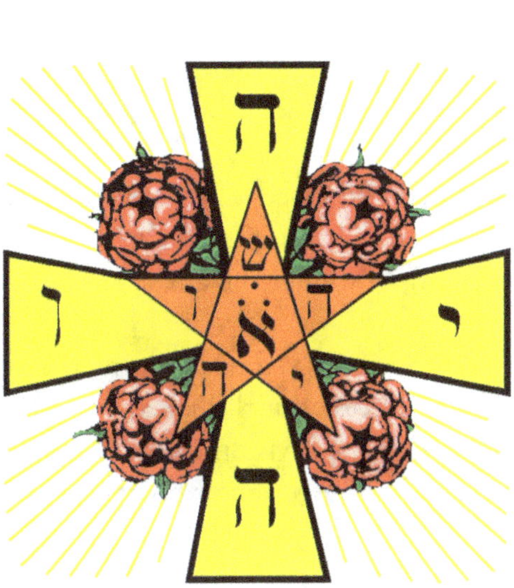


Figure B36 - Rose Cross Lamen

Figure B37 - Rose Cross Lamen (front)

Figure B38 - Jewel of the Rose Cross - after the Jewel of the 18° of the Scottish Rite of Freemasonry

Figure B39 - A Rosicrucian Crucifixion

## Stones of Discomfort

**6. Therefore do ye fret yourselves because of this.**

Note the plural form of the address. Adonai addressed V.V.V.V.V. directly, but now says "**ye**" and "**yourselves**". Here, He is speaking to Crowley the servant, those who would follow him, as well as the advocates of the other spiritual system indicated.

The Master of the Temple V.V.V.V.V. is above the veil of illusion wherein such differences in viewpoint are pangs of discomfort. But the servant and the advocates of other systems are equally troubled by the division in the word. As may be expected, very often there is vast difference between their points of view.

## The Dying God

Each of these last four stones contain the symbolism of the Dying God.

The golden yellow *topaz* is the colour of the Sun ☉ of Tiphereth, which was formerly associated with the crucified and resurrected Jesus.

The purple colour of the *amethyst* is that of piety and royalty, the combination of which found expression in the Great Sorcery that wedded Roman Imperialism and the Roman Church, culminating in the exaltation of the Papacy and its attempts to dominate the entire world.

The *gray sapphire*, with its somber sorrowful shade, points also to Tiphereth and Jesus, the "man of sorrows." This is even more so when the gray sapphire displays the six-rayed star.

These emblems are further carried out in the *deep blue of the dark sapphire with a tinge of blood*, suggesting the associations with the *Hanged Man* of Tarot, another Archetype of the Dying God.

No doubt that Adonai could have given other examples of symbolic stones representing the various religions and philosophies of the world, but He seemed to be making a very particular point.

These stones specifically represent *Christianity* and its host of symbols. Yet, in this place, I make haste to say that Adonai did not indicate *dogmatic Christianity* here, but rather *Mystical Christianity*. The suggestion of negative aspects that are inherent in Dogmatic Christianity is not present in the stones utilized by Adonai in these verses.

Dogmatic Christianity could well have been represented by a chunk of *coal*, sufficient to provide heat to the poor huddled masses, but leaving its unmistakable and persistent stain on its surroundings, and polluting the atmosphere.

How do we know that it is Mystical Christianity?

The answer to this question requires only a simple question in return. If Dogmatic Christianity were intended, why should we, who have accepted the Law of Thelema, "**fret**" over this? We are admonished to dismiss it outright as it is cursed by the Book of the Law.

What then is there to fret over?

The Mystical Christianity to which I refer is that which is found in philosophies and organizations that incorporate arcane and Hermetic typology, specifically those conceptually modeled after the earliest witnesses of *original* Rosicrucianism. All of these operated under the formulae of the Old Aeon; the Dying God, Glorification through Suffering and Sacrifice, and the crucified Rose upon the Cross.[84] The most significant recent examples are found in the *Orden des Gold und Rosenkreutz* ("Order of the Golden and rosy Cross"), which flourished in Germany circa 1710-1800 e.v., the 18° of the Scottish Rite of Freemasonry called *Knight Rose Croix*, the *Societas Rosicruciana in Anglia* ("Rosicrucian Society of England," sometimes called the SRIA), founded in 1865 and still in existence, and the *Hermetic Order of the Golden Dawn*, which was founded in 1888 and survived in sporadic forms until its final lineage in New Zealand ceased operation in 1978 e.v.[85]

The root of our "problem," and what causes some of us great discomfort, is that the systems of Thelema have incorporated symbols and imagery that evolved from a cursed religion. For some individuals, these are strange bed-fellows indeed.

Crowley himself was reared in a very strict dogmatic Christian household and grew up with an extreme distaste for anything related to Jesus, regardless if such references were dogmatic or mystical. However, once he attained Mastery, he realized that one need not throw out the baby with the bathwater. He understood that there *is* Truth in Mystical Christianity, sometimes aspects of the

---

84 No opinion is offered on the earliest witnesses of Rosicrucianism, as to whether they were literal or symbolic expressions. It is sufficient to state that such luminaries as Michael Maier and Robert Fludd contributed an inordinate amount of labor supporting the premise of that Order, which if chimerical, would be odd in the extreme. Conversely, it is clear that both of these meritorious scholars knew well that the House of the Holy Spirit had as its cornerstone the *Lapis Invisibilis*, that it was built on a high mountain at the ends of the earth, and that it was οἰκίαν ἀχειροποίητον αἰώνιον ἐν τοῖς οὐρανοῖς.

85 Pascal Beverly Randolph (1825-1875 e.v.) considered himself a Rosicrucian, and founded the *Fraternitas Rosae Crucis* in San Francisco circa 1856 e.v., the earliest Rosicrucian Order in the United States. The Order later fell into the hands of Reuben Swinburne Clymer, a medical quack and dissembler, whose writings continue to be promulgated by the Order which still exists. As Aesop said, the cocked hat does not make a warrior, and the *Fraternitas Rosae Crucis* is no more a Rosicrucian Order than the Lion's Club is a group of experts in the *Pantherinae*.

same Truth as that of Thelema, just in different garments.

But he never ceased to have difficulties with it *intellectually*. This was so, even though inspiration for his initial Magical Motto (*Perdurabo*, "I will endure") was probably the *Gospel of Matthew* 24:13,[86] and *The Book of the Law* itself, in Chapter II, Verse 57 contains a direct paraphrase of *Revelation* 22:11.[87]

Aside from the intellectual difficulties of his vessel, *To Mega Therion* Understood and fretted not.

*Figure B40 - Emblems of the 18° of Scottish Rite Masonry - Knight Rose Croix*

Freemasonry is not Rosicrucianism, despite the name, regalia and symbolism of the 18° degree of Knight Rose Croix (*Prince Rose Croix*). Nevertheless, the degree incorporates important Rosicrucian elements in the teachings of that degree, which are clearly Mystically Christian oriented. The legendary Masonic scholar Albert Pike described the central emblems of this degree to his brother Masons as,

86 "But he that shall endure unto the end, the same shall be saved." (KJV)

87 "He who is unjust, let him be unjust still: and he which is filthy, let him be filthy still: and he that is righteous, let him be righteous still: and he that is holy, let him be holy still." *(KJV)* Compare with *Liber AL*, II:57: "He that is righteous shall be righteous still; he that is filthy shall be filthy still."

> The Degree of Rose ✠ teaches three things; - the unity, immutability and goodness of God; the immortality of the Soul; and the ultimate defeat and extinction of evil and wrong and sorrow, by a Redeemer or Messiah, yet to come, if he has not already appeared...
> The Rose was anciently sacred to Aurora and the Sun. It is a symbol of Dawn, of the resurrection of Light and the renewal of life, and therefore of the dawn of the first day, and more particularly of the resurrection: and the Cross and Rose together are therefore hieroglyphically to be read, the Dawn of Eternal Life which all Nations have hoped for by the advent of a Redeemer. The Pelican feeding her young is an emblem of the large and bountiful beneficence of Nature, of the Redeemer of fallen man, and of that humanity and charity that ought to distinguish a Knight of this degree.[88]

At the time this was penned by Albert Pike, his "brother Masons" of this degree did not include those who were Jewish, only Christians. True to the typical Christian spirit of universal brotherhood, Jews were not allowed in the 18° or beyond.[89]

In his early years, Crowley had passed through the Adeptus Minor Ritual of the Hermetic Order of the Golden Dawn, a Ritual steeped in Christian Mysticism. In that Ritual, the Chief Adept embodied Christian Rosenkreutz, whose name was said to signify "the Rose and Cross of Christ, the Fadeless Rose of Creation, the Immortal Cross of Light."[90]

The Chief Adept was entombed in the Vault of the Pastos, the Key of which is "the word I.N.R.I.," which was based on the initials on the placard placed over the head of Jesus in his crucifixion. Originally intended to signify the Latin words, *IESVS NAZARENVS REX IVDÆORVM* ("Jesus of Nazareth, King of the Jews"),[91] it has been interpreted metaphorically over the centuries in numerous ways.

To the Alchemists it concealed *Igne Natura Renovatur Integra, All of Nature is renewed by Fire.* The Golden Dawn presented it as the Key Word to the Vault of the Pastos: "I.N.R.I., Yod, Nun, Resh, Yod."[92] Crowley offered *Intra Nobis Regnum deI, The Kingdom of God is within us.*[93]

The Candidate for this Initiation was then bound physically to the "Cross

---

88 Pike, *Morals and Dogma of the Ancient and Accepted Scottish Rite of Freemasonry*, p 287, 291.

89 De Hoyos, *Albert Pike's Morals and Dogma of the Ancient and Accepted Scottish Rite of Freemasonry Annotated Edition*, p. 364, n. 69.

90 *The Equinox*, Vol. 1, No. 3. He was here also identified with "Osiris Onnophris, the Justified One," i.e. *Asar-un-nefer* of the Egyptians, thereby indicating the purely symbolic identification with Jesus Christ.

91 See *Figure B29* above.

92 *The Equinox*, Vol. 1, No. 3, pp. 211-212, or *Liber O vel Manus et Sagittae, sub figura VI, Section IV, The Lesser Ritual of the Hexagram (II).*

93 *The Equinox*, Vol. 1, No. 1, p. 160.

Figure B41 - The Cross of Suffering at the Base of the Pastos

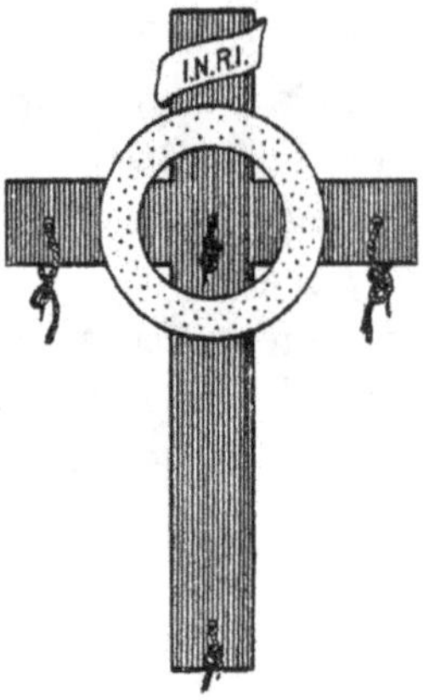


Figure B42 - The Cross of Suffering

of Suffering" and was admonished, "If ye be crucified with Christ, ye shall also reign with him." When the Chief Adept of the Temple arose from the Tomb in the climax of the Ritual, he recited *John* 11:25-26 from the *King James Bible* verbatim:

> I am the Resurrection and the Life. He that believeth in me, though he were dead, yet shall he live. And whosoever liveth and believeth in me, shall never die.[94]

Crowley published a synopsis of that Ritual in *The Equinox*, Volume 1, Number 3. The preface to the text read,

> The ritual of the 5° = 6° is of considerable length, and of such profundity and beauty that it is difficult to conceive of any man not being a better and more illuminated man for having passed through it.

It had a profound effect upon him; but this was in January of 1900 e.v., four years prior to the reception of *The Book of the Law*. After he had finally accepted his mission dictated by *Liber AL*, it became more difficult for him to intellectually resolve his conflict with the Christian symbols found throughout the magical system which he had been admonished to reconstruct.[95]

He dutifully revised the system of Initiation and followed the Instruction he had received to cast away the "evil ones" and to purge the "good ones."[96] The former Initiation Ritual of the Adeptus Minor was ejected, and in its

94 *Ibid.*, p. 218. The text in the Equinox has a typographical error in the last sentence, reading "on me," rather than "in me."

95 *Liber AL*, I:49-50, II:5.

96 See *Liber AL*, II:5.

place, the simple Oath of an Adeptus Minor with its sublime Task to attain to the Knowledge and Conversation of the Holy Guardian Angel. The physical temple of the "old time" was replaced by the bodily Temple of the Initiate.

Some motifs of the Old Aeon were cast aside, such as the "Cross of Suffering."[97]

Other significant figures were retained. The great emblem of the crucified Rose upon the Cross was the central emblem of the Inner Order, R.R. et A.C., *Rosae Rubæ et Auræ Crucis.*

It still is.[98]

*Figure B43 - The Rose Cross of A.'.A.'.*

*Figure 44 - Rose Cross Applique of the Inner Order Adepti of A.'.A.'.*

All Adepti of the Inner Order of A.'.A.'. wear a form of this figure on their breast, configured as the red five-petalled *Rosa Mundi* upon a golden Cross.

Two other great emblems, identified with V.V.V.V.V. and 666, include the inscription I.N.R.I. as well as the Crucified Rose: the *Lamen of V.V.V.V.V.* (*Figure B45*) and the Seal Ring of the Praemonstrator of A.'.A.'. (*Figure B46*) which is the *Ring of Amethyst* described in *The Wake World:*

---

97 See Gunther, *Initiation in the Aeon of the Child,* pp. 26-29.

98 See *Figure B43*. Students of A.'.A.'. should note that the lower arm of the Rose Cross Lamen is now solid bright green, as opposed to the former four-coloured lower arm of the previous Aeon which signified the quadrants of Malkuth (Cf. *Figures B37* and *B4* above, and the commentary thereon.)

*Figure B45 - The Lamen of V.V.V.V.V.*

*Figure B46 - The Ring of Amethyst*

> Now you must know that my Fairy Prince is my lover, and one day he will come for good and ride away with me and marry me. I shan't tell you his name because it is too beautiful. It is a great secret between us. When we were engaged he gave me such a beautiful ring. It was like this. First there was his shield, which had a sun on it and some roses, all of kind of bar; and there was a terrible number written on it. Then there was a bank of soft roses with the sun shining on it, and above there was a red rose on a golden cross, and then there was a three-cornered star, shining so bright that nobody could possibly look at it unless they had love in their eyes; and in the middle there was an eye without an eyelid. That could see anything, I should think, but you see it never could go to sleep, because there wasn't any eyelid. On the sides were written I.N.R.I. and T.A.R.O., which means many strange and beautiful things, and terrible things too. I should think any one would be afraid to hurt any one who wore that ring.[99]

The adherents of Mystical Christianity continue to have great difficulty in seeing any Truth in Thelema as well, for they are shackled by their adherence to the paradigms of the fallen Aeon of Osiris.

Likewise, many of Crowley's followers continue to fret themselves because of various Mystical Christian symbols throughout the systems of the OTO and A∴A∴ because they are blinded by their hatred of dogmatic Christianity and confound the symbolic with the literal.

---

99 Crowley, *Konx Om Pax*, pp. 3-4.

Adonai was acknowledging the tendency for his children to be concerned and troubled by the many variant forms in which Truth can sometimes be veiled. It is especially difficult for those who adhere to a strict doctrinal viewpoint that fails to acknowledge that other approaches may also contain valid points of view. Unfortunately, these are normally overshadowed and obscured by the false doctrines in which they are contained.

Students of Thelema should not be confused when they see Thelemic Orders using Symbols that have been traditionally associated with the methods and practices of the Old Aeon.

*Liber LXI vel Causæ* A.∴A.∴ addresses this very issue:

> Now the Great Work is one, and the Initiation is one, and the Reward is one, however diverse are the symbols wherein the Unutterable is clothed. (Verse 5)

> Should therefore the candidate hear the name of any God, let him not rashly assume that it refers to any known God, save only the God known to himself. Or should the ritual speak in terms (however vague) which seem to imply Egyptian, Taoist, Buddhist, Indian, Persian, Greek, Judaic, Christian, or Moslem philosophy, let him reflect that this is a defect of language; the literary limitation and not the spiritual prejudice of the man P.
> We labour earnestly, dear brother, that you may never be led away to perish upon this point; for thereon have many holy and just men been wrecked. By this have all the visible systems lost the essence of wisdom. We have sought to reveal the Arcanum; we have only profaned it. (Verses 23-24)

*Figure B47 - Igne Natura Renovatur Integra*

# § C. ASCENSVS VII-XI

7. Be not contented with the image.
8. I who am the Image of an Image say this.
9. Debate not of the image, saying Beyond! Beyond!
   One mounteth unto the Crown by the moon and by
   the Sun, and by the arrow, and by the Foundation,
   and by the dark home of the stars from the black earth.
10. Not otherwise may ye reach unto the Smooth Point.

THE ADEPT WAS INSTRUCTED that the truth he sees is only an image, a reflection of the Truth seen through many veils. Likewise, the Mystical Christian viewpoint is also only a pale image. It too possesses elements of the truth, as do many systems of attainment - some more than others. The Adept was urged not to debate on these images. But there is more to this injunction than first meets the eye.

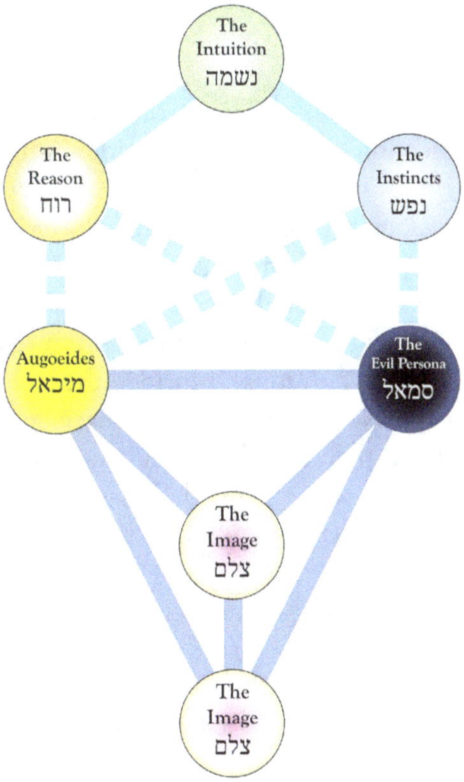

*Figure C1 - The Tzelim*

The diagram in *Figure C1* was created by Éliphas Lévi and elaborated by S. L. Mathers.[1] It illustrates a mystery of the **צלם**, *Tzelim*, or "image" of the soul.

At the top of the illustration are the three divisions of the human soul: **נשמה**, *Neshamah*, or Intuition, **רוח**, *Ruach*, or Reason, and **נפש**, *Nephesh*, or Instincts.

1 Lévi, *La clef des grands mystères* (1861), p. 389 and Mathers, *Kabbala Denudata, The Kabbalah Unveiled* (1887) plate facing page 37.

Next, just below on the left, is The *Augoeides* or Holy Guardian Angel. On the right is the *Evil Persona*, which Jungian Analysts call "The Shadow," the negative aspects of the personality.

Our Reason, as well as our Instincts, attempt to perceive the Augoeides. This is shown by the dotted line connecting the Reason as well as the Instincts. But notice that our Reason and Instincts likewise can perceive the Evil Persona; a dotted line also connects the Evil Persona to our Reason and our Instincts. These lines are not "solid" but "dotted" which indicates an imperfect and undeveloped link.

Therefore, an image forms from the imperfect perception of Augoeides as well as an image from the imperfect perception of the Evil Persona.

This image is *doubled* because of two divisions of the human soul, the Reason and the Instincts.

The initial Tzelim,"image," is a reflection of *both* Augoeides and the Evil Persona.

The second Tzelim or image which is shown below the first image is a reflection of not only Augoeides and the Evil Persona, but of *the first image as well.* This lower image is *the image of an image.*

The key here is that *neither image* is the real thing. If aspirants succumb to either one they are chasing a phantom in a house of mirrors. Neither image is pure for they are but Shells, *Qliphotic* shadows, with only glimmers of the real thing, whether it be Augoeides, the Evil Persona, or *BOTH.*[2]

Hence, Adonai informed the Adept that he must not be content with **the image**. Note that the word "image" here is written with a lower case "i." Then Adonai then called Himself the **Image of an Image.** The initial letter of both occurrences of the word "Image" is here written in the Uppercase. This means that his *True Image*, which is not the Tzelim that we have been talking about, is still but *a Reflection of a Reflection of the Divine*, albeit above the Abyss beyond the Realm of the Intellect or Instincts.

The message of Adonai is clear: **"Debate not of the image..."**

Again, note the lower case "i" here. This image of which he spoke here is a Tzelim, any of the false images that cannot be trusted.

Debate or argument is futile, for language also is limited and faulty. Neither the Reason or the Instinct can grasp the essence of the Truth, for that Truth is entirely above the Abyss that separates the human from the divine. One cannot argue about that which is "Beyond." Notice here that Adonai used this word twice: **"Beyond! Beyond!"** This stresses the world of duality in which we live and which limits our perceptions.

---

2 צלם also has the meaning of "shadow." Cf. *Gesenius*, p. 710b.

The "**Crown**" is Kether, the first Sephira on the Tree of Life. The Path of initiation leads ultimately to the Crown, but to attain to this one must put aside intellectual debates and aspire in the proper manner, which is by directed, earnest labor. The Path described above is that of the Middle Pillar.

# The Smooth Point

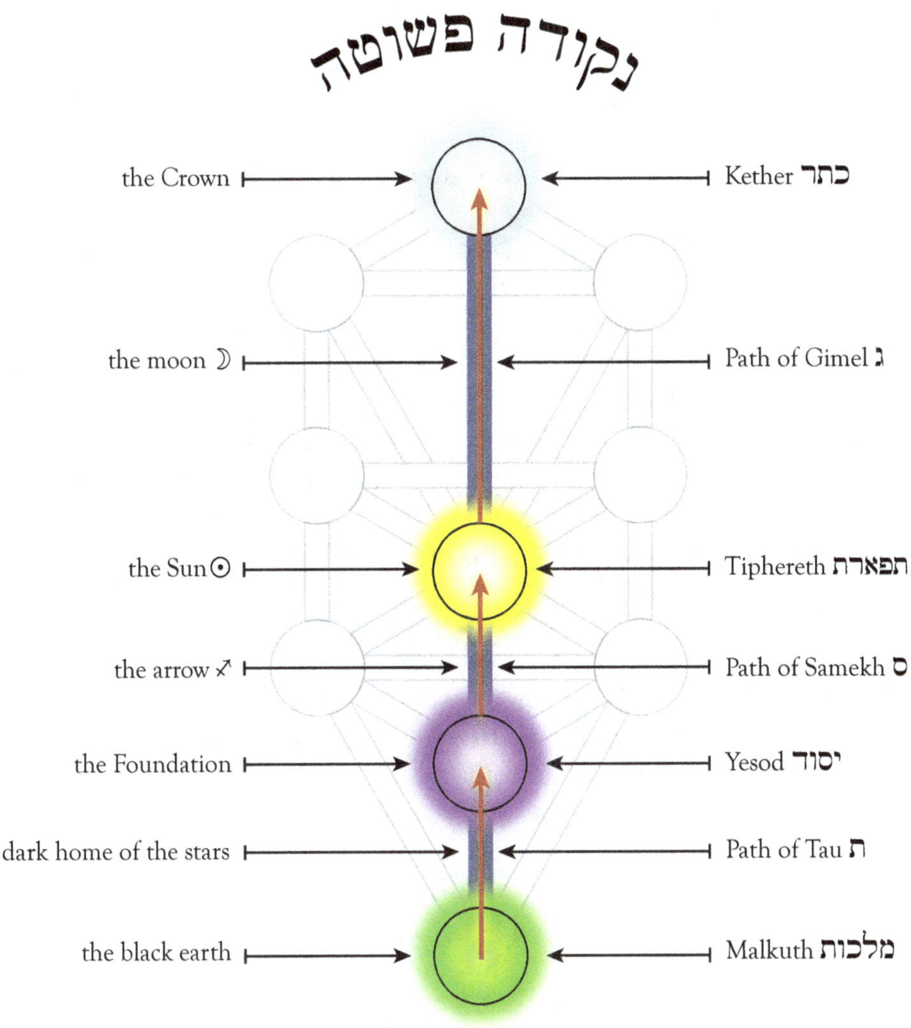


*Figure C2 - The Tree of Life - The Way of the Middle Pillar*

**One mounteth unto the Crown** which is כתר, *Kether*, and **by the moon** - the Path of ג, *Gimel*, which is referred to the ☽ moon, **and by the Sun** ☉ which is תפארת, *Tiphereth*, **and by the arrow**, the Path of ס, *Samekh*, which is attributed to ♐ Sagittarius, **and by the Foundation** יסוד, *Yesod*, which means “foundation” in Hebrew, and by **the dark home of the stars** which is the Path of ת, *Tau*, attributed to the tarot card *The Universe*, and lastly, **the black earth**, which is Malkuth, referred to the four elements of earth.

Now, note that the Path as described is in *reverse* of that of the Path of the Great Return. Adonai expressed that Path in the order of *manifestation* of the Tree of Life, as a ladder *let down* unto the earth. In other words, He described it from his perspective. However, we have the task of ascending that ladder *back* unto נקודה פשוטה, *Nequdah Peshutah*, the “Smooth Point,” which is a name for Kether, the Crown.[3] In fact, *Liber LXV* tells us that we cannot reach the Smooth Point in *any other way!*

**Not otherwise may ye reach unto the Smooth Point.**

*Any system* that utilizes the trances of the Middle Pillar (as we call them), is acceptable. The goal can be attained therein.

The “Smooth Point” refers to Kether as a Monad manifested from אין, *Ain, Nothing*. It is a perfect name to signify Kether as *The One* compared to its opposite, which is *The Many*.

Here, we should also consider the final aphorism given in *Liber Trigrammaton*, which follows the descriptions of all manifestation and speaks of the Great Return. Kether is called **the Smooth Point** in *Liber LXV*, whereas in *Liber Trigrammaton* it is called the “Stainless Abode.”

☷

**Therefore was the end of it sorrow; yet in that sorrow a sixfold star of glory whereby they might see to return unto the stainless Abode; yea, unto the Stainless Abode.**

3 Ginsburg, *The Kabbalah, its Doctrines, Development and Literature (1865 e.v.)*, pp. 7-8 & 11. נקודה פשוטה is sometimes rendered “simple point.” Adolf Franck called it the point “par excellence” (*La kabbale*, p. 185.) This term was misspelled by S.L. Mathers, *The Kabbalah Unveiled*, p. 23 and followed by Crowley in 777 *Revised* (p. 138) and in *Sepher Sephiroth* under numerical value 945. The earliest source of the phrase I have located is in ספר פרדס רימונים, *Sepher Pardes Rimonim* (*Book of the Garden of Pomegranates*), by Moses Cordova (edition of 1591 e.v.): הכתר לרוב העלמו לא נתגלה כי אם בקוצו של יו״ד, “Kether (the Crown) was not revealed unto the world except at the end of a *Yod*...,” לא תצדק צורת אות כלל אלא נקודה פשוטה ידייק כיון שבחכמה, “Because in Wisdom (*Chokmah*) the shape of a letter will not be justified at all, except as a Simple Point (*Nequdah Peshutah*).” *Sepher Pardes Rimonim*, 20:11:2.

# The Royal Matter

**11. Nor is it fitting for the cobbler to prate of the Royal matter. O cobbler! mend me this shoe, that I may walk. O king! if I be thy son, let us speak of the Embassy to the King thy Brother.**

Verse eleven tells us that the task of **the cobbler** is to mend shoes, not to prate of things beyond his or her skill, such as the **Royal matter**, that which is "Beyond."

This is a common mistake made by young aspirants who daydream of attainments far beyond their abilities. All of us who have aspired in the Great Work have done so. It is perfectly natural to dream of a better life with an increase in wisdom and understanding. For the sincere aspirant it is essential not to fill one's hours with fantasies rather than working on the basic practices needed to fulfil that aspiration. We must not forget that it is called the *Great Work* – not the *Great Speculation*!

We must follow the Path by means of disciplined motion, manifesting the fifth power of the sphinx which is *IRE*, a Latin word meaning, "to Go." It is the Power that crowns the Four Virtues, which are the *Four Powers of the Sphinx: AUDERE (to Dare), SCIRE (to Know), VELLE (to Will) and TACERE (to Keep Silent.)* The fifth Power *IRE* referred to ⊛ Spirit, which when awakened, enables us to consolidate the Four Virtues of the Adept and transform them into the tools of persistent spiritual labor, and fortify us for the journey.

*Figure C3 - Powers of the Sphinx*

The task of the cobbler is not very romantic, but it is absolutely necessary.

We must make our shoes ready for the journey, and this means finding and mending the weak spots in our lives. The word "cobble" means "patch up," yet it is derived from an older word which means, "to join together." It is a word of Union.[4]

---

4 *Cobble* is derived from the Old French *cobler, coubler*, "to join together" and is connected to the Old French *cople*, from which the English word *couple* is derived. (*Skeat*, p. 96b.)

*Figure C4 - Ceremonial Ankh*

The , *ꜥnḫ*, *Ankh*, the ancient Egyptian word for "life,"[5] according to the eminent Egyptologist Sir Alan Gardiner, is actually a representation of a *sandal strap*.[6] It was a man-made object, formed by a cobbler, that bound to the sole of the shoe protecting the feet of *Osiris* as he proceeded on his journey.

We know from the symbolic language in *The Egyptian Book of the Dead* that *rigidity* was the hallmark of the torpidity of the grave; motion to the limbs signified life.

In ancient Egyptian, the sole of the foot was called , *ṯbw*. The word for "sandals" was , *ṯbwty*. Sandals were considered clothing for the feet, made by a craftsman known as , *ṯbw*, a "sandal-maker," that is, a "cobbler." A cobbler was one who clothed the feet.

Note the following words:[7]

, *ṯbw* - "sole of the foot"

, *ṯbwty* - "sandals"

, *ṯbw* - "sandal-maker (cobbler)" One who clothes the feet

, *ꜥnḫ* - "life" - depicts a sandal strap

The god of all craftsmen, including cobblers, was , *ptḥ*, *Ptah*. As a verb, the Egyptian word , *ptḥ* , means "create, to fashion, to form, to shape."[8]

In the 'Proclamation of the Perfected One', which is a magical incantation derived from spell 42 of *The Egyptian Book of the Dead*, the candidate proclaims, "My feet are the feet of *Ptah*!"[9] In other words, I have mended my own shoes that I may walk. It is I that Go that I may have *life*.

(Verse 11 continued:)

---

5 *CDME*, p. 43.

6 Gardiner, *Life and Death (Egyptian)* in *Encyclopedia of Religion and Ethics*, Vol. VIII, p. 19-21 and Gardiner, *Egyptian Grammar*, p. 508. Cf. Gunther, *The Angel & The Abyss*, pp. 19-23.

7 *CDME*, p. 304.

8 Demotic *(CDD*, 8, p. 171*)* Cf. Coptic **ⲫⲱⲧϩ** (*Crum 276b*, under **ⲡⲱⲧϩ**, "carve, engrave, depict" and Hebrew **פתח**, "engraver."(*Jastrow*, Vol. 2, 1251b.) An 18th dynasty stela in the British Museum is inscribed with a Hymn to Amun which includes a phrase that illustrates this usage: , *ptḥ=tw nb=k ḥꜥw=k*, "thou hast fashioned (*ptḥ*) thy limbs." BM EA826, 2nd register, Line 3. (Edwards, *Hieroglyphic Texts from Egyptian Stelae*, Part VIII, p. 24.)

9 See Gunther, *Initiation in the Aeon of the Child*, Appendix I.

**O king! if I be thy son, let us speak of the Embassy to the King thy Brother.**

*Figure C5 - The Egyptian God Ptah*

Note that the first **"king"** is written with a lower case 'k'. The second is written with the upper case 'K'. This indicates that *two different kings* are being discussed. However, *both* are aspects of the Candidate, but at different levels of attainment.

**"O king!** with the lower case "k" is **חסד**, *Chesed*, the fourth Sephira which is attributed to ♃, Jupiter. It is the *Exempt Adept* $7^\circ = 4^\square$ the highest Grade of the Inner College.

**"if I be thy son"** - This is **תפארת**, *Tiphereth*, the sixth Sephira, the *Adeptus Minor* $5^\circ = 6^\square$, attributed to **ו**, *Vau* of **יהוה**, *Tetragrammaton*, who is called the "prince."

**"let us speak of the Embassy"** - the *Embassy*, here used in the sense of the word as a mission to a foreign government - here, it signifies the journey beyond the Abyss.

**"to the King thy Brother"** - This King, with the upper case "K," refers to **חכמה**, *Chokmah*, the Magus $9^\circ = 2^\square$, and **י** *Yod* of *Tetragrammaton* **יהוה**.

For clarity, the following diagram places these concepts on the Tree of Life.

What then, is the essential meaning of this portion of Verse 11?

The **cobbler** must mend shoes; this is the task of each aspirant.

The *prince*, a son of the king, has the station to speak of royal matters, but through "proper channels" and "proper decorum." We must not attempt to reach beyond our means by vain effort, but only by serious and trained methods.

The Neophyte, for example, has a task to do and it is not to daydream and chatter about the Inner College or the Supreme College. These are matters for the Adept and the Master of the Temple respectively.

Yet, even when Neophytes attain to the Grade of Adeptus Minor $5^\circ = 6^\square$, although being a *prince*, they are expected to follow protocol, and complete their assigned Task.

If they desire to speak to the **King** (upper case 'K', the Magus $9^\circ = 2^\square$) , it will be through the **king** (lower case 'k', the Exempt Adept $7^\circ = 4^\square$).

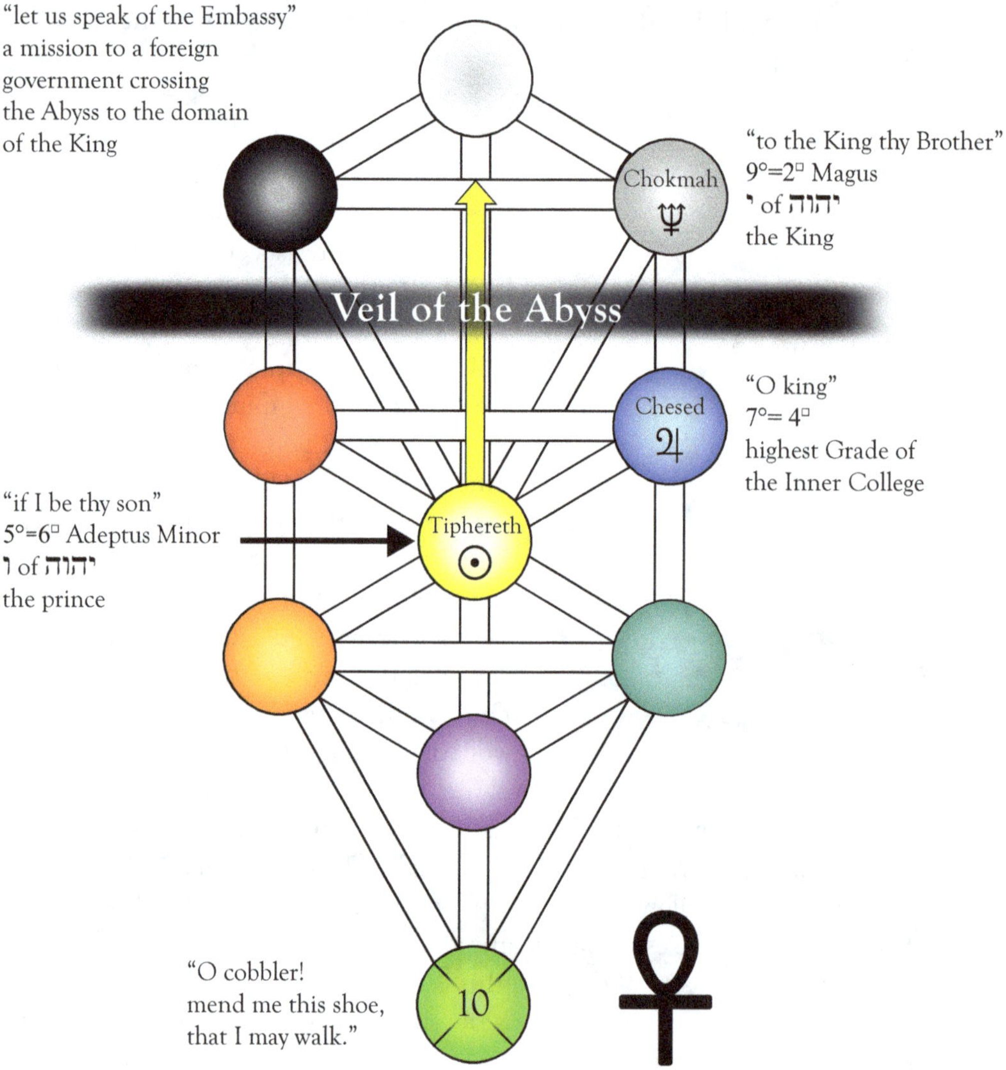


*Figure C6 - O king! if I be thy son, let us speak of the Embassy to the King thy Brother*

# § D. FALLAX IMAGO
# XII-XVIII

**12. Then was there silence. Speech had done with us awhile. There is a light so strenuous that it is not perceived as light.**

THE ADEPT RETURNED TO HIS CONTEMPLATIVE state, meditating in silence on what he had just heard. He contemplated the imperfection of the vehicles that *feel and perceive* (the Nephesh and the Ruach.)

*Figure D1 - The Silent Watcher*

In this particular verse, it is unclear if the speaker in verse 12 was Adonai, or a contemplation of the Adept. However, it seems probable that the first sentence in this verse is the voice of the Adept, followed by an instruction by Adonai, which then continues with verse 13.

The first contemplation pertains to the nature of light.

At either end of the colour spectrum there is the light that cannot be seen by the human eye. Below the red spectrum is the infra-red, and at the opposite end above the violet is the ultra-violet. These lights are examples of *the limitation of perception*, a reality entirely beyond the means of the individual to perceive them in their natural state. Thus, here begins instructions pertaining to such perceptual limitations.

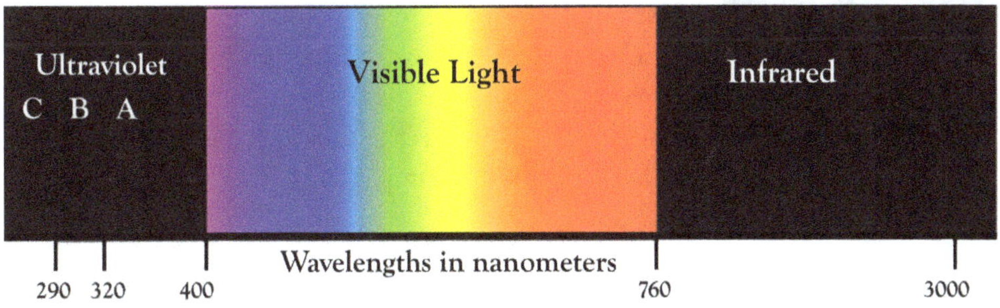


*Figure D2 - The Light Spectrum*

# The Piercing Poison

**13. Wolf's bane is not so sharp as steel; yet it pierceth the body more subtly.**

Wolf's bane (aconitum) derives its name from the Greek word ἀκόνιτον.[1] It is a plant that is also called *monkshood* or *friar's cap* due to the shape of its flower which is shaped like the hood of a robe.

*Figure D3 - Wolf's Bane*

Traditional interpretation considers the hood of the monk, or Hermit, to suggest the Hebrew letter י *Yod*. This is vividly portrayed in *The Hermit* card as it was interpreted by Paul Foster Case for the tarot deck of *The Builders of the Adytum*. (*Figure D4*)

Thus, in its outer form, wolf's bane or monkshood, is a reminder of the secret seed. While Yod, is the smallest of all Hebrew letters, it is the letter from which all others derive their shape.

*Figure D4 - Trump 9, The Hermit*

The secret seed can indicate the subtle, quiet influence of the Angel. It is what we call The Still Small Voice.[2]

The etymology of the Greek word ἀκόνιτον is uncertain, but it may in fact derive from ἀκόντιον, "a dart or javelin."[3] This is highly suggestive in the symbolic context of verse 13. Historically, wolf's bane was used to poison the tips of arrows.

Wolf's bane contains large quantities of the highly poisonous *aconitine* and related alkaloids, particularly in the roots. Poisoning from wolf's bane can also occur from merely picking the leaves of the plant without wearing gloves. The toxins are readily absorbed directly into the skin.[4] The deadly effect is thus capable of entering the body 'more subtly' than penetration by a steel weapon.

---

1 Specifically, *Aconitum Napellus. LSJ*, p.52b.

2 Cf. Gunther, *Initiation in the Aeon of the Child*, p. 191.

3 *LSJ*, p.52b-53a.

4 Amory & Emerson, *Wharton and Stille's Medical Jurisprudence, Vol. 2 Poisons, Aconitin (Monkshood; Wolfsbane)*, pp. 559-564.

The analogy continues, similar to that made concerning the nature of *light* in verse 12. That which is obvious to the external senses may be incomplete or misleading.

In the case of wolf's bane, the beauty of the plant conceals a deadly quality invisible to the eyes. This is one of the analogies of *Liber LXV* that deals with the "masks of reality"; things are not always what they appear to be, whether in nature, or within the soul of man.

Moreover, the descriptions given in verses 12-17 all partake of the character of "destruction," which is the function of the Work in the Outer College of A.·.A.·..

## Infectious Words

**14. Even as evil kisses corrupt the blood, so do my words devour the spirit of man.**

Adonai compared His **words** with **kisses** from a carrier of an infectious disease which invades the body through intimate contact. Such a contagion spreads invisibly throughout the entire organism carried by the bloodstream. In the description in verse 14, the contagion stems from the *words* of Adonai which infect the spirit of man and ultimately consume it. Adonai is thus a centre of pestilence.

*Figure D5 - Fermentatio*

The inspirational quality of the Word of the Lord partakes of this nature, which is like unto the alchemical operation called *Fermentatio*. In the same manner as the introduction of leaven into bread flour, the ferment assimilates itself to the mass, eventually penetrating it entirely. Martin Ruland in his Lexicon defined the alchemical operation of Fermentatio, "And so, as is the nature of the ferment, so too is the matter fermented."[5] In other words, when we are infected with the contagion that Adonai carries, we too become carriers of that dis-ease.

In this alchemical engraving from the *Philosophia Reformata* of 1622, note that *Fermentatio* is associated with the *Clangor Buccinæ*, or "sound of the horn" of *the* angel of final judgement. While the husbandman sows the seed into the plowed earth, the angel sounds the trump to raise the dead, here represented as the *Philosophical Sun* and *Philosophical Moon*.

This same motif is represented in an engraving called the *Eighth Key of Basil Valentine*, from the *Tripus Aureus* of Michael Maier printed four years earlier in 1618. The angel of the resurrection blows the trumpet awaking the dead, who rise like the grain sprouting up from the earth.

This image echoes the words in the first verse in *Liber LXV*: **"I await the awaking! The summons on high From the Lord Adonai, the Lord Adonai!"**

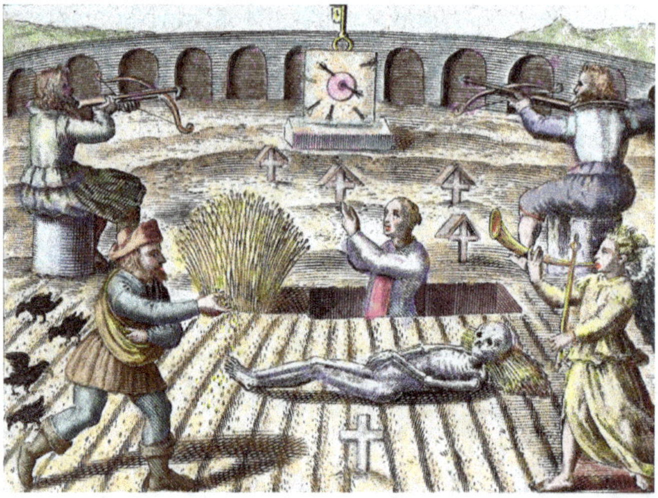

*Figure D6 - Eighth Key of Basil Valentine*

Additionally, in the background of this engraving, there are depicted two archers aiming for the bulls-eye of the target, over which is a key. There are seven arrows lodged in the target with two more arrows readied to be shot

5 *Quale itaque fermentum, tale et fermentatum.* (Ruland, *Lexicon Alchemiæ sive Dictionarium Alchemisticum*, p. 211.)

from the bows of the archers. That is a total of nine arrows, the number of the Sephira Yesod the foundation, from which the Path of Sagittarius ♐, the arrow, ascends to Tiphereth.

The emblem of the bulls-eye in the target looks strikingly like the symbol of ☉ Sol, the Sun, attributed to Tiphereth. The arrow is the emblem of straight and true aspiration which is a key to the Great Work.

In the words of *Liber VII*, Chapter I, Verse 37:

**I shoot up vertically like an arrow, and become that Above.**

These latter analogies - which align with our qabalistic system - were not an intentional reference by the engraver, but rather an example of archetypal synchronicity. Nevertheless, that does not diminish the significance of such examples but rather emphasizes their universal character.

## Dis-ease

**15. I breathe, and there is infinite dis-ease in the spirit.**

The "breath" or "inspiration" from Adonai is the source of the contagion described above in verse 14. It causes the **dis-ease in the spirit**, or uneasiness in the Ruach of men and women. The word **spirit** is derived from the Latin *spiritus*, "breath." The English word "inspiration" means literally "to breathe in."[6]

Those who seek the Truth through the process of Initiation should not expect peace of mind. The training of the Adept requires that one divest oneself of all preconceived notions and false concepts of what *Truth* really is, and do the preparatory work in order to receive that which is genuine. For most people, this is a tumultuous process, and brings unrest rather than peace, requiring the courage to confront the actual Truth, rather than hide behind the veils of more comfortable falsehoods. Confronting that Truth and embracing it brings dis-ease.

This breath from Adonai and its resulting discomforts are not limited to an initial and finite period of inspiration, it is "infinite," that is to say, it is continuous, as we will see in Verses 16 and 17.

---

6 Cf. *Skeat*, p. 459b, "aspire" derived from "Spirit."

# Dissolution

**16. As an acid eats into steel, as a cancer that utterly corrupts the body; so am I unto the spirit of man.**
**17. I shall not rest until I have dissolved it all.**

The purpose for the transmission of the Word, the planting of the *secret seed*, is that it may transform the entire world. This Word is of course *Thelema*. The influence of the Word is a **dis-ease**, a ferment which penetrates all throughout the aspirant until union is complete.

All who aspire to the Great Work, thus described, should note carefully that once one truly steps upon this Path, there is no turning back. The ferment of the Angel continues to work even like unto a cancer that metastasizes throughout the human body. The words of Adonai here are a promise as well as a warning.

Ultimately, if a True aspirant endures unto the end, it is a promise that this will lead them to the frontier of the Abyss and the requirement of the passage thereof, wherein the ego is annihilated, resulting in coition with our lady BABALON.

Those dilettantes who take a step upon the Path and seek to retreat to their old, familiar gray world of the *Qliphoth* should understand that the ferryman Χάρων, *Charon*, must one day be paid his due fee.[7] Whether in this lifetime, or another, or another, the Oath and Task must be fulfilled, and that original Oath and Task lead unfailingly to the lonely towers of the Abyss. Adonai will not rest until dissolution is complete. One can never really look back.

As Crowley himself might say, "Remember Lot's wife!"[8]

7 It should be remembered that Χάρων, *Charon*, the ferryman of Ἅδης, *Hades*, is the son of Νύξ, NOX. "Wherefore I charge you that ye come unto me in the Beginning; for if ye take but one step in this Path, ye must arrive inevitably at the end thereof." (*Liber Cheth*, 19).

8 *Genesis* 19:26. Even though *Yahweh* provided the *Sulphur*, and Lot's wife provided the *Salt*, it is doubtful that Lot himself distilled the *Mercury*.

# NOX

**18. So also the light that is absorbed. One absorbs little, and is called white and glistening; one absorbs all and is called black.**

Here again is another lesson about an illusion within nature. In Western traditions **white** is considered a colour of purity, happiness and good, while **black** suggests the impure, the sorrowful or evil. The custom of wearing black at a funeral dates back to the Roman Empire.

The Eastern religions designate white as the funeral colour, precisely because they consider it the colour of Purity.

But from the perspective of Adonai, absorbing all perceptions is the goal. White is the *reflection* of all colours in the visible spectrum; it absorbs nothing. Black, on the other hand, absorbs *all* of them.

Hence, the methodology of Horus is the formula of NOX, "night," not LVX, "light." The formula of LVX was the hallmark of the Aeon of Osiris. The central formula of Horus is NOX. The Angel does not diminish the sacred character of the **white and glistening** that is LVX. But he does remind us that the white is that which absorbs little. The black absorbs **all**.

This calls to mind Chapter 40 from *The Book of Lies*:

> A red rose absorbs all colours but red; red is therefore the one colour that it is not. This Law, Reason, Time, Space, all Limitation blinds us to Truth. All that we know of Man, Nature, God, is just that which they are not; it is that which they throw off as repugnant.

# § E. NOCTIS LAVDATIO XIX-XXIV

**19. Therefore, O my darling, art thou black.**
**20. O my beautiful, I have likened thee to a jet Nubian slave, a boy of melancholy eyes.**

Here, Adonai was speaking about His beloved, V.V.V.V.V. The colour of Binah is black in the Queen Scale of colour. Since V.V.V.V.V. is a perfect Magister Templi (as well as a perfect Adeptus Minor), He therefore appears black to all below the Abyss. V.V.V.V.V. is also likened unto the colour black which reflects no colours but absorbs all. This is also the nature of the Holy Guardian Angel.

**Jet** is a black gemstone, a mineraloid that is derived from wood subjected to high pressure for millennia. As an adjective, "jet" or "jet-black" means something as black as possible - the blackest black.[1]

*Figure E1 - Head of a Nubian Boy*

In this verse, there is the distinct suggestion of the Nubian slave boy as an object of sexual desire. The Nubian people were slender and athletic, with handsome features and extremely black skin. In the first century BCE, slaves taken from among the Nubians by marauding invaders were highly prized in those countries where dark skin was a rarity. Because of the colour of their skin and their beautiful features they were considered exotic and precious "property" of their owners.

The imagery of a Nubian slave also appears in *Liber VII*, Chapter II, verses10-12. Herein, the aspiring Babe of the Abyss describes his God as a desirable Nubian female slave:

1 *New Shorter Oxford English Dictionary*, Vol. 1, p. 459b.

**Thou art not worth an obol in the agora; yet Thou art not to be bought at the ransom of the whole Universe.**
**Thou art like a beautiful Nubian slave leaning her naked purple against the green pillars of marble that are above the bath.**
**Wine jets from her black nipples.**

## Fear and Defamation

**21. O the filthy one! the dog! they cry against thee.**
**Because thou art my beloved.**

Because the nature of V.V.V.V.V. represents a wholeness which encompasses the black as well as the white, there will be many who fear Him and His influence. Here, in verse 21, Adonai is speaking to V.V.V.V.V. about how the uninitiated populace will call Him **the filthy one**, and **the dog**. But this sentence applied equally to the scribe Aleister Crowley.

Note that the first letter of both the word **thee** and **thou** are in lower case. This was also the case in verse 20. The lower vehicles, those below the Abyss, take on the character of the Magister once union has been achieved. When the masses attacked our Prophet, unwittingly they were attacking V.V.V.V.V. and Adonai.

Hatred was leveled at Aleister Crowley the scribe in part because his behavior and his rhetoric often violated the social norms of the day. As an unconventional advocate of sexual liberty and freedom of choice in all areas of social and private life, he was branded a hedonist and heretic. It must be admitted that he often proved to be his own worst enemy, often by presuming a level of intelligence among his general readership which was non-existent. A perfect example is in Chapter XII of *Magick in Theory and Practice*, "Of the Bloody Sacrifice, and of Matters Cognate." After stating that the sacrificial animal should "therefore be killed within the Circle," he followed this with, "A male child of perfect innocence and high intelligence is the most satisfactory and suitable victim." The footnote to this passage informed the reader that "It appears from the Magical Records of Frater Perdurabo that He made this particular sacrifice on an average about 150 times every year between 1912 e.v. and 1928 e.v."[2] Not a few fools considered this to be a confession that Crowley had murdered over 2,500 children in a Black Mass. Crowley naively assumed

2 See Crowley, *Magick, Liber ABA, Book 4, Part 3, Magick in Theory and Practice*, Chapter XII, p. 207. The gullibility, stupidity or animosity of some readers led editor Hymenaeus Beta to add, "Crowley specifies self-sacrifice that does not result in serious injury or death; his remarks also have a sex-magical interpretation. He is advocating neither suicide nor ritual murder."

that an intelligent person reading this chapter carefully would realize that the author was engaged in a bit of gleeful leg-pulling, as well as veiled symbolism, and that no such literal interpretation was intended. It was an overly-generous assumption.[3]

While Crowley's uninhibited writing sometimes added fuel to the fire of his enemies, the animosity he encountered, then as well as now, has a deeper unconscious provenance. Hatred was leveled at Aleister Crowley the scribe, because of his union with the Master V.V.V.V.V. The populace was too ignorant and fearful of this Truth to comprehend anything other than what appeared before their blind eyes.[4]

We read in Verse 18 of this chapter that **One absorbs little, and is called white and glistening; one absorbs all and is called black**. It is our natural inclination to gravitate toward the light instead of the darkness. It is part of our genetic inheritance that causes us to prefer the light and fear the dark.[5]

Occasionally, any Thelemite may encounter this reaction as well. Some people who first come into contact with Thelema and its representatives experience an inexplicable fear. Confounded by their own limitations of perception, they may sense it to be evil. This is due to an unconscious realization that Thelema represents a threat to their ego. The weak often hate what they fear or cannot understand. This is a lesser aspect of what we call the **Fear Invisible**.[6]

Later, in the 5th Chapter of *Liber LXV*, in Verse 6 (fifth chapter, verse 6 no less!) we read:

> **Through the midnight thou art dropt, O my child, my conqueror, my sword-girt captain, O Hoor! and they shall find thee as a black gnarl'd glittering stone, and they shall worship thee.**

He shall be found as a *black* stone, gnarl'd and glittering. Note that *Hoor*

---

3 This type of vile nonsense was long-lived. In 1976 e.v., I visited a museum at San Francisco's Fisherman's Wharf. The *pièce-de-résistance* was a life-sized wax figure of Crowley with evil countenance, in the setting of a Christian church, standing behind a casket and exposed corpse, in the act of performing a "black mass"; the "Wickedest Man in the world" desecrating a church and violating a corpse. To call it disgusting would be an understatement.

4 Crowley was forewarned of such things in *Liber AL*: "Fear not, o prophet, when these words are said, thou shalt not be sorry. Thou art emphatically my chosen; and blessed are the eyes that thou shalt look upon with gladness. But I will hide thee in a mask of sorrow: they that see thee shall fear thou art fallen: but I lift thee up. Nor shall they who cry aloud their folly that thou meanest nought avail; thou shall reveal it: thou availest: they are the slaves of because: They are not of me." (*Liber AL*, II:53-54)

5 See Gunther, *Initiation in the Aeon of the Child*, pp. 32-36.

6 See *Liber LXV*, V:36.

is described as falling through the midnight, *the darkest hour of the night.* He doesn't fall to the earth openly or visibly in the light; he has to be *found*. Those who desire Him, must *search* for Him. And then they will worship Him.

Note the words of Nuit in *The Book of the Law,* Chapter I:60

> **My colour is black to the blind, but the blue & gold are seen of the seeing. Also I have a secret glory for them that love me.**

## The Eyes of Adonai

> **22. Happy are they that praise thee; for they see thee with Mine eyes.**

Verse 22 of *Liber LXV*, Chapter One, tells us that there are those who are able to see the Truth in the word of V.V.V.V.V., praise Him, and experience the joy that this knowledge brings.

The word **Mine** in this verse is written with the Upper Case "M." Those that praise Him, see Him with the eyes of Adonai. Yet, once again, we see both instances of the words **thee** have their initial letter in the lower case: **they that praise thee; for they see thee**. This represents those whose perspective is that of one below the Abyss, in the world of duality. They praise V.V.V.V.V., instinctively perceiving Him as Adonai envisions Him, yet their perceptions are limited.[7]

Because Aleister Crowley was the chosen of V.V.V.V.V., in like fashion, those that praise our Prophet, Aleister Crowley, see him also with the eyes of Adonai the Lord.[8]

## Three Types of Praise

> **23. Not aloud shall they praise thee; but in the night watch one shall steal close, and grip thee with the secret grip; another shall privily cast a crown of violets over thee; a third shall greatly dare, and press mad lips to thine.**

---

7 Cf. *Liber VII,* IV:49, "I catch Thee by instinct, though my eyes fail from Thy glory."

8 Again, cf. *Liber AL,* II:53.

This is a perfect description of the various ways in which Candidates come to know V.V.V.V.V. through The Holy Guardian Angel. Note that this speech is that of Adonai speaking to V.V.V.V.V.

All of the methods of coming to know Him are silent, personal and private. Some might even say "secret." **Not aloud shall they praise thee...** In other words, "silently" shall they praise thee. Then we are presented with three different ways this is accomplished.

## The Night Watch

The **night watch**, or Νύχευμα,[9] was an ancient military and nautical tradition of posting a guard in the night, in either a city, or on board a ship.

The night watch among the Jews consisted of three periods: From sunset unto 10:00 p.m., the middle watch from 10 p.m. until 2:00 a.m., and the final watch from 2:00 a.m. until sunrise. The Romans used four night watches, each of three hours duration that corresponded with the changing of the guard.

*Figure E2 - The Night Watch*

9 *LSJ*, p. 1185b. In Hebrew, אשמורה בלילה, "a watch in the night." (The phrase occurs one time in the *Old Testament*, in *Psalm* 90:4) Cf. *Gesenius* אשמרה (p. 87a) < שמר (p. 838a), also ליל (p. 438a).

The illustration above is the famous painting by Rembrandt named "The Night Watch." Ironically, it received that name because, at some point, someone painted it over with a dark varnish, which led everyone to believe it was a representation of the night watch guard heading out after sunset.

After the painting was restored, and they removed the dark varnish, they discovered it was a day scene! Things are not always how they appear.

Be that as it may, there are some lovely verses in the *Song of Solomon* in the *Bible* that speak of seeking the beloved during the night watch.

Crowley was very conversant with the *Bible*. the *Song of Solomon* was one book that he admired for the quality of its verse. Without doubt, he knew these verses quite well:[10]

> By night on my bed I sought him whom my soul loveth: I sought him, but found him not.
> I will rise now, and go about the city in the streets, and in the broad ways I will seek him whom my soul loveth: I sought him, but I found him not.
> The watchmen that go about the city found me: to whom I said, Saw ye him whom my soul loveth? It was but a little that I passed from them, but I found him whom my soul loveth: I held him, and would not let him go, until I had brought him into my mother's house, and into the chamber of her that conceived me.[11]

In reading this verse, when we think of the one whom "my soul loveth" we think of Adonai, the Lord. But please note, this verse of *Liber LXV* refers to V.V.V.V.V. the *beloved* of Adonai (Cf. Verses 21-22) and not specifically to Adonai Himself.

So what are we to understand from this?

Serious aspirants are urged to carefully read *The Wake World*, where it is abundantly clear that the Angel, the Prince of the soul, is One with V.V.V.V.V.

23. Not aloud shall they praise thee; **but in the night watch one shall steal close, and grip thee with the secret grip;** another shall privily cast a crown of violets over thee; a third shall greatly dare, and press mad lips to thine.

---

10 Late in his life, Crowley penned a letter to his son Aleister Ataturk who had just turned ten years old. In this letter, Crowley wrote, "The best models of English writings are Shakespeare and the *Old Testament*, especially the book of *Job*, the *Psalms* and *Proverbs*, *Ecclesiastes*, and the *Song of Solomon*. It will be a very good thing for you to commit as much as you can of these books and of the best plays of Shakespeare to memory, so that they form the foundation of your style." (Kaczynski, *Perdurabo*, p. 545.)

11 *Song of Solomon*, 3:1-4 (A.V.).

*Figure E3 - I found Him whom my Soul Loveth*

*Figure E4 - The Five Points of Fellowship*

The Candidate gripped Him with **the secret grip**. In the words of the *Song of Solomon*, “I held him and would not let him go.”[12]

The term **secret grip** suggests to me, solely on the expression used, something akin to the secret grip of a Master Mason in the Old Aeonic system of Freemasonry, where it is called the “real grip.” It is also called the “Lion’s Paw” grip. It is this Masonic grip by which the Candidate, who is symbolically Hiram Abiff, is raised from the dead at graveside.

The “Lion’s Paw Grip” is received in the position known as “The Five Points of Fellowship”: foot to foot, knee to knee, breast to breast, hand to back, and cheek to cheek (or mouth to ear).

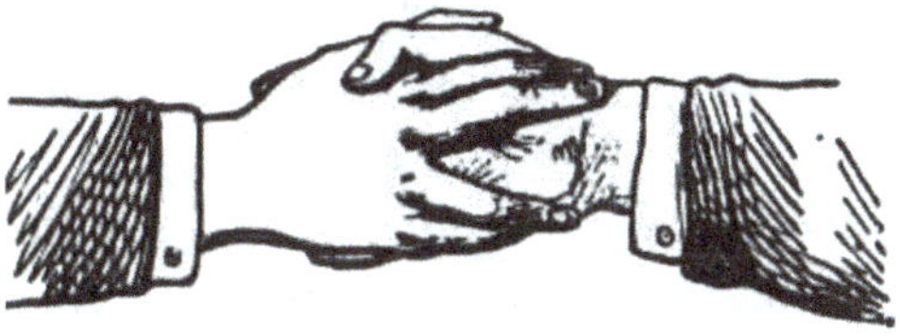

*Figure E5 - The “Lion’s Paw” Grip*

It is in this position that the Secret Word of Freemasonry is transmitted.

Of course, this is of an Old Aeonic system. As Crowley himself said, “the Secret (i.e. of Freemasonry) pertains to the Past. It is part of the heritage of Humanity. But the Rites of Freemasonry are, after all, those of Osiris, the

12 אחזתיו, “I held him,” from אחז, “take hold, grip.” (*Gesenius*, p. 30a).

Dying God."[13] But Crowley was well-versed in the ritual protocols, postures and "secret grips" of Freemasonry, and a form of this practice was also used in the Hermetic Order of the Golden Dawn. I think that it is more than likely that the term "secret grip" triggered an association with that ritual formality, where it formed such an important symbol of Brotherhood and transmission of a hidden word. The Freemasons called it the "Lions Paw grip." This likely would have resonated with Crowley by reason of his intrinsic identification with Leo.

In this context, these "Five Points of Fellowship" bring to my mind the name of five letters, V.V.V.V.V.

Within the system of Freemasonry, this "secret grip" was the grip of *Brother to Brother*. I personally think that this correspondence carries over to the meaning of this verse. One who steals close and grips with a secret grip, known only to another within a closed fraternity, is identifying himself as a Brother.

## A Crown of Violets

23. Not aloud shall they praise thee; but in the night watch one shall steal close, and grip thee with the secret grip; **another shall privily cast a crown of violets over thee;** a third shall greatly dare, and press mad lips to thine.

Another aspirant will crown Him with **a crown of violets** in an act of adoration.

Among the Greeks, a crown of violets was a sign of Aphrodite, goddess of love and beauty.[14]

The crown of violets is a *feminine* crown; it was cast upon the goddess as a symbol of love for her, and as a symbol that she represented love herself.

Here, our nameless aspirant casts this crown upon V.V.V.V.V. **privily**, which is to say "confidentially" or "secretly."

This type of aspirant adores the Lord quietly, without obvious outward expression, and worship in the privacy of their own Temple, which is to say, in their Heart.

13 Crowley, A Past Grand Master, "The Crisis in Freemasonry," *The English Review*, Vol. XXXVI (August 1922), pp. 127-134.

14 In Hesiod's *Homeric Hymn VI, To Aphrodite*, she is called ἰοστεφάνου Κυθερείης, "violet-crowned Cytherea." The Term *Cytherea*, "lady of Cythera," was an epithet for *Aphrodite*, for the Island of Cythera was one location proclaimed as her birthplace.

Thou art standing as it were upon a pinnacle at the edge of some fortified city. I am a white bird, and perch upon Thee.
Thou art My Lover: I see Thee as a nymph with her white limbs stretched by the spring.
She lies upon the moss; there is none other but she:
Art Thou not Pan?
I am He. Speak not, O my God! Let the work be accomplished in silence.
Let my cry of pain be crystallized into a little white fawn to run away into the forest!
Thou art a centaur, O my God, from the violet-blossoms that crown Thee to the hoofs of the horse.

*Liber VII, I:-3-9*

## The Daring Lover

23. Not aloud shall they praise thee; but in the night watch one shall steal close, and grip thee with the secret grip; another shall privily cast a crown of violets over thee; **a third shall greatly dare, and press mad lips to thine.**

The third type of aspirant is that of a lover who, overcome with yearning, mad with desire, dares all to kiss the beloved.

Aleister Crowley was this kind of aspirant, as should be obvious from the example of his life.

Such an aspirant sometimes throws caution to the wind, with a feeling of desperate yearning for the Beloved. "Here am I Lord! Take me!"

But Oh! I love Thee.
I have thrown a million flowers from the basket of the Beyond at Thy feet, I have anointed Thee and Thy Staff with oil and blood and kisses.
I have kindled Thy marble into life – ay! into death.
I have been smitten with the reek of Thy mouth, that drinketh never wine but life.

*Liber VII, I:43-46*

Come to me now! I love Thee! I love Thee!
O my darling, my darling – Kiss me! Kiss me! Ah! but again.

*Liber VII, II:50-51*

This type of aspirant is somewhat rare. Few are the greyhounds, many are the snails. But in the end, the manner of aspiration is inconsequential, as long as one attempts to manifest the Fifth Power of the Sphinx – To Go.

> **Let not the failure and pain turn aside the worshippers. The foundations of the pyramid were hewn in the living rock ere sunset; did the king weep at dawn that the crown of the pyramid was yet unquarried in the distant land?**
>
> *Liber LXV, V:51*

## NOX

> **23. Not aloud shall they praise thee; but in the night watch one shall steal close, and grip thee with the secret grip; another shall privily cast a crown of violets over thee; a third shall greatly dare, and press mad lips to thine.**
>
> **24. Yea! the night shall cover all, the night shall cover all.**

All three sacred acts are concealed by the Night of Pan (NOX). Remember that black reflects no light; it absorbs all light. So none of these methods of adoration are reflected audibly or visibly to the outside world. They are performed under the cloak of sacred darkness and silence.

Notwithstanding, the shielding darkness is not only a concealer, it is a secret *revealer* for those that can perceive Him, for such is the character and nature of the Holy One.

Compare *Liber VII*, Chapter IV, verses 48-49:

> **Excellent is Thy love, Oh Lord! Thou art revealed by the darkness, and he who gropeth in the horror of the groves shall haply catch Thee, even as a snake that seizeth on a little singing-bird.**
> **I have caught Thee, O my soft thrush; I am like a hawk of mother-of-emerald; I catch Thee by instinct, though my eyes fail from Thy glory.**

He is "revealed by the darkness." Here, in this verse quoted from *Liber VII*, the Angel is not the one compared to the snake, it is the aspirant and his method of seeking the Angel. The Angel is likened unto a little singing bird, a "soft thrush" pursued by that aspirant who then compares himself to a predatory hawk of mother-of-emerald.[15] He catches the Angel by "instinct" (i.e. the Nephesh, for the candidate is ה *Heh Final* of יהוה to which the Nephesh is attributed) because his eyes are blinded by the glory of The Holy Guardian Angel. Yet, it is the darkness itself that reveals the Holy One, the ambassador of Pan.[16]

As seekers of the Holy Guardian Angel, we cannot rely on "evidence" or "proof" of His existence or His presence. We cannot rely on our eyes, which are our windows to the manifest world of duality, for they cannot behold His glory.[17] We first must rely on our spiritual Instinct.

15 Again, compare *Liber Tzaddi*, 0-3: "In the name of the Lord of Initiation, Amen. I fly and I alight as an hawk: of mother-of-emerald are my mighty-sweeping wings. I swoop down upon the black earth; and it gladdens into green at my coming. Children of Earth! rejoice! rejoice exceedingly; for your salvation is at hand." See also Verse 4 of *Liber LXV* above, and the commentary thereon. By this self-comparison, the Candidate (here Frater Perdurabo, Aleister Crowley) identifies Himself with the *Lord of the Aeon* and with V.V.V.V.V., His Messenger.

16 Cf. *The Book of Lies*, Cap 11, THE GLOW WORM; "The reflection of All is Pan: the Night of Pan is the Annihilation of the All. Cast down through The Abyss is the Light, the Rosy Cross, the rapture of Union that destroys, that is The Way. The Rosy Cross is the Ambassador of Pan." See also *The Vision & the Voice*, 12th Æthyr.

17 Remember Verse 12 of *Liber LXV*, Chapter I: "There is a light so strenuous that it is not perceived as light."

# § F. COR VNIVERSVM XXV-XXVIII

**25. Thou wast long seeking Me; thou didst run forward so fast that I was unable to come up with thee. O thou darling fool! what bitterness thou didst crown thy days withal.**

ADONAI ISSUED A SWEET REBUFF TO HIS beloved V.V.V.V.V., and at the same time, to His servant, the Adept, Frater O.M. (as well as the scribe Frater Perdurabo.) For even as the Master, so the disciple.

What you must remember in order to understand this verse is that Aleister Crowley was an exceptional candidate. Unlike most candidates for initiation who drag their feet endlessly along the Inward Journey, Crowley tried to storm the gates of heaven.

He sought his Angel with such fierceness of aspiration that the Angel could not come up with him. In his case, he hampered his own success by over-eagerness. That is an exceptionally rare attribute among students.

## Now I Am With Thee

**26. Now I am with thee; I will never leave thy being.**
**27. For I am the soft sinuous one entwined about thee, heart of gold!**

Continuing His address, Adonai spoke to V.V.V.V.V. as well as O.M. and Frater Perdurabo here. By default, this applies to all of us who attain to the Knowledge and Conversation of The Holy Guardian Angel.

We first achieve union with The Holy Guardian Angel in Tiphereth. However, this union is made *permanent* when the daughter ה, *Heh Final*, is set upon the Throne of the mother Binah, ה *Heh Prima* of the Tetragrammaton יהוה - in other words, when the aspirant attains to Master of the Temple in Binah.

The Angel and the aspirant are then united as One and None under the Night of Pan in the City of the Pyramids. This is what is meant earlier when it was said the Magister was perfect Adeptus Minor.

And the Angel gave us this wonderful promise, **I will never leave thy being**. The fully attained Adept is called a **heart of gold**, that is, Tiphereth realized in all its fullness.

The Angel compared Himself again to the Serpent of Wisdom, entwined softly and lovingly about the heart of the aspirant.

There are some who foolishly claim that *everyone* has a Holy Guardian Angel. These people have not read the Holy Books carefully and prayerfully. They mistakenly quote *Liber LXV*, Chapter II, verse 60: **I waited patiently, and Thou wast with me from the beginning.**

Indeed.

But the **beginning** of what? The universe? The formation of the Earth? Conception by one's parents? Physical birth upon this planet?

No. None of these things.

Would it not be very convenient if we were all born with a Holy Guardian Angel like a good fairy? We would not have to do anything; we would not have to aspire to the Angel, we would not have to make the temples of our souls fit for the presence of God.

We could just sit down on our lazy backsides puffed up with pride and self-aggrandizement, blinded by the illusion that we were one with the Lord, or even worse, believing that the Holy Guardian Angel is some exalted idea of ourselves.[1] And we would go to our graves believing a lie, and a potential life of aspiration would be wasted.

Note that the Angel said, ***Now* I am with thee...**

If we always had a Holy Guardian Angel, the emphatic time-stamp "**Now**" would be unnecessary.

For any of us who aspire to know the Angel and converse with the Angel, we came to know that *the instant we firmly set our foot upon the Path*, the Angel was with us.

Once we took that step, He was with us, but we were not yet with Him.

We had to strive, to work, to enflame ourselves with prayer in order to cleanse the temple of our souls, as best we could, to make it fit for the presence of The Holy One.

For any of us who do that, we will then be able to hear those glorious words for ourselves: ***Now* I am with thee; I will never leave thy being.**

Then we will know that He was with us from the time we declared our aspiration and set a trembling foot upon the Path of the Inward Journey. We had been just too blind to see, too deaf to hear, too shackled by the chains of Ego to say, "It is I that go" and come to know that soft, sinuous one entwined lovingly about our hearts.

---

1 See again the passage from Crowley, *Magick Without Tears*, Chap. 42, quoted in the Introduction to this book, pp. 6-7.

Yet, note that in Chapter III of *Liber LXV*, in verses 17 through 20, the Adept cries:

> **Then I beheld myself compassed about with the Infinite Circle of Emerald that encloseth the Universe.**
> **O Snake of Emerald, Thou hast no time Past, no time To Come. Verily Thou art not.**
> **Thou art delicious beyond all taste and touch, Thou are not-to-be-beheld for glory, Thy voice is beyond the Speech and the Silence and the Speech therein, and Thy perfume is of pure ambergris, that is not weighed against the finest gold of the fine gold.**
> **Also Thy coils are of infinite range; the Heart that Thou dost encircle is an Universal Heart.**

The heart that is entwined is not *just* the heart of an Initiate, but the heart *of all mankind* – a **Universal Heart**, that is to say, the company of Heaven. The coils of the Emerald Snake are Infinite.

## Linea Viridis Gyrat Universa

This **Infinite Circle of Emerald** is the *linea viridis gyrat universa*, "The green line circles the universe."[2] Note the words in this verse that have initial Upper Case letters:

**"Infinite Circle of Emerald"; "Snake of Emerald"; "Past"; "To Come"; "Heart"; "Universal Heart."**

Likewise, all of the *second person pronouns* are in Upper Case: "**Thou**" and "**Thy**." This tells us that we are dealing with Hyper-Abyssic concepts. They transcend human Reason, and are beyond individual consciousness.

This symbol of the green line circling the universe is one of those mystical concepts that students will encounter occasionally in Qabalistic or magical books. Numerous contemporary authors mention it, rarely saying anything meaningful about it, and never giving its source, if they are even aware of it.

It is worthwhile to take a brief diversion here and investigate the history of the *linea viridis gyrat universa*. It is the history of the phrase, its origin and interpretations, that are vital to a real understanding of its true meaning, and how those early explanations impact the current use of the phrase.

---

2 Cf. also, *Liber LXV*, Chapter III, verses 1-2 where this "green line" is first introduced in this Holy Book.

The **Infinite Circle of Emerald that encloseth the Universe** mentioned in Chapter III of *Liber LXV* refers to a motif in the 36th Qabalistic axiom given by Johann Pistorius the Younger in his work *Artis Cabalisticæ hoc est Reconditæ Theologiæ* published in 1587:

*Figure F1 - Johann Pistorius the Younger*

> Quod dicitur à Cabalistis, quòd linea viridis girat vniuersum, conuenientissim dicitur ad conclusionem vltimam, quam diximus ex mente Porphyry.[3]

This axiom with a very brief commentary was published by Eliphas Levi in *La science des esprits* in 1865 e.v.

There, he translated the Latin to French as "La ligne verte circule autour de toutes choses." ("The green line circles about everything.")

Levi's brief commentary was,

> Les kabbalistes, dans leurs pantacles, représentent la couronne divine par une ligne verte qui entoure les autres figures. Le vert est l'alliance des deux couleurs principales du prisme, le jaune et le bleu: figures des Eloïm ou grandes puissances qui se résument et s'unissent en Dieu.

> The kabbalists depict the divine crown in their pantacles by means of a green line encircling the other figures. Green is the union of the two principal colours of the prism, yellow and blue: symbols of the Elohim, or great powers which are summed up and united in God.[4]

The source of Levi's Qabalistic assertion was not given, yet it was probably *Jean De Mons*:

> Ce qui semble estre designé par celuy qui en la vision de l'Evangiste est assis au milieu des sept chandeliers dorez, semblable au fils de l'homme, qui a les yeux comme la flãme du feu, qui est ceint d'une ceinture doree à l'endroit des mãmelles, à l'entour duquel il y a un Iris ou arcq resplẽdissant cõme l'Esmerade, qui est verte, laquelle couleur les Cabalistes ont grandement

---

3 Pistorius, *Artis Cabalisticæ hoc est Reconditæ Theologiæ (1587)*, p. 863. Translation, same as given below on page 197

4 *Science des Esprits (1865)*, p. 170. Translation by Matthew Andrews.

estimé, pource qu'ils ont creu qu'il y a une ligne verte qui meut & faict tourner tout l'univers, & que de sa seule proprieté & vertu depēd le mouvemēt de tous les orbes & Spheres celestes: Ceste ligne estāt cōme une supreme couronne (qu'aucuns d'eux pour ceste cause ont appellé Cheter Elion) dont premierement descendēt & à dextre & à senestre toutes les influences divines, laquelle puissance & vertu le Prophete Ieremie semble auoir appellé Royne du Ciel: Ayans ces anciens Hebreux voulu signifier par ceste ligne verte (ainsi que l'on a interpreté) l'Ame du monde, & principalement du premier mobile, c'est à dire, une vertu admirable & occulte du Createur, cause causante seule & premiere de la subsistāce de toute creature...

That which seems indicated by he who in the vision of the Evangelist is seated in the middle of the seven golden chandeliers, like the son of man, who has eyes like the flame of fire, who is girt with a golden belt in the place of the breasts, around whom there is an Iris or arc resplendent like Emerald, which is green, which colour the Cabalists greatly admired, for they believed that there is a green line which moves the whole universe and makes it turn, and from whose sole domain and virtue depends the movements of all the orbs and celestial Spheres: This line being like a supreme crown (for this reason, none of them called it Kether Elion) from which firstly descends, both on the right and on the left, all the divine influences, whose power and virtue the Prophet Jeremiah seems to have called Queen of the Sky: these ancient Hebrews having wanted to signify by this green line (so it was interpreted) the Soul of the world, and principally of the primum mobile, that is to say, an admirable and occult virtue of the Creator, sole causing cause, and first of the sustenance of all creation.[5]

Levi's brief translation of the axiom from Pistorius was later included by A.E. Waite in the revised and enlarged second edition of Eliphas Levi's *The Mysteries of Magic* in 1886 e.v.[6]

In the phrase *linea viridis gyrat universa*, the word *gyrat* is the verbal form of the noun *gȳrus*, "circle, circuit." It is derived from the Greek γῦρος, which means "a ring or a circle"[7] The verb *gyrat* implies motion, "to circle," "to wheel around," "to go around," whereas the nominal form *gȳrus* implies a static "circle" or "ring."[8]

5 Jean De Mons, *La sextessence diallactique et potentielle tirée par une nouvelle façon d'alambiquer, suivant les préceptes de la saincte magie et invocation de demons, (Paris, 1595)*, p. 300. Translation by Matthew Andrews.

6 Levi, *(trans. A.E. Waite), The Mysteries of Magic (1886)*, p. 133.

7 *LSJ*, p. 364a.

8 In *Appleton's Latin Dictionary of 1904* e.v., *gyrus* is defined as "a circular course" or *gyrum trahere*, that is "circular undulations" (of a snake), p. 245b.

The verbal form used in this phrase implies something in constant motion, that is to say, an ongoing process.

*Figure F2 - Giovanni Pico della Mirandola*

Pistorius was not the originator of this reference. He was quoting the Qabalistic "Conclusions" of Giovanni Pico della Mirandola (1463-1494 e.v.) which was published in1486 e.v.[9] Fortunately, these axioms were later reprinted in a volume of his complete works, *Opera Omnia Ioannis Pici Mirandulæ* (Basil 1557 e.v.).

It was fortunate because the original publication from 1486 e.v. was condemned by Pope Innocent VIII in 1487 e.v. in a Papal Bull,[10] the first instance of a printed book banned by the Roman Catholic Church. Nearly all copies were burned as a result.[11] Only two copies are known to exist; one in the Vatican Library, the other in the British Library.

In this work, Mirandola first mentioned the *cœlum lineam viridem* as the 7th axiom in *Conclusiones Cabalisticæ numero XLVII.*[12]

> 7. Cum dicit Salomon in oratione sua in libro regum, Exaudi o cœlum, per cœlum lineam uiridem debemus intelligere, quæ girat uniuersum.

> 7. When Solomon said in his prayer in the book of *Kings*, "Listen, O heaven," by heaven we should understand a green line which circles the universe.[13]

---

9 Mirandola, *Conclusiones Philosophicæ, Cabalisticæ et Theologicæ* (1486).

10 *Damnatio nonnullarum propositionum Ioannis Pici, cum in hibitione illas imprimendi ac legendi, sub-poena excommunicationis, Innocentius VIII. Dat. die 4 augusti 1487, pontif. anno III.* The Bull of interdiction had 8 Sections of condemnations. (Thomassetti & Cocquelines, *Bullarum Diplomatum et Privilegiorum Sanctorum Romanorum Pontificum Taurinensis Editio, Vol. 5 (1860)*, pp. 327-329).

11 Hanegraaf, *Esotericism and the Academy*, p. 54.

12 The full title of this section is, *Conclusiones Cabalisticæ numero XLVII, secundum secretam doctrinam sapientum Hebreorum Cabalistarum, quorum memoria sit semper in bonum* (*Opera Omnia Ioannis Pici, Mirandulæ*, pp. 80-81).

13 Probably a reference to *I Kings*, 8:32 (named *Regum Liber III* in the Vulgate edition of the *Bible*) which begins, *tu exaudies in cælo*, "then hear thou in heaven." The phrase is repeated several times up through verse 45. (*Biblia Sacra Vulgatæ Editionis Sixti V et Clementis VIII (1774)*, p. 253). Translation by Matthew Andrews.

In the same book, he then discussed the famous line in question as the 29th axiom in *Conclusiones Cabalisticæ numero LXXI.*[14]

> 29. Quod dicitur à Cabalistis, quod linea uiridis girat uniuersum, conuenientissimè dicitur ad conclusionem ultimam, quam diximus ex mente Porphirij.
>
> 29. That which is said by the Kabbalists, that a green line circles the universe, applies most suitably in reference to the final conclusion which we related from the thought of Porphyry.[15]

The *original* source for the *Linea viridis gyrat universa* is the חגיגה, *Chagigah*, one of the tractates comprising the מועד, *Moed* ("Festivals"), second of the six orders of the משנה, *Mishnah* ("repetitive study"), or collection of Jewish traditions in theתלמוד, *Talmud* ("instruction").[16]

Note the following passages:

> עשרה דברים נבראו ביום ראשין ואלי הן שמים וארץ
> תהו ובהו אור וחשך רוח ומים מדת יום ומדת לילה
>
> Ten things were created on the first day of Creation, and they are as follows: Heaven and earth; **tohu**[17] and **bohu;**[18] light and darkness; wind and water; the length of day and the length of night.
>
> תהו קו ירוק שמקיף את כל העולם כולו, שממנו יצא
> חשך שנאמר: (תהלים יח ,יב) ישת חשך סתרו סביבותיו

---

14 The full title of this section is, *Conclusiones Cabalistice numero LXXI, secundum opinionem propriam, ex ipsis Hebreorum sapientum fundamentis Cristianam religionem maxime confirmantes. (Opera Omnia Ioannis Pici, Mirandulæ, p. 110.)* These 72 'Conclusions' were reproduced by *Archangelus de Burgo Nuovo* in *Apologia Pro Defensione Doctrinæ Cabalæ*, (published in Bologna in 1564 e.v., prior to the publication by Pistorius in 1587 e.v.), which was a defense of Mirandola in response to an attack published in Rome in 1489 by *Pedro Garcia*, Bishop of Ussellus, addressed to *Pope Innocent VIII*: (*Petri Garsie Episcopi Usselen. ad sanctissimum patrem et dominum Innocentium papam VIII in determinationes magistrales contra conclusiones apologiales Ioannis Pici Mirandulani Concordie Comitis proemium*). The apologia by Archangelus de Burgo Nuovo was reprinted again in Basil in 1600 e.v.

15 Translation by Matthew Andrews.

16 *Gesenius*, pp. 457a, *Jastrow* 857a, 1672a. The Talmud = תלמוד בבלי, *Babalonian Talmud.*

17 תהו, tohu, "chaos" (Cf. *Gesenius*, p. 857a.)

18 בהו, bohu, "void" (*Gesenius*, p.104a-b.)

> **Tohu** is a green line that encompasses the entire world, and from which darkness emerged, as it is said (*Psalms* 18:12): "He made darkness His hiding place round about Him"[19]
>
> *The Babylonian Talmud*, חגיגה *(Chagigah), Chapter 2, 12a*[20]

It is likewise described this way in the *Midrash Konen*, a midrash composed in the 11th Century e.v.:[21]

> ותהום עומד על תהו ותהו דומה לקו ירוק ומקיף את כל
> העולם כולי כחוט
>
> And an abyss stands in Chaos (**tohu**) and Chaos (**tohu**) resembles a **green line encircling the world as a thread**."[22] (emphasis added)
>
> *Midrash Konen, 2:8*

The word תהו, *tohu* ("chaos") paired with בהו, *bohu* ("void"), is first encountered in the first chapter of *Genesis* in verses 1 and 2, describing the initial state of creation prior to the formation of day and night:

> בראשית ברא אלהים את השמים ואת הארץ:
> והארץ היתה תהו ובהו וחשך על־פני תהום
>
> In the beginning Elohim created the heavens and the earth: The earth was chaotic (תהו, *tohu*) and void (בהו, *bohu*) with darkness over the surface of the abyss.[23]

As expressed in the *Chagigah*, the tohu or "chaos," is called the "green line that encompasses the entire world," and by means of a partial quote of *Psalms* 18:12, is identified as the source of darkness. The complete verse from *Psalms* is more descriptive:

---

19 *Psalms* 18:12, JPS Hebrew-English *Tanakh*. In Christian Bibles, this verse is *Psalms* 18:11.

20 *Wiliam Davidson Talmud (Sefaria.org) Chagigah*. Chapter 2, 12a. Cf. Rodkinson, *The Babylonian Talmud*, Vol. 6, *Tract Hagiga*, p. 22, and Streane, *Translation of the Treatise Chagigah from the Babylonian Talmud*, pp. 58-59. (For Hebrew text, see *Masechet Chagiga min Talmud Bavli*, p. 41).

21 The first edition was in Gikatilla, ספר ארזי לבנון, *Sepher Arze Lebanon*, published in Venice in 1601 e.v.

22 Jellenik, בת המדרש, *Beth ha Midrash*, Vol. 2, מדרש כונן, *Midrash Konan*, author's translation.

23 בראשית, *Genesis* (1:1-2), *Tanakh*, JPS (1999 e.v.), author's translation. In the *King James* version of the *Bible*, Tohu is translated "formless." Cf. Daniel C. Matt, *The Zohar* Vol. 1, *Parashat Be-reshit* I:16a (Pritzker Edition), pp. 118-121 for additional interpretations of *Tohu wa-Bohu*.

ישת חשך סתרו סביבותיו סכתו חשכת־מים עבי שחקים׃

He made darkness his hiding place round about Him; His canopy dark waters, thick clouds of the sky.[24]

This hiding place of darkness, with a canopy of חשכת־מים, *dark waters* and עבי שחקים, *thick clouds of the sky*, indicates a heavy thunderstorm. Here is an obvious parallel with *Typhon*, the great Serpent of the ravening storm in *Liber LXV*, verse 1.

**Ah me! but the glory of ravening storm**
**Enswathes thee and wraps thee in frenzy of form.**

In this quote from Chapter III of *Liber LXV*, and evaluating the original sources of *linea viridis gyrat universa*, we have seen that this "green line" is tohu "chaos," and that tohu is none other than the **Snake of Emerald** entwined about the **Universal Heart.**[25] Originating prior to the moment of creation, in the *chaos* and *void*, this snake has **no time Past** nor **time To Come**. He is "not" (i.e. bohu, "void").

*Figure F3 - Ouroboros Surrounding Mount Meru & the Earth Carried by the World Tortoise*

This is a universal Archetype that has many varying representations in different cultures. Here is an illustration designed by a Brahman, showing the world tortoise bearing the earth and Mount Meru, surrounded by the same ouroboric snake – *linea viridis gyrat universa*.

Herein is also a reflection of the "orphic egg" emblem, which symbolized the cosmos surrounded by the serpent of the creative spirit. This Greek myth proclaimed that the universe was hatched from a cosmic egg. In this, we see the soul of the aspirant to the mysteries, and the serpent, the wisdom of the ages. The egg is Tiphereth, the Heart.

---

24 *Psalms* 18:12. In Christian Bibles, this is *Psalms* 18:11.

25 Note that אדם, Adam + חוה, Eve + נחש, Nehesh the serpent = 422, the value of קו ירוק, "green line," the definition of *Tohu* in the *Chagigah*. Of course the word משיח, *Messiah* could be substituted for נחש, *Nehesh*, and the numerical value would be the same.

# The Celestial Virgin

**28. My head is jewelled with twelve stars; My body is white as milk of the stars; it is bright with the blue of the abyss of stars invisible.**

In this verse, Adonai proclaimed that He is crowned with the zodiac, which is a circular, starry symbol of wholeness. The Holy Guardian Angel is vastly superior to the angelic hierarchies familiar to us from the Qabalah. He cannot be identified with a particular sign of the zodiac, for His nature is universal.

The number twelve is that of the Hebrew word הוא, *HVA*, which means, "He." It is a title of Kether, which is thereby identified with the zodiac, the "home of twelve stars."

*Fig. F4 - Ophis et Ovum Mundanum, Tyrionum*

Note that He says, **My head is jewelled with twelve stars**. The head corresponds to Kether, the Crown.

The overall image in Verse 28 of *Liber LXV* echoes that of the *woman clothed with the sun* from the *New Testament* book of *Revelation*, Chapter 12:

> Καὶ σημεῖον μέγα ὤφθη ἐν τῷ οὐρανῷ γυνὴ περιβεβλημένη τὸν ἥλιον καὶ ἡ σελήνη ὑποκάτω τῶν ποδῶν αὐτῆς καὶ ἐπὶ τῆς κεφαλῆς αὐτῆς στέφανος ἀστέρων δώδεκα·
>
> And a great Sign appeared in the heaven; a woman clothed with the sun, and the moon under her feet, and on her head a crown of twelve stars."[26]

It is interesting to note that in *Figure F5*, the representation of this symbol painted by artist J. Augustus Knapp for Manly Palmer Hall's *The Secret Teaching of All Ages*, he chose to depict the celestial virgin with the moon under her feet which in turn rests upon the orphic egg.

The hierarchy of the Roman Catholic Church appropriated this symbol and confounded it with their own perverted doctrine some time after 1615 e.v. when the feast of the *immaculate conception* was established.

26 *Revelation* 12:1.

The painting of the virgin Mary by Francisco Pacheco *(Figure F6)* is an example of the Catholic Church's approved iconography for the virgin of the immaculate conception.

This Archetypal figure described in *The Apocalypse* was never intended to be a representation of the virgin Mary. It is an unfortunate modern corruption appropriated to support a vile, despicable doctrine.

She is the celestial virgin, the virgin of all men, the heavenly harlot of all the world.

In *Liber VII*, Chapter I, verse 36 the Holy Guardian Angel is described as,

> **a beautiful thing, whiter than a woman in the column of this vibration.**

*Figure F5 - The Celestial Virgin with the Sun God in Her Arms*

And in the final chapter of *Liber LXV*, Verse 65, Adonai is described as follows:

> **He is like the Woman that jetteth out the milk of the stars from her paps...**

*Figure F6 - Immaculate Conception*

All of these symbols are intended to demonstrate the unlimited, all-encompassing character of the Angel, partaking of the unbounded nature of Nuit, the goddess of **Infinite Space and the Infinite Stars thereof,**[27] **- all pleasure and purple, and drunkenness of the innermost sense,**[28] with the secret Serpent flaming therein.

Now, continuing on to Verse 29, we will see that Adonai changed the subject from Himself.

27 *Liber CCXX*, I:22

28 *Liber CCXX*, I:61

# § G. NVNTIVS
# XXIX-XL

**29. I have found that which could not be found; I have found a vessel of quicksilver.**

NOTE CAREFULLY THE SPEAKER HERE. This was the Voice of Adonai speaking about his Servant, V.V.V.V.V., *not* His servant Aleister Crowley. How do we know that the subject is V.V.V.V.V. and not Aleister Crowley himself? This is clear from the verse which immediately follows, where Crowley is called "**thy servant**."

Quicksilver is another name for *Mercury*, the only metal which is liquid under normal temperature and pressure. In Greek it was called ὑδράργυρος, which means, "watery silver."[1]

Although it is a metal, it cannot take permanent shape, thus it represents continual change and fluidity of form. In contrast to most of us who are prone to rigidity of thought and torpidity in form, *Adonai* praised V.V.V.V.V. whom he recognized as a vessel capable of embodying his presence without limitation or restriction.

Each of us are the sacred vessel which we are to prepare for the indwelling of God. From our perspective, we are the Cup of Reception. Yet, none of us, no matter how receptive we are, or how open we are for internal change, deserve to be called "**a vessel of quicksilver**." Even the Prophet himself, although he was the Magus of the Aeon, which is attributed to Mercury, and even though he manifested V.V.V.V.V., was still bound by the limitations of physical incarnation. We will see a description of this limitation later, in Verse 44.

From the words of Adonai it is apparent that a Servant with such characteristics is rare and precious. It suggests to us that He had been in quest of one who could fulfill the demands of such a requirement. He found it in V.V.V.V.V.

1 Cf. *LSJ*, p. 1844b.

## Admonition to the Magister

**30. Thou shalt instruct thy servant in his ways, thou shalt speak often with him.**

**31. (The scribe looketh upwards and crieth) Amen! Thou hast spoken it, Lord God!**

The Magister, V.V.V.V.V., was admonished by Adonai that he should communicate frequently with the Adept and teach him that which the Adonai teaches unto the Magister. The scribe of course heard this Instruction to the Magister and he raised his voice to affirm that he would be a willing recipient of such instruction.[2]

## Adonai and V.V.V.V.V. in the World of Humankind

**32. Further Adonai spake unto V.V.V.V.V. and said: Let us take our delight in the multitude of men!**

**33. Let us shape unto ourselves a boat of mother-of-pearl from them, that we may ride upon the river of Amrit!**

Adonai spoke again unto the Magister V.V.V.V.V.. Examine carefully what he said.

Adonai suggested that He and V.V.V.V.V. "**take delight**" in the multitude of men. He was speaking of the mystery of manifestation – "**in the**

---

2 In his short commentary to this verse of *Liber LXV*, Crowley wrote: "Seems an injunction to the Holy Guardian Angel to keep in close touch with the Adept." Marcello Motta, in his commentary to this verse, contradicted Crowley: "Not so: It is an injunction to the Adept to keep in close touch with the "scribe" - his physical instrument of manifestation." (Motta, *Liber LXV Commented*, p. 58) Motta was dead wrong. He did not clearly understand the difference between the scribe, the Adept, and the Magister V.V.V.V.V. Crowley's comment itself seems to have been made in haste, for the line of communication in this verse is clearly indicated by *Liber LXV* itself. The speaker was Adonai, addressing V.V.V.V.V., who was admonished to instruct His servant (the Adept) and speak often with him. The scribe, in turn, is the servant of the Adept. Our normal human consciousness (the scribe) is the servant of our Adept Consciousness. Since the scribe is the one recording this conversation, he personally replied to Adonai, speaking for himself, as well as for the Adept whom he served. The scribe was doubtless pleased that Adonai admonished V.V.V.V.V. to speak often with his Adept Self for he too benefits from that communication. That the speaker in this Verse is Adonai addressing V.V.V.V.V. is proved by Verse 32 immediately following: "**Further** Adonai spake unto V.V.V.V.V. and said…" (Emphasis added.)

**multitude of men.**" This should not be confused with the mysteries of incarnation or reincarnation. It is a mystery of direct *Spiritual Communication*, in which V.V.V.V.V. worked through the Magister, who in turn communicated to the Adept, who was incarnated as the scribe.

It may be seen from this verse that such manifestation among humankind was not considered by Adonai to be an unseemly or undesirable option. He found it delightful to mingle with the people of the earth.

Why? Because the Angel is also continually learning and growing, as is the Master of the Temple. And he has promises to keep. One might even possibly assume that these things are part of an ongoing experiment, where Adonai's own knowledge of the "old grey land" is augmented.

Let us examine carefully the wording of the second sentence of verse 33:

> **"Let us shape unto ourselves a boat of mother-of-pearl *from them* that we may ride upon the river of Amrit!"** (Emphasis added.)

The river of *Amrit* is, in one sense, the अमृत नदी, *amṛta naḍī*, which is Sanskrit for "river of immortality."[3] The river of Amrit is the sacred dew of immortality that may flow in the **सुषुम्णा नाडी**, *suṣumṇā naḍī*, when the **कुण्डलिनी**, *kuṇḍalinī*, has risen, piercing the *cakras* and opening the **सहस्रार चक्र**, *sahasrāra cakra*, the thousand-petalled lotus.[4] It is a tiny drop of divine nectar that may unite man and God in *samādhi*. This is a microcosm of the River Amrit that flows invisibly through the world in which humankind is incarnated.

Thus, in order for Adonai and the Magister to "**ride**" upon this river of Amrit, the Magister must be incarnate in the *flesh*. Hence, Adonai told V.V.V.V.V. that they would make the boat **from them**, that is, *from the flesh of mankind*. He took flesh first in the form of the Adept, Frater O.M.,[5] who was served by his scribe, Frater Perdurabo – Aleister Crowley.

So, in this sense, the river here signified the River of Life, bound eternally to the wheel of **संसार**, *saṃsāra*, the Wheel of Necessity.[6] But by an act of will,

---

3 अमृत, *amṛta*, 'immortal, नदी, *naḍī*, "river." (*Monier-Williamsm*, pp. 82b & 526a).

4 See above, §A, and *Figure A14*.

5 It was necessary that Frater O.M. successfully cross the Abyss and attain the Grade of *Magister Templi* and be cast out into the Sephira of Chesed in order to fully perfect this union with V.V.V.V.V. The initial contact had already been made by Frater Perdurabo when he attained to the Grade of *Adeptus Minor Within*, taking the Motto *Christeos Luciftias*. Upon attaining to Magister Templi, he assumed a Motto with the initials V.V.V.V.V. to affirm this union.

6 संसार, *saṃsāra*, "wandering through, transmigration" (*Ibid.*, p. 1119b-c). In Hinduism, it signifies the wheel of reincarnations.

V.V.V.V.V. was able to manifest in the world of humankind, through His chosen recipient, and ride upon this eternal river.

In the second chapter of *Liber LXV*, in verse 7, we see the river again:

> **Moreover I beheld a vision of a river. There was a little boat thereon; and in it under purple sails was a golden woman, an image of Asi wrought in finest gold. Also the river was of blood, and the boat of shining steel.**

*Figure G1 - Mother of Pearl*

Here, the river is clearly defined as *a river of blood*, the river that is the river of consciousness for one incarnate in the flesh.

Mother-of-pearl is a substance called nacre, which is found inside oyster shells. It is very strong and iridescent in colour. It is important to note that the Oyster Shell is that which harbors the Pearl, and the Pearl itself is an emblem of the Master of the Temple. Crowley wrote:

> The Pearl is referred to Binah on account of its being the typical stone of the sea. It is formed by concentric spheres of hard brilliant substance, the centre being a particle of dust. Thus, that dust which is all that remains of the Exempt Adept after he has crossed the Abyss, is gradually surrounded by sphere after sphere of shining splendour, so that he becomes a fitting ornament for the bosom of the Great Mother.[7]

In Chapter 3 of *The Book of Lies*, called *The Oyster*, the oyster is given as a symbol of the Great Mother Binah. Therein, it is written:

> The Brothers of A∴ A∴ are one with the Mother of the Child. The Many is as adorable to the One as the One is to the Many.

This chapter in *The Book of Lies* emphasizes the point that Adonai did not find the world of humankind undesirable. We are as adorable to the One, that is the Angel, as the One is to us.

It is highly significant to realize that verses 32 and 33 of Chapter I of *Liber LXV* refer to a *previous event in time*, one that took place immediately prior to the Adeptship of Aleister Crowley.

---

7 Crowley, *Liber 777*, p. 102 (*Notes to Column XL, Precious Stones*).

We are granted a look at the moment when the Holy Guardian Angel and the Master that revealed Himself to Aleister Crowley discussed returning to the earth again, to take their delight in the multitude of men. And part of that delight was to bring to the earth the Law of Thelema. We read of this also in *Liber Porta Lucis*:

> **I behold a small dark orb, wheeling in an abyss of infinite space. It is minute among a myriad vast ones, dark amid a myriad bright ones. I who comprehend in myself all the vast and the minute, all the bright and the dark, have mitigated the brilliance of mine unutterable splendour, sending forth V.V.V.V.V. as a ray of my light, as a messenger unto that small dark orb.**[8]

The Lord of the Aeon sent V.V.V.V.V. into the world as His messenger, His chosen Angel, who bore a mandate of the ages. Despite the magnificence and glory of the Magistry of V.V.V.V.V., He was described as *a single ray of light*, in comparison to Adonai Himself, and His "**unutterable splendour**." This should give us all pause, so that with genuine humility, we may reflect upon our own position in this exalted Hierarchy. We are the inhabitants of that "**small dark orb**", the benefactors of that single ray of light. Would that we be worthy of it.

## The Unfading Flower

> **34. Thou seest yon petal of amaranth, blown by the wind from the low sweet brows of Hathor?**
> **(The Magister saw it and rejoiced in the beauty of it.) Listen!**
> **35. (From a certain world came an infinite wail.)**
> **36. That falling petal seemed to the little ones a wave to engulph their continent.**

Suddenly, Adonai directed the attention of V.V.V.V.V. (here called the "**Magister**") to a distant, single petal of **amaranth**, floating upon the breeze. The name of the plant amaranth is derived from the Greek ἀμάραντος, which means "unfading flower."[9] This flower signifies that which is imperishable, thus symbolizing eternity.

---

8 *Liber Porta Lucis*, 1-2.

9 *LSJ*, p. 77a.

In Greece, as well as many other places, the variety of amaranth that grows is the *amaranthus viridis*, or "green amaranth." Here is another, and very specific, example of the *benedicta viriditis*, or "blessed greenness" discussed previously in verse 5.

It was blown by the wind, that is to say, by the *spirit*, from the "**low sweet brows of Hathor**".

*Hathor* bore the title , *nbt ỉmntt*, *Mistress of the West*, and she was a goddess of love, sex, art, music, and significantly, *childbirth*. Her name in ancient Egyptian , *ḥwt-ḥrw*, literally means, "house of Horus."[10] In the Sahidic dialect of Coptic, her name was written **ϩⲁⲑⲱⲣ**, *Hathōr*; in the Bohairic dialect it was **ⲁⲑⲱⲣ**, *Athōr*. Among the Greeks her name was written 'Αθῦρ.[11] In the Hermetic Order of the Golden Dawn, her name was "magically" spelled as **ⲁϩⲁⲑⲱⲱⲣ** (*Ahathōōr*), a tradition which Crowley continued.[12] This was the divine name the Golden Dawn assigned to the Invisible Station of the Kerub of Air.[13] Prefacing her historic name with an additional Coptic Alpha **ⲁ**, was said to emphasize the *Airy* nature of the name, since **ⲁ** = Hebrew **א**, attributed to △, the element Air. The latter part of this magical name, **ϩⲁⲑⲱⲱⲣ**, is actually the plural form of the Sahidic **ϩⲁⲑⲱⲣ** that corresponds to her name as found in the Egyptian , *tꜣ sfḫt ḥwt-ḥrwyw, the seven Hathors.*[14] The final portion of that name, **ϩⲱⲱⲣ**, is derived from another "magical" spelling used by the Golden Dawn, for the name *Hōōr* (i.e. *Horus*).[15] The name *Horus* in Coptic is actually **ϩⲟⲣ**, *Hor*,

*Figure G2 - Amaranthus Viridis*

*Figure G3 - The Egyptian Goddess Hathor*

10 *Allen 524b*, Wilkinson, *The Complete Gods and Goddesses of Ancient Egypt*, pp. 139-145. Sometimes translated "mansion of Horus" or even "enclosure of Horus" (*Allen* § *3.6.*)

11 *Vicichl*, p. 291a.

12 It occurs in *Liber LXV*, IV:23 and the adorations in *Liber* CCXX, III:38, paraphrased from the Stele of Revealing.

13 Regardie, *The Golden Dawn (1986 e.v.)*, p. 353.

14 *Vycichl*, p. 291b. The Seven Hathor goddesses, who were said to be present at the birth of children, signified "fate." They were worshipped in seven cities in Egypt and corresponded to the star cluster of the *Pleiades* ("the seven sisters") in the constellation of *Taurus.*

15 Regardie, *The Golden Dawn*, p. 352.

derived from the Egyptian , *ḥrw.*[16]

The phrase, "**the low sweet brows of Hathor**" is curious. The goddess is most commonly depicted as a cow, or with the head of a cow, and her brow carries her horns, which suggest the crescent Moon.[17] This crescent embraces the emblem of , *rʿ*, the Sun god, to whom she gave birth each day at dawn. At sunset, it was said that *Ra* would reenter her body in the West, journey through the night of the Duat, and be reborn each morning in the East. During this eternal journey, Ra travelled on the great eternal river that flowed from East to West, through the Day and through the Night. This too was a symbol of the River of Life and the journey of all humankind, from Birth to Death and eventually to Rebirth.

There is a historical reference to the brow of Hathor used as something of a poetic and symbolic device, other than a literal reference. It occurs on the reverse side of a stela created for a craftsman from Thebes named , *ỉpwy*, *Ipuy* (18th Dynasty)[18] in which he recounted a dream of Hathor. The stela is badly damaged, but the pertinent passage is essentially intact.

*sḏm.n=st ỉt=st ỉmn sprtw=st nb ḥtp [............]*

*Her father Atum listens to all her petitions peacefully [............]*

*[... wbJn=f ẖr ntrw=st ỉr=f ḫsbdw n šnw=s*

*[...] when he [rises] through her beauty. He created lapis lazuli for her hair,*

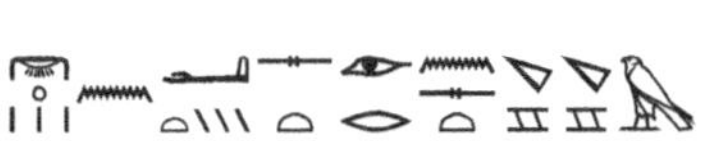

*nbw n ʿtw ỉr.n=st ỉdby ḥrw*

*gold for her arms. The Two Banks of Horus were created for her*

---

16 The early Egyptian form , *ḥrw*, demonstrates the graphic transposition employed in the spelling of the name. We know that it was actually vocalized from *ḥwr*, with the semi-vowel preceding the final consonant. Hence the Coptic ϩⲟⲣ and the Greek ῟Ωρος. (See *Vycichl*, p. 307b.)

17 In andromorphic form, Hathor's crown has the Horns mounted on a low modius atop her head, often surmounting the vulture headdress and tripartite wig.

18 In the *Kunsthistorisches Museum* in Wien, Austria, Inventory No. 8390.

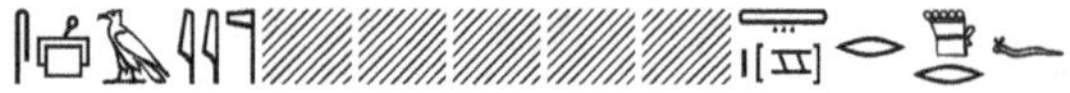

*sꜣy nṯr … … … … … … tꜣ r ḏr=f*

*so that the god may prepare [............]   the land to its limit*

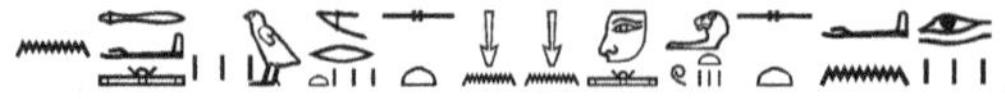

*n ꜥꜣw mrwt=st snsn ḥnt ḥꜣwty=st ꜥnw*

*for the magnitude of her love. Her brow shall bind with the beauty*

*n ḥr=f mry [............ ]*

*of his beloved face [............]"*[19]

The latter portion of the inscription, "Her brow shall bind with the beauty of his beloved face," means that the crescent-shaped Horns upon her brow[20] are united with the Solar Disc,  , which symbolizes the Moon ☽ united with the Sun ☉, another form of our modern symbol ◉, the Sun in the arms of the Moon, *Kteis* under *Phallos*, or love under Will.[21]

In this verse, the falling petal of amaranth represents the Law of Thelema, brought by V.V.V.V.V. as the Messiah of the New Aeon, symbolically born from the brows of Hathor, the "house of Horus," from an act of Divine Unity ◉, as a flower of eternity, an emissary of the Holy Ones to bring the Law of Thelema to humankind. It was **"blown by the wind"** (the Spirit) from **"the low sweet brows of Hathor"** in the West, carried through the Night (NOX) and was born into the world in the East, the place of birth and life:

---

19 Stela of *Ipuy*, Reverse, lines 17-19. Hieroglyphic text in Satzinger, *Zwei Wiener Objekte mit bemerkenswerten Inschriften*, in *Mélanges Gamal Eddin Mokhtar*, p. 253.

20 In Egyptian, one of the words for "brow" is 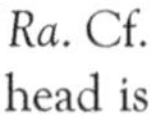 , *wpt*. This same word can also mean "horns." *CDME*, p. 73.

21 Traditionally, *Hathor* was also described as the daughter of *Ra*, emerging from his brow as a uraeus serpent. She is also described as the eye of *Ra*. Cf. B. Lesko, *The Great Goddesses of Egypt*, p. 120 The Archetype of birth from the brow or head is recounted in the myths of the Greek goddess *Athena*, who was said to have been born from the head of Ζεύς, *Zeus*, and the Hindu goddess काली, *Kālī*, was born from the brow of दुर्गा, *Durgā*, the mother goddess. See Smith, *Dictionary of Greek and Roman Biography and Mythology*, Vol. 1, pp. 397-398 and Devadatta *Kālī*, देवीमाहात्म्यम्, *In Praise of the Goddess, The Devīmāhātmya and Its Meaning*, 7.6.

**Ra-Hoor-Khuit hath taken his seat in the East at the Equinox of the Gods; and let Asar be with Isa, who also are one. But they are not of me. Let Asar be the adorant, Isa the sufferer; Hoor in his secret name and splendour is the Lord initiating.**

*Liber AL, III:49*

As we see from this verse, and from the previous discussion of *Liber Tzaddi*, Verses 0-3, His appearance was likened unto that of a hawk, the image of Horus. That appearance was the birth of a new child, and that child was the New Aeon.

**In the name of the Lord of Initiation, Amen.**
**I fly and I alight as an hawk: of mother-of-emerald are my mighty-sweeping wings.**
**I swoop down upon the black earth; and it gladdens into green at my coming. Children of Earth! rejoice! rejoice exceedingly; for your salvation is at hand.**

*Liber Tzaddi, 0-2*

This same event is described also in *Liber Porta Lucis*, verses 1-5, with an additional description of its immediate result:

**I behold a small dark orb, wheeling in an abyss of infinite space. It is minute among a myriad vast ones, dark amid a myriad bright ones.**
**I who comprehend in myself all the vast and the minute, all the bright and the dark, have mitigated the brilliance of mine unutterable splendour, sending forth V.V.V.V.V. as a ray of my light, as a messenger unto that small dark orb.**
**Then V.V.V.V.V. taketh up the word, and sayeth:**
**Men and women of the Earth, to you am I come from the Ages beyond the Ages, from the Space beyond your vision; and I bring to you these words.**
**But they heard him not, for they were not ready to receive them.**

Later, in *Liber LXV*, Chapter V, verses 1-3, there is yet another description with parallels to those of *Liber Porta Lucis* and *Liber LXV* Chapter I:

> **Ah! my Lord Adonai, that dalliest with the Magister in the Treasure-House of Pearls, let me listen to the echo of your kisses.**
> **Is not the starry heaven shaken as a leaf at the tremulous rapture of your love? Am not I the flying spark of light whirled away by the great wind of your perfection?**
> **Yea, cried the Holy One, and from Thy spark will I the Lord kindle a great light; I will burn through the grey city in the old and desolate land; I will cleanse it from its great impurity.**

In *Liber AL*, the Hierophant of the New Aeon is Ra-Hoor-Khuit, a form of Horus. The Lord of Initiation is declared to be *Hoor in his secret name and splendour.* In *Liber Tzaddi*, in the name of the Lord of Initiation, He is compared to a hawk with sweeping wings of mother-of-emerald. In *Liber Porta Lucis*, He is compared to a ray of the light of the Lord of the Aeon. In the fifth chapter of *Liber LXV*, he is described as a spark of the Lord's light carried upon the great wind, that same wind described in *Liber LXV*, I:34 that carried the flower petal, symbolic of eternity, to a world not yet ready to undergo the birth pangs of a New Age. This "**wind**" is the eternal Spirit of Divine Inspiration and presence.

The Magister beheld the beautiful flower petal floating on that wind and rejoiced in its beauty. But then He heard the voice of Adonai again, who interrupted his reverie, saying, "**Listen!**" Then from a "**certain world**" they heard an "**infinite wail**", a vast cry of anguish.

The word "**infinite**" is important here. In this place, it means something that cannot be measured or counted. It was a worldwide cry of agony. Note carefully the parallel words of *Liber LXV*, Chapter V, verses 30-33:

> **Also Adonai spake unto V.V.V.V.V. saying: O my little one, my tender one, my amorous one, my gazelle, my beautiful, my boy, let us fill up the pillar of the Infinite with an infinite kiss!**
> **So that the stable was shaken and the unstable became still.**
> **They that beheld it cried with a formidable affright: The end of things is come upon us.**
> **And it was even so.**

This "**certain world**" is the world of **עשיה**, *Assiah*,[22] the world of humankind. The Messiah[23] came and brought the Law of Thelema gently to the earth like a soft petal of amaranth blown by the wind. He was a ray of the light of the

---

22 *See* § A. *EXORDIUM*.

23 Students are here reminded that the word "Messiah" means "Anointed One," and has nothing whatsoever to do with Christian connotations. They should not "fret" over the word.

Lord of the Aeon, a flying spark upon the wind of Adonai's perfection – that is, the perfected *spirit of Adonai.* Yet, the Word that he articulated was accompanied by the birth pangs of a New Aeon. In *Liber VII*, Chapter IV, verse 44, the sound of that Voice is described:

**This is the voice which shook the earth.**

The stability of the old Aeon of Osiris was shattered and began to crumble immediately as we see in those verses from *Liber LXV*, Chapter V, verses 30-33 quoted above.

## Burden of the Servant Aleister Crowley

**37. So they will reproach thy servant, saying: Who hath set thee to save us?**
**38. He will be sore distressed.**

Returning to Chapter One of *Liber LXV*, Verse 37, we see it prophesied that the people of the old grey land, the followers of the doctrines of the Old Aeon, would reproach the servant Aleister Crowley.[24] This came to pass.

As every avatar who preceded him, he heard the people of the Old Aeon say, "Why should we listen to you? Who made you the savior?" And it depressed him.

Now, V.V.V.V.V. experienced no distress over this. He is beyond the frailty of such human emotions. But Aleister Crowley the man, despite all of his bluster, leg-pulling and jousting with wind-mills, cared deeply about the spiritual development of humankind. Being called the "wickedest man in the world," being branded a "Satanist," an advocate of "child sacrifice" and all the rest of the nonsense, caused him great distress.

In one sense, this is just another example of that cynical question: Can anything good come from Nazareth? It is recounted in the *New Testament* that when Jesus began his ministry, some of his first followers were excited by his message, and wanted to share that excitement with their friends.

---

24 The Practicus of A∴A∴ should pay close attention to the construction of the sentence, "Who hath set thee to save us?" and the unusual use of the word "set" in this place.

ἦν δὲ ὁ Φίλιππος ἀπὸ Βηθσαϊδά, ἐκ τῆς πόλεως Ἀνδρέου καὶ Πέτρου. Εὑρίσκει Φίλιππος τὸν Ναθαναὴλ καὶ λέγει αὐτῷ. Ὃν ἔγραψεν Μωσῆς ἐν τῷ νόμῳ καὶ οἱ προφῆται εὑρήκαμεν, Ἰησοῦν τὸν υἱὸν τοῦ Ἰωσὴφ τὸν ἀπὸ Ναζαρέτ.καὶ εἶπεν αὐτῷ Ναθαναήλ, Ἐκ Ναζαρὲτ δύναταί τι ἀγαθὸν εἶναι; λέγει αὐτῷ Φίλιππος, Ἔρχου καὶ ἴδε.

Now Phillip was from Bethsaida, the city of Andrew and Peter. Phillip found Nathanial and said unto him, 'We have found him of whom Moses wrote about in the Law and the Prophets – Jesus, the son of Joseph, from Nazareth. And Nathanial said unto him, 'Can anything good be from Nazareth?" Phillip said unto him, "Come and see."[25]

Later, when Jesus was in his own country and began to teach in the synagogue, his kinsmen were offended at his words because they knew him only as a carpenter, the son of Mary. Jesus responded to them,

ἔλεγεν δὲ αὐτοῖς ὁ Ἰησοῦς, Ὅτι οὐκ ἔστιν προφήτης ἄτιμος, εἰ μὴ ἐν τῇ πατρίδι αὐτοῦ καὶ ἐν τοῖς συγγενέσιν καὶ ἐν τῇ οἰκίᾳ αὐτοῦ.

A prophet is not dishonored except in his hometown, among his relatives, and in his house.[26]

This example, using the myth of Jesus, is just to emphasize the problem that so many Holy and Just men and women have faced over the centuries. Why should we listen to this "nobody from nowhere?" And there is a bit of the old-fashioned proverb, "familiarity breeds contempt." There have been numerous times in my life when I encountered this type of skepticism or outright rejection when I mentioned that Aleister Crowley was the Prophet of the New Aeon or even sought out his books.

Once, in California in 1970 e.v., I was thrown out of a book store by the owner because I asked her for a copy of *The Book of the Law*. "That evil man? That drug addict? If you are a follower of Aleister Crowley, then you are as bad as he was! Get out of my store and never come back!"

Years later, I would think about this event, and recall the words of *Liber LXV*, I:22, "**Happy are they that praise thee; for they see thee with Mine eyes.**"

---

25 *John* 1:44-46.

26 *Mark* 6:4. This text is the oldest of the four Gospels, hence it is quoted here. See *Book IV, Part IV*, p. 421 where Crowley quoted the account of this event from the King James translation of *Matthew* 13:55-57 in relation to V.V.V.V.V..

# The Boat of Mother-of-Pearl and the Yew-Groves of Yama

**39. All they understand not that thou and I are fashioning a boat of mother-of-pearl. We will sail down the river of Amrit even to the yew-groves of Yama, where we may rejoice exceedingly.**

**40. The joy of men shall be our silver gleam, their woe our blue gleam – all in the mother-of-pearl.**

Adonai explained to V.V.V.V.V. that the world would not understand their mission, and of course, the scribe Crowley hearing this message, understood that it applied to him as well. The world at large would not see the plan that would unfold as the New Aeon. The limited faculties of the populace were unable to comprehend the designs of the Supreme Chiefs. Adonai and V.V.V.V.V., following their *pure will*, were symbolically sailing down the river of immortality, in a boat of mother-of-pearl, unto the yew-groves of *Yama*.

Let us examine these symbols carefully.

The boat wherein they travel is of **mother-of-pearl**. Mother-of-pearl is the natural opalescent material which comprises the Pearl, a symbol of Binah. It is incredibly strong, and it is iridescent. It is the iridescence that reflects different colours depending on the angle at which it is viewed. This is a vitally important clue. Adonai told us at the very beginning of this chapter in verse number 3 (the number of Binah), "**For the colours are many, but the light is one.**"

The vessel of the Masters sailed from the Great Sea of Binah, that they might transmit the light and word of Truth unto humankind.

We must remember that the colours we behold are but *reflections* in the mother-of-pearl, and the words we hear are but the *echoes* of the kisses of Adonai, as described in *Liber LXV*, V:1:

> **Ah! my Lord Adonai, that dalliest with the Magister in the Treasure-House of Pearls, let me listen to the echo of your kisses.**[27]

---

27 The "Treasure-House of Pearls" refers to دار الجلال , *Dār al-Jalāl*, "House of Glory," one of the Seven Heavens of the Arabs, which is said to be made of Pearls. See *Liber 777, Columns CXXVII and CXXVIII*, where *Dār al-Jalāl* is attributed to the Supernal Triad of Kether, Chokmah and Binah. الجلال , *al-Jalāl*, "the Glorious," is a Sufi term that expresses the state of God beyond the world of Reason. (Hughes, *A Dictionary of Islam*, p. 225).

*Figure G4 - Yew Trees in a Graveyard*

The **Yew** is an ancient tree revered by mankind throughout history. Evidence of the existence of the Yew tree may be found in fossils of the Jurassic period, which dates back 160,000,000 years.[28] The Yew is traditionally a sacred tree in numerous cultures. Yew groves were planted by Druids to create sacred conventicles.

Old church yards and graveyards in England, Ireland and France were filled with Yew trees.

The Yew is called "the death tree," because almost every part of it is poisonous: the seed, the wood, the bark and the nettles.[29] The only part of the tree that is not poisonous is the red berry that surrounds the seed.[30]

In days past, Yews were planted in these old churchyards simply to keep the common folk from grazing their cattle there! Apparently, it worked very well.

Alfred Lord Tennyson drew upon the symbolism of the Yew in Part II of his famous poem, *In Memoriam A.H.H.*:

Old Yew, which graspest at the stones
    That name the underlying dead,
    Thy fibres net the dreamless head,
Thy roots are wrapt about the bones.
The seasons bring the flower again,
    And bring the firstling to the flock;
    And in the dusk of thee, the clock
Beats out the little lives of men.

O not for thee the glow, the bloom,
    Who changest not in any gale,
    Nor branding summer suns avail
To touch thy thousand years of gloom:
And gazing on thee, sullen tree,
    Sick for thy stubborn hardihood,
    I seem to fail from out my blood
And grow incorporate into thee.[31]

---

28 Chong Dong, *Middle-Late Jurassic fossils from northeastern China reveal morphological stasis in the catkin-yew,* p. 1765-1766.

29 Cf. Amory & Emerson, *Wharton and Stille's Medical Jurisprudence,* Vol. 2 Poisons, Taxus Baccata (Yew), p. 546.

30 Lowe, *The Yew Trees of Great Britain and Ireland,* pp. 136-153.

31 Tennyson, *In Memoriam A.H.H. Obit* MDCCCXXXIII. (Thackery, *The Complete Poetical Works of Alfred, Lord Tennyson* (1884), p. 105. This poem was a memorial written for the British Poet Arthur Henry Hallam, a close friend of Tennyson who died suddenly at age 22.

*Figure G5 - The Angel of Death Points the Way to the Stone of the Philosophers*

The wood of a Yew is very strong. Anciently it was used to manufacture long-bows.[32] The same tree served to make poison for poison-tipped arrows.[33]

Recall how The Holy Guardian Angel compared Himself to poisonous substances in *Liber LXV*, Chapter I, Verses 13-17. This is another example of that type of symbolism - beautiful, strong, utilitarian, and a deadly poison.

It should be remembered that the Holy Guardian Angel is also the Angel of Death: "For thou wilt find a life which is as Death: or a Death which should be infinite."[34]

He leads the Way to the Fifty Gates of Binah, and the Name of every Gate is Death.

## Yama

Y*ama* refers to यम, *Yama*, the Hindu god of death.[35] In the mythology of the Vedas, Yama was the first human being who died and found the way to the celestial abodes.[36] As a result, he became the ruler of the dead.

According to Post-vedic mythology, Yama is the judge and punisher of the dead, and is thus called धर्मराज, *dharmarāja*, ("just or righteous king"[37]) or धर्म, *dharma* ("that which is established or firm, law, righteous, just.")[38]

*Figure G6 - यम, Yama, the Hindu God of Death*

32 Lowe, *The Yew Trees of Great Britain and Ireland*, Chapter 9, passim.

33 Pliny, *Historia Naturalis*, XVI.20.

34 *The Vision & the Voice*, 30th Æthyr.

35 Sometimes also called यमराज, *Yamarāja*.

36 *Ṛgveda*, Hymn 33, "The Funeral Hymn." See Doniger, *The Rig Veda: An Anthology: One Hundred and Eight Hymns*, pp. 42-46.

37 *Monier-Williams*, p.511c.

38 *Ibid.*, p.510c. Corresponds to the Egyptian word , *m3ʿt, maat* (*CDME*, p.101).

*Figure G7 - Yama Turning the Wheel of Life*

As the lord of the underworld, he is the equivalent of the Greek ᾞδης, *Hades* or Πλούτων, *Pluto.*[39]

He is commonly shown as the one who governs and turns the wheel of life to which all humankind is bound by कर्म, *karma.*[40]

Sailing to the yew groves of Yama, the sacred *conventiculum* of धर्म, *dharma*, is a journey to the place of the Lord of Death, the place of the Master of Illusion and The Lord of the Wheel of Life.

It is a place sacred to the Lord of the Aeon.

The god Yama is dedicated to maintaining harmony and balance, essential characteristics of Tiphereth.

## Silver Gleam and Blue Gleam

39. All they understand not that thou and I are fashioning a boat of mother-of-pearl. We will sail down the river of Amrit even to the yew-groves of Yama, where we may rejoice exceedingly.

**40. The joy of men shall be our silver gleam, their woe our blue gleam - all in the mother-of-pearl.**

Emotional states of humankind are but pale reflections of reality. We are urged by our doctrine not to care for fools of men with their woes, which are balanced by weak joys, for they feel little, because they are but reflections.[41]

The creation of the world is division for love's sake, for the chance of union. The pain of division is really as nothing, but the joy of dissolution is all.[42]

So it was seen by Adonai and V.V.V.V.V., as but glimmers of **silver** or **blue** in the mother-of- pearl, the boat whereby they sailed upon the river of Amrit.

---

39 *Monier-Williams*, p. 846a.

40 कर्मन *karman*, "product, result, effect" (i.e. that which has been made). Commonly and erroneously called "fate." Cf. *Monier-Williams*, p. 258b.

41 See *Liber AL*, I:31.

42 See *Liber AL*, I:29-30.

But why is the joy of men their "**silver gleam**"? And why is the woe of men their "**blue gleam**"? Remember, nothing in a Class A Holy Book is without meaning.

A brief digression will be necessary here for us to understand the meaning of these things. We need to briefly examine one of the fundamentals of Qabalistic doctrine: the Four Worlds.

In accordance with the Holy Name יהוה, which we call the *Tetragrammaton*, the four-lettered Name of God, the universe was said to have been created in four worlds or divisions, each corresponding to a letter of that divine name.

The first is the world of אצילות, *Atziluth*, the world of "emanations." It corresponds to י *Yod* of *Tetragrammaton*.

The second is the world of בריאה, *Beriah*, the world of "creation." It corresponds to ה *Heh Prima* of *Tetragrammaton*.

The third is the world of יצירה, *Yetzirah*, the world of "formation." It corresponds to ו *Vau* of *Tetragrammaton*.

The fourth and final one is the World of עשיה, *Assiah*, the world of "action." It corresponds to ה *Heh Final* of *Tetragrammaton*.

| | | | |
|---|---|---|---|
| World of *Atziluth*<br>"Emanations" | אצילות | 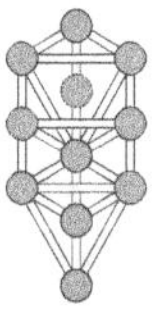 | י of יהוה |
| World of *Beriah*<br>"Creation" | בריאה | 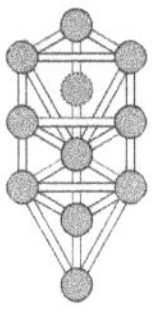 | ה of יהוה |
| World of *Yetzirah*<br>"Formation" | יצירה | 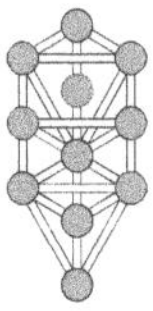 | ו of יהוה |
| World of *Assiah*<br>"Action" | עשיה | 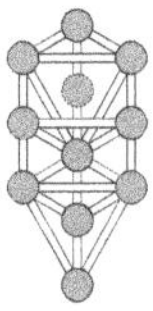 | ה of יהוה |

*Figure G8 - The Four Worlds*

Each Tree of Life in the four worlds has 22 Paths, and to these Paths we attribute the 22 letters of the Hebrew alphabet. They are attributed to the same Paths in each of the four worlds.

The Path of the Hebrew Letter ג, *Gimel*, connects כתר, *Kether*, the Crown, to תפארת, *Tiphereth*, Beauty (and the heart), in each of the four worlds. Furthermore, each of the four worlds has a unique colour scale for both the Sephiroth and the Paths of that world.

In the Queen scale of colour, that is to say, from the viewpoint of the world of Beriah, the Creative World, the Path of Gimel is **silver**.

In the King scale of colour, that is to say from the viewpoint of the world of Atziluth, the World of Emanations, the Path of Gimel is **blue.**[43]

Remember that in Hebrew, ג, *Gimel*, means "camel." In *The Book of Lies*, Crowley called the five initials V.V.V.V.V. the "footprints of a Camel."[44] The Queen scale here signifies the viewpoint of V.V.V.V.V. – the "**joy of men**," their "**silver gleam**," in the Path of Gimel in the world of Beriah.

The King scale signifies the viewpoint of Adonai. The "**woe**" of men is their "**blue gleam**," in the Path of Gimel in the world of Atziluth.

From these lofty perspectives, humankind's feeble joys or woes are but faint glimmers in the mother-of- pearl, the boat whereby Adonai and V.V.V.V.V. sailed upon the river of *Amrit*.

---

43 See *Liber* 777, Columns XV-XVI.

44 Crowley, *The Book of Lies*, Chapter 42.

## § H. CEDERE
## XLI-XLVI

**41. (The scribe was wroth thereat. He spake:**
**O Adonai and my master, I have borne the inkhorn and the pen without pay, in order that I might search this river of Amrit, and sail thereon as one of ye. This I demand for my fee, that I partake of the echo of your kisses.)**

**42. (And immediately it was granted unto him.)**

HEARING THIS EXPRESSION of the Master's non-attachment, the scribe Aleister Crowley felt alienated and became angry. After all, he was one of those whose joy or sorrow is viewed as merely two faint reflections in the mother-of-pearl, inconsequential in the greater scheme of things.

Consequently, he addressed Adonai directly, reminding him that as the scribe, he has done his duty, and acted selflessly that he might record these holy words for mankind, so that one day, he too might be as one of the gods.

Then he boldly demanded that he be given a *samādhi* for his fee.

**And immediately, it is granted unto him.**

His bold requirement was fulfilled because the relationship of the scribe with the Angel is not one of slavery, but one of mutual service and love. This is, in fact, the same for any of us who attain to the Knowledge and Conversation of the Holy Guardian Angel. As aspirants, we serve the Masters for a very specific reason, and that is to eventually become a Master ourselves. The Masters serve us, not because they are utterly altruistic, but because they also grow and become wiser Masters thereby. The relationship is completely reciprocal and is mutually beneficial. We are not slaves to the Masters, nor they to us.

But notice that the scribe did not ask for riches, or fame, or glory – any of the things that you might expect Aleister Crowley to request.

No. He humbly asked that he might partake of the **echo** of the kisses of V.V.V.V.V. and Adonai. He did not even ask for a direct kiss – just the **echo** *of a kiss* – a distant, faint share of the direct intimacy experienced by the Magister and his God.

## The Admonition to Yield

**43. (Nay; but not therewith was he content. By an infinite abasement unto shame did he strive. Then a voice:)**
**44. Thou strivest ever; even in thy yielding thou strivest to yield – and lo! thou yieldest not.**
**45. Go thou unto the outermost places and subdue all things.**
**46. Subdue thy fear and thy disgust. Then – yield!**

But immediately after receiving *samādhi* for his fee, the scribe made a mistake. Remember the one who was described in verse 25 as trying to run forward so fast that the Angel couldn't come unto him? Here, Crowley was doing the same thing. He was not content with the *samādhi* he had been granted; he wanted even more bliss. He had asked only for an **echo** of the kisses of V.V.V.V.V. and Adonai. But he was not satisfied when that wish was granted.

Even when he should have yielded, he was told that he "**strivest to yield**."

Yielding is not striving. They are opposites of one another. Yielding is of the *Yoni*; striving is the *Lingam*. In *The Book of Lies*, in Chapter 4, the Master says,

> Soft and hollow, how thou dost overcome the hard and full!

"**Abasement**" means to lower one's self. His error was so egregious in this that it is called "**an infinite abasement unto shame**".

Now, for most of us, making the same mistake the scribe made would not be judged so seriously. But the scribe had been chosen by the Holy Ones as their Prophet. The bar set for him was certainly higher than the rest of us might expect.

If any of us had committed that error, the Supreme Chiefs might look at us and say, "Oh well, what can one expect?" But looking at the scribe, the Prophet, they said that he abased himself unto **shame**.

We get an idea of the nature of his problem in the next verses. He was instructed to go into the **outermost places** and subdue his fear and disgust, and then to ***yield***.

He was being open to impressions, but not *all* impressions. He had not completed the task of confronting all of his internal fears and aversions – they lay in the "**outermost places**", that is to say, in a distant strata of his psyche.

This is common to all of us. These aspects of our psyche constellate into groups of factors that psychologists call "complexes." As Carl Jung said,

> The complex must therefore be a psychic factor which, in terms of energy, possesses a value that sometimes exceeds that of our conscious intentions, otherwise such disruptions of the conscious order would not be possible at all.[1]

Jung also said that the signs of a complex are "fear and resistance."

Complexes congregate in that part of our psyche that Analytical Psychology calls the *Shadow*, where they remain undeveloped and unintegrated until they are confronted and one performs the often difficult task of *conscious integration*. The Shadow represents an unconscious aspect of the personality with which the conscious ego does not identify. Jung said that *all of us* have complexes, some more significant or serious than others. But the only really practical question is what we do with our complexes.[2]

The question of "what to do" is exactly what Crowley was told: subdue his fear and disgust and confront each of them. The word "**subdue**" means to "overcome," to "quieten," to bring under "control." Then the voice told him that he had to **yield**, in other words, confront his fear and resistance and integrate these negative aspects of his psyche.

We do not know whose voice it was in verses 43-46. *Liber LXV* does not indicate that. It just indicates that he heard "**a voice**." We may be assured, however, that it was a voice of Authority, an Utterance of one of the Holy Ones.

---

1 Jung, *The Structure and Dynamics of the Psyche*, (paragraph 200).

2 Jung, *The Symbolic Life*, (paragraph 94).

# § J. PARABOLA DE NOVA NATIVITATE XLVII-XLIX

**47. There was a maiden that strayed among the corn, and sighed; then grew a new birth, a narcissus, and therein she forgot her sighing and her loneliness.**

**48. Even instantly rode Hades heavily upon her, and ravished her away.**

*Figure J1 - The Rape of Proserpine (Persephone)*

ABRUPTLY, ADONAI BEGAN A PARABLE, and the subject of his parable is Persephone. We know immediately that the maiden who **strayed among the corn** is Persephone, because verse 48 tells us that the maiden was "ravished away" by Hades, the god of the Underworld.

The two characters of Persephone and Hades comprise two of the *dramatis personae* of one of the more well-known myths from ancient Greece, a tale beloved for centuries; a myth that, in its simplest form, explains why there are different seasons in the year.

In the myth, the innocent goddess Persephone was gathering flowers in a meadow in Nysa with the daughters of Oceanus. In the meadow grew many beautiful flowers, including the Narcissus, a radiant flower which had been placed to be a snare for Persephone. It was a dangerous blossom, sacred to Hades, the Lord of Hell. No sooner than she had picked the deadly flower than,

> χάνε δὲ χθὼν εὐρυάγυια Νύσιον ἂμ πεδίον, τῇ ὄρουσεν ἄναξ Πολυδέγμων ἵπποις ἀθανάτοισι, Κρόνου πολυώνυμος υἱός. ἁρπάξας δ' ἀέκουσαν ἐπὶ χρυσέοισιν ὄχοισιν ἦγ' ὀλοφυρομένην
>
> the wide-pathed earth gaped along the plain of Nysa. There the Lord, the All-receiver, darted forth with his immortal steeds - Kronos' son, worshipped under many names. He snatched her away against her will, and carried her off upon his golden chariot as she wailed.[1]

*Figure J2 - Proserpine (Persephone)*

In grief, vegetation began to die, and soon after, winter came with its icy chill.

> Herald of winter's reign.
> Persephone is called to the hollow earth.
> It is the season of the sombre masque.[2]

With the outcry of protest for the abduction of Persephone, Hades falsely offered her freedom to return to her mother upon the earth. But to ensure that Persephone must return to him, Hades tricked her into eating a pomegranate seed.

> αὐτὰρ ὅ γ' αὐτὸς ῥοιῆς κόκκον ἔδωκε φαγεῖν μελιηδέα λάθρῃ, ἀμφὶ ἓ νωμήσας, ἵνα μὴ μένοι ἤματα πάντα αὖθι παρ' αἰδοίῃ Δημήτερι κυανοπέπλῳ.
>
> But he stealthily gave her a honey-sweet pomegranate seed to eat... so that she might not remain there for all time with the revered, dark-robed Demeter.[3]

Desperate for her daughter to be returned to the earth, Demeter asked Persephone,

---

1 *Homeric Hymn II, To Demeter*, 16-20. Translation by Matthew Andrews.

2 Gunther, *Northern Cross* (unpublished).

3 *Homeric Hymn II, To Demeter*, 370-374. Translation by Matthew Andrews.

τέκνον, μή ῥά τι μοι σύ γε πάσσαο νέρθεν ἐοῦσα βρώμης; ἐξαύδα, μὴ κεῦθ', ἵνα εἴδομεν ἄμφω: ὣς μὲν γάρ κεν ἐοῦσα παρὰ στυγεροῦ Ἀίδαο καὶ παρ' ἐμοὶ καὶ πατρὶ

My child, I do hope you did not taste any food when you were down below? Speak and hide nothing, that we may both know. For if you have not, you can be free from abominable Hades, and live with me and your father...

Persephone answered,

τοιγὰρ ἐγώ τοι, μῆτερ, ἐρέω νημερτέα πάντα:... αὐτὰρ ὃ λάθρῃ ἔμβαλέ μοι ῥοιῆς κόκκον, μελιηδέ' ἐδωδήν, ἄκουσαν δὲ βίῃ με προσηνάγκασσε πάσασθαι.

Well then, mother, I will tell you everything truthfully...he stealthily gave me a pomegranate seed, that honey-sweet food, and with force he constrained me to taste it against my will."[4]

As a result of Persephone violating the rule of taking no food in the underworld, Hades did not free her, but he allowed her to return to the earth for a time. But she was required to remain under the earth for a third part of the year.

*Figure J3 - The Return of Persephone*

The third portion of the year was the winter season. Pseudo-Apollodorus confirmed this time period:

Περσεφόνη δὲ καθ' ἕκαστον ἐνιαυτὸν τὸ μὲν τρίτον μετὰ Πλούτωνος ἠναγκάσθη μένειν, τὸ δὲ λοιπὸν παρὰ τοῖς θεοῖς.

Persephone was forced to remain with Pluto (i.e. Hades) for a third of every year, while for the rest she remained with the gods.[5]

Thus, it is said that each year, when she is returned to the surface, Spring comes with her, followed by the Summer of the year.

---

4 *Ibid.* 406, 411-413. Translation by Matthew Andrews. For a magical interpretation of a portion of this myth, see *The Vision & the Voice*, 8th Æthyr.

5 Apollodorus, *Bibliotheca* 1,5,3.Translation by Matthew Andrews.

# The Name Persephone

It is helpful to examine the figure of Persephone herself in order to help give a better idea of what she represents in this place.

The name Persephone is commonly written in Greek as Περσεφόνη. This is the Ionic form of her name in the epic literature.[6]

In *Magna Graecia* she was known as Προσερπίνε, *Proserpinē*, from whence the Romans derived her name and legend, calling her *Proserpina*:

> Terrena autem vis omnis atque natura Diti patri dedicata est, qui Dives, ut apud Graecos Πλούτων, quia et recidunt omnia in terras et oriuntur e terris. Cui Proserpinam nuptam, quod Graecorum nomen est; ea enim est, quae Περσεφόνη Graece nominatur, quam frugum semen esse volunt absconditamque quaeri a matre fingunt.
>
> All earthly and natural power is dedicated to Father Dis, in Greek Πλούτων, because all things arise from the earth and return to it. To whom Proserpine was married, which is a Greek name, for she is the one whom the Greeks call Περσεφόνη, by which they mean the seed of corn, who was hidden, and sought by her Mother.[7]

In *The Odyssey*, Homer called her Περσεφονεία, *Persephoneia*.[8] In other dialects she was known under other names that were quite different.

In his tragedy Ἀντιγόνη, *Antigone*, Sophocles called her Φερσέφασσα, *Phersephassa*.[9]

Aristophanes, in his comedy, Βάτραχοι, *The Frogs*, gave her name as Φερσέφαττα, *Phersephatta*.[10]

In *Cratylus*, *Plato* called her Φερέπαφα, *Pherepapha*, writing,

> ʽΦερέπαφα᾽ οὖν διὰ τὴν σοφίαν καὶ τὴν ἐπαφὴν τοῦ φερομένου ἥ θεὸς ἄν όρθῶς καλοῖτο, ἤ τοιοῦτόν τι.

---

6 *LSJ* 1395b.

7 Cicero, *De Natura Deorum*, 2.26. Translation by Matthew Andrews.

8 *LSJ* 1395b. Cf. *The Odyssey*, Book 11, 47.

9 Sophocles, *Antigone*, 894. Greek text in Dindorf, *ΣΟΦΟΚΛΕΟΥΣ ΑΝΤΙΓΟΝΗ - Sophoclis Antigone*, p. 262.

10 *Ranae*, 671. Greek text in Plaistowe, *Aristophanes: Ranae*, p. 42.

> Thus, on account of her wisdom and because she touches upon that which is in motion, the goddess might rightly be called 'Pherepapha,' or some such name.[11]

*Cratylus* is a dialogue about the correctness of names, hence the discussion concerning Persephone. Yet, the discourse concerning this goddess is quite telling in a very specific way other than the fact that her name was surrounded with taboo. In Euripides' *Helena*, she is called, ἀρρήτου κούρας, *the maiden (Korē) whose name may not be spoken.*[12] In Homer's *Iliad* she is called ἐπαινὴ Περσεφόνεια, *dread Persephone.*[13]

All of these variations of her name suggest to us that the Greeks had difficulty in pronouncing her original name. No doubt this was because her original name had a *pre-Greek origin*, from the time *before* Proto-Greek speakers occupied that region. It is a very ancient name with historical roots in pre-history.[14] For example, in the Linear B script of Mycenaean Greek, which predates the Greek alphabet by several hundred years, the names of Persephone and Kore have been proposed for 𐀟𐀩𐁁 ("*pe-re-swa*") and 𐀒𐀷 ("*ko-wa*").[15]

In other words, her proper name very probably originated during the *Aeon of Isis*.

To continue, we note that Xenophon, in the 6th book of his *History of Greece*, referred to her by the name of Κόρη, *Korē*.[16] This last name is important to us, because it literally means "maiden,"[17] as in the "**maiden that strayed among the corn**," that is, Persephone. It is a confirmation that this verse in *Liber LXV*, without a doubt, refers to Persephone.

But there is something very interesting here. The name *Korē* as a substitute for Persephone came about because uttering the name Persephone became *taboo*.

The Greeks were frightened to speak the name Hades aloud, hence he was referred to by various epithets instead. We can see that clearly in the account of Persephone given in the Homeric Hymn quoted above. In this text, he is called two such names, Πολυδέγμων, *All-receiver*, and Κρόνου πολυώνυμος υἱός,

---

11 *Cratylus*, 404d. Greek in Stallbaum, *Platonis Opera Omnia Uno Volumine Comprehensa*, p. 138a. Plato was utilizing a typical etymology from antiquity: φερομένου ("*what is in motion*") + ἐπαφὴν ('*touching*') = Φερέπαφα', "Pherepapha." Translation and etymology by Matthew Andrews.

12 ἀρρήτου κούρας, literally, "the unspoken maiden." Euripides, *Helena*, 1307.

13 Homer, *Iliad* 9.457.

14 Chadwick, *The Mycenaean World*, pp. 95 ff.

15 This proposal continues to be debated by scholars.

16 Dindorf, *ΞΕΝΟΦΟΝΤΙΣ ΕΛΛΗΝΙΚΑ. Xenophontis Historia Graeca, Liber VI*, Cap. 3, 6, p. 204.

17 *LSJ*, p. 980b.

*Kronos' son worshipped under many names,* in order to avoid using his cursed name.

After her abduction, Persephone became the consort of Hades, and therefore she was considered the terrible Queen of the Dead. They also began to refer to her euphemistically as *Korē*, "the maiden," because it wasn't considered safe to utter her real name either.[18]

We can understand that taboo from the ancient past. But why is that of interest to us now?

Because the name of Persephone does not appear in these verses in *Liber LXV*. She is only called **"a maiden"**, that is, *Korē*.

Does the absence of the name in this place represent a taboo? Or does it point us in another direction?

## The Maiden

**47. There was a maiden that strayed among the corn, and sighed; then grew a new birth, a narcissus, and therein she forgot her sighing and her loneliness.**

Persephone, or *Korē*, the **maiden**, symbolizes the "earth-bound soul," that is to say, one who is not an initiate. She represents the part of the soul we call the **נפש**, *Nephesh*, the so-called "animal soul" or the instincts.

The verse tells us that she **"strayed among the corn"**. Here is the key word to understanding this verse. That word is **"strayed"**.

"There was a maiden that ***strayed*** among the corn." To stray means to *wander,*[19] that is, *to go beyond some established limit.* It means to go somewhere *you are not supposed to go.* It is connected to our word "astray" - off of the desired or correct path - in her case, the path that she had followed for countless years - since the *Aeon of Isis*.

Her name originated in the Aeon of Isis. For *millennia* she had a proper place, a proper way to behave - all formed during the Aeon of the Mother.

But now we see that Persephone had ***strayed***.

Persephone was the goddess of innocence, but she ***strayed*** into the fields of her mother. Archetypically, that suggests that she was attempting to abandon childhood and become a woman. Not surprisingly, *Liber LXV* said explicitly

---

18 They also feared that uttering her name would awaken the wrath of her mother, the grieving Demeter.

19 *Skeat*, p. 472b.

*Figure J4 - Demeter Mourning for Persephone*

that she **"grew a new birth."**

As long as people could remember, the corn had been the domain of Persephone's Mother Δημήτηρ, *Demeter*,[20] the queen of the bountiful harvest.[21]

Here, I am reminded of the Greek word νεόφυτος, *neophyte - newly planted.*[22]

The Neophyte begins to grow a new birth, like a new plant.

The Holy Book tells us that her new birth was that of a **Narcissus** flower. Becoming the **Narcissus, she forgot her sighing and loneliness** - her former condition of isolation and despair - the condition of the exiled שכינה, *Shekinah*, the soul cut off from union with God.[23] Hesiod's lengthy second Homeric Hymn to *Demeter* recounts how Persephone was bending down to pick a **narcissus** when she was abducted by Hades.[24]

---

20 *LSJ*, p.385b.

21 *Homeric Hymn XIII*, Δημήτηρ' ἠύκομον, σεμνὴν θεάν, ἄρχομ' ἀείδειν, αὐτὴν καὶ κούρην, περικαλλέα Περσεφόνειαν. "Of the lovely-haired Demeter, I being to sing - both of her and her daughter, the exceedingly beautiful Persephone." (Translation by Matthew Andrews.) See also *Orphic Hymn No. 40*: Δήμητρος Ἐλευσινίας...Δηώ, παμμήτειρα θεά, πολυώνυμε δαῖμον,σεμνὴ Δήμητερ, κουροτρόφος, ὀλβιοδῶτι, πλουτοδότειρα θεά, σταχυοτρόφε, παντοδότειρα, εἰρήνη χαίρουσα καὶ ἐργασίαις πολυμόχθοις, σπερμείη, σωρῖτις, ἀλωαίη, χλοόκαρπε. "To Eleusinian Demeter...Deo, divine mother of all, goddess worshiped under many names. O revered Demeter, you are the nursing mother and bestower of bliss; divine giver of riches, you who nourish the ears of corn, giver of all. While rejoicing both in peace and in toilsome labor, you preside over the seeds, the corn heaps, the threshing floor and the unripe fruit." (Translation by Matthew Andrews.) One of her Epithets was, "she of the grain." (Aelian, *Varia Historia*, 1.27. Cf. *Eustathius of Thessalonica*, *Scholia on Homer's Iliad*, 265, 30).

22 *LSJ*, p.1170a.

23 שכינה, *Shekinah*, "indwelling," derives from שכן, "to dwell, rest." In post-biblical texts it came to signify the Divine Presence. (*Jastrow*, Vol. 2., p.198b.) Qabalists identified the *Shekinah* with *Heh Final* of *Tetragrammaton*, attributed to Malkuth, the tenth Sephira on the Tree of Life and the Bride of God. With the destruction of the Temple in Jerusalem and the subsequent Babylonian exile there arose the doctrine of Shekinah abandoning God to go with her children into exile until the Temple be rebuilt. It thus symbolizes the Soul cut off from the Divine Presence, which in our System would equate to one who has not attained to the Knowledge and Conversation of the Holy Guardian Angel.

24 Hesiod, *Theogony*, 913-914. and *Homeric Hymn II, to Demeter*.

This myth was briefly mentioned by Hesiod in his *Theogony*, and at greater length in the *Homeric Hymn to Demeter*. According to the geographer Pausanias, the Athenian poet Pamphos said,

> Κόρην τὴν Δήμητρος φησιν ἁρπασθῆναι παίζουσαν καὶ ἄνθη συλλέγουσαν, ἁρπασθῆναι δὲ οὐκ ἴοις ἀπατηθεῖσαν ἀλλὰ ναρκίσσοις.
>
> The maiden daughter of Demeter was snatched up while playing and collecting flowers - she had been tricked into being abducted not by violets but by the narcissus flower.[25]

*Figure J5 - Narcissus*

## Narcissus - the Young Man

The tale of *Narcissus* is another well-known myth. He was a handsome youth who rejected the love of the beautiful nymph *Echo* who was much admired by the goddess *Venus*, and did so vehemently, crying,

"Hands off! Embrace me not! May I die before I give you power over me!"[26]

When Narcissus thus mocked Echo, he had, in effect, mocked the other nymphs of the countryside. One of the scorned nymphs prayed unto heaven, "So may he love himself, and not gain the thing he loves!"[27]

The goddess Νέμεσις, *Nemesis,* [28] heard this prayer, and caused Narcissus to fall in love with his own reflection in a pool of water.

So he fell in love with the image of himself and he wasted away unto death, never being able to abandon his own reflection.[29]

We have generally become so accustomed to the common use and misuse of the Freudian term *narcissism* that we are likely to miss a valuable point of the myth of Narcissus.

---

25 Pausanias, *Description of Greece*, 9.31.9. Translation by Matthew Andrews.

26 Ovid, *Metamorphoses*, Liber 3, 370-391.

27 "Sic amet ipse licet, sic non potiatur amato!" Ovid, *Metamorphoses, Liber 3, 405.*

28 Νέμεσις, *Nemesis*, was the goddess of Divine Retribution against mortals who succumbed to hubris, thus offending the gods. (*LSJ*, p. 1167a.) She was called *Adrastia*, the "chastiser of evil deeds and the rewarder of good actions." in *Ammianus Marcillinus*, 14,11:25. For Ἀδράστεια, see *LSJ*, p. 23b.

29 Ovid, *Metamorphoses, Liber 3, 402-505.*

*Figure J6 - Echo and Narcissus*

The Jungian analyst Edward Edinger brilliantly made this point in his book *Ego And Archetype.*[30] Edinger pointed out that Narcissus represents the alienated ego that cannot love because it has not yet related to itself. It does not know itself.

Consider the ancient Greek aphorism Γνῶθι Σεαυτόν,"know thyself." It was the most important of the three axioms inscribed on the pronaos of the temple of Apollo at Delphi.[31]

To know yourself does not mean to be familiar with your own image; unless we are blind, we all know what we look like in the mirror.

This does not mean being captivated or entranced by our own image. We are talking about actually coming to know *who we are* – to be in possession of our self.

If you are in love with the *reflection* of yourself, you are not yet in possession of yourself. Remember what *Liber LXV* tells us in Chapter I, verse 7: **"Be not contented with the image."**

The implication of Narcissism is not that of a useless excess of self-love, but rather frustration and desire for a *self-knowledge* which does not exist. The unfulfilled yearning of Narcissus will only disappear with the experience of self-love. Γνῶθι Σεαυτόν. "Know Thyself."

In the Gnostic *Gospel according to Thomas*, Isa said,

---

30 Edinger, *Ego and Archetype*, p. 161 ff.

31 *Pausanias Description of Greece*, Book X: 24,1. See Jones, *Pausanias Description of Greece*, Vol. 4, Books VIII-X, p. 507.

*Figure J7 - The Temple of Apollo at Delphi*

**ⲉϣⲱⲡⲉ ⲇⲉ ⲧⲉⲧⲛⲁⲥⲟⲩⲱⲛ ⲧⲏⲩⲧⲛ̄ ⲁⲛ ⲉⲉⲓⲉ ⲧⲉⲧⲛ̄ ϣⲟⲟⲡ` ϩⲛ̄ ⲟⲩⲙⲛ̄ⲧϩⲏⲕⲉ ⲁⲩⲱ ⲛ̄ⲧⲱⲧⲛ̄**

If you do not know yourselves, then you dwell in poverty and you are poverty.[32]

**ⲇⲉ ⲡⲉⲧⲥⲟⲟⲩⲛ ⲙ̄ⲡⲧⲏⲣϥ` ⲉϥⲣ̄ ϭⲣⲱϩ ⲟⲩⲁⲁϥ ⲣ̄ ϭⲣⲱϩ ⲙ̄ⲡⲙⲁ ⲧⲉⲣϥ`**

Whoever knows the All but fails to know himself, lacks everything.[33]

Edinger reminded us that fulfilled self-love is a prerequisite to being able to genuinely love anyone or anything. To unite with the image in the water requires that we descend into the unconscious. That is what Narcissus could not do. We have the basic idea in the vernacular of English when we say that someone, "couldn't take the plunge." You have to dive in.

After he died, Narcissus became the flower called Narcissus. The name Νάρκισσος, *Narcissus,* is from the Greek ναρκάω, "to be stiff or dead."[34] The Narcissus is a death flower.

There is another fact that is most interesting in this context. The etymology of the name Persephone is said to be φέρειν φόνον, which means "to bring or cause death."[35]

This flower was sacred to Hades and opened the doors to the Underworld. Thus, when Persephone picked the narcissus flower she unknowingly invoked the lord of Hell.

---

32 *The Gospel according to Thomas*, 81,3-4.

33 *Ibid*, 93, 18-19.

34 *LSJ*, p.1160b. *Skeat*, p. 301a-b. The modern English word "narcotic" is also related.

35 Smith, *Dictionary of Greek and Roman Biography and Mythology*, Vol. 3, p. 204.

As Edinger pointed out, the inescapable conclusion is that in order to enter the realm of the unconscious, one must experience *Narcissus in the soul.*

What did Edinger mean by that statement?

It meant that you must first have a fulfilled expression of self-love - that is, self-knowledge, if you are to truly find love - and by love, I mean Union. This self-love or self-knowledge includes going into the outermost places and confronting your fears and your disgust, the weaknesses of your character.

Remember *Liber LXV*, I:45-46, the verses that *immediately* precede our parable.

## Preparation for the Parable

**45. Go thou unto the outermost places and subdue all things.**
**46. Subdue thy fear and thy disgust. Then - yield!**

Preparing us to receive the parable of Persephone, we are given verses 45 and 46.

When we do this difficult task, we begin to spiritually "grow up." We will have "**strayed among the corn**" so to speak, and will begin to grow a "**new birth.**"

We must be willing to leave our old life behind and seek a new one - still uncertain and unknown. As I have described it many times, we must abandon the **death** which the world calls **life**, and embrace the **life** which the world calls **death**.

Once again, in the Gnostic *Gospel according to Thomas*, we find a similar expression:

**ϫⲉ ⲓ̅ⲥ̅ ϫⲉ ⲡⲉⲧⲁϩⲥⲟⲩⲱⲛ ⲡⲕⲟⲥⲙⲟⲥ ⲁϥ` ϩⲉ ⲉⲩⲡⲧⲱⲙⲁ ⲁⲩⲱ ⲡⲉⲛⲧⲁϩϩⲉⲉ ⲁⲡⲧⲱ ⲙⲁ ⲡⲕⲟⲥⲙⲟⲥ ⲙ̅ⲡϣⲁ ⲙ̅ⲙⲟϥ ⲁⲛ**

Isa said: Whoever has known the world has found a corpse, and whoever has found a corpse, the world is not worthy of him.[36]

You must not become confused with this symbolic language. You are *not* embracing death. You are embracing ***life***. Remember that the etymology of Persephone's name meant to "cause or bring death?" Yes, but she **grew a new birth**. Your new birth is a new flower in the fields, which the world will call Narcissus, the "death flower," because they cannot see the ineffable glory of the Path of the Adept, and its nameless goal. As it is written in *Liber Porta Lucis*, verse 15:

36 *Loc Cit*, 90, 30-31.

> **Even as a man ascending a steep mountain is lost to sight of his friends in the valley, so must the adept seem. They shall say: He is lost in the clouds. But he shall rejoice in the sunlight above them, and come to the eternal snows.**

If you begin to ascend the mountain, from that moment on, if you persist in the Path, you will be dead to the world, and the world with its former sense of values will be dead to you. The things of the world will not mean the same thing to you anymore. They will never have the same meaning for you *ever again.*

Then, and only then, will you be ready to yield to the Holy Guardian Angel, and the little new plant will blossom into a beautiful flower. This is that which is written in *Liber VII*, Chapter III, verses 56-57:

> **Thou shalt crush me in the wine-press of Thy love. My blood shall stain Thy fiery feet with litanies of Love in Anguish. There shall be a new flower in the fields, a new vintage in the vineyards.**

The new flower in the fields, the new vintage in the vineyards, is the Candidate, the "newly planted" one grown up – the Neophyte readied for the central Initiation. In the symbolism of the Neophyte Initiation Ritual of A∴A∴ the dead one *Asar*, the Lord of the Dead, transformed with self- knowledge to become *Asar un Nefer, myself made perfect.*[37]

In the text of this Parable in *Liber LXV*, Persephone picked the death plant. She experienced the Narcissus in her soul. She changed and grew a **new birth**. Then what happened?

The god of Hell came roaring out of the bowels of the earth and snatched her out of her sweet little former life, and forcibly carried her off into the depths of the underworld.

Note how the text of Verse 48 describes the appearance of Hades - "**Even instantly**" he rode heavily upon her.

---

37 In *Liber Samekh*, in Point I, Section A, no. 5, Crowley wrote, "Thou art ASAR-UN-NEFER" ("Myself made Perfect"). The source document for *Liber Samekh* was a papyrus in the British Museum (*Greek papyrus XLVI*), published in 1852 e.v. under the name *Fragment of a Graeco-Egyptian Work Upon Magic*, translated by Charles Wycliffe Goodwin. In 1928 e.v. it was included in Karl Preisendanz' publication, *Papyri Graecae Magicae*, Vol. 1, pp. 184-186. An English translation of the PGM was published in 1986 e.v. as *The Greek Magical Papyri In Translation*, by Hans Dieter Betz. Lines 96-172 of the papyrus fragment comprise the section that has come to be known as *The Bornless Ritual.* Lines 101-102 read, Σὺ εἶ 'Οσορόννωφρις, ὅν οὐδεὶς εἶδε πώποτε, "Thou art Osoronnophris whom none hath ever seen." The name 'Οσορόννωφρις is a Greek corruption of the Egyptian 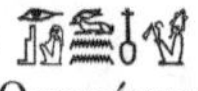 , *isir-wn-nfr*, "Osiris the beautiful," or *Asar-un-nefer*. Crowley changed the corrupt 'Οσορόννωφρις to *Asar-un-nefer* for *Liber Samekh*, adding his magical interpretation, "Myself made Perfect."

In the representation of this myth in *Liber LXV*, who does Hades signify?

Hades signifies the Holy Guardian Angel.

In my first book, *Initiation in the Aeon of the Child*, in Chapter 8, which is entitled "Wormwood." I quoted *The Vision & The Voice* from the 22nd Æthyr, where the *Sevenfold Arrangement of Hoor* is revealed. I began with the revelation of the *three aspects*, which correspond to *Introversion*, *Extraversion* and *Centroversion*.

*Introversion* is "a turning within." In the system of Thelema it is *Mysticism* as opposed to *Magick*.

*Extraversion* is "a turning outward." It is the practice of *Magick* as opposed to *Mysticism*. *Centroversion* is "a turning to the Center." This is a practice which combines the methods of Introversion and Extraversion in balanced application.

Introversion represents certain characteristics of the Aeon of the Mother Isis.

Extraversion carries certain characteristics of the Aeon of the Father Osiris. Centroversion is a characteristic of the Aeon of the Child Horus.

Here is what is written in *The Vision & The Voice*:

> **My arms were out in the form of a cross, and that Cross was extended, blazing with light into infinity. I myself am the minutest point in it. This is *the birth of form*.**

The birth of form is the conception of the Self in extension - that is, Extraversion.

> **I am encircled by an immense sphere of many-coloured bands; it seems it is the sphere of the Sephiroth projected in the three dimensions. This is *the birth of death*.**

The birth of *death* is the conception of the Self extended into the negative circle or sphere of Nuit - that is, Introversion. This death is a death which should be *infinite* as *The Vision & The Voice* tells us.[38] The death of the external world leads us to The Inward Journey.

And lastly, we see the Third and final aspect:

> **Now in the centre within me is a glowing sun. That is *the birth of hell*.**

This is referred to Centroversion - the perception of one's innermost nature.

It is particularly referred to the Aeon of the Child.

Look at the words of this verse carefully. "in the centre within me is a glowing sun."

---

38 "For thou wilt find a life which is as Death: or a Death which should be infinite." *Liber 418*, 30th Æthyr.

That is an image of Tiphereth, the sixth Sephira on the Tree of Life to which we attribute the sun – the "glowing sun" – the centre of humankind, the *heart*.

It is the Sephira that corresponds to the Knowledge and Conversation of the Holy Guardian Angel. This is the birth of *hell*.

What does *Liber Tzaddi* verses 15 through 17 tell us?

**I have hidden myself beneath a mask: I am a black and terrible God. With courage conquering fear shall ye approach me: ye shall lay down your heads upon mine altar, expecting the sweep of the sword. But the first kiss of love shall be radiant on your lips; and all my darkness and terror shall turn to light and joy.**

Those who will dare to "stray" among the corn, grow a **new birth** – the narcissus – have the promise of the Lord of the Aeon in *Liber Tzaddi*, verses 27-30:

**O my children, ye are more beautiful than the flowers: ye must not fade in your season.**
**I love you; I would sprinkle you with the divine dew of immortality.**
**This immortality is no vain hope beyond the grave: I offer you the certain consciousness of bliss.**
**I offer it at once, on earth; before an hour hath struck upon the bell, ye shall be with Me in the Abodes that are beyond Decay. (Emphasis added)**

We are offered this *at once*. Before an hour hath struck upon the bell. Look at this verse from *Liber Tzaddi* closely. Look at the last sentence. There are three words written with initial letters in the Upper Case in mid-sentence.

**Me, Abodes**, and **Decay**.
**M.A.D.**

The letters M.A.D. spell the Enochian word MAD, *mad*, which means "GOD."

Before an hour hath struck upon the bell, *ye shall be with God*.

The death flower, the narcissus, will then be transformed into the *Chrysanthemum* – the Golden Flower.

Ye shall be a new flower in the fields

*Figure J8 - Chrysanthemum*

## Narcissus In the Heart

**49. (Then the scribe knew the narcissus in his heart; but because it came not to his lips, therefore was he shamed and spake no more.)**

Hearing and seeing these things, the scribe knew and understood the narcissus in his heart, but he was not able to bring it to his lips. This means he was unable to convert this wonderful experience into words. Crowley stated that he was seized with the beauty of these ideas, and wanted to write a poem worthy of it, but was unable to do so.

So he assumed the sign of silence.

Nevertheless, he recorded his experience in the beautiful words of *Liber LXV*, which is indeed poetry more than worthy of the moment. However, it seems to me that he spoke these words from the viewpoint of Aleister Crowley the man, the poet, and not that of the Adept. The words of the poet failed him, whereas the Words of the God did not.

# § K. VINDEMIA
# L - LXV

**50. Adonai spake yet again with V.V.V.V.V. and said: The earth is ripe for vintage; let us eat of her grapes, and be drunken thereon.**

AS WE HAVE SEEN, THE NEW FLOWER in the fields, the new vintage in the vineyards, is the Candidate, the "newly planted" one, the Neophyte ready for initiation.

Adonai urged V.V.V.V.V. to reap the harvest with Him, "**and be drunken thereon.**" Recall what I said earlier about our relationship with the Angel? We are as adorable to the One, as the One is to the many.

Seeing that the earth was ready for harvest, Adonai desired to go among the people of the earth and "**eat of her grapes**". This is the symbolic language that Adonai used to describe his desire to deliver unto mankind a new Word that will reap a new harvest of "**grapes**". This new harvest would be those who are ripe and potentially suitable for the new Law, and they will comprise the fruit chosen for vintage.

However, being "ripe and ready," so to speak, does not mean that all of the harvested fruit of the vineyard will be chosen for the wine vat. It was also understood that this "first harvest" of the new grapes would be small, as is common when a fine wine is being developed. Only the most select of the fruit of the vineyard would be harvested, and even a small portion of those would be culled. We learn this from the words of *Liber Porta Lucis*, Verses 9-10:

**This Knowledge is not for all men; few indeed are called, but of these few many are chosen.**
**This is the nature of the Work.**

# The Subtle Word

**51. And V .V .V .V .V . answered and said: O my lord, my dove, my excellent one, how shall this word seem unto the children of men?**

**52. And He answered him: Not as thou canst see.**
**It is certain that every letter of this cipher hath some value; but who shall determine the value? For it varieth ever, according to the subtlety of Him that made it.**

Responding, V.V.V.V.V. asked Adonai how this new **word** would be received by mankind. We should realize that we are reading an account of a conversation that was intended to serve as a learning opportunity for the Adept and scribe.

In this verse, V.V.V.V.V. was looking ahead to the time subsequent to the harvesting of the grapes, when the fine wine had fermented, and delivered unto the marketplace, that is, the world of humankind. The question is a simple one: "how will the children of men judge the wine?"

V.V.V.V.V. being above the Abyss, knew *precisely* how all this would seem to the children of men. He was asking this question for the benefit of the Adept, who had the unenviable task of delivering this word to the world. The Magister V.V.V.V.V. knew perfectly well what kind of reaction Thelema would receive from Christians, just to mention one group.

Adonai naturally replied, not to V.V.V.V.V., but *directly to the Adept* (note the lower case "**t**" in "**Not as thou canst see**"). He stated that the Adept does not have the ability to see the entirety of this mystery, because it is written with such subtlety by the Magister – "**Him that made it.**" (Upper Case "**H**" here.) It is operative on multiple levels at the same time. Such is the quality of Class A documents, which are limited only by the subtlety of their author, Adonai himself.

# Mystery of the Oppositorum

**53. And He answered Him: Have I not the key thereof? I am clothed with the body of flesh; I am one with the Eternal and Omnipotent God.**

**54. Then said Adonai: Thou hast the Head of the Hawk, and thy Phallus is the Phallus of Asar. Thou knowest the white, and thou knowest the black, and thou knowest that these are one. But why seekest thou the knowledge of their equivalence?**

**55. And he said: That my Work may be right.**

Once again, V.V.V.V.V. took the initiative and responded to Adonai by asking the question he knew was in the mind of the Adept. The Magister proffered that He possessed the key to the mystery of comprehending the word, being one with the Eternal and Omnipotent God while manifest in the flesh of his Adept and scribe, Aleister Crowley.

Adonai acknowledged that His Magister's knowledge bridges the Abyss that separates the Realm of the Actual from the Realm of the Ideal. He is at once divine, having the **Head of the Hawk** (Horus), and human, having the **Phallus of Asar** (Osiris), capable of fertilizing Isis or Nature.

He also knows the mystery of the *oppositorum*, which is the understanding of their ultimate identity. To attain Mastery, one must unite the opposites of their Nature, the human and the Divine, in order to comprehend their ultimate equivalence.

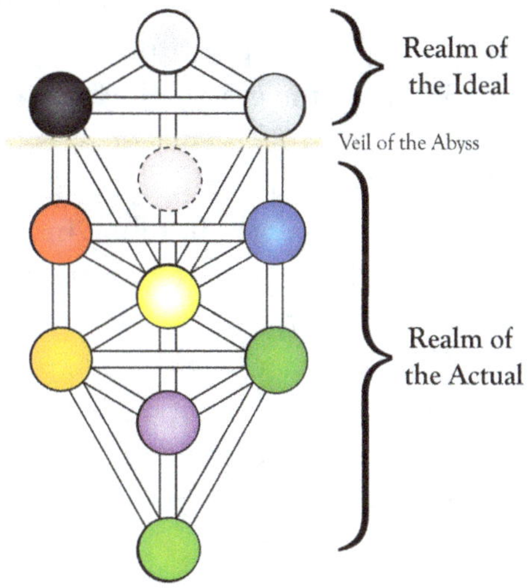


*Figure K1 - The Two Realms*

Adonai answered the Magister, again with an instruction intended for the Adept. His reply was also in the form of a question – "**why seekest thou**" (lower case "**t**", the Adept)

He asked why he should seek to find equations which attempt to explain the relationships between such diverse symbols, knowing that in the end, they are not bound to such limited definitions.

Naturally, the answer came from the Adept, not V.V.V.V.V. "**And he said: That my Work may be right.**" Note that "**he**" has an initial lowercase letter, while "**Work**" is written with an initial uppercase letter. The Adept understood that the Great Work ultimately transcends the Abyss. But hearing this question, the Adept answered it from his point of view, which is *below* the Abyss. The response comes from human consciousness (the Adept), but the Work itself is the Path to the Divine Realm, the Path of the Inward Journey.

The Adept meant that he felt that he needed to Understand the illusion, for being incarnate, he dwelled in the illusory world, the world of duality.

Adonai responded immediately with a short parable about the reapers of grain.

## Parable of the Reaper and the Wise Man

**56. And Adonai said: The strong brown reaper swept his swathe and rejoiced. The wise man counted his muscles, and pondered, and understood not, and was sad.**
**Reap thou, and rejoice!**

**57. Then was the Adept glad, and lifted his arm.**
**Lo! an earthquake, and plague, and terror on the earth!**
**A casting down of them that sate in high places; a famine upon the multitude!**

**58. And the grape fell ripe and rich into his mouth.**

In this parable, the "**strong brown reaper**" signifies the Adept, who is doing his Task, fulfilling his *pure will* without intellectualizing it, which would deprive it of *prāṇa* and render it ineffectual. He knows that if Power asks why, then Power is weakness. He also knows that reason is a lie.[1]

The "**wise man**" on the other hand, is the type of aspirant who intellectualizes the Task, the method and the means. The "wisdom" of such a person is not received from Chokmah (Pure Will), nor is it Understood through Binah (Neshamah, the Intuition). This kind of "wisdom" does not come from above the Abyss; note that "**wise**" is written with a lower-case "**w.**"

This type of "wisdom" is simply Daath, or "knowledge," the dust of the Abyss. Accordingly, the so-called "**wise man**" placed his trust in that false wisdom, and he failed to *act*. As a result, nothing was done, and the result was failure and unhappiness.

---

1 *Liber AL*, II:27-33.

Ending this short parable, Adonai admonished the Adept and his servant: "**Reap thou, and rejoice!** " (Note the lower case "**t**" in "**thou**").

The Adept, who had been listening to this instructional conversation between Adonai and V.V.V.V.V., promptly took this advice and continued to act and not intellectualize.

It is the Adept-self that dwells in the world of duality, and must fulfill the Task as inspired by the Magister and Adonai, not the false rationale of human intellect.

Thus, the Adept did not "ponder" and become lost in a maze of meaningless intellectual evaluations.

He acted. He swept his swathe, which is the Path cut by his scythe.[2] He fulfilled his function and task, and in parallel symbolism, harvested the grapes which were ready for the ripe vintage without worrying about how it would be seen by the children of men.

**Do what thou wilt shall be the whole of the Law.**

The result, in the case of this particular Adept, was the reception of *The Book of the Law* and the fall of the Aeon of Osiris.

The earth was shaken, and the structures erected by the Aeon of the Father began to crumble.[3] The spiritual food being fed to the masses was revealed for what it really was – not the body and blood of God, but worm-eaten bread and vinegar mingled with gall from the Father of lies.[4]

And thus, there was famine upon the multitude.

Now, you must not forget that this entire conversation began when Adonai urged the Adept to reap the new harvest of **grapes**. It was then that V.V.V.V.V. responded by asking Adonai the question that was in the mind of the Adept and scribe: how will the Word of the Law would seem unto mankind?

The answer was ultimately this: "the Law is for all", yet not all will hear and prepare themselves accordingly.[5]

But those that do hear, and ready themselves, are the *fruit of the new vintage*, which is judged by its *quality*, not its quantity.

And the grape will fall ripe and rich into their mouths.

In *Liber VII*, Chapter VI, verses 40-41, we are told:

---

2 It is significant that the scythe which cuts the swathe is the sign of Saturn ♄ by shape. Saturn is referred to the Abyss. The Path of the Adept leads across the Abyss.

3 Cf. *Liber AL*, I:11, I:31, I:41-42, I:49-50, I:53, II:25, II:44-47, III:3-8.

4 Cf. *Liber AL*, I:41, I:58, II:5, II:17-21, III, 49-59.

5 Cf. *Liber AL*, I:33-40.

**There are few men; there are enough.**
**We shall be full of cup-bearers, and the wine is not stinted.**

*Figure K2 - Italian Midday*

If you become discouraged and disheartened in trying to promulgate the Law of Thelema, remember this verse. If you feel lonely and isolated in trying to accomplish the Great Work, remember this verse. I have had to tell myself to recall the promise of this verse countless times in my life.

Today, there are few of us compared to the world population. There are countless numbers of people who contemplate great wisdom, and do nothing but grow old and die. And there are those among us who claim to be workers in the fields, but only sow discord, delusion and hatred.

But there are enough among us, whose hearts are true, that we may accomplish the Task that has been given to us today. And tomorrow, there will be more. We will, one day, be filled with cup-bearers who reap the harvest of new grapes and bring the wine of the new vintage to the world. And we, like our beloved Master, shall all be drunken thereon.

## Tincture of the Grape

59. **Stained is the purple of thy mouth, O brilliant one, with the white glory of the lips of Adonai.**
60. **The foam of the grape is like the storm upon the sea; the ships tremble and shudder; the shipmaster is afraid.**
61. **That is thy drunkenness, O holy one, and the winds whirl away the soul of the scribe into the happy haven.**
62. **O Lord God! let the haven be cast down by the fury of the storm! Let the foam of the grape tincture my soul with Thy light!**

Enraptured by the Beatific Vision, the Adept-scribe was permitted to behold the nature of the Law of Thelema and its ultimate impact upon the world, and he cried out with these inspired words.

The **purple** of the harvested grape is upon the mouth of V.V.V.V.V., the "**brilliant one,**" the ray of light, the flying spark of light of the Lord of the Aeon.[6] It is he that had to mingle with mankind, and manifest among them. (This is why "**brilliant one**" has lower-case initial letters.)

He bore the purple stain of the harvested grapes upon his mouth from previous millennia and countless years in Service to Adonai. Yet, the stain upon his lips came from **the white glory of the lips of Adonai** his Lord.[7] The colour white suggests Kether, the Crown of the Tree of Life.

> **I have been smitten with the reek of Thy mouth, that drinketh never wine but life.**
> **How the dew of the Universe whitens the lips!**
>
> *Liber VII, I:46-47*

The storm of change, the "**tempest of years**" experienced by the world, is the slow, deliberate fermentation of the individual grapes of humankind into a New Wine.

The "**ships**" upon this sea, that is, *the religions of the world*, shudder amid the churning waves of the New Aeon.

Here we see the little boat of "**mother-of-pearl**" that bore Adonai and V.V.V.V.V. contrasted with the mundane **ships upon the sea**. The shipmasters, the religious leaders of all faiths, are afraid, for the end of their time is upon them.

> **Also Adonai spake unto V.V.V.V.V. saying: O my little one, my tender one, my little amorous one, my gazelle, my beautiful, my boy, let us fill up the pillar of the Infinite with an infinite kiss!**
> **So that the stable was shaken and the unstable became still.**
> **They that beheld it cried with a formidable affright: The end of things is come upon us.**
> **And it was even so.**
>
> *Liber LXV, V:30-33*

---

6 *Liber Porta Lucis*, 2 and *Liber LXV*, V:2-3.

7 Cf. *Liber VII*, III:47-50.

Figure K3 - Stormy Sea at Night

This is the drunkenness of the Lord, and the soul of the Adept and Magister will be carried away into a haven of peace, apart from the turmoil experienced by the masses.

Yet, the Adept requested that he *not* be sequestered from the effects of the change, but that he be allowed to experience firsthand the presence of Adonai. He wanted the transformative kiss of Adonai to permeate his *entire* being, that he might Understand the complete nature of the ravening storm.

## Bacchus, Silenus and Pan

**63. Bacchus grew old, and was Silenus; Pan was ever Pan for ever and ever more throughout the æons.**

**64. Intoxicate the inmost, O my lover, not the outermost!**

It is difficult to tell from this verse who is the speaker. In his hastily written commentary to this verse, Crowley wrote that he thought this was "presumably" once more the voice of the Angel speaking to the Adept.

But if you read this verse and the verse immediately following, it seems probable that this is the voice of The Adept continuing his plea to Adonai from verse 62. He used the analogy of the myths of Bacchus, Silenus and Pan.

Figure K4 - Bacchus

The Roman god of the vine was Bacchus, the god who inspired ritual drunkenness and ecstatic worship.

His Greek name Bacchus (Βάκχος) was adopted by the Romans. He was also known as *Dionysus* (Διόνυσος).

*Silenus* (Σειληνός) was the companion and tutor of Dionysus, and a notorious drunk.[8] He was depicted as much older than the satyrs in the following of

8 See *The Orphic Hymn, number 53*, a hymn to Silenus. He is there called "foster-father and nurse" of Bacchus. Ovid, in *Metamorphoses, Book 11* described Silenus as "stumbling with the weight of years and wine."

Dionysus, and was thus called Πάππος Σειληνός, *Pappo Silenus* ("grandfather Silenus")[9] and represented as a fat, drunken old fool.

Both of these figures signify *external intoxication* of the most superficial type. One young superficial drunk took another elder drunkard as his companion and advisor. The young became as the old. A young fool became an old fool. And they passed from the earth like vapor.

*Figure - K5 - The Drunken Silenus*

The joy of wine has its place; intoxication of the senses can be pleasurable for its own sake, if refined by decorum and common sense.[10]

It can also be bent into the service of the Lord. Yet there is something beyond this that we should seek. Compare the wanton drunkenness of Bacchus and Silenus to the divine madness of *Pan*, the god whose name in Greek, ΠΑΝ, means *ALL*.

*Figure K6 - Pan and Psyche*

We should seek that *innermost intoxication* of the Spirit and not be content with the external intoxication of the physical senses, for the "madness of Pan" is beyond this. It is eternal and beyond rational distinction.

I feel certain that in this verse, this was what the Adept was asking Adonai to do; not let him be satisfied with drunkenness of the external senses, the glories of which are impermanent and fade away to be lost in memory. Pan symbolizes divine intoxication of the Spirit, not external debauchery and revelry. This intoxication lives eternally, untouched by the ravages of time.

*Pan* is beyond the limitation of time and space, beyond the bounds of bodied bliss. This is our desire, to reach beyond shallow intoxication to become drunk on the wine of God, the drunkenness of the innermost sense – to make our soul, our *psyche*, drunken upon the endless presence of the divine.

---

9 Pollux, *Onomosticon*, 4:142.

10 Cf. *Liber AL*, II:70.

# The Peeled Wand

**65. So was it – ever the same! I have aimed at the peeled wand of my God, and I have hit; yea, I have hit.**

This final verse is without doubt the voice of the Adept. He spoke of the *magical wand*, which is the symbol of the *pure will.*

The old grimoires gave instructions to make the magic wand from pure wood, to cut from the branch of a tree with a single stroke of the knife. The bark was to be removed, and the wand smoothed down with the holy oil, emblematic of Spirit. [11]

By removing the unseemly bark on the shaft, we signify banishing the Qliphoth – the "shells," which are the components of the unbalanced Tree of Life. The Hebrew word קליפה, *Qliphah*, means literally, "bark" or "husk."[12]

The Adept aimed at the pure balanced wand of his God – he fired the arrow of aspiration again, even as he has done through many incarnations, in many forms, in many names, always ever the same. He sealed up the word of Adonai into his blood, and became the chosen of Adonai.[13]

*Figure K7 - A∴ A∴ Seal*

For the **Thought of Adonai** is a **Word** and a **Deed**, and the Adept bound together his words and his deeds, so that in all was **one Thought**, the **delight** of **Adonai.**[14]

---

11 Mathers, *The Key of Solomon the King*, Book 2, Chapter 8. See also Crowley, *Magick Without Tears*, Chapter XXIII.

12 *Jastrow*, Vol. 2, p. 1377a.

13 See *Liber LXV*, V:59.

14 *Liber LXV*, V:58-59.

In the great Order of A∴A∴, the aspirant signs a document which is a sacred Oath, but also confirms Tasks that be accomplished to seal that Oath.

Our words must be bound by deeds.

All of us who aspire to know Adonai try our best to "*mend our shoes that we may walk.*"

We who have set out upon the long Inward Journey, make every effort to bind our words by our deeds.

I, who write these words, humbly bear the Cup of His gladness.

To all of you I say, drink thereof, and become even as my Lord, my beautiful, my desirable one.

There is no wine like unto this wine.

I give all of you my sincere best wishes.

May your life be the Life which abideth in Light, yea, the Life which abideth in Light.

And with this, Speech has done with us for awhile.

# Ever the Heart

## An Essay on the Symbolism of The Heart of Blood

Gwen Gunther

# Ever the Heart
## An Essay on the Symbolism of The Heart of Blood

By Gwen Gunther

Cover Art: *Ever the Heart* by Elena Bortot,
after a study by Gwen Gunther

# CHAPTER I

## The Heart of Blood

### AS A THREE-FOLD ELEMENTARY SYMBOL

*My heart of my mother!*
*My heart of my mother!*
*My Consciousness of my existence upon the earth!*[1]

A triangle is a simple three-side polygon that is one of most ubiquitous shapes in theoretical and practical applications worldwide. For instance it is widely used to express various mathematical properties and formulas, and forms one of the shapes of basic geometry. Thus it is used in a wide variety of practical applications, from children's learning toys to complex engineering plans. In general the conventional attitude is that this three-angled form is merely a simple shape whose properties are clearly defined and – although useful – it is not particularly interesting or mysterious. In short the triangle is ordinary.

But if we can transcend the ordinary and examine it as extraordinary – that is as a *symbolic* emblem – then we have a doorway to the creative and mysterious world of the psyche. In discussing the intangible value of symbols, Carl Jung in his essay *Approaching the Unconscious* relays the following:

> What we call a symbol is a term, a name, or even a picture that may be familiar in daily life, yet that possess specific connotations in addition to its conventional and obvious meaning. It implies something vague, unknown, or hidden from us.... Thus a word or an image is symbolic when it implies something more than its obvious and immediate meaning. It has a wider "unconscious" aspect that is never precisely defined or fully explained. Nor can one hope to define or explain it. As the mind explores the symbol it is led to ideas that lie beyond the grasp of reason.[2]

Symbols are the language of the Unconscious, emissaries of the Archetypes they represent; they therefore manifest from the primordial realm. Such Images

---

1 *The Book of the Dead*, Spell 30 The Sarcophagus of Ankhefenkhonsu (Cairo CG, 41001). Translation by J. Daniel Gunther.

2 Jung, *Man and His Symbols*, (Dell Publishing 1968).

are capable of weaving together diverse and seemingly unconnected elements.[3] The Heart of Blood that is the subject of this essay, is a prime example of this phenomenon. It is an ordinary shape that conceals a numinous wellspring of Thelemic doctrine. It is *how* the Heart of Blood is defined in symbolic form that connects the triangle to its occult significance. In other words, this simple three-angled formation should be seen as glyph whereby one can consciously investigate its mystery.

Written words are a good example of using glyphs to communicate something much more than the shapes of letters employed. It is the mind and the emotions that give them life beyond simple figures on a piece of paper. From the written word most sacred to Thelemites, *The Holy Books of Thelema*, this symbol emerges. The prevalent appearance of the "heart" motif throughout the text of the *Holy Books of Thelema* tells the reader that something important is being imparted. Initially, and in a general sense, the physical heart and the metaphysical traits attached to it by contemporary society are likely to come to mind. Beyond the general idea of the "heart" the assiduous student of the Mysteries will be compelled to dive deeper into the message and discover for themselves the subtle and sublime nuances of each occurrence of the word. It is with this attitude of discovery that I embark on this inquiry into the mysteries contained within *The Heart of Blood.*

The specific Book within the Foundational Thelemic Corpus that marks the first and only appearance of the phrase "Heart of Blood" is found in **LIBER LIBERI - VEL - LAPIDIS LAZULI SUB FIGURÂ VII.**[4]

> **There is the Heart of Blood, a pyramid reaching its apex down beyond the Wrong of the Beginning.**[5]

In the Holy Book,[6] **LIBER CORDIS CINCTI SERPENTE - VEL LXV SUB FIGURÂ אדני**[7] received shortly after *Liber VII*, a complementary description is given.

> **The red three-angled heart hath been set up in Thy shrine;**[8]

---

3 Neumann, *The Great Mother*, pp. 3-17 (Bollingen 1974).

4 *Liber VII. Liber Liberi vel Lapidis Lazuli, Adumbratio Kabbalæ Ægyptiorum sub figurâ VII. Book 7. The Book of the Free Man, or of Lapis Lazuli, an Adumbration of the Qabalah of the Egyptians, under the figure 7.* - Translation by Matthew Andrews.

5 *Liber VII*, V:42.

6 The time frame for the reception of the *Holy Books* is given in the Preface to the 1983 *The Equinox III:9*.

7 *Liber LXV. Liber Cordis Cincti Serpente. Book 65. The Book of the Heart Girt with a Serpent.* - Translation by Matthew Andrews.

8 *Liber LXV*, III:28.

From the many occurrences of the heart within the text of *The Holy Books of Thelema*, these two verses stand out as interrelated descriptions that serve to communicate the basic significance of this symbol. They will be used as the basis of this investigation into the Heart of Blood which is specific to the Initiatic experience in the Aeon of the Child.

The first and most basic feature of the Heart of Blood is that it is three-angled. In the most elementary way, this means its nature is threefold. While I began this essay with the general description of the triangle, we must examine it more closely to find its deeper meaning. Both verses from the Holy books that distinguish the symbol give it both form and function. One of these is "three angled" and the other description is "a pyramid". The emblem on the Robe that adorns the Heart of the Neophyte is a descending red triangle which is aligned with "three angled heart". In the mystical unveiling given in *Liber VII* it takes the form of a Pyramid. This point is not to be construed as a difference between the triangle and the pyramid. Rather it should be viewed as a structural development that expresses the living function of this symbol. Consider it as a triangle projected into three dimensions, that is to say, as a triangular pyramid. Geometrically, it would be described as a Tetrahedron.

An example of the ritualistic use of a triangular pyramid is given in the published book titled: *Liber DCCCLX, John St. John. The Record of the Magical Retirement of* G.H. *Frater* O.·. M.·..[9] During Aleister Crowley's magical retirement he worked on the Initiation Ritual published under the name *Liber Pyramidos.* Upon building the magical Pyramid during the opening of the Temple he states: *All this they affirm; and in affirming the triangular base of the Pyramid, find they have mysteriously affirmed the Apex thereof whose name is Ecstasy.*[10]

The Pyramid base structure of three points as opposed to four is an important distinction to consider. In magical theory and practice, both the three and four angled designs contain their own separate yet harmonious principles. The observation that the base is defined as tripartite is very important. To understand this we have to look at the esoteric meaning of three in contrast to four, in order to show their separate values.

The number four is generally thought of as a number of stability, representing a fixed idea or a stationary place. In Qabalistic terms, the fourth Sephira, חסד, *Chesed*, shows the establishment of the Universe in three dimensions – that is, below the Abyss.[11]

---

9 Aleister Crowley's Exempt Adept Motto, ΟΥ ΜΗ. G.H. stands for Greatly Honored.

10 Crowley, *Liber DCCCLX* (Weiser 2006).

11 Crowley, *The Book of Thoth*, p. 213 (Weiser 2000 edition).

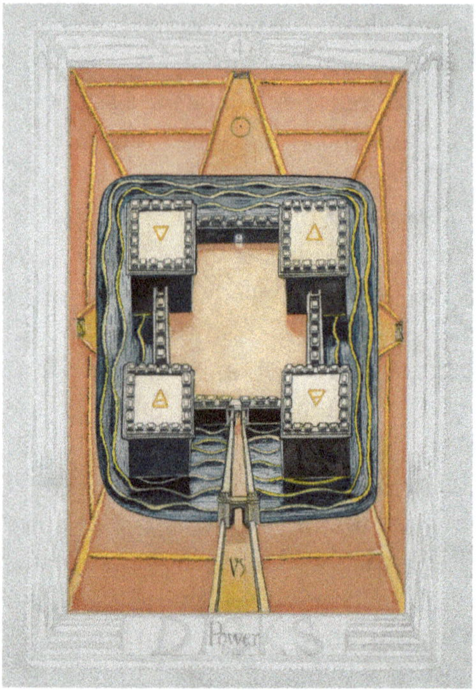

*Figure EH2 - Power*

The projection of four into the material world of עשיה, *Assiah*[12] is aptly represented in the Thoth Tarot card *Power*. This card is attributed to the element Earth and the Tarot suit of Disks. Astrologically this card is ruled by Sol in Capricorn, which signifies energy in limitation, and therefore structured life, in the Sephira of מלכות, *Malkuth*.

When examining the symbolism of this card, we should note that it signifies a fortress which upholds established law and order. This is represented as a medieval castle with four square turrets, one in each of the four corners; these indicate the disks of the elements. In order to emphasize the stable energy of the Four of Disks, Crowley noted: *The disks themselves are square; revolution is very opposite to the card.*[13]

In this figure, the number four serves to solidify the number three. Magically, this fourfold stability points to a very important function that we term *The Powers of the Sphinx*. The Powers of the Sphinx are represented as four living creatures, of which three are animals, and one is human.[14] In summary, while the number four partakes of the number three its nature and therefore its function are static.[15]

Contemplating the psychological relationship between three and four, Jungian analyst Edward F. Edinger discusses the dynamic between these two numbers in his book *Ego and Archetype*. In the chapter titled, *The Trinity Archetype and the Dialectic of Development*, he stated:

> The threefold rhythm of the developmental process deserves greater attention. Let us consider that this ternary symbol is a separate and valid entity within itself. In this case the archetype of the trinity or threefoldness

---

12 Or as *Olam Asiyah*, עולם עשיה "World of Action."

13 Crowley, *The Book of Thoth*, p. 213 (Weiser 2000).

14 Gunther, *Mend Me this Shoe*, (TBP).

15 Compare this to the *Oxford* Physics definition "concerned with bodies at rest or forces in equilibrium."

> and the archetype of quaternity or fourfoldness would refer to two different aspects of the psyche, each valid, appropriate and complete in its own realm. The quaternity image expresses the totality of the psyche in its structural, static and eternal sense, whereas the trinity image expresses the totality of psychological experience in its dynamic, developmental, temporal aspect.[16]

The preceding Thoth Tarot card in the Suit of Disks is the Three of Disks, called *Works.* Keep in mind that all cards in this suit are attributed to the element Earth. Astrologically, the Three of Disks is ruled by Mars in Capricorn, that is, energy in construction, and therefore animated life in the Sephira of Malkuth. It differs from the inverted position of the Heart of Blood as it is shown from the viewpoint of the apex. This was done in order to draw attention the most importance aspect of this card, which is the base.

> The influence of Binah in the sphere of Earth shows the material establishment of the idea of the Universe, the determination of its basic form. It is ruled by Mars in Capricornus; he is exalted in that Sign, and therefore at his best. His energy is constructive, like that of the builder or engineer. The card represents a pyramid viewed from above the apex. The base is formed by three wheels Mercury, Sulphur, and Salt; Sattvas, Rajas, and Tamas in the Hindu system; Aleph, Shin, and Mem–Air, Fire, and Water–the three Mother letters of the Hebrew alphabet. This pyramid is situated in the great Sea of Binah in the Night of Time,[17]

*Figure EH3 - Works*

Although the meaning of this card diverges somewhat from the subject of this essay,[18] it nonetheless serves to lay the groundwork for the basic components inherent in this symbol. It clarifies the tripartite structure,

16 Edinger, *Ego and Archetype*, p. 182 (C. G. Jung Foundation 1972).

17 *The Book of Thoth*, pp. 212-13 (Weiser 2000).

18 This is primarily due to its point of view, which is limited to the element of Earth in the Sephira of Malkuth.

identifies its changeful nature, and reinforces the connection between Binah, Malkuth and The Heart of Blood. This connection is vital to understanding its meaning and the very important role it plays in the structure of the Initiatic system of A∴A∴ and its symbolism within Thelema in general.

The ternary base represents the inherent nature and function of its energy, which is creative, vital, and dynamic. Note that the base of the Pyramid is situated on three wheels, as seen on the Three of Disks. The three-fold interacting forces from the Hindu system, सत्त्व *Sattva*, रजस् *Rajas*, and तमस् *Tamas*,[19] collectively formulate the गुण, *Guṇas*.[20] These forces are said to be in constant motion, with each *Guṇa* striving against the other for dominance.

In his book *The Angel and the Abyss*, J. Daniel Gunther discusses both the mystical and practical attributions and application of these three energies. The chapter *The Forces of Life* is a good source for anyone wishing to study this subject. Specific to the point of this essay he states:

> Being threefold, we immediately recognize the Guṇas as an Archetype of the Divine Realm. The number Three is a number aligned with Divinity, not as a conscious association, but as an unconscious reality.[21]

In Qabalistic terms, the third Sephira בינה, *Binah*, dwells in the Supernal realm.[22] This reveals that the basis of this Symbol is of a transcendent nature beyond that of Rational Thought. This, I believe, is a fundamental quality to consider about the symbol we call The Heart of Blood.

*Figure EH4 - Threefold Knot of the Guṇas*

The threefold dynamic of the Guṇas generally represent the three rotating Forces of Life that govern the changes of the natural world. ☿ Mercury, 🜍 Sulphur, and 🜔 Salt are typical symbols of alchemy in its psychospiritual

19 "*Sattva* सत्त्व means 'lucidity', and represents clarity, fluidity and equability. *Rajas* रजस् means 'activity', and signifies excitability and energy. *Tamas* तमस् means 'obscurity' and is inaction, sluggishness and torpor." Gunther, *The Angel and the Abyss*, p. 135 (IBIS Press 2014).

20 "In Sanskrit, the word Guṇas गुण means literally, "thread," signifying a single stand of a more complex, intertwining cord. We interpret the Guṇas as modes of action, or tendencies, rather than actual qualities. These three together are the threads of tendencies for the phenomenal universe." See *The Angel and the Abyss, Forces of Life*, p. 135 (IBIS Press 2014).

21 Gunther, *The Angel and the Abyss*, p. 135 (IBIS Press 2014).

22 Binah contains all of the Three Primary Elements - א (Air) from Kether, ש (Fire) from Chokmah, מ (Water) from Binah.

form, and in one sense signify the constant distillation of a substance to bring it to perfection. Distillation is a process of circulation induced by an uninterrupted application of heat in order to release the fine matter from the raw matter.

This process of Circulatio, which is analogous to the Great Work, occurs within an alchemical vessel. An excellent representation of such an alchemical vessel of change is the *Vas Pellicanicum* (Pelican Vessel) which is suggestive of the feminine form. Vessels of varying types are predominantly symbols of the Primordial Feminine Archetype. From prehistoric time various figures of woman-like vessels in honorific and ritualistic form have been discovered which help to shed light on the unrecorded Matriarchal Aeon. Some of these figures linger into the epoch of the Father and further help to reveal the development of human consciousness toward the elementary Matriarch.

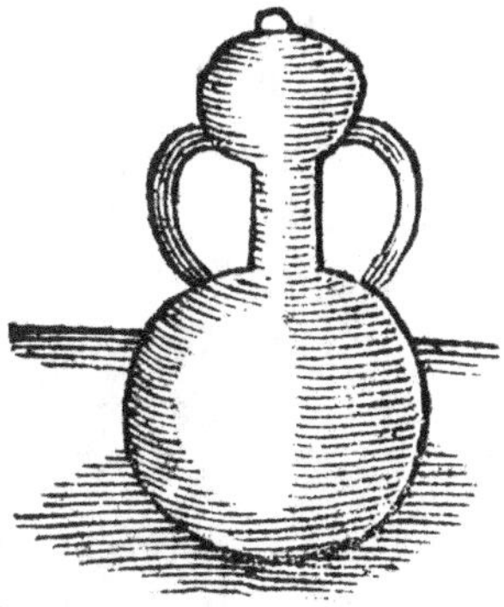

*Figure EH5 - The Form of a Pelican*

There has sometimes been the tendency to devalue and deflate the worth of "The Vessel". This is an inherited limitation from the past Aeon, that of the Father. But those newborn to the Aeon of the Child have the opportunity to see this motif with new eyes. Some basic associations of the Great Feminine vessel that appear in the forms of Nature are the cave shielding the mystery of the unknown; the egg of unborn animal life; the Earth as the fertile and fecundating great round of terrestrial life; the sea holding both plant and animal life in its depths; the Moon as a luminary filling and emptying with the light of the Sun; and even the empty sky by day upholding the chariot of the Sun, and by night covering the earth with Her body of stars. All of these grand expressions impress upon consciousness the idea that containment is the central symbol of the Primordial Feminine Archetype.

Contained within the Great Round of this small orb in space is the most important representation of this central feminine mystery, the human body. You will note that I said the human body, not only the female body. Erich Neumann wrote a well-rounded and informative book on this subject titled *The Great Mother, An Analysis of the Archetype.* In the chapter, *The Central Symbol of the Feminine* he states the following.

> This central symbol is the *vessel*. From the very beginning down to the latest stages of development we find this archetypal symbol as the essence of the feminine. The basic symbolic equation woman = body = vessel corresponds to what is perhaps mankind's - man's as well as woman's – most elementary

experience of the Feminine. The experience of the body as vessel is universally human and not limited to woman. What we have designated as "metabolic system"[23] is an expression of this phenomenon of the body as a vessel.[24]

Within the human body lies a world of its own, a little world, hidden from the outside whose internal function is complex and dynamic. Within this inner world exists the physical wonder of the heart. The heart is the central representation of the elementary feminine vessel as it exists in nature and as it relates to human life. The heart in connection with the circulatory system is an excellent exemplification of the constant motion of the three fold dynamic – which is not a separate thing from the vessel but *is* the natural function of the vessel.

Thus we can see that this Archetype in its structural manifestation is not static, but vigorous and robust. It offers the sacrament of incarnation, and both nourishes and enlivens the temporal individual life both male and female. The heart is therefore an embodiment of *Magna Mater*, which as progenitress of life in turn endows her offspring with a heart – the Heart of their Mother. This three-fold mother, son, daughter heart is poetically expressed in *Liber LXV, I:1.*

**O heart of my mother, my sister, mine own,**

In the commentary on Chapter I, which precedes this essay, the attributions are:

- **heart of my mother** = Isis as the Supernal Mother and ה Prima of יהוה
- **my sister** = the little world, the daughter as ה Final of יהוה
- **mine own** = Osiris, the son as ו of יהוה

From these attributions we can see the grand Archetype of the heart as encompassing the totality of the body as well as the instincts and consciousness. When we view both the body and psyche as structural vessels of life – both functions of the whole human being – these seemingly diverse modes of existence form a unifying harmony.

---

23 The text gives this reference: "My *Origins and History of Consciousness*" pp. 28 ff., 290 ff.

24 P. 39 (First Princeton/Bollingen 1974).

# CHAPTER II

## The Heart of Blood

### AS A TRANSFORMATIVE MANA SYMBOL

*All the formulae of Horus are Mysteries of the Averse, at least from the point of view below the Abyss. Any apparent paradox is resolved in practice only with the reconstellation of the aspirant's psyche.*[1]

Special attention should be paid to the distinct characteristic of Inversion. Inversion implies something within, below & hidden – all of which are correct associations of this symbol. In *Liber VII*, Chapter V, the chapter assigned to Mercury, the treasured Lapis is revealed in its principal location, the *Inverted Palace*, the Sephirah of Binah, which is also contains the *Secretest Chamber of the Palace*. It is this verse that gives this symbol its well-known title: Heart of Blood.

> **There is the Heart of Blood, a pyramid reaching its apex down beyond the Wrong of the Beginning. Bury me unto Thy Glory, O beloved, O princely lover of this harlot maiden, within the Secretest Chamber of the Palace!**[2]

The Initiatic mysteries presented in the verse above exceed the scope of this essay, it is enough to note the inverted and hidden ideas associated with the Heart of Blood. Relevant to this subject is the doctrinal comprehension that the Mountain of Abiegnus[3] resides above the Abyss in the bosom of the Great Mother. The subsequent descent of the apex reaches down into Malkuth, the world of the actual where it is realized. It is this relationship that embodies the harmony between Binah, Malkuth and The Heart of Blood. In figurative language, the triangle, kinetically considered, is a symbol of directed force.[4]

---

1 Gunther, *Initiation in the Aeon of the Child*, p. 50 (IBIS Press 2009).

2 *Liber VII*, V:42-43 Note: A brief designation in Qabalistic terms of the *Wrong of the Beginning* is necessary. The *Wrong of the Beginning* refers to the first Sephira Kether since its existence marks the first deviation from the perfection of Nothing.

3 The symbolic mountain of God in the center of the Universe. See Gunther, *Initiation in the Aeon of the Child*, Glossary, 193.

4 Crowley, *The Book of Lies*, Chapter 69 (Weiser 1970).

The descending Heart of Blood therefore signifies the Inverse Initiatic Current governing the formula of progress in the New Aeon. The Formula of Progress within the Magical and Mystical system of A∴A∴ follows the averse path that is contrary to the pattern of manifestation; The Path of the Great Return.

*Figure EH6 - My Wine is Poured Out*

In a very personal way, the aspirant to A∴A∴ who experiences the Neophyte Ceremony, comes into direct contact with the Averse current of Hoor and as such is fitted to wear the emblem called the Heart of Blood upon his or her breast. Thusly adorned they are reminded of their commitment to

The Path of the Great Return which represents directed movement toward the goal of Initiation. In the most general terms the goal of the traveler on this journey is to move from a state of complexity and disorder to one of simplicity and equilibrium. Aleister Crowley analyzing this situation in numerical, or Qabalistic terms wrote:

> Now the Aspirant to Magic is displeased with this state of things. He finds himself but a creature, the farthest removed from the Creator, a number so complex and involved that he can scarcely imagine, much less dare to hope for, its reduction to the One.[5]

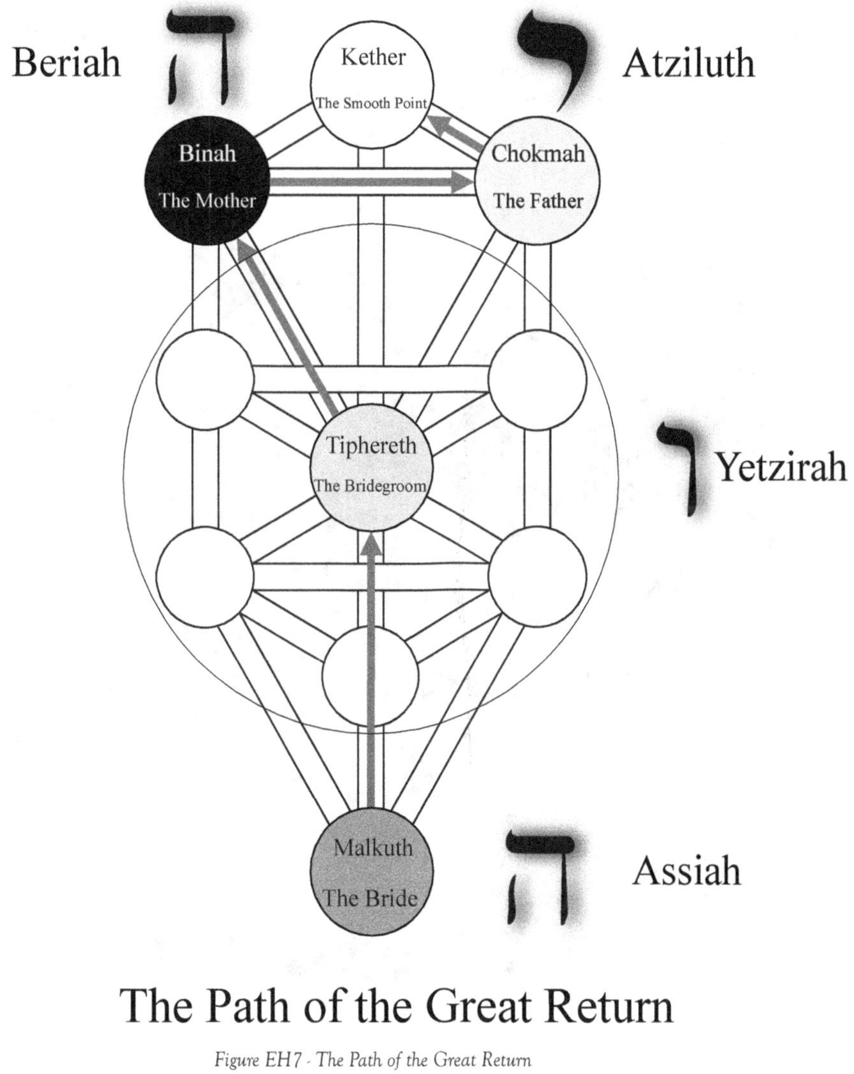


*Figure EH7 - The Path of the Great Return*

5 Crowley, *777 and Other Qablistic Writings of Aleister Crowley*, p. 38 (Weiser 1997).

This idea was summed up when Crowley later says *I am Malkuth. I wish to become Kether.* Likewise in this essay he touched on the redemptive formula of Tetragrammaton יהוה though the transformation of ה the Daughter to ה the Mother. This doctrine of ה ה and the term *The Mother is the Daughter, the Daughter is the Mother*[6] conceals the experiential narrative of the aspirant to A.'. A.'.. This Initiatic doctrine has been developed and detailed all throughout *The Inward Journey Series*, by J. Daniel Gunther. However, it is in *Book II, The Secret of V*, that this Averse Formula is clearly explained. For those who have not studied this series I will quote a brief summary.

> Each aspirant is ה Final, the Daughter. Our task is to set the Daughter upon the Throne of the Mother, which is ה Prima or Binah. This awakens the Eld of the All-Father Chokmah, which corresponds to י (Yod). The reunion of Yod the All-Father and Heh the All-Mother is the Perfect and the Perfect uniting to form One Perfect in Kether, which is thus None, the attainment of a condition of Nothingness, which I have termed *Nulliversion*. This entire sequence is what I have called THE PATH OF THE GREAT RETURN.[7]

*Figure EH8 - Demeter, Enthroned in Benediction*

6 Crowley, *777 and Other Qablistic Writings of Aleister Crowley*, p. 40 (Weiser 1997).

7 Gunther, *The Angel and the Abyss*, p. 282 (IBIS Press 2014).

Thus far in my essay I have repeatedly invoked the symbolism of the Feminine Archetype, and so it will likely be apparent that the Heart of Blood is principally a glyph of the Feminine Mysteries. It is likewise a symbol synonymous with the letter ה, within the teachings of A∴A∴. Notice that I chose the term *Feminine Archetype* and **not** *Great Mother*. This distinction is important since I mean to include the totality of the Archetype in Her various forms, which both include and exceed the venerable mystery of motherhood.

In the prior chapter I aligned the threefold configuration of the base of the pyramid with the elementary character of the vessel and with Primordial Goddess. With the transition to the Aeon of Horus there was a psychic development of the Yin principle in harmony with the Yang principle. With this change there is a new and vibrant unfolding of the Feminine Mana[8] Figure in the central nexus of spiritual development which I call *The Return of the Great Goddess.*

The mother–daughter relationship as containing an Initiatic formula is not original to Thelema. Perhaps the best known example is to be found in the *Eleusinian Mysteries*. While much of the knowledge of the Eleusinian Mysteries is unknown, I surmise that the ritual centered around the natural phenomena of the seed and the plant, with the purpose of imparting the spiritual meaning of death and rebirth.

In this teaching the earthy dominant Feminine Archetype was represented by Δαμάτηρ, *Demeter*. She was the Mother whose power of fertility governed plant, mineral, and animal life. She was the embodiment of the fertile earth and the guardian of the secret that transformed seed into grain. She was the guardian of the knowledge of immortality.

Her virgin daughter Περσεφόνη, *Persephone*, in the first bloom of womanhood, stood at the threshold of this same secret. Unknown to Persephone, she had caught the eye of the *Host of Many*, a terrifying suitor from the depths of the Underworld. The Host of Many was a euphemism for Ἅδης, *Hades*, Lord of the dead.[9]

*Figure EH9 - Persephone's Return*

In this myth Hades represented the numinous phallic principle which caught the eye of the maiden

8 Oxford definition: *a spiritual power, authority or energy within people, places or things*. My use of this word is intended to mean: *numinous and influential*.

9 *Hymn 2 to Demeter*, p. 289 (Hugh G. Evelyn-White).

in the form of a seductive and radiant flower called the νάρκισσος, narcissus.[10] The attraction to the flower was also indicative of the awakening of the libidinal fire within the maiden. Upon succumbing to the instinct to reach for this flower she was immediately ravished away not to the starry overworld, but to the chthonic dark world in her epic descent into Hell.

While in that dark world she partook of a single pomegranate seed which bound her forever to the Lord of Hell and to the realm of the dead. The daughter Persephone was thus initiated into the mystery of fertility and motherhood.

In order to understand this transformation attention should be given the corporal experience of Womankind, whom nature has endowed with the mysterious power of generation and nourishment of life. Of the sexes, it is the woman who intimately *experiences* the whole circle of life as the vessel of life.

In other words, the Woman experiences herself, as described by Neumann:

> It is important for the basic understanding of the magical efficacy of woman and of woman as a mana figure to bear in mind that woman necessarily experienced herself as subject and object of mysterious processes and as a vessel of transformation. The mysterious occurrences in her body, the instinctual mysteries of her existence, are exclusively the possession of woman.[11]

The Eleusinian Mysteries developed during the Aeon of Isis, and prospered in the Aeon of Osiris. It has blossomed in the Aeon of Horus. This same mother–daughter mystical dynamic was reborn from the Unconscious in new and numinous garments specific to Thelema.

Contemplating these mysterious processes within the mother–daughter dynamic in its sublimated and spiritual correlation opens the door to a *new and vibrant unfolding of the Feminine Mana Figure in the central nexus of spiritual development.* What I mean by "new" is that there is an expansion of Initiatic consciousness, as the formula of ה ה expresses a widening of the horizon of aspirational development for every initiate male and female equally. Spiritually, every aspirant that passes through the Neophyte Initiation is Persephone, while the abduction by Hades represents the opening of the Grade of Malkuth.

The mystical descent into Hell is a twofold dynamic which sets in motion the *reconstellation of the aspirant's psyche.* Figuratively, it signifies a descent *into* the Mother Vessel, as an alembic of spiritual alchemy[12] wherein the threefold Forces of Life become the Forces of Transformation within this *Body of the*

---

10 Liddell-Scott, *Greek-English Lexicon*, p. 991a.

11 Neumann, *The Great Mother*, p. 291 (First Princeton/Bollingen 1974).

12 See *Liber X*, 20.

*Pelican.*[13] This descent *within* the individual signifies a "turning inward" to the heart, the center of one's innermost self. The heart center of the Self is called *Hell* within the doctrine of Thelema.[14] In this way the candidate is led into the *spiritual feminine transformative character, which leads though suffering*[15] *and death, sacrifice and annihilation, to renewal, rebirth and immortality.*[16]

In the vision of The Ninth Æthyr [17] the seer was led to the Palace of the Virgin who was enthroned in Binah. He described Her as *proud and delicate and beyond imagination fair.*

More importantly, it was said that her body IS the Palace.

In this Vision, instruction was given to the seer concerning the volatile movement of the Spirit in the psyche of the aspirant, beginning with the opening of the Gates of Malkuth. [18]

> **They also tremble that are without, and they are shaken from without by the earthquakes of his judgement. They have set their affections upon the earth, and they have stamped with their feet upon the earth, and cried: It moveth not. Therefore hath earth opened with strong motion, like the sea, and swallowed them. Yea, she hath opened her womb to them that lusted after her, and she hath closed herself upon them. There lie they in torment, until by her quaking the earth is shattered like brittle glass, and dissolved like salt in the waters of his mercy, so that they are cast upon the air to be blown about therein, like seeds that shall take root in the earth; yet turn they their affections upward to the sun.** [19]

The Earth, that is Malkuth, transforms into the sea, which symbolizes a dramatic event called the "volatizing of the fixed." Within the framework of the Path of the Great Return the "volatizing of the fixed" followed by the "fixing of the volatile" are terms used to describe the ongoing process of movement through the Grades.[20] This "process" is exemplary of what I discussed in the

---

13 An example of this "Body of the Pelican" is the Tree of Life as the cohesive structure of the Grades of A∴ A∴.

14 Concerning the Thelemic doctrine of Hell, see *The Vision & the Voice*, The 22nd *Æthyr* (Weiser 1998). Also see *Parables of Thelema*, pp. 19-51 (Wennofer House 2023).

15 It is important to keep in mind the proper attitude toward suffering. See: Gunther, *Initiation in the Aeon of the Child, Skeleton of a New Truth* (IBIS Press 2009).

16 Neumann, *The Great Mother*, p. 291 (First Princeton/Bollingen 1974).

17 Crowley, *The Vision & the Voice*, pp. 172-177 (Weiser 1998).

18 The Neophyte Grade comprises the whole of the Outer College.

19 Crowley, *The Vision & the Voice*, p. 177 (Weiser 1998).

20 For a study in more detail on this process see: Gunther, *Initiation in the Aeon of the Child*, chap. One, Four & Five.

first chapter: *This process of Circulatio, which is analogous to the Great Work, occurs* ***within*** *an alchemical vessel.*

In this way, the formula of ה ה is sympathetic with that which Neumann expressed: *woman necessarily experiences herself as subject and object of mysterious processes and as a vessel of transformation,* if we understand these *mysterious processes* as a two-fold dynamic of the archetypical vessel. This is where one experiences *Cor Mulieris Mysteriorum*[21] as the Macrocosmic Transformative Vessel and their own individual heart as a microcosmic vessel of that Transformation.

*Figure EH10 - Die Sünde*

So far the mother-daughter duality has served as the basis of the link between ה Prima and ה Final, within the formula of יהוה, Yet in order to discover the wholeness of this symbol we have to look at it in a way that is independent of the generational function. That is to say, as its own self-contained quality.

The most striking and oppositional aspects[22] of the Feminine Archetype which have emerged in this Aeon with fresh charisma,[23] are the harlot and the virgin.

The concept of virgin is aligned with maiden, and since *Liber VII* uses the term harlot – maiden this is the form I will use going forward. The forms of this quaternary, mother – daughter – harlot – maiden, are all unique reflections of OUR LADY BABALON, BLESSED BE HER NAME.

The elements of this diametrically opposed paradigm may at first seem to be internally incompatible with each other. However, when they are examined by the symbolic significance of the Heart of Blood, a unification occurs. The inverted triangular form by its shape suggests the vulva and the womb, and therefore the feminine libido and creative force. This is the obvious and material

21 "The Heart of the Woman of the Mysteries" signifies the Feminine Instructive Principle. The "Woman of the Mysteries" is also a title of Babalon from *Liber LXV,* III:58.

22 Synonymous with the mother–daughter motif we have been discussing.

23 From Greek χάρισμα (*chárisma*), which means "favor freely given" or "gift of grace."

interrelation between them. Within this quaternary are the dual phases, harlot and maiden, as the self-governing and self-contained twin libido; also present are the mother and daughter as the creatrix-creatus through unification with the masculine counterpart. This representation of the quaternary serves to solidify the feminine aspect of the tripartite Heart.

What this reveals is that Feminine Libido, no longer shrouded with taboo and restriction, has developed an autonomous presence in the human psyche.[24] What I mean by libido is not limited to the sex instinct[25] but is intended to be understood in a broader sense: as *psychic energy*, mana, life energy.[26]

Magically, they both embody the Cup, which is the distinguishing attribute of ה, and therefore represents a mystical unity between them. It also expresses a universality in the magical formula of Tetragrammaton. For the Cup is a circle and seeks to expand infinitely. In the loftiest sense it is representative of the emptiness and vastness of Space. In its ability to receive it is the desire for the fulfillment of every possibility and so emblematic of the lust for union. As the great transformer of the seed it is the abundant cornucopia of life, and so becomes the Pantacle of the Earth. All of this is prefigured in the little Chalice in the arsenal of the Magician, and in the Heart of Blood upon the Robe of the Neophyte.

> The Robe of the Neophyte of the A∴A∴ is therefore adorned with a descending Red Triangle that is a Heart of Blood, affirming commitment to the Great Work and the ultimate outpouring of that blood into the Cup of Babalon of which it is likewise an emblem.[27]

The magical substance of the Cup is the mystical element of Water, with the qualities of fluidity, change, transmutation, and reflection—all of which give the Cup a Mercurial virtue. Alchemically, Mercury is a metal that is fluid, a paradox of nature. In another sense it is representative of the senses: the sensorium, the thoughts, the emotions, the complexities of consciousness, all of which lead to the final contemplation of this chapter and a sacral and material mystery of the Heart of Blood.

---

24 This universal autonomy is new, and still has to be realized by the individual and by the traditional customs of humankind. This will take time.

25 At first glance one may assume the libido is limited to the sexual impulse and the sex organ, and therefore solely of the nature of the Nephesh. However, the libido is not limited to sex. There are also other subjective impulses that are products of this force, such as desire, drive, attraction and other random impulses that lie hidden within the individual psyche until they "burst out," so to speak.

26 See Jung, *The Structure and Dynamics of the Psyche, On Psychic Energy* (Princeton University Press 1970).

27 Gunther, *Initiation in the Aeon of the Child,* p. 124 (IBIS Press 2009).

Figure EH11 - Yogi in Tantric Meditation

It is one that is found in the etymological connection between the words *sacral* and *sacrum*. Both share the meaning of being sacred. The Latin phrase *Os Sacrum* translates as "holy bone," from Greek ἱερὸν ὀστέον (*hieròn ostéon*). The sacrum bone along with the coccyx in the body reside at the base of the spine. These bones in the human body form the shape of an inverted triangle. The sacrum acts as a fulcrum of support for the extended serpentine spinal column up to the cranium. This bone in female anatomy is referred to as the "gate of life," as its flexibility is instrumental in opening the birthing canal. The close proximity to the womb and the pivotal role it plays in giving life imbued it from prehistoric times with a numinous and sacred status.

This linguistic and ritualistic association is not only found in the European continent but also in Mesoamerica. In a paper titled, *The Mesoamerican Sacrum Bone: Doorway to the Otherworld*,[28] the cultural importance of the sacrum bone and the spinal column are documented. Concerning the linguistic etymology, it states:

> In those Mayan languages for which we have translations of sacrum and coccyx, the words usually relate the sacrum to notions of "god" and "sacred", while the coccyx is related to "fire". For example, Yucatec Maya has a word for sacrum, k'ul, which also means "sacred" and "holy" (Barrera Vasquez 1980). Itzá Maya has the word k'uul "hip, tail bone" (Hoffling and Tesucún 1997:402), which surely derives from the Itzá root k'u "sacred, holy". The Tojolabal Maya word for sacrum s-bah h-wawtik (literally "sacred image, sacred self") is based on the verb wawtikan "to worship, deify," and ultimately derives from the root waw "man" (Lenkersdorf 1979 (2):666; (1):395).

28 Brian Strauss, *The Mesoamerican Sacrum Bone: Doorway to the Otherworld* Chapter: *The Holy Sacrum: Evidence From Language* (University of Texas at Austin, 2007.) http://research.famsi.org/aztlan/uploads/papers/stross-sacrum.pdf.

This chapter on the linguistics of the "sacred bone" is summed up as follows:

> However, through information preserved in language and in narrative, particularly when in written form, we are able to determine that some Old World perceptions of the sacrum and pelvic region, if not identical, were at least similar and comparable to those in Mesoamerica, and that data from the Old World links the "holy bone" or sacrum directly to resurrection, which implies passage through at least a figurative cosmic portal or doorway between this world and the other world.

The sacrum (sacrum and coccyx) is the place where the *kuṇḍalinī*, the serpentine Magical Force, resides in its passive state. As a reservoir of physic energy she is figured as a coiled serpent at the base of the spine and residing in the *mūlādhāra cakra*.

> In the pericarp of that Adhara lotus is a very beautiful triangular yoni, kept secret in all tantras. The great goddess Kundalini is there, in the form of a streak of lightning. Coiled three and one-half times, she is delicate and resembles a snake.[29]

*Figure EH12 - Virtue*

This Yogic view of transformation through the awaking of this mysterious fire is a direct and efficacious method which has been subsumed within the teaching and testing Order of A.∴ A.∴. Although the Kundalini is traditionally viewed as a goddess, and therefore feminine, it is a force that is present in both men and women, representing a cosmic and universal power of the soul. Note that I used the term "power of the soul," which is meant to point to the aspect of the soul called the נפש, *Nephesh*, which corresponds to ה the daughter in the hierarchy of Tetragrammaton. Some attributes of the Nephesh are the emotions and the instincts of the individual. Perhaps one of the best descriptions of this mysterious fire is given in the Tarot comment on the Three of Wands: primeval Energy.

---

29 शिव संहिता, *Śiva Saṃhitā*, p.31. (VogaVodya first edition, translated by James Mallinson 2007).

> This card refers to Binah in the suit of Fire, and so represents the establishment of primeval Energy. The Will has been transmitted to the Mother, who conceives, prepares, and gives birth to, its manifestation. It refers to the Sun in Aries, the Sign in which he is exalted. The meaning is harmonious, for this is the beginning of Spring. For this reason one sees the wand taking the form of the Lotus in blossom. The Sun has enkindled the Great Mother.[30]

The awaking of the serpentine force and the subsequent opening of the *cakras* is emblematic of the flower that is planted in Malkuth and blooms in the light of the Sun. The Master Therion, 666, in his book on Magick[31] aligns the potency of this mysterious energy to the Magical Cup. This chapter gives a myriad of analogies on its complexity and examples of what the Great Work of the Magical Cup is, yet there is only One aspiration of the Cup, which is to receive Truth. It is the Divine Kiss of the Holy One that awakens the magical soul on the *corpse of Osiris afloat in tomb*! Much like the opening of the earth in the symbolism of the Ninth Æthyr, the awaking sets in motion the transformation of the *seeds that shall take root in the earth; yet turn they their affections upward to the sun.*

---

30 Crowley, *The Book of Thoth*, p. 190 (Weiser 2000).

31 Crowley, *Book IV* (Weiser 1994).

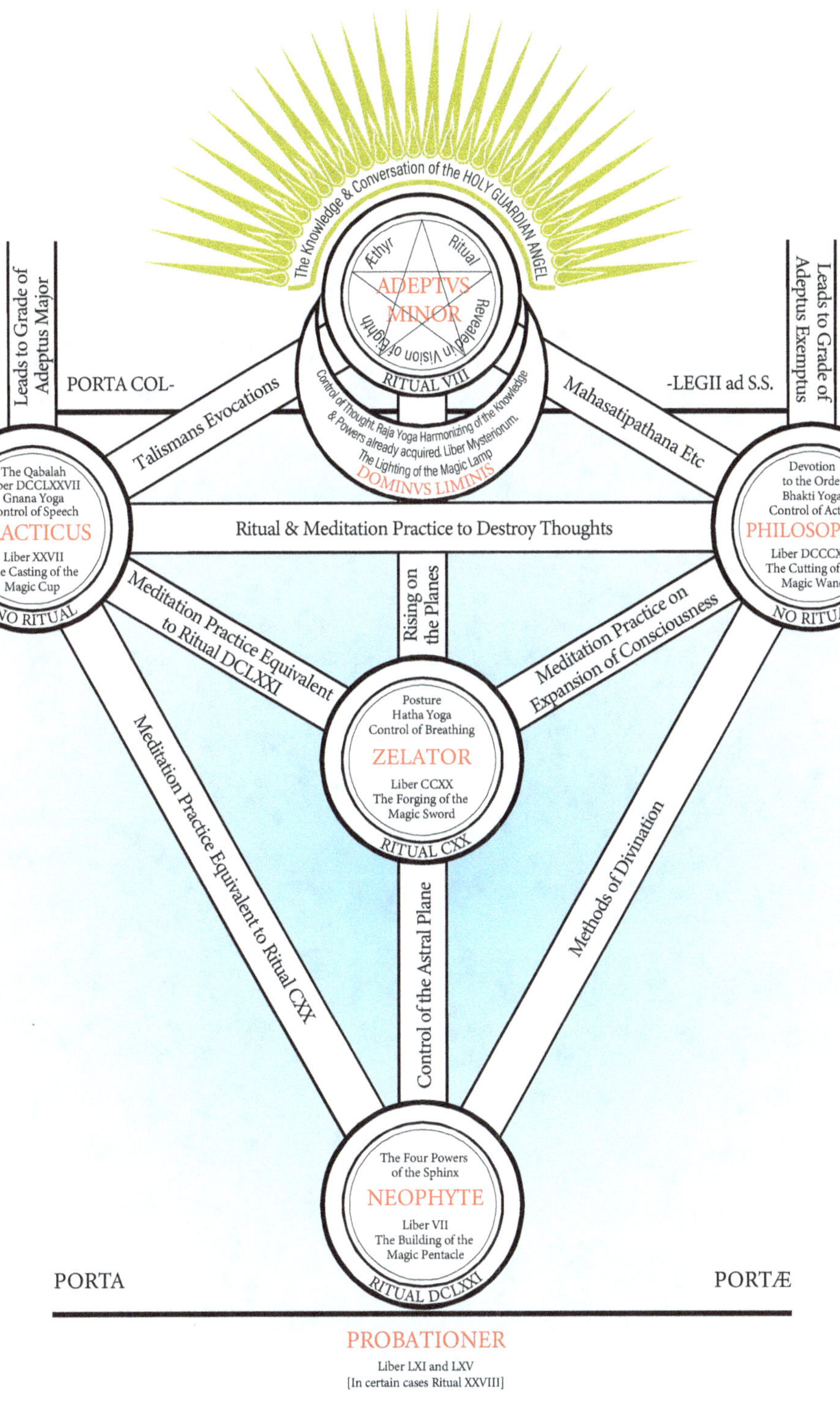


*Figure EH13 - Graduum Montis Abiegni*

# CHAPTER III

## The Heart of Blood

### AS THE TREASURED LAPIS

*Oh my Lord, let us sail upon the sea of blood!*[1]

The most striking visual component of this symbol is the colour. Red usually denotes warmth, love, passion, action, danger, and – most relevant to this symbol – life. For the blood is the life.[2]

In *Liber LXV*, III: 28, this figure is described as the red three-angled heart. We know that the colour red specifically means blood, and the three angles refer to its basic structure. The potency of blood and the threefold structure are both characteristics which reinforce the vibrant and energetic qualities of the Heart of Blood. The number three expresses a lofty idea and the substance of blood a very human reality, thus emblematic of the spiritual life of the aspirant.

*Figure EH14 - The Red Triangle of the Neophyte Robe*

In contemplating both verses there is a noticeable difference in the way this Heart is presented to the reader. In *Liber VII* the initiate is led to it and it is addressed in upper case, designating "Heart of Blood" as the title proper. In *Liber LXV* the heart is referred to in the lower case. Furthermore, the heart is **set up** in the shrine, signifying to the reader that it was deliberately placed there. It will be worthwhile to note that the subject of *Liber VII* is the initiation of the Master of the Temple, while *Liber LXV* is that of the Adept.[3]

1 *Liber LXV,* III:41.

2 *Deuteronomy,* 12:23 KJV.

3 This is a generalization for analysis, however, keep in mind that all Holy Books of Thelema transcend the reasoning faculty. See the comment on the 1909 edition of *Thelema* concerning *Liber LXV,* "The full knowledge of the interpretation of this book is concealed from all, save only the Shining Triangle." The Shining Triangle refers to the Supernals.

**The red three-angled heart hath been set up in Thy shrine; for the priests despised equally the shrine and the god.**

The red three-angled heart signifies the heart of man in the Temple of the Neophyte,[4] which in one sense is the shrine of Osiris. The heart is *set up*, that is elevated, so that attention can be drawn to it. The very first perception of the god in the shrine is as the corpse of Osiris. He is the natural man clothed in the garment of death in the shrine of the sorrow of Isis. On this sorrow Crowley said: *This trance is not simple and definite; indeed, it commonly begins in a limited selfish form. The imagination cannot pierce beyond terrestrial conditions, or the sense of self grasp more than the natural consciousness.*[5] Yet it is the initial perception of sorrow by means of the instincts (Nephesh) and the intellect (Ruach) that prompt the Intuition to look beyond the veil of mortality and for some, to seek Initiation. In a practical way the shrine serves to "show the way," which gives the conscious Self a destination to orient to. The Neophyte of A.·.A.·. will know this shrine when he comes face to face with the Guardians of the Three Points of the Triangle.

But this is all very preliminary.[6] More important is the use of the upper case "T" in ***Thy** shrine* which reveals that it is the shrine of the Angel. The word "shrine" comes from the Anglo-Saxon word *scrin* and from the Latin *scrinium*,[7] meaning a chest or box and thus implying an object made intentionally for a specific purpose. It is something man-made, that is, something intellectually constructed. The word shrine understood in its modern use means an erected structure. It typically serves to represent something sacred, something holy. In the midst of the *great-city*, the priests of **אדני**, *Adonai*, have erected the shrine of L.V.X. to serve Him, and to serve mankind. The great city represents all the seven Sephiroth below the abyss, of which **תפארת**, *Tiphereth*, is the center. In the lyrical expression from *Chapter III* of *The Book of the Heart Girt with a Serpent* the great city is called *the city of the violets and the roses*.

**I, and Me, and Mine were sitting with lutes in the market-place of the great city, the city of the violets and the roses.**[8]

Tiphereth as the center of this great city is called the "market-place;" it is also referred to as "the agora."[9] Yet, this public display of the deific image earns

4 Gunther, *Angel and the Abyss*, p. 161 (IBIS Press 2018).

5 Crowley, *Little Essays Toward Truth, on Sorrow*, p. 21 (Facsimile Edition 1985).

6 Perhaps it is better to say that the identification with Osiris is simply a veil of the shrine.

7 Skeats, *Etymological Dictionary*, p.411.

8 *Liber LVX*, III:21.

9 *Liber VII*, II:10.

the scorn of the priests. That which is sacred has become subject to the faults and limitations of the individual. Note it says that the Priest despised equally the shrine and the god, as any formula or imago of Adonai is insufficient. Why? Verse 26 tells us exactly why this is so.

**For there is no Symbol of Thee.**[10]

The verse that follows the display of the heart in the market-place shows why the heart was *set up in Thy shrine* and how it ultimately serves to reveal the Truth.

**Yet all the while Thou wast hidden therein, as the Lord of Silence is hidden in the buds of the lotus.**[11]

The Shrine of *L.V.X.*, is an outward display of something that can never be revealed openly. It only serves to draw attention to what it conceals. This hidden virtue is likened to the Lord of Silence which is a twin aspect of the Pantomorphous Lord of the Aeon whose known attribute is Strength.[12] In seeking to understand this mystery special attention should be paid to this solar babe and the lotus who represented the rebirth of Osiris through the intervention of Isis in Egyptian mythology.

*Figure EH15 - Emerging from the Lotus*

First note that the Lord of Silence is Harpocrates who was typically represented as a babe in an egg of the freshly risen Sun. Although he was represented anthropomorphically his primary attribute was solar.

In this Aeon He is the expression of Hoor that takes a fully human form. This indicates His Archetype is capable of conscious manifestation, albeit hidden within the Lotus. His Solar nature reveals that He is a Star, and thus immortal and imperishable though wrapped in the illusion of death and rebirth. Thus the Star child is emblematic of the transpersonal center of the self and the three fold birth of *form, death and hell* kindled into life by the Lord of Hell.[13]

In commenting on this symbol, 666 stated that "*The red three angled heart*" *is the peculiar symbol of Ra-Hoor-Khuit*; and that *Not until nineteen years later did*

10 *Liber LVX*, III:26.

11 *Liber LVX*, III:29.

12 *Liber CCXX*, III:70.

13 *Parables of Thelema*, p. 45-50 (Wennofer House 2023).

*he fully realize that the Holy Guardian Angel was concealed in this symbol Ra-Hoor Khuit.*[14] One meaning of this comment is that the red three angled heart both conceals and reveals the Heart of Hoor. Just as the Heart of Blood on the Robe of the Neophyte represents both the individual Cup and the Universal Cup, so this heart set up in the market-place is likewise an emblem of the heart of man and the Heart of the Initiator. [15] The link between them is the transformation of the heart of Osiris, that is the heart called ***mine own,*** by the pivotal experience in Tiphereth on the Path of the Great Return.

> We symbolically begin this Journey as Asar, or Osiris, the Lord of the Dead. The death of Osiris is first celebrated in the Ritual of the Pyramid. From the ceremony of the Pyramid we arise as Asar-un-Nefer, which being interpreted is *Myself Made Perfect.* We then loosen the swathings of the corpse, unbind the feet of Osiris, so that with continued aspiration and initiation, the Candidate symbolically becomes the flaming god Hoor, the Child, who may rage through the universe with his fantastic spear.[16]

Second, note that He is *hidden* in the lotus upon the Water. Thus He is eternally connected to the regenerative powers of the cosmic womb. The divine child on the lotus is a mythological expression of the divine birth motif. Psychologically, symbolic birth from a flower carries a very important spiritual significance:

*Figure EH16 - Lotus Blossom*

> The bond between woman and plant can be followed though all the stages of human symbolism. The psyche as flower, as lotus, lily, and rose, the virgin as flower in Eleusis, symbolize the flowerlike unfolding of the highest psychic and spiritual developments. Thus birth from the female blossom is an archetypical form of divine birth, whether we think of Ra or Nefertem in Egypt, or of the Buddhist "divine treasure in the lotus," or, in China and the modern West, of the birth of the self in the Golden Flower.[17]

---

14 Crowley, *Commentaries to the Holy Books and Other Papers*, pp. 123-4 (Weiser 1996).

15 *Liber AL Vel Legis* I:49 "Hoor in his secret name and splendour is the Lord initiating."

16 Gunther, *The Angel and the Abyss*, p. 285 (IBIS Press 2014).

17 Neumann, *The Great Mother*, p. 262 (First Princeton/Bollingen 1974).

Notice that the symbol of the flower has appeared all throughout this essay in varying forms. Wherever there is a flower there is a transformation of sorts, and so it is emblematic of the development of the aspirant and the transformations of the heart. There is the narcissus of Persephone as the flower of Malkuth. There are the lotuses of the *cakras*, the magick Cup and the flower of the Nile Water. The violets of Aphrodite in the great city as the secret flower flame of love and adoration for the Angel. Lastly there is the Rose. Concerning the Mystery of the Rose, I will be silent.

This brings me to the last and most important quality of the Lord within the lotus which is *Silence*. It is therefore impossible to say more. Mere analysis will fail to capture the Truth, and the rituals alone will not make true initiation happen. It is by communion with the Silence in the Eden of one's soul that the Arcanum is revealed.[18] Concerning this, the Master Therion stated:

> Of all the magical and mystical virtues, of all the graces of the Soul, of all the attainments of the Spirit, none has been so misunderstood, even when at all apprehended, as Silence. It would not be possible to enumerate the common errors; nay, it may be said that to think of it at all is in itself an error; for its nature is Pure Being, that is to say, Nothing, so that it is beyond all intellection or intuition. Thus, then, the utmost of our Essay can be only a certain Wardship, as it were a Tyling of the Lodge wherein the Mystery of Silence may be consummated.[19]

*Figure EH17 - Rose Upon the Cross*

18 *Liber LVX*, V:7.

19 Crowley, *The Book of Thoth*, p. 120 (Weiser 2000).

Throughout this essay I have tried to tie together varying and sometimes contrary aspects of this one symbol, into a harmony that is perceivable and relatable. So far I have discussed its elementary tripartite structure, its Initiatic Archetypes, and its personal meaning to the aspirant. At this point I endeavor to discuss in more detail the very lofty and sacred mystery of The Heart of Blood. To do this I will start by reinforcing a distinction I made earlier: The Heart of Blood that adorns the Robe of the Neophyte is emblematic of ה Final, and relates to the Microcosm. Its function is personal devotion to the Great Work and most importantly service to others. This is the act of pouring the individual life into the Golden Cup of Babalon. The Heart of Blood as a symbol of the Macrocosm corresponds to ה Prima. It signifies that which is poured out from Her Cup for the worshiper and offers the mystic Union with God.

*Figure EH18 - Commitment to the Great Work*

Heh final of Tetragrammaton is attributed to Pentacles, or Coins. The "redemption" of Heh final is the restoration of the Daughter Malkuth to the Throne of the Mother Binah. The messenger of Babalon who delivered that Word of the Scarlet Woman unto the world was V.V.V.V.V., and that Word embodied the means of crossing the Abyss. It is not accomplished by vicarious atonement and faith in the labors of another; within the crucible of each individual heart the coin must be redeemed by self-sustained effort. The price is paid with our own blood, not by faith in the blood of another. The Robe of the Neophyte of the A.∴ A.∴ is therefore adorned with a descending Red Triangle that is a Heart of Blood, affirming commitment to the Great Work and the ultimate outpouring of that blood into the Cup of Babalon of which it is likewise an emblem.[20]

Leading the way to the Heart of Blood in its appearance in *Liber VII*[21] is the child of Aphrodite, the god Ἔρος, *Eros*. He is the embodiment of passion,

---

20 Gunther, *Initiation in the Aeon of the Child*, p. 124 (IBIS Press 2014).

21 The distinction I made earlier - concerning *Liber LXV* and *Liber VII* is important to keep in mind.

desire, and love, from whence we get the English word "erotic."[22]

Notice that there is a dramatic sequence of events which sets the stage for the revelation of The Heart of Blood.

> **Then, O my God, the breath of the Garden of Spices. All these have a savour averse. The cone is cut with an infinite ray; the curve of hyperbolic life springs into being. Farther and farther we float; yet we are still. It is the chain of systems that is falling away from us. First falls the silly world; the world of the old grey land. Falls it unthinkably far, with its sorrowful bearded face presiding over it; it fades to silence and woe. We to silence and bliss, and the face is the laughing face of Eros. Smiling we greet him with the secret signs. He leads us into the Inverted Palace. There is the Heart of Blood, a pyramid reaching its apex down beyond the Wrong of the Beginning.**

A detailed commentary on the meaning of the verses would require an essay in itself. However, relevant to this subject is the observation that silence and woe, characterized by the sorrowful bearded face,[23] so dominant in the world of the old grey land fade away. These characteristics are also synonymous with those of the Eastern concept of the *Wheel of Karma*, and so this event is also described as *the chain of systems that is falling away*.[24] In the stillness the Virtues of silence and bliss, personified as *Eros*, show the way into the Primordial Heart of Blood.[25]

*Figure EH19 - Cupid Triumphant*

The appearance of this erotic god in the Inverted Palace of Binah represents the awakened Eld of the All-Father in חכמה, *Chokmah*, by the

22 *Liber VII*, V:32-42.

23 The sorrowful bearded face is an imago of the dying god.

24 *Liber VII*, V:36.

25 The Vault of the Masters.

presence of the harlot maiden. The harlot maiden has another name in the system of A.'. A.'., which is: *Scarlet Woman.* It is important to remember that *all Masters of the Temple are Scarlet Women.*[26]

She is ה Final the Bride who through union with ו the Bridegroom, is transformed in the Palace of Beauty. Upon entry into the Inverted Palace she consummates the union with י the All-Father and so becomes ה Prima the All-Mother.[27] This sequence of events signifies the fulfillment of the experiential narrative I discussed in the prior chapter: *The Mother is the Daughter and the Daughter is the Mother.* Thus the individual heart is joined with the Mystery of the Great Mother Babalon in the City of the Pyramids and becomes an Universal Heart.

This joyous event is expressed beautifully in the ecstatic cry of *Liber LXV*:

> **Let Kheph-Ra sound his sharded drone! let the jackals of Day and Night howl in the wilderness of Time! let the Towers of the Universe totter, and the guardians hasten away! For my Lord hath revealed Himself as a mighty serpent, and my heart is the blood of His body.**[28]

In The Vision of the 12$^{th}$ Æthyr Frater Perdurabo encounters the Charioteer bearing the Sangraal from the Supernal abode of the Great Mother Babalon by the Path of ח. As the Cup takes center stage in the unfolding of the Vision, an all pervasive perfume fills the Aire.

> **And there is a marvelous perfume in the Aire, like unto the perfume of Ra-Hoor-Khuit, but sublimated, as if the quintessence of that perfume alone were burnt. For it hath the richness and voluptuousness and humanity of blood, and the strength and freshness of meal, and the sweetness of honey, and the purity of olive-oil, and the holiness of that oil which is made of myrrh, and cinnamon, and galangal.**[29]

---

26 Gunther, *Initiation in the Aeon of the Child,* p. 208 (IBIS Press 2014). "Scarlet Woman A technical name for any Master of the Temple who, under the Night of Pan in the City of the Pyramids, has sacrificed every drop of his Blood into the Cup of Babalon..."

27 Gunther, *Angel and the Abyss,* p. 285 (IBIS Press 2014) "The newly-formed Master of the Temple is conceived as the Mother who awakens the Eld of the All-Father, uniting in Love as the Perfect and the Perfect becoming One Perfect which is None."

28 *Liber LXV,* IV:26.

29 Crowley, *The Vision & the Voice,* p. 149 (Weiser 1998).

The scent is made from the comingling of the elements of the Eucharist into One Substance, the Wine of the Sabbath. In one sense it represents the spiritual potency of the material substance of the Eucharist upon the Altar. Yet there is a distinct and overwhelming sense of humanity conveyed in this description. It is one that gives voice to the profoundly human experience of the initiate. The blood represents the blood sacrifice of the saints; *for the wine of the cup is the blood of the saints.*

> **With the breath of her kisses hath she fermented it, and it hath become the wine of the Sacrament, the wine of the Sabbath; and in the Holy Assembly hath she poured it out for her worshipers, and they have become drunken thereon, so that face to face have they beheld my Father. Thus are they made worthy to become partakers of the Mystery of this holy vessel, for the blood is the life.**[30]

In the natural world the process of fermentation takes an ordinary substance and changes it into something exciting and stimulating. It is as if the substance is imbued with a mysterious essence, hence the name "spirits" that is applied to fermented beverages. The Fermentation process on both an Archetypical and practical plane is aligned with the potencies of the Great Feminine, and was the particular domain of women in ancient times. In his book *The Great Mother, Spiritual Transformation*, Eric Neumann explains that the practices of gathering, storing and containing the fruits and seeds yielded the knowledge of fermentation. It was an art that was perfected though time and practice. Thus the knowledge of medicines, intoxicants and poisons all belonged to the special power of the feminine.

From this perspective the dual goddess Demeter and Persephone embodied the mystery of the grain; as grain = daughter and fermentation = mother forms. All of these natural processes have a spiritual correlation in the cup, bowl or cauldron in the hands of the priestess on a cosmic level. Yet *nothing can be built up without blood*, as shown below:

> The kettle of transformation is identical with the sacrificial blood bowl whose content the priestess requires in order to achieve her magical purpose. Here the blood has not yet the later "spiritual" significance of a sacrificial offering, but a magical significance; it "contains" the soul, as the *Bible* still teaches. The necessity of its use rests on the matriarchal belief that even in the womb no life can be built up without blood.[31]

---

30 Crowley, *The Vision & the Voice*, p. 149 (Weiser 1998).

31 Neumann, *The Great Mother*, p. 288 (First Princeton/Bollingen 1974).

This magical practice from ancient times expresses in material terms the spiritual necessity of giving ones blood to the Cup of Babalon in order to re-enter the womb of the Great Mother. It also relays the practical need for the Babe of the Abyss to lie in a state of fermentation through this time of change. Likewise, every initiate who progresses through the grades experiences this fermentation, though in a lesser way, through giving their heart to the Work and yielding to the transformations. *Liber LXV* instructs the soul to be still.

**Be still, O my soul! that the spell may dissolve**[32]

The fermentation of the Blood in the Cup though the *breath of her kisses* sets it aside from ordinary blood. The statement *it hath become* represents a process, one that is likened to the alchemical method of bringing the Stone to its Quintessence. This is the consecrated Cup that gladdens the heart of the weary one and awakens the youth of the All-Father. It thus becomes the Eros Chalice of deadly Poison, for the Substance of this most holy vessel is the conjoined essence of יה.

On an Primordial level the symbolism of this Cup takes an archaic form of the vessel and serpent as the womb and phallus.

Edmund Spenser in his epic story called *The Faerie Queene* would use similar imagery to paint an evocative and magical mood in "bygone" poetic fashion.

*Figure EH20 - Fidelia and Speranza*

She was araièd all in lilly white,
And in her right hand bore a cup of gold,
With wine and water fild up to the hight,
In which a Serpent did himself enfold,
That horrour made to all, that did behold;
But she no whit did chaunge her constant mood:
And in her other hand she fast did hold
A booke, that was both signd and sealed with blood,
Wherein darke things were writ, hard to be understood.[33]

The symbolism employed is one of danger and intrigue. Students to the mysteries, and practitioners of magick will no doubt find the imagery of the woman and the poison cup seductive and emblematic of primal and potent magick.

32 *Liber LVX*, I:1.

33 *The Faerie Queene* by Edmund Spenser.

Figure EH21 - Lust

This primordial idea is more aptly expressed in the Thoth Tarot card *Lust*, which is assigned to the zodiacal sign of Leo, the element of Fire, and the luminary of the Sun. It is said to represent the most critical of all magical and alchemical operations and brings to bear the influence from above through the divine birth of the divine child. We know this Cup to be the Cup of Babalon, the Queen of the Night of Pan in the City of the Pyramids. She bears the Holy Graal full of the consecrated and fermented Blood of the saints, the sacrament of the new Aeon. It is full of the Dew of Love that abhors limitations and brings all to perfection, yet it is also the cup of Death and the poison of the Serpent.

In the description of *Atu XI, Lust* attributed to ט, To Mega Therion stated:

> There is in this card a divine drunkenness or ecstasy. The woman is shown as more than a little drunk, and more than a little mad; and the lion also is aflame with lust. This signifies that the type of energy described is of the primitive, creative order; it is completely independent of the criticism of reason. This card portrays the will of the Aeon. In the background are the bloodless images of the saints, on whom this image travels, for their whole life has been absorbed into the Holy Grail.[34]

This is the Poison Cup in which the arrows of Eros are dipped, and the weapon in the hand of the Initiatrix which is likewise a bow. This connection is discussed in the complementary Tarot card of this same Archetype, *The High Priestess*, whose luminous Crown is the Moon.[35] Luminous bodies have had a penetrating effect on the psyche ever since the dawn of human consciousness. The Moon with its close link to the womb of generation and the ebb and flow of terrestrial life is therefore a symbol of the transcendent feminine powers.

34 Crowley, *The Book of Thoth*, p. 95 (Weiser 2000).

35 Crowley, *The Book of Thoth*, pp. 72-75 (Weiser 2000).

The bow and the arrow, imbued with the power of enchantment, are the magical weapons of the Moon Priestess. As such they are representative of the influence of the substance of the Cup that descends from the Supernals. She is both the Maiden and the Harlot, and from her bow is shot the poison arrow of Eros into the heart of man.

Yet being beyond the realm of reason it is impossible to approach this Mystery though the faculty of the intellect. Remember, this energy *is completely independent of the criticism of reason.* In writing on this Mystery of the most August and Austere Order of A.'. A.'., I will rely on the words of the Voice and the spirit of the Vision granted to the seer of the Second Æthyr, the prophet of the lovely Star:

> **Every man that hath seen me forgetteth me never, and I appear oftentimes in the coals of the fire, and upon the smooth white skin of woman, and in the constancy of the waterfall, and in the emptiness of deserts and marshes, and upon great cliffs that look seaward; and in many strange places, where men seek me not. And many thousand times he beholdeth me not. And at the last I smite myself into him as a vision smiteth into a stone, and whom I call must follow.**[36]

In this description, man is identified with *a stone,* which in alchemical terms signifies the *prima materia* or the *lapis vulgaris.* It is the uncomely stone which the builders rejected because it was not useful. The vision is emblematic of the piercing poison of wolf's bane which *pierceth the body more subtly.*[37] It is the agent of change that acts like a subtle poison which sets in motion the transformation of the stone.[38] The stone, refined and perfected, becomes the *Lapis Philisophorum,* the Stone of the Philosophers. This is the treasured lapis which dwells within the heart of man.

---

36 Crowley, *The Vision & the Voice,* pp. 242-243 (*The Equinox IV(II)*).

37 *Liber LXV,* I:13.

38 Gunther, *Initiation in the Aeon of the Child,* pp. 127-158 (IBIS Press 2009).

Figure EH22 - Round and Square

Our Stone dwells within the Heart of man which is also called the Garden of Eden. Adam, the three אדם which is four אדאם, the round who is square, is crucified on the Cross of the four rivers flowing outward from Eden. For the heart or center of Man, that is אדם, is the letter ד which has the value of 4. And the 4 rivers of Eden go into Havilah where that is Gold. Know from this that you must first reduce the Stone into 4 elements. And unite it again into One. This they say, is the whole of the Magistry.[39]

This image from *Opus Alchymicum* depicts the heart of אדם as three-fold which manifest as אדאם upon the four-fold Cross. Here we encounter the archetype of threefoldness extended into a quaternary which assists to fix or anchor its energy. The number three serves to represent forces that are of the creative, volatile, and dynamic sort. The number four is aligned with the qualities of stability, structure, and manifestation. The number three is aligned with divinity and the number four with humanity. This is a motif of the dynamic, transcendent and spiritual heart that is realized in the actual and static reality of incarnation. The meaning of being nailed to the cross represents fixation and solidification.[40]

This is a point I made earlier in the opening chapter, as it was important to isolate the symbol of the Heart of Blood in order to understand its meaning and function. Now, as I come to the end of the essay it is necessary to re-unite the "three" and the "four" to solidify the meaning of Heart Heart of Blood symbol – to unite the spiritual idea with the human reality.

---

39 Gunther, *Opus Alchymicum*, Figure 3, pp. 16,17 (Wennofer House 2023).

40 Gunther, *Initiation in the Aeon of the Child*, p. 41 (IBIS Press 2014). "Fixation was often represented by impaling with nails or a sword." The footnote relays the following source: "57 Cf. *Speculum veritatis* f.9 & 10. The illustrations have been reprinted in Alchemy *The Secret Art by Stanislas Klossowski de Rola*. The volatile matter was also occasionally depicted as a serpent."

Note that this drawing depicts *two* serpents. They represent opposing ideas united as one. In this case it expresses the unification of the "three" and the "four."

For the aspirant, the spiritual essence of the Heart cannot only be a lofty aspiration removed from reality. In order to *be* a Heart of ***Blood*** – it must be manifest in flesh and blood.

> The blood is the life, and the Spirit must have life if it is to dwell in the world. The Candidate is of course the vehicle of Life for the indwelling Spirit. Now here, we are not talking about passive participation in the process; that would amount to what might be aptly described as vampirism and possession. This is not part of the program. We are talking about a process wherein the Candidates enflame themselves with prayer, and actively seek interaction with the Divine Influence. If we think of this only as the dramatic encounters that are often described as visions or trances, we fail to consider the extremely important yet subtle interaction that guides our feet upon the path. Not only through prayer and practices, but in careful study of the Holy Books, all things must be directed constantly and patiently toward the Divine. It must be made part of daily life at all times; it must be sealed up in the Heart in order to have a genuine, living experience.[41]

The aspirant must always remember that pouring forth their blood into the Cup of Babalon is an act of yielding to the change that Initiation brings. It is equally a yielding that requires active participation in the Work, to BE THE HEART. In *Liber LXV*, V:21 the Adept is commanded to always be the heart.

> **Thou shalt be ever the heart, and I the serpent will coil close about thee.**

To the aspirant upon the Path of the Great Return who seeks to **be ever the heart,** I offer the words of a Master who lived long ago. When confronted by the question: *Master, which is the greatest commandment in the law? Isa said unto him, thou shalt love the Lord thy God with all thy heart, and with all thy soul, and with all thy mind.*[42]

And for now, speech has done with us for a while.

---

41 Gunther, *Initiation in the Aeon of the Child*, p. 131 (IBIS 2009).

42 *Matthew* 22:36,37. Διδάσκαλε, ποία ἐντολὴ μεγάλη ἐν τῷ νόμῳ; ὁ δὲ ἔφη αὐτῷ Ἀγαπήσεις Κύριον τὸν θεόν σου ἐν ὅλῃ καρδίᾳ σου καὶ ἐν ὅλῃ τῇ ψυχῇ σου καὶ ἐν ὅλῃ τῇ διανοίᾳ σου·

# Bibliography of Works Consulted

## I. Published Editions by Aleister Crowley (including The Equinox)


*777 and other Qabalistic Writings* (ed. I. Regardie) New York: Weiser (1986)

*The Book of Thoth. A Short Essay on the Tarot of the Egyptians.* The Master Therion [pseud.] New York: Weiser (1974)

*Commentaries to the Holy Books and Other Papers* (ed. Hymenaeus Beta), *The Equinox IV(1).* York Beach, ME: Weiser (1996)

*The Equinox.* Volume I. 10 Vols. New York: Weiser (1974)

*The Equinox.* Volume III. New York: Weiser (1973)

*The Heart of the Master & Other Papers.* Scottsdale, AZ: New Falcon Publications (1992)

*Konx Om Pax, Essays in Light.* Chicago: The Teitan Press (1990)

*The Law is for All.* (ed. Louis Wilkinson & Hymenaeus Beta) Tempe, AZ: New Falcon Publications (1996)

*Liber Aleph vel CXI. The Book of Wisdom or Folly* (ed. Karl Germer & Marcelo Motta) *The Equinox* III (6), Barstow, CA: Thelema Publishing Co., 1961. rev. 2nd edition, ed. Hymanaeus Beta. New York, 93 Publishing (1991)

*Liber CCCXXXIII. The Book of Lies which is also falsely called Breaks.* Frater Perdurabo [pseud.] New York: Weiser (1972)

*Little Essays Toward Truth.* London: O.T.O. (1938)

*The Magical Record of the Beast, 666: the diaries of Aleister Crowley, 1914-1920.* (ed. John Symonds & Kenneth Grant) Third Edition. London: Duckworth. (1993)

*Magick. Book 4, Parts I-IV.* second rev. edition (ed. Hymenaeus Beta) York Beach, ME: Weiser (1994)

*Magick in Theory and Practice.* Paris: Lecram Press. (1929)

*Magick Without Tears* (ed. Karl Germer) Hampton, NJ. Thelema Publishing Co. (1954)

*The Tao Te Ching. Liber CLVII.* (trans. Aleister Crowley, ed. Hymenaeus Beta) *The Equinox III(8).* York Beach, ME: Weiser (1995)

ΘΕΛΗΜΑ: *The Holy Books of Thelema* (ed. Hymenaeus Alpha & Hymenaeus Beta) York Beach, ME: Weiser (1983)

*The Vision & The Voice with Commentary and other papers.* (ed. Hymenaeus Beta) *The Equinox IV(2).* York Beach, ME: Weiser, 1998.


## II. General Works


אלפא ביתא דבן סירא. Krakau (1896)

Abbott, Jacob. *Nero.* New York: Harper & Brothers (1904)

Abdel-Hadi, Yassar A. "Astronomical Interpretation of the Winding Canal in the Pyramid Texts," Cairo: *Journal of Astronomy and Astrophysics, Special Issue, April.* Cairo: National Research Institute of Astronomy and Geophysics (2009)

Abdel-Haleem, Muhammad. *The Qur'an: A New Translation.* Oxford: Oxford University Press. (2004)

Abdel-Magiud, R. Zakariya. "Two Hymns of [A]doring Ra," *SHEDIT, Vol. 3, Issue 3.* Faiyum: Fayoum University (2016)

Agrippa, Henry Cornelius. *De Occulta Philosophia Libri Tres*. Cologne (1533)

_____. (trans. James Freake). *Three Books of Occult Philosophy, written by Henry Cornelius Agrippa, of Nettesheim, Counseller to Charles the Fifth, Emperor of Germany and Judge of the Pregorative Court*. London (1651)

Alciati, Andrea. *Omnia Andreae Alciati V.C. Emblemata*. Antwerp (1577)

Ali, Maulvi Muhammad. *The Holy Qur-án, third edition*. Woking, Surry: Unwin Brothers Gresham Pres. (1935)

Allen, James P. *The Ancient Egyptian Language, an Historical Study*. Cambridge: Cambridge University Press (2013)

_____. *Ancient Egyptian Phonology*. Cambridge: Cambridge University Press (2020)

_____. *The Ancient Egyptian Pyramid Texts*. Atlanta: Society of Biblical Literature (2005)

_____. *Coptic, A Grammar of Its Six Major Dialects*. University Park, PA: Eisenbrauns (2020)

_____ *Middle Egyptian. An Introduction to the language and Culture of Hieroglyphs. Third Edition*. Cambridge: Cambridge University Press (2014)

Allen, Thomas George. *The Book of the Dead or Going Forth by Day. Third Edition*. Chicago: University of Chicago Press (1974)

_____. *The Egyptian Book Of The Dead Documents In The Oriental Institute Museum At The University Of Chicago* (OIP 82). Chicago (1960)

_____. "Some Egyptian Sun Hymns," *Journal of Near Eastern Studies, Vol. 8, No. 4, pp. 349-352*. Chicago: University of Chicago Press. (1949)

Allen, W. Thomas. *Homeri Opera, Vol. 5, Hymnos Cyclum Fragmenta Margiten Batrachomyomachiam Vitas Continens*. Oxford: The Clarendon Press (1912)

Amory, Robert & Robert L. Emerson. *Wharton and Stille's Medical Jurisprudence, Vol. 2 Poisons. Fifth edition*. Rochester, NY: The Lawyers' Co-operative Publishing Co. (1903)

Anonymous. *Auriferae Artis, quam Chemiam Vocant, Vol. 1*. Basil: Petrum Pernam. (1572)

Anonymous. *Das Buch mit Sieben, Vol. 1*. Manly Palmer Hall Collection of Manuscripts (ca. 1700)

Anonymous. *F De La Rose. Croix* , Manly Palmer Hall Collection of Manuscripts (ca. 1700)

Anonymous. *Geheime Figuren Der Rosenkreutzer aus dem 16ten und 17ten Tahrhundert*. Altona (1785)

Anonymous. *Rosarium Philosophorum, Secunda Pars Alchimiæ de Lapide Philosophico Vero Modo preparando, continens exactam eius scientiæ progressionem. Cum Figuris rei perfectionem ostendentibus*. Frankfurt (1550)

Anonymous. *The Greek Ecclesiastical Historians of The First Six Centuries of the Christian Era. 6 Vols., I. Eusebius's Life of Constantine, Oration etc., II. Eusebius's Ecclesiastical History, to 324 A.D., III. Socrates Scholasticus's History, from about 305 to 445 A.D., IV. Sozomen's Narrative, 324 to about 440 A.D., V. Theodoret's Ecclesiastical History, from 322 to 428 A.D., VI. Evagrius's Ecclesiastical History, from 431to 594 A.D*. London: Samuel Bagster and Sons (1846)

Archangelus de Burgo Nuovo. *Apologia Pro Defensione Doctrinæ Cabalæ*. Bologna (1564)

Assmann, Jan (trans. David Lorton). *Death and Salvation in Ancient Egypt*. Ithica: Cornell University Press (2001)

Athanassakis, Apostolos N. *The Orphic Hymns, Text, Translation and Notes*. Missoula, MT: Scholors Press for The Society of Biblical Literature (1988)

Avalon, Arthur (pseud. Sir John Woodroffe). *The Serpent Power being the* ṢAṬ-CAKRA-NIRŪPAṆA and PĀDUKĀ-PAÑCAKA. New York: Dover Publications (1974)

Avery, William T. "The *Adoratio Purpurae* and the Importance of the Imperial Purple in the

Fourth Century of the Christian Era." *Memoirs of the American Academy in Rome, Vol. 17, pp. 66-80.* New York (1940)

Avinoam (Grossman), Reuben. *Compendious Hebrew-English Dictionary.* Tel-Aviv: The Dvir Publishing Co. (1938)

Babbitt, Frank Cole. *Plutarch: Moralia.* 15 Vols. London: Harvard University Press (1936)

Baker, G. P. *Constantine the Great and the Christian Revolution.* London: Eveleigh Nash & Grayson Limited (1931)

Baluze, Etienne. *Stephani Baluzii Miscellaneorum Liber Secundus, Hoc est, Collectio Veterum monumentorum quæ hactenus latuerant in variis codicibus ac bibliothecis.* Paris (1679) < *Editio Princeps* of *Lactantii De Mortibus Persecutorum*>.

Barchusen, Johann Conrad. *Elementa Chemiæ Quibus Subjuncta est Confectura Lapidis Philosophica Imaginibus Repræsentata.* Leiden (1718)

Baret, M Eugene. *C. Soll. Apollinaris Sidonii Œpera. Ouevres de Sidoine Apollinaire Texte Latin.* Paris: Libraire du Collége de France (1879)

Barker, William D. *Isaiah's Kingship Polemic: An Exegetical Study in Isaiah 24-27.* Tübengen: Mohr Siebeck (2014)

Barnett, R.D. & John R. Hinnells (eds.). *Mithraic studies: Proceedings of the first International congress of Mithraic studies.* Vol. 2, Manchester: Manchester University Press. (1975)

Barnaud, Nicolaus. *Lambsprink, De Lapide Philosophica.* Frankfurt (1677)

Bauer, Walter. *A Greek-English Lexicon of the New Testament and Other Early Christian Literature.* (trans. William F. Arndt & F. Wilbur Gingrich*), 2nd ed. rev. and augmented.* Chicago: Univ. of Chicago Press (1979)

Beato, George: *Azoth, sive Aureliæ Occultæ Philosophorum.* Frankfurt (1613) <Attributed by some to Basil Valentine>.

Bekker, Immanuel. *Apollodori Bibliotheca.* Leipzig: Tuebner (1854)

_____. *Aristoteles Graece. Vol. 2.* Berlin: George Reimer (1831)

_____. *Iullii Pollucis Onomasticon.* Berlin: Libraria Friderici Nicolai (1846)

_____. *Photii Bibliotheca. Vol. 1.* Berlin: George Reimer (1824)

_____. *Zosimus.* Bonn: Weber (1837)

Berry, George Ricker. *Interlinear Greek-English New Testament.* Reading, PA: Baker Book House (1981)

Besant, Annie. *The Bhagavad Gîtâ or The Lord's Song.* London: Theosophical Publishing Society (1896)

Bethe, Erich. *Pollvcis Onomasticon.* 3 Vols. Leipzig: Teubner (1900-1937)

Betz, Hans Dieter. *The Greek Magical Papyri in Translation including the Demotic Spells.* Chicago: University of Chicago Press (1986)

Bhaktivedanta, A.C. Swami Prabhupada. *The Bhagavad Gîtâ As It Is.* Los Angeles: United States: Bhaktivedanta Book Trust. (1989)

_____. *Śrīmad Bhāgavatam. 12 Vols. (Cantos 1-12).* United States: Bhaktivedanta Book Trust. (1970-1977)

*Biblia Sacra Vulgatae Editionis, Sixti V et Clementis VIII. Editio Nova, versiculis Distincta.* Paris (1774)

Bierbrier, M. L. *The Late New Kingdom in Egypt* (c. 1300-664 B.C.), Warminster: Aris & Phillips Ltd. (1975)

Blavatsky, H. P. *Isis Unveiled: A Master Key to the Mysteries of Ancient and Modern Science and Theology. 2 Vols.* New York: Theosophical Publishing Society (1877)

______. *The Secret Doctrine: The Synthesis of Science, Religion and Philosophy. 2 Vols.* New York: Theosophical Publishing Society (1888)

_____. *The Theosophical Glossary*. New York: Theosophical Publishing Society (1892)

_____. *The Voice of the Silence being Chosen Fragments from the 'Book of the Golden Precepts'* London: Theosophical Publishing Company (1889)

Boak, Arthur E.R. *A History of Rome to 565 A.D.*. New York: The Macmillan Company (1921)

Boegart, Abraham. *De Roomsche Monarchy, Vertoont In de Muntbeelden der Westersche en Oostersche Keizeren; beginnende van Cesar, en Eidigende met Leopoldus, den Tegenwoordigen Roomschen Keizer.* Ultrecht: Halma & Van de Water (1697)

Böhme, Jakob. *Der Weeg zu Christo: verfasset in neun Bücklein*. Amsterdam (1682)

Boisacq, Émile. *Dictionnaire Étymologique de la Langue Greque*. Heidelberg: Carl Winters (1916)

Boissard, Jean Jacques. *Icones Quinquaginta Viroum Illustrium Doctrina & Eruditione Præssantium ad Vivum Effictæ, Cum Eorum Vitis Descriptis. Frankfurt (1597)*

_____. *Tractatus Posthumus Jani Jacobi Boissardi Vesuntini De Dviniatione & Magicis Præstigiis, Quarum Veritas ac Vanitas solide exponitur per Descriptionem.* Oppenheim (1615)

Bonomi, J. and S. Sharpe: *The Alabaster Sarcophagus of Oimeneptah I., King of Egypt* (London, 1864) <The Sarcophagus of Sety I>

Bostock, John & H.T. Riley, *The Natural History of Pliny, 6 Vols.* London: George Bell & Sons. (1893)

Breasted, James Henry. *The Dawn of Consciousness*. Charles Scribner's Sons. New York (1933)

_____. *The Philosophy of a Memphite Priest.* in *Zeitschrift für Agyptische Sprache un Ältertumskunde* 39, pp.39-53. Leipzig (1901)

Bremmer, J. N. "The Vision of Constantine," *Land of Dreams. Greek and Latin Studies in Honour of A.H.M. Kessels, pp. 57-79.* Leiden: Koninklijke Brill (2006)

Bright, William. ΕΥΣΕΒΟΥ ΤΟΥ ΠΑΜΦΙΛΟΥ ΙΣΤΟΡΑΣ ΕΚΚΛΗΣΙΑΣΤΙΚΗΣ ΛΟΓΟΙ ΔΕΚΑ. *Eusebius' Ecclesiastical History according to the text of Burton.* Oxford: The Clarendon Press (1872)

_____. ΣΩΚΡΑΤΟΥΣ ΣΧΟΛΑΣΤΙΚΟΥ ΕΚΚΛΗΣΙΑΣΤΙΚΗ ΙΣΤΟΡΙΑ *Socrates' Ecclesiastical History according to the text of Hussey*. Oxford: The Clarendon Press (1893)

_____. *The Canons of the First Four General Councils of Nicæa, Constantinople, Ephesus and Chalcedon, with Notes.* Oxford: The Clarendon Press (1892)

Brooks, Francis. *Marci Tulli Ciceronis, De Natura Deorum*. London: Methuen & Co. (1896)

Brown, Francis. *A Hebrew and English Lexicon of the Old Testament with an appendix containing the Biblical Aramaic*. Oxford. (1939)

Brown, Leslie (Ed.) *New Shorter Oxford English Dictionary. 2 Vols.* Oxford: The Clarendon Press (1993)

Browne, Henry. *Triglot Dictionary of Scriptural Representative Words in Hebrew, Greek and English.* New York: James Pott and Co. (1901)

Brugsch, Heinrich. *Recueil de monuments Égyptiennes, Vol. 2.* Leipzig: J. C. Hinrichs (1863)

_____. *Reise nach der Grossen Oase el Kargeh in der Libyschen Wüste*. J. C. Hinrichs Buchhandlung (1878)

Brunner, Heinrich. "Das Constitutum Constantini," *Festgabe for Rudolf von Gneist, pp. 2-36.* Berlin: Julius Springer (1888)

Bryant, Edwin Francis. *Krishna: A Sourcebook*. Oxford: Oxford University Press (2007)

Bryant, Jacob. *A New System, or an Analysis of Ancient Mythology. 3 Vols.* London (1774)

Budge, E.A. Wallis. *An Account of the Sarcophagus of Seti I* (London, 1908)

_____. *An Egyptian Hieroglyphic Dictionary. 2 Vols.* New York: Dover Publications, Inc. (1978). Facsimile reprint of the edition published by John Murray, London. (1920).

_____. *The Book of the Dead. The Chapters of Coming Forth by Day. 3 Vols.* London: Kegan Paul, Trench, Trübner & Co. (1898)

_____. *The Book of the Dead. Facsimiles of The Papyri of Hunefer, Ánhai, Ḳerāsher and Netchemet.* London: Harrison & Sons. Trustees of the British Museum (1899)

_____. *The Book of the Dead. Facsimile of The Papyrus of Ani in the British Museum.* Second Edition. London: Longmans & Co. (1894)

______. *The Chapters of Coming Forth by Day or The Theban Rescension of The Book of the Dead. The Egyptian Hieroglyphic Text edited from numerous papyri. 3 Vols.* New York: AMS Press Inc. (1976) Facsimile Reprint of the 1910 edition published by Kegan Paul, Trench, Trübner & Co. < Typeset Hieroglyphic texts only, no translations.>

_____. *Coptic Apocrypha in the Dialect of Upper Egypt.* London: Trustees of the British Museum (1913)

_____. *The Egyptian Heaven and Hell (3 Vols.* in *Books on Egypt and Chaldea Vol. XX through XXII.)* London (1905)

_____. *The Gods of the Egyptians; or, Studies in Egyptian Mythology. 2 Vols.* London: Methuen & Co. (1904)

_____. *The Papyrus of Ani in the British Museum.* London: Kegan Paul, Trench, Trübner & Co. (1895)

Bulić, Nada and Maria Mariola Glavan. "Lustration Rituals in Ancient Rome and Cosmogonic Myth," *Vjesnik za Arheologiju i Historiju Dalmatinsku, Vol. 112, Issue 1, pp. 151-166.* Delmatia, Croatia (2019)

Bunte, Bernhard. *Hygini Astronomica.* Leipzig: T. O. Weigel (1875)

Burnet, Gilbert. *A Relation of the Death of the Primitive Persecutors. Written Originally in Latin by L.C.F. Lactantius.* Amsterdam (1687)

Bury, R.G. *Plato in Twelve Volumes.* London: Harvard University Press (1975)

Caley, Earle R. & John F. C. Richards. *Theophrastus On Stones. Introduction, Greek Text, English Translation, and Commentary.* Columbus, OH: The Ohio State University (1956)

Cameron, Averil & Stuart G. Hall. *De Vita Constantini, Eusebius' Life of Constantine.* Oxford: The Clarendon Press (1999)

Carrier, Claude. *Les papyrus de livre des morts de l'égypte ancienne de Neferoubenef (Louvre III 93) et de Soutymès (Bnf, égyptien «38-45»).* Montigny-le-Breetonneux: Imprimerie PAM, BREST. (2014)

_____. *Les papyrus de livre des morts de l'Égypte ancienne de Ptahmès (Milan, coll. Busca) et de Hounefer (BM EA 9901).* Montigny-le-Breetonneux: Imprimerie PAM, BREST. (2015)

_____. *Reproduction de 17 Papyrus de l'Égypte ancienne.* Montigny-le-Breetonneux: Imprimerie PAM, BREST. (2014)

_____. *Série des papyrus du livre des morts de l'Égypte ancienne. Vol. I: Le Papyrus de Nouou (BM EA 10477).* Paris: Cybele (2010)

_____. *Série des papyrus du livre des morts de l'Égypte ancienne. Vol. I: Le Papyrus d'Any (BM EA 10470).* Paris: Cybele (2010)

_____. *Série des papyrus du livre des morts de l'Égypte ancienne. Vol. III: Le papyrus de Nebseny (BM EA 9900).* Paris: Cybele (2011)

_____. *Série des papyrus du livre des morts de l'Égypte ancienne. Vol. IV: Le papyrus de Iouefânkh (Turin, cat. n 1791).* Paris: Cybele (2010)

_____. *Textes des Pyramides de l'Égypte ancienne. Tome I: Textes des pyramides d'Ounas et de Téti.* Paris: Cybele (2009)

______. *Textes des Pyramides de l'Égypte ancienne. Tome II: Textes de la pyramide de Pépy Ier.* Paris: Cybele (2009)

_____. *Textes des Pyramides de l'Égypte ancienne. Tome III:Textes de la pyramide de Pépy II.* Paris: Cybele (2010)

_____. *Textes des Pyramides de l'Égypte ancienne. Tome IV: Textes des pyramides de Mérenrê, d'Aba, de Neit, d'Ipout et d'Oudjebten.* Paris: Cybele (2010)

Cartari, Vincenzo. *Le Imagani Degli Dei Degli Antichi.* Padua: Lorenzo Pasquati (1608)

Cary, Earnest. *Dio's Roman History, Vol. 8.* London: William Heinemann (1925)

Černý, Jaroslav. *Coptic Etymological Dictionary.* London: Cambridge University Press (1976)

Černý, Jaroslav & Sarah Israelet Groll. *A Late Egyptian Grammar. Fourth edition.* Rome: Pontificao Instituto Biblico (1993)

Chadwick, John. *The Mycenaean World.* Cambridge: Cambridge University Press (1976)

Champollion, Jean François & Léon Jean Joseph Dubois. *Pantheon Égyptien, collection des personnages mythologiques de l'ancienne Égypte d'après les monuments.* Paris: de Imprimerie de Firmin Didot. (1823)

Charles, R.H. *Apocrypha & Pseudepigrapha of the Old Testament. in English. 2 Vols.* Oxford: Oxford University Press (1978)

_____. *The Apocalypse of Baruch, translated from the Syriac.* London: Adam & Charles Black (1896)

_____. *The Book of Enoch, translated from Professor Dillmann's Ethiopic Text.* Oxford: The Clarendon Press (1893)

Chassinat, Émile. *Le temple d'Edfou, Vol. 4.* Cairo: L'institut Français d'archéologie orientale (1929)

Chatelain, Emile & Paul Legendre. "Hygini Astronomica," *Bibliothèque de L'Ecole Des Hautes Études*, Issue 118. Paris: Honoré Champion (1909)

*Chicago Demotic Dictionary (CDD)*, (ed. Janet H. Johnson). https://isac.uchicato.edu/research/publications/chicago-demotic-dictionary.

Chong Dong, Gongle Shi, Fabiany Herrera, Yondong Wang, Patrick s. Herendeed, Peter R. Crane. "Middle-Late Jurassic fossils from northeastern China reveal morphological stasis in the catkin-yew," *National Science Review, Vol. 7, Issue 11, November 2020, pp. 1765-1767.*

Choul, Guillaume du. *Sopra la castrametatione, & Bagni antichi de i Greci, & Romani.* Venice (1582)

Clarke, Emma C., John M. Dillon & Jackson P. Hershbell, *Iamblichus On The Mysteries*, Atlanta, GA: Society of Biblical Literature. (2003)

Coleman, Charles. *The Mythology of the Hindus.* London: Parbury, Allen & Co. (1832)

Coleman, Christopher Bush. "Constantine the Great and Christianity. Three Phases: The Historical, the Legendary, and the Spurious." *Studies in History, Economics and Public Law, Vol. 60, No. 1. Whole Number 146.* New York: The Columbia University Press (1914)

_____. *The Treatise of Lorenzo Valla on the Donation of Constantine, text and translation into English.* New Haven: Yale University Press (1922)

Conybeare, F. C. *Philostratus, The Life of Apollonius of Tyana. 2 Vols.* London: William Heinemann (1912)

Cooper, W.R. *The Serpent Myths of Ancient Egypt.* London: Robert Hardwicke (1873)

Cordovera, Moses ben Jacob. ספר פרדס רימונים, *Sefer Pardes Rimonim, "Book of the Garden of Pomegranates."* Cracow (1591)

Crum, W. E. A *Coptic Dictionary.* Oxford: Oxford University Press (1979)

Cumont, Franz. *Textes et monuments figurés relatifs aux mystèries de Mithra, Vol. 1.* Brussels: H. Lamertin (1899)

Cureton, William. *History of the Martyrs in Paletine, by Eusebius, Bishop of Caesarea, Discovered in a Very Antient Syriac Manuscript.* London: Williams and Norgate (1861)

Dalton, O.M. *The Letters of Sidonius. Vol. 2.* Oxford: The Clarendon Press (1915)
Dan, Joseph. "Samael, Lilith, and the concept of Evil in Early Kabbalah," *AJS Review, Vol. 5, pp. 17-40.* Philadelphia: Penn Press (1980)
Daniels, Peter T & William Bright (eds.) *The World's Writing Systems.* Oxford: Oxford University Press (1996)
Davies, Norman de Garis. *The Temple of Hibis in El Khargeh Oasis, Part III, The Decoration.* New York: Metropolitan Museum of Art Egyptian Expedition (1953)
DeBuck, Adrian. *The Egyptian Coffin Texts. 7 Vols.* Chicago: University of Chicago Press (1935-1961)
De Fresne, Charles. *Glossarium Ad Scriptores Mediæ et Infimæ Latinitatis, Vol. 2, Part 2. Frankfurt am Main (1710)*
Deitsch, Heinrich Rudolf. *Eutropii Breviarium Historiae Romanie.* Leipzig: B.G. Teubner (1883)
De Jancigny, M. Dubois & M. Xavier Raymond. *L'Univers. Histoirie et des tous les peuples: Inde.* Paris: Firmin Didot Fréres (1845)
De Jong, Helena. *Michael Maier's Atalanta Fugiens: sources of an alchemical book of emblems.* York Beach, ME: Nicolas-Hays, Inc. (2002)
De Mons, Jean. *La sextessence diallactique et potentielle tiree par une nouuelle façon d'alambiquer, suiuant les preceptes de la saincte magie & invocation demons.* Paris (1595)
Devadatta Kālī. देवीमाहात्म्यम् *In Praise of the Goddess, The Devīmāhātmya and Its Meaning.* Berwick, ME: Nicolas Hays, Inc. (2003)
Dewsbury, Laura May. *Invisible Religion in Ancient Egypt.* Birmingham: Unpublished Doctorial Thesis, Department of Classics, Ancient History and Archaeology. (2016)
*Dictionary of Deities and Demons in the Bible Second Edition* (eds. Karel van der Toorn, Bob Becking & Pieter. W. van der Horst) Grand Rapids: Wm B. Erdmans Publishing (1999)
Dillmann, August. *Lexicon Linguae Aethiopicae.* Leipzig: T. O. Weigel (1865)
_____. *Liber Henoch, Aethiopice, Ad Quinque Codicum Fidem Editus, Cum Variis Lectionibus.* Leipzig (1851)
Dindorf, Karl Wilhelm. **ΣΟΦΟΚΛΕΟΥΣ ΑΝΤΙΓΟΝΗ**, *Sophoclis Antigone.* Leipzig: Teubner (1873)
Dindorf, Ludwig. **ΞΕΝΟΦΩΝΤΟΣ ΕΛΛΗΝΙΚΑ**, *Xenophontis Historica Graeca.* Leipzig: Teubner (1876)
Doniger, Wendy. *The Rig Vegda: An Anthology: One Hundred and Eight Hymns.* London: Penguin (1981)
Du Cange, Charles Du Fresne. *Glossarium Ad Scriptores Mediæ & Infimæ Latinitatis, Vol. 2, Part 2.* Frankfurt am Main (1710)
Duff, J. D. *Lucan, The Civil War, Books I-X (Pharsalia).* London: William Heinemann (1962)
De Hoyos, Arturo. *Albert Pike's Morals and Dogma of the Ancient and Accepted Scottish Rite of Freemasonry, Annotated Edition.* Washington, DC: The Supreme Council 33°, Southern Jurisdiction (2013)
Duncan, Malcolm C. *Duncan's Masonic Ritual and Monitor or Guide to the Three Symbolic Degrees of the Ancient York Rite. Third Edition.* New York: Dick & Fitzgerald (1866)
Edinger, Edward. *Anatomy of the Psyche. Alchemical Symbolism in Psychotherapy.* La Salle, IL: Open Court Publishing Co. (1985)
_____. *Ego and Archetype. Individuation and the Religious Function of the Psyche.* New York: G. P. Putnam's Sons (1972)
Edwards, I.E.S. *British Museum, Hieroglyphic Texts from Egyptian Stelae, etc. Part VIII.* London: The British Museum (1939)
Eichholz, D. E. *Pliny Natural History. Vol. X, Libri XXXVI-XXXVII.* Cambridge: Harvard

University Press (1971)

Einstein, J.D. *Ozar Midrashim. Vol. 1*, 1 - a. New York: J. D. Einstein (1915) < Contains the Hebrew text of אלפא ביתא דבן סירא, "*Alpha Beta Ben Sira.*" >

Eleazar, Abraham. *Uraltes Chymiches Werk*. Erfurt (1735)

Emerton, J. A. "Leviathan and Ltn: The Vocalization of the Ugaritic Word for the Dragon." *Vetus Testamentum,Vol. 32, pp. 327-331*. Leiden: E. J. Brill (1982)

*Encyclopedia Brittanica, Tenth Edition, 35 Vols*. Cambridge: Cambridge University Press (1902)

_____. *Eleventh Edition, Vol. 1*. Cambridge: Cambridge University Press (1917)

*Encyclopedia of Religion and Ethics, Vol. VIII* (James Hastings, ed.) New York: Charles Scribner's Sons (1916)

*Encyclopedia of Hinduism* (Denise Cush,Catherine Robinson & Michael York eds.) London: Routledge, Taylor & Francis Group (2008)

Erman, Adolf. *Wörterbuch der Aegyptischen Sprache, im Auftrage der deutschen Akademien hrsg. von Adolf Erman und Hermann Grapow. 7 Vols*. Leipzig/Berlin: Hinrichs's Buchhandlung (1950-1971)

Eusebius of Caesarea. *Historia Ecclesiastica*. Strasburg (circa 1475-1480) < Latin translation by *Rufinus*>.

_____. **ΕΚΚΛΗΣΙΑΣΤΙΚΗΣ ΙΣΤΟΡΑΣ.** *Ecclestiasticae Historiae, Eiusdem de vita Constantini, Socratis, Theodoriti episcopi Cyrensis, Collectaneorum ex historia eccles. Theodori Lectoris, Hermii Sozumeni, Euagrii*. Paris: 1544. < *Editio Princeps* of the Greek text by *Stephanus*.>

Evelyn-White, Hugh G. HESIOD, *The Homeric Hymns and Homerica*. London: William Heinemann (1914)

Fairclough, H. Rushton. *Virgil, 2 Vols*. London: William Heinemann (1922)

Fairman, H. W. & Bernhard Grdseloff. "Texts of Ḥatshepsut and Sethos I inside Sepos Artemidos." *The Journal of Egyptian Archaeology, Vol. 33, pp. 12-33* (1947)

Faulkner, R.O. *A Concise Dictionary of Middle Egyptian*. Oxford: Griffith Institute (1962)

_____. *The Ancient Egyptian Coffin Texts. 3 Vols*. Warminister: Aris & Phillips (1973-1978)

_____. *The Ancient Egyptian Pyramid Texts*. Oxford: Clarendon Press (1969)

_____. "The Book of Overthrowing Apep," *The Journal of Egyptian Archaeology, Vol. 23, pp. 166-185* (1937) and *Vol. 24, pp. 41-52* (1938)

_____. "The Papyrus Bremner-Rhind (British Museum No. 10188) The Book of Overthrowing Apep," *Bibliotheca Aegyptiaca III, pp. 42-88*. Brussels: Édition de la Fondation Égyptologique Reine Elisabeth. (1933)

Faulkner, R. O. & Ogden Goelet, Jr. *The Egyptian Book of the Dead, the Book of Going Forth by Day, Twentieth Anniversary Edition, revised and expanded, with A Survey of Egyptian Scholarship by* J. Daniel Gunther. San Francisco: Chronicle Books (2015)

Fell, John. *Caecilii Firmiani Lactantii De Mortibus Persecutorum*. Oxford (1680)

Fischer, Henry George. *Egyptian Titles of the Middle Kingdom, A Supplement to Wm. Ward's Index*. New York: The Metropolitan Museum of Art (1997)

Fletcher, William. "The Works of Lactantius, Vol. 2.," *Ante-Nicene Christian Library: Translations of the Writings of the Fathers down to 325. Vol. XXII*. Edinburgh: T. & T. Clark (1871)

Forster, Thomas. *The Lives of the Twelve Cæsars by C. Suetonius Tranquillus; To which are added, His Lives of the Grammarians, Rhetoricians, and Poets*. London: Henry G. Bohn (1855)

Fowler, Harold N. *Plato in Twelve Volumes. 12 Vols*. Cambridge: Harvard University Press (1925)

Franck, Adolphe. *La kabbale du la philosophie religieuse des hébreux*. Paris: L. Hachette (1843)

_____. *The Kabbalah or The Religious Philosophy of the Hebrews*. New York: The Kabbalah Publishing Company (1926) <English translation of the French title above.>

Frazer, James George. *Apollodorus, The Library. 2 Vols.* London: William Heinemann (1921)

Freese, J. H. *The Library of Photius, Vol. 1.* New York: The Macmillan Company (1920)

Gaisford, Thomas. **ΕΥΣΕΒΙΟΥ ΤΟΥ ΠΑΜΦΙΛΟΥ ΕΥΑΓΓΕΛΙΚΗΣ ΠΡΟΠΑΡΑΣΕΥΣ** ΛΟΓΟΙ ΙΕ. *Eusebii Pamphili Evangelicæ Præparationis Liber XV*. Oxford: Typographeo Academico (1843)

Garcia, Pedro. *Petri Garsie Episcopi Usselen. ad sanctissimum patrem et dominum Innocentium papam VIII in determinationes magistrales contra conclusiones apologiales Ioannis Pici Mirandulani Concordie Comitis proemium*. Rome (1489)

Gardiner, Alan. *The Admonitions of an Egyptian Sage, from a Hieratic Papyrus in Leiden (Pap. Leiden 344 recto).* Hildesheim: Georg Olms Verlag (1969)

_____. *Egyptian Grammar. Being an Introduction to the Study of Hieroglyphs. Third edition revised.* Oxford: Griffith Institute (1978)

Gardiner, Alan & T. Eric Peet. *The Inscriptions of Sinai, Vol. 1, Introduction and Plates*. London: The Egyptian Exploration Fund (1917)

Gardiner, Alan, T. Eric Peet & *Jaroslav Černý*. *The Inscriptions of Sinai, Vol. 2, Translations and Commentary*. Oxford: Oxford University Press (1955)

Garnot, Jeane Sainte-Fare. "*Notes on the Inscriptions of Suty and Ḥor,*" *Journal of Egyptian Archaeology, Vol. 35, pp. 43-49.* London: The Egypt Exploration Society. (1949)

Gauthier, Henri. *Catalogue général des antiquites égyptiennes du musée du caire, nos. 41042-41072 Cercueils anthropoides des prètres de Montou. 2 Vols.* Cairo: De L'Institute Français (1913)

_____. *Dictionanaire des noms géographiques contenus dans les textes hiéroglyphiques. 7 Vols.* Cairo: Société Royale de Géographie d'Egypte (1925-1931)

Gerondi, Jacob ben Sheshet. ספר האמונה והבטחון, *Sefer ha-Emunah veha-Bitahon, "The Book of Faith and Confidence."* Warsaw: Be-defus D. Sklover (1842)

Gertner, M. "Terms of Scriptural Interpretation: A Study in Hebrew Semantics."*Bulletin of the School of Oriental and African Studies, University of London. Vol. 25, No. 1/3, pp. 1-27.* London: Cambridge University Press (1962)

*Gesenius' Hebrew-Chaldee Lexicon to the Old Testament Scriptures* (Samuel Prideaux Tregelles ed.). Grand Rapids, MI: Baker Book House (1979)

Gibbon, Edward. *The History of the Decline and Fall of the Roman Empire. Vol. 2.* London: W. Strahan & T. Cadell (1781)

Gifford, E. H. *Eusebii Pamphili Evangelicae Praeparationis Libri XV, Vol. 3, Part 1.* Oxford: Oxford University Pess (1903)

Gikatilla, Joseph be Abraham. ספר ארזי לבנן, *Sefer Arze Lebanon, "Book of the Cedar of Lebanon."* Venice: (1601) <includes מדרש כונן, *Midrash Konen &* ספר האמונה והבטחון, *Sefer ha-Emunah veha-Bitahon.*>

_____. ספר גנת אגוז, *Sefer Ginnat Egoz, "Book of the Garden of Nuts."* Hanau (1615)

_____. ספר שערי אירה, *Sefer Sha'arei Orah, "Book of the Gates of Light."* Offenbach (1715)

_____. (trans. Paulo Riccio) *Portae Lvcis, h[a]ec est porta Tegragram[m]aton iusti intrabu[n]t p[er] eam.* Augsburg: (1516)

Ginsburg, Christian D. *The Kabbalah: its Doctrines, Development, and Literature*. London: Longmans, Green, Header and Dyer. (1865)

Glotzer, Leonard R. *The Fundamentals of Jewish Mysticism*. Northvale, New Jersey: Jason Aronson Inc. (1992)

Godfroy, Jacques. *Philostorgii Cappadocis, Veteris sub Theodosio Ivniore Scriptoris, Ecclestiasticæ Historiæ*. Geneva (1643)

Goodwin, Charles Wycliffe. *Fragment of a Graeco-Egyptian Work upon Magic*. Cambridge:

Deighton, Macmillan and Co. (1852)

_____."Upon an Inscription of the reign of Shabaka," Chabas, *Mélanges Égyptologiques, 3rd Series, Vol. 1, pp. 247-285.* < defective translation of *BM 498*>

Grant, Mary. *The Myths of Hyginius*. Lawrence, KS: University of Kansas Publications. (1960) <Includes the 2nd book of *Poetica Astronomica.*>

Gray, Louis Herbert (ed.) *The Mythology of All Races, Vol. I, Greek and Roman*. Boston: Marshall Jones Co. (1916)

Green, Jay P. *The Interlinear Bible Hebrew/English. 3 vols.* Grand Rapids, MI: Baker Book House (1976)

Grenfell, Alice. "The Ka on Scarabs," *Recueil de travaux relatifs a la philologie et a l'archéologie Égyptiennes et Assyriennes. Vol. 37. pp. 77-93.* Paris: Honoré Champion (1915)

Grimes, John. *Concise Dictionary of Indian Philosophy*. Albany: Suny Press (1996)

Guillaumont, A., H.-Ch Puech, G. Quispel, W. Till & Yassah 'Abd Al Masīh. *The Gospel According to Thomas*. New York: Harper & Row Publishers. (1959)

Gunn, Battiscombe. "The Religion of the Poor in Ancient Egypt," *The Journal of Egyptian Archaeology, Vol. 3, pp. 81-94*. London: The Egypt Exploration Fund (1916)

Gunther, J. Daniel: *The Angel & The Abyss*. Lake Worth, FL: Ibis Press (2014)

_____. *Initiation in the Aeon of the Child, The Inward Journey*. Lake Worth, FL. Ibis Press (2009)

_____. *Opus Alchymicum, An Illuminated Epistle on the Stone of the Philosophers*. Wennofer House (2023)

_____. *Parables of Thelema. Lecture Series Vol. 1.* Wennofer House (2022)

_____. *The Visions of the Pylons, A Magical Record of Exploration in the Starry Abode*. Lake Worth, FL: Ibis Press (2018)

Haaren, John H. and A.B. Poland. *Famous Men of Rome*. New York: American Book Company (1904)

Haleem, M.A.S. Abdel (trans.) *The Qu'ran*. Oxford: Oxford University Press (2005)

Hall, Manly Palmer. *The Secret Teachings Of All Ages*. Los Angeles: The Philosopical Research Society, Inc. Facsimile of First Edition (1971)

Hanegraff, Wouter J. *Esotericism and the Academy, Rejected Knowledge in Western Culture.* Cambridge: Cambridge University Press (2012)

Harris, J. R. *Lexographical Studies in Ancient Egyptian Minerals*. Berlin: Akademie Verlag (1961)

Hart, George. *The Routledge Dictionary of Egyptian Gods and Goddesses*. London: Routledge Taylor & Francis Group. (2005)

Hays, Harold M. *The Organization of the Pyramid Texts, Typology and Disposition. 2 Vols.* Leiden: Brill (2012)

Heinichen, Frederich Adolph. *Eusebii Pamphili de Vita Constantini Libri IVet Panegyricus atque Constantini ad Sanctorum Coetum Oratio*. Leipzig: G. C. Nauckius (1830)

Henderson, Bernard W. *The Life and Principate of the Emperor Nero*. London: Methuen & Co (1903)

Hennecke, Edgar (trans. R. McL. Wilson). *New Testament Apocrypha. 2 Vols.* Philadelphia: The Westminster Press (1963)

*The Holy Bible. Authorized Version. (ed. C. I. Schofield)*. New York: Oxford University Press (1945)

*The Holy Bible containing The Entire Canonical Scriptures According to the Decree of the Council of Trent; translated from The Latin Vulgate: The Old Testament, First Published by the English College at Douay, A.D. 1609. The New Testament, by the English College at Rheims, A.D. 1582. Revised and Corrected According to the Clementine Edition of the Scriptures.* Chicago:

William M. Farrar (1875)

Hone, William. *The Aprocryphal New Testament, being all the Gospels, Epistles, and other Pieces now extant, attributed in the first four Centuries to Jesus Christ, his Apostles, and their Companions, and not included in the New Testament by its Compilers.* London: Ludgate Hill (1820)

Horner, George. *Pistis Sophia.* Society for Promoting Christian Knowledge. London (1924)

Hornung, Erik (trans. David Lorton). *The Ancient Egyptian Books of the Afterlife.* Ithica, NY. Cornell University Press (1999)

_____. *The Egyptian Book of Gates.* Zurich: Living Human Heritage Publications (2014)

Hughes, Thomas Patrick. *A Dictionary of Islam, being A Cyclopaedia of the Doctrines, Rites, Ceremonies, and Customs, together with the Technical and Theological Terms, of the Muhammadan Religion.* London: W.H. Allen & Co. (1885)

Hussey, Robert. **ΕΡΜΕΙΟΥ ΣΟΖΟΜΕΝΟΥ ΕΚΚΛΗΣΙΑΣΤΙΚΗ ΙΣΤΟΡΙΑ.** *Sozomeni Ecclesiastica Historia. 2 Vols.* Oxford: Typhographeo Academico (1860)

Hyginius, Gaius Julius. *Poeticon Astronomicon.* Cologne: Johannes Soter (1539)

_____. FABVLARVM. Lyon: Gaasbekios (1570)

*Index Librorum Prohibitorum, Sanctissimi Domini Nostri pii Sexti Pontificis Maximi Jussu editus.* Rome (1786)

Jastrow, Marcus. *A Dictionary of the Targumim, the Talmud Babli and Yerushalmi, and the Midrashic Literature. 2 Vols.* London: Luzac and Co. (1903)

Jellinek, Adolph. בית המדרש, *Bet ha-Midrash Vol. 2.* Leipzig: F. Nies (1853) <includes מדרש כונן, *Midrash Konen*>

Jerram, C.S. *Euripides, Helena.* Oxford: Clarendon Press (1882)

Jones, A. H. M. *The Later Roman Empire 284-602 A Social Economic and Administrative Survey. 3 Vols.* Oxford: Basil Blackwood (1964)

Jones, Horace Leonard. *The Geography of Strabo. Vol. 8.* London: William Heinemann Ltd. (1967)

Jones, W.H.S. *Pausanias Description of Greece. Vol. 4.* London: William Heinemann Ltd. (1935)

_____. *Pliny Natural History. Vols. 6-9.* Cambridge: Harvard University Press (1951-1963)

*JPS Hebrew-English Tanakh.* Philadelphia: Jewish Publication Society (1999)

Jung, Carl (trans. R.F.C. Hull), *Aion. Second Edition.* Princeton: Princeton University Press (1978)

_____. *Alchemical Studies. Second Edition.* Princeton: Princeton University Press (1976)

_____. *Archetypes of the Collective Unconscious. Second Edition.* Princeton: Princeton University Press (1980)

_____. *Mysterium Coniunctionis. Second Edition.* Princeton: Princeton University Press (1976)

_____. *Psychology and Alchemy.* Princeton: Princeton University Press (1977)

_____. *The Structure and Dynamics of the Psyche. Second Edition.* Princeton: Princeton University Press (1978)

_____. *The Symbolic Life, Miscellaneous Writings.* Princeton: Princeton University Press (1980)

_____. *Symbols of Transformation. Second Edition.* Princeton University Press (1990)

_____. *The Basic Writings of C.G. Jung.* (Violet Staub De Laslo ed.) New York: Random House (1959)

Junge, Freidrich (trans. David Warburton). *Late Egyptian Grammar, an Introduction.* Oxford: Griffith Institute (2005)

Kammerer, Winifred. *A Coptic Bibliography.* Ann Arbor: University of Michigan Press (1950)

Kaplan, Aryeh. *Sefer Yetzirah, The Book of Creation.* York Beach, ME: Samuel Weiser, Inc.

(1990)
Kaczynski, Richard. *Perdurabo. The Life of Aleister Crowley*. Berkeley: North Atlantic Books (2010)
Kane, Thomas Leiper. *Amharic-English Dictionary. 2 Vols*. Wiesbaden: Otto Harrassowitz (1990)
Keightley, Thomas. *The Mythology of Ancient Greece and Italy. Second Edition*. London: Whittaker and Co. (1838)
Kerényi, Carl. *The Gods of the Greeks*. London: Thames and Hudson (1951)
King, C. W. *The Natural History of Gems or Decorative Stones*. Cambridge: Deighton, Bell & Co. (1867)
_____. *The Natural History, Ancient and Modern, of Precious Stones and Gems, and of the Previous Metals*. London: Bell and Daldy (1865)
Kircher, Athanasius. *Œdipus Ægyptiacus. 3 Vols. (4 books)*. Rome (1652-1654)
Kirwan, L.P. "A Survey of Nubian Origins." *Sudan Notes and Records, Vol. 20, No. 1*. Cairo: Hadarat al-Sudan Press (1937):
Kitchen, K.A. *Ramesside Inscriptions Historical and Biographical. 7 Vols*. Oxford: B.H. Blackwell Ltd. (1975-1989)
Kittel, Rudolph. תורה נביאים וכתובים, *Biblia Hebraica. 2 Vols*. Leipzig: J. C. Hinrichs (1906)
Klossowski de Rola, Stanislas. *Alchemy the Secret Art.* : London: Thames and Hudson Ltd. (1973)
_____. *The Golden Game. Alchemical Engravings of the Seventeenth Century*. New York: George Braziller, Inc. (1988)
Knorr von Rosenroth, Christian. *Kabbala Denudata seu Doctrina Hebræorum Transcendentalis et Metaphysica Atque Theologica. 3 Vols. (4 Books)*. Sulzbach: Abrahaam Lichtenthaler (1677)
Lacau, M. Pierre. "Apocalypse de Barthélemy." *Mémoires de l'institut Français d'Archéologie Orientale du Caire.Vol 9. pp. 39 ff.* Cairo (1904)
Lake, Kirsopp & J. E. L. Oulton. *Eusebius. The Ecclestiacal History. 2 Vols*. London: William Heinemann (1926 & 1942)
Lambdin, Thomas O. *Introduction to Sahidic Coptic*. Macon, GA: Mercer University Press (1983)
Lambert, Wilfred G. "Leviathan in Ancient Art." *Shlomo, Studies in Epigraphy, Iconography, History and Archaeology in Honor of Shlomo Moussaieff, pp. 147-154*. Tel Aviv: Archaeological Center Publications (2003)
Lapp, Gunther. *Catalogue of the Books of the Dead in the British Museum,Volume 1, The Papyrus of Nu*. London: Trustees of the British Museum (1997)
Laurence, Richard. *Libri Enoch Prophetæ Versio Æthiopica*. Oxford: Typis Academicis, Impensis Editoris (1838)
_____. *The Book of Enoch The Prophet*. London: Kegan Paul, Trench & Co. (1883)
Layton, Bentley. *The Gnostic Scriptures*. New York: Doubleday (1987)
Lee, Sidney (Ed.) *Dictionary of National Biography. Vol. 51 (Scoffin-Sheares)*. London: Smith, Elder & Co. (1897)
Legrain, Georges. "Textes recueillis dans quelques collections particulières. I. Collection Sabattier," *Recueil de travaux relatifs a la philologie et a l'archéologie Égyptiennes et Assyriennes. Vol. 14, pp. 54-66*. Paris: Emile Bouillon (1893)
Leibovitch, Joseph. "Gods of Agriculture and Welfare in Ancient Egypt," *Journal of Near Eastern Studies, Vol. XII, No. 2*. Chicago: University of Chicago Press (1953)
Lepsius, Karl Richard. *Das Todtenbuch der Ägypter nach dem Hieroglyphischen Papryus in Turin.*

Leipzig: George Wgiand (1842)
Lesko, Barbara. *The Great Goddesses of Egypt.* Norman, OK: University of Oklahoma Press. (1999)
Lesko, Leonard H. *A Dictionary of Late Egyptian. 4 Vols.* Providence, RI.: B.C. Scribe Publications (1982-1989)
Lete, Gergorio del Olmo & Joaquin Sanmartin. (trans. & ed.) Wilfred G.E. Watson) *A Dictionary of the Ugaritic Language in the Alphabetic Tradition. Third revised edition.* Leiden: Brill (2015)
Leunclavius, Johannes. *Zosimi Comitis ex Exadvocati Fisci, Historiae Novae.* Basil (1576)
Lévi, Éliphas. *Dogme et rituel de la haute magie. 2 Vols.* Paris: Germer Baillière (1861)
_____. *La clef des grands mystères.* Paris: Germer Baillière (1861)
_____. *La science des esprits.* Paris: Germer Baillière (1865)
_____. (trans. A.E. Waite).*The Mysteries of Magic. Second edition, revised and enlarged.* London: Kegan Paul, Trench, Trübner & Co. (1897)
Lewis, Charlton T. and Charles Short. *A Latin Dictionary.* Oxford: The Clarendon Press (1945)
Lichtheim, Miriam. *Ancient Egyptian Literature. 3 Vols.* Berkeley: University of California Press (1973-1980) <Vol. 1, pp. 51-57 includes translation only of *BM 498*>
Liddell, George H. & Scott, Robert. *A Greek-English Lexicon.* Oxford: The Clarendon Press (1968)
Lieblein, Jens. *Dictionnaire de noms hiéroglyphiques en ordre généalogique et alphabétique. 2 Vols.* Leipzig: J. C. Hinrichs (1871-1892)
Liftin, Bryan M. "Eusebius on Constantine: Truth and Hagiography at the Milvian Bridge." *Journal of the Evangelical Theological Society, Vol. 55, No. 4, pp. 773-792.* Scottsville, AZ (2012)
Lightfoot, John. *A Commentary On the New Testament From The Talmud and Hebraica.* Grand Rapids: Baker Book House (1979) Facsimile of the Oxford 1859 edition
Loomis, Louise Ropes. *The Book of the Popes (Liber Pontificalis), Vol. I, To the Pontificate of Gregory I.* New York: Columbia University Press (1916)
Lowe, John. *The Yew-Trees of Great Britain and Ireland.* London: Macmillan and Co. (1897)
Lucas, A. *Ancient Egyptian Materials & Industries. Second edition revised.* London: Edward Arnold & Co. (1934)
Macdermot, Violet. *The Concept of Pleroma in Gnosticism.* Leiden: E. J. Brill (1981)
Macdonell, Arthur. *A Sanskrit – English Dictionary.* London: Longmans Green & Co. (1893)
_____. *Hymns From the Rigveda.* Calcutta: Association Press (1922)
Mackey, Albert G. *A New and Revised Edition of An Encyclopedia of Freemasonry and its kindred sciences comprising the whole range of arts, sciences and literature as connected with the Institution. 3 Vols.* Chicago: The Masonic History Company (1921)
Maier, Michael. *Arcana Arcanissima hoc est Hieroglyhica Aegyptio-*Graeca. London (1614)
_____. *Atalanta Fugiens.* Oppenheim: (1617)
_____. *De Circulo Physico, Qadrato.* Oppenheim (1618)
_____. *Secretioris Naturæ Secretorum Scrutinium Chymicum.* Frankfurt (1687)
_____. *Symbola Aureæ Mensæ Duodecim Nationum.* Frankfurt (1817)
_____. *Tripus Aureus, Tres Tractatus Chymici Selectissimi.* Frankfurt (1618)
_____. *Viatorium, Hoc Est, De Montibus Planetarum Septem Seu Metallorum.* Oppenheim (1618)
_____. *Viridarium Chymicum.* Frankfurt (1688)
Mallinson, James. *The Shiva Samhita, a Critical Edition and An English Translation.* Woodstock,

NY: YogaVidya.com (2007)

Mansour, Ahmed. "The Serabit el-Khadim Inscriptions, Formulaic Approach." *Abgadiyat, Issuue No. 6, 2011.* Leiden: Brill.

Marchant, J.R.V. and Joseph F. Charles (ed.). *Appleton's Latin Dictionary*. New York: D. Appleton and Company. (1904)

*Masechet Chagiga min Talmud Bavli*. Prague: Druck und Verlag des M.I. Landau (1841)

Maspero, Gaston. "Notes sur quelques points de grammaire et d'historie," *Recueil de travaux relatifs a la philologie et a l'archéologie Égyptiennes et Assyriennes,Vol. 2, pp.105-120.* Paris: F. Vieweg (1880)

Mathers, S.L. Macgregor. *Kabbala Denudata, The Kabbalah Unveiled*. London: George Redway. (1887)

_____. *The Key of Solomon the King (Clavicula Salomonis)*. London: George Redway (1889)

Matt, Daniel C. *The Zohar Pritzker Edition. 12 Vols.* Stanford: Stanford University Press (2003-2017)

McLean, Norman. *The Ecclesiastical History of Eusebius in Syriac*. Cambridge: Cambridge University Press (1898)

Mendelssohn, Ludwig. *Zosimi comitis et exadvocati fisci Historia Nova*. Leipzig: Teubner (1887)

Merry, W. Walter. *Homer's Odyssey. 2 Vols.* Oxford: The Clarendon Press (1886)

Meyer, Leo. *Handbuch der Griechischen Etymologie. 4 Vols.* Leipzig: Hirzel (1901-1902)

Meyer, Marvin W. *The Mithras Liturgy*. Missoula, MT: Scholars Press (1976)

*Midrash Konen*: **מדרש כינן**, *On the Creation, the Heavens and Hell*. Vilna: Abraham Isaac Dvoretz (1836)

Migne, Jaques Paul. *Patrologiae Cursus Completus. Series Graeca, Vol. 96,* **ΙΩΝΝΟΥ, ΤΟΥ ΔΑΜΑΣΣΚΗΝΟΟΥ**, *Joannis Damasceni, Opera Omnia quae exstant.* Paris (1864)

_____. *Patrologiae Cursus Completus. Series Latina, Vol.7, Lucii Cæcilii Firmiani Lactantii Opera Omnia.* Paris: (1844)

_____. *Patrologiae Cursus Completus. Series Latina, Vol. 103. S. Benedicti / Sedulii Junioris Natione Scoti.* Paris (1864)

Milan, S. C. *The Book of Adam and Eve, also called, The Conflict of Adam and Eve With Satan*. G. Norman & Son. London (1882)

Miles, Margaret R. *A Complex Delight: The Secularization of the Breast, 1350-1750*. Berkeley: University of California Press (2008)

Miller, Frank Justus. *Ovid, Metamorphoses, Vol. 1.* Cambridge: Harvard University Press (1951)

Milton, John. *Paradise Lost. A Poem in Twelve Books*. London (1746)

Moakley, Gertrude. *The Tarot Cards Painted by Bonifacio Bembo for the Visconti-Sforza Family*. New York: The New York Public Library (1966)

Mohr, Paul. C. *Sollius Apollinaris Sidonius*. Leipzig: B. G. Teubner (1895)

Molen, Rami van der. *A Hieroglyphic Dictionary of Egyptian Coffin Texts*. Leiden: E. J. Brill (2000)

Möller, Georg. *Hieratische Paläographie*. 4 Vols. Leipzig: J. C. Hinrichs'sche Buckhandlung (1909-1936)

Mombrizio, Bonino (Mombritius). *Santuarium seu Vitate Sanctorum, Vol. 2.* Paris: Albert Fontemoing (1910) <includes *Vita Silvestri*.>

Monier-Williams, Monier. *A Sanskrit-English Dictionary*. Oxford: Oxford University Press (1960)

Moret, Alexandre. *Catalogue général des antiquites égyptiennes du musée du caire, n$^{os}$. 41001-41041, sarcophages de l'epoque bubastite a l'epoque saite, Vol. 2.* Cairo: De L'Institute Français

(1913)
Most, Glenn W. *Hesiod, Theogony, Works and Days, Testimonia.* Cambridge: Harvard University Press (2006)
Müller, Max (trans. & ed.) *The Sacred Books Of The East. Vols 1 and 15, The Upanishads Part I & II.* Oxford: The Clarendon Press (1879 and 1884)
_____. (trans. & ed.) E. H. Palmer) *The Sacred Books Of The East. Vols VI and IX, The Qur'ân Parts 1 & 2.* Oxford: The Clarendon Press (1880)
Murray, A.T. *Homer, The Iliad.* Vol. 1. Cambridge: Harvard University Press. (1946)
*Musæum Hermeticum Reformatum et Amplificatum.* Frankfurt: Hermann Sande (1678)
Mylius, Johann Daniel. *Anatomia Auri sive Tyrocinium Medico-Chymicum.* Frankfurt: Lucas Jennis (1628)
______. *Philosophia Reformata.* Frankfurt: Lucas Jennis (1622)
*Nag Hammadi Tractate_II, 2_The Gospel of Thomas*
*Nag Hammadi Tractate_II, 4_The Hypostasis of the Archons*
*Nag Hammadi Tractate II, 5 On the Origin of the World*
*Nag Hammadi Tractate III, 2 & IV, 2. The Gospel of the Egyptians*
*The Nag Hammadi Library in English* (trans. Members of the Coptic Gnostic Library Project for the Institute for Antiquity and Christianity) San Francisco: Harper & Row (1977)
Naville, Edouard. *Das aegyptische Todtenbuch der XVIII bis XX Dynastie. 3 Vols.* Elibron Classics, facsimile reprint of 1886 edition.
Nelson, Harold Hayden. *The Great Hypostyle Hall at Karnak (Oriental Institute Publications, Vol. 106).* Chicago: The Oriental Institite of the University of Chicago (1981)
Nelson, R. J. *Eutropius and Aurelius Victor, with vocabulary.* Edinburgh: Oliver & Boyd (1865)
Neumann, Erich (trans. Ralph Manheim). *The Great Mother. An Analysis of the Archetype.* Princeton, NJ: Princeton University Press (1974)
_____. (trans. R.F.C. Hull). *The Origins and History of Consciousness.* Princeton, NJ: Princeton University Press (1973)
*New Shorter Oxford English Dictionary. 2 Vols.* (ed. Leslie Brown). Oxford: Clarendon Press (1993)
Olivelle, Patrick. *The Early Upanishads, annotated text and translation.* Oxford: Oxford University Press (1998)
Olmo Lete, Gregorio del & Joaquín Sanmartín. *A Dictionary of the Ugaritic Language in the Alphabetic Tradition, Part One [a/i/u – k].* Leiden: E. J. Brill (2003)
Ouda, Ahmed M. Mekawy. "Did Werethekau 'Great of Magic' have a Cult?: A Disjunction between Scholarly Opinions and Sources," Cairo: *The German Archaeological Institute Cairo, Young Researchers' Lecture Series (2013).*
_____. "Werethekau and the votive stela of *p3-n-'Imn* (Bristol Museum H 514)," London: *British Museum Studies in Ancient Egypt and Sundan 22* (2015)
_____. "Who or What is Werethekau 'Great of Magic', A Problematic Inscription (UC 16639)." Cairo: *Papers from the Institute of Archaeology, pp. 1-7.* (2013)
*Oxford Arabic Dictionary* (Tressy Arts ed.) Oxford: Oxford University Press (2014)
*Oxford Latin Dictionary.* (A.N. Bryan-Brown ed.) Oxford: The Clarendon Press (1968)
Paley, F.A. *The Epics of Hesiod.* London: Bell & Sons (1883)
Parker, Samuel. *Eusebius Pamphilus His Ten Books of Ecclesiastical History, Faithfully and Abridg'd from the Original.* London *(1703)*
Parthey, Gustav. *Jamblichi, De Mysteriis Liber.* Leipzig. Teubner (1857)
Patai, Raphael. *Encyclopedia of Jewish Folklore and Traditions.* New York: Routledge (2013)

Paton, W.R. *The Greek Anthology. Vol. 3*. London: William Heinemann (1925)

Peck, A. L. *Aristotle Historia Animalium, Vol. 2 (Books IV-VI)*. Cambridge: Harvard University Press (1984)

Pelam, Henry Francis (ed. F. Haverfield). *Essays by Henry Francis Pelham*. Oxford: The Clarendon Press (1911) < includes *The Early Roman Emperors (Caesar-Nero)*>

Pelle, Stephen Anthony. *Continuity and Renewal in English Homiletic Eschatology, ca. 1150-1200*. Toronto: Centre for Medieval Studies, University of Toronto (2012)

Pernety, Antoine Joseph. *Dictionnaire Mytho-Hermétique. 2 Vols*. Paris: Bauche (1758)

Pesenti, Giovanni. *De Mortibus Persecutorum*. Turin: In Aedibus Io. Bapt.Paraviae et Sociorum (1922)

Pettigrew, Thomas Joseph. *On Superstitions connected with the History and Practice of Medicine and Surgery*. Philadelphia: Barrington and Haswell (1844)

Piankoff, Alexander. *Mythological Papyri. 2 Vols. Bollingen Series 40*. Princeton University Press, New York (1957)

_____. *The Tomb of Rameses VI. Bollingen Series 40/1*. Pantheon Books, New York (1954)

Pichlmayr, Franciscus. *Sexti Aurelii Victoris Liber de Caesaribus, Praecedunt Origo Gentis Romanae et Liber De Viris Illustribus Urbis Romae Subsequitur Epitome De Caesaribus*. Leipzig: B.G. Teubner (1911)

Pico della Mirandola, Giovanni. *Opera Omnia, Ioannis Pici, Mirandvlæ*. Basil (1557)

Piel, Karl. *Inscriptions Hiéroglyphiques. Premiere Partie: Planches*. Leipzig: J.C.Hinrich'sche Buckhandlung

Pike, Albert. *Morals and Dogma of the Ancient and Accepted Scottish Rite of Freemasonry*. Washington, DC: The Supreme Council 33°, Southern Jurisdiction (1916)

Pistorius, Johann. *Artis Cabalisticæ: hoc est, Reconditæ Theologiæ et Philosophiæ. Vol. 1*. Basil (1587)

Plaistowe, F.G. *Aristophanes: Ranae*. London: W.B. Clive (1896)

Pogue, Joseph E. "The Turquoise. A Study of its History, Mineralogy, Geology, Ethnology, Archæology, Mythology, Folklore, and Technology." *National Academy of Sciences, Volume XII, Part II, Third Memoir*. Washington, DC (1915)

Povarsky, Rabbi Baruch Dov., ספר בד קודש חידושים וביאורי סוגיות בבא בתרא,"*The Book of Holy Cloth. Innovations & Explanations. Baba Batra.*" Bnai Brak, Israel: Institute for the Translation of Hebrew Literature. (2009)

Preisendanz, Karl. *Papyri Graecae Magicae*, Vol. 1. Leipzig: Teubner (1928)

Price, Richard. "In Hoc Signo Vinces: The Original Context of the Vision of Constantine," *Signs, Wonders, Miracles: Representations of the Divine Power in the Life of the Church. Studies in Church History 41. pp. 1-10*. Woodbridge, UK: The Boydell Press (2004)

Quarles, Francis. *Emblems Divine and Moral*. London (1790)

Quirke, Stephen. *Egyptian Literature 1800 BC questions and readings*. London: Golden House Books (2004)

_____. *Going out in Daylight, prt m hrw, the Ancient Egyptian Book of the Dead, translation, sources, meanings*. Croydon, London: Golden House Books (2013)

Rackham, Harris. *Aristotle, The Nichomachean Ethics*. Cambridge: Harvard University Press (1926)

_____. *Cicero in Twenty-eight Volumes. Vol. 19. De Natura Deorum Academica*. Cambridge: Harvard University Press (1933)

_____ *Pliny, Natural History. Vols. 1-5 & 9*. Cambridge: Harvard University Press (1938-1952)

Ranke, Hermann. *Die Ägyptischen Personennamen*. 3 Vols. Glückstadt: J. J. Augustin (1935-

1976)

Raymond, Xavier M. *Inde, par M. Dubois de Jancigny*. Paris: Firmin Didot Frères (1845)

Read, F.W. and A.C. Bryant."A Mythological Text from Memphis," *Proceedings of the Society of Biblical Archaeology. Vol. XXIII, pp. 160-187.* London: (1901) < defective translation of BM 498>

Reed, J. Eugene. *The Lives of The Roman Emperors and Their Associates from Julius Cæsar (B.C. 100) to Augustulus (A.D. 476)*. Philadelphia: Gebbie & Co. Publishers (1884)

Regardie, Francis Israel. *The Golden Dawn. Fifth edition.* St. Paul: Llewellyn (1986)

Reichel, Oswald J. *The See of Rome in the Middle Ages*. London: Longmans, Green, and Co. (1870)

Reitemeier, Johann Friedrich: *Zosimus Historiae Graece et Latine*. Weidmann (1784)

Renou, Jean D. (Renodaeus). *Dispensatorium Medicum, Continens Institutionum Pharmaceuticarum*. Frankfort (1615)

Respour, P. M. *Versuche vom Mineral-Geist* (1772)

Richardson, John, Charles Wilkins & Francis Johnson. *A Dictionary, Persian, Arabic, and English.* London: (1829)

Rodkinson, Michael L. *New Edition of the Babylonian Talmud, 10 Vols*. New York: New Talmud Publishing Co. (1899) <incomplete translation of the Babylonian Talmud.>

Rodrigues, E.A. *The Complete Hindoo Pantheon, comprising the Principal Deities worshipped by the Natives of British India throughout Hindoostan, being a Collection of the Gods and Goddesses, Accompanied by a Succint History and Descriptive of The Idols. Deduced from Original and Authentical Manuscripts and also Extracts from Standard Authors.* Vepery (1842)

Rolfe, John C. *Ammianus Marcellinus. 3 Vols.* London: William Heinemann Ltd. (1935-1939)

_____. *Suetonius. 2 Vols*. Cambridge: Harvard University Press (1979)

Roth, Karl Ludwig. *C. Suetoni Tranquilli quae supersunt omnia.* Leipzig: B. G. Teubner (1875)

Rudolph, Kurt. *Gnosis, The Nature and History of Gnosticism.* San Francisco: Harper SanFrancisco (1987)

Ruland, Martin. *Lexicon Alchemiæ sive Dictionarivm Alchemisticvm.* Frankfurt: Zacharias Palthenius (1612)

_____. (ed. A. E. Waite). *A Lexicon of Alchemy*. York Beach, ME: Weiser (1984)

Russell, Bertrand. *History of Western Philosophy and its Connection with Political and Social Circumstances from the Earliest Times to the Present Day.* London: George Allen & Unwin Ltd. (1955)

Rustafjaell, Robert. *The Light of Egypt, From Recently Discovered Predynastic and Early Christian Records*. London: Kegan Paul, Trench Trübner & Co. (1909)

Sarwar, Ghulam. *Translation of The Holy Qur-an*. Woking, Surry: S.M.S. Faruque (1930)

Satzinger, Helmut. *Zwei Wiener Objekte mit bemerkenswerten Inschriften*, in *Mélanges Gamal Eddin Mokhtar, pp. 249-254.* Cairo: Institut Français d'Archéologie Orientale. (1985)

Schaff, Philip and Henry Wace (eds.) *A Select Library of Nicene and Post-Nicene Fathers of the Christian Church. Second Series. Vol. 1. Eusebius: Church History, Life of Constantine the Great, and Oration in Praise of Constantine. Vol. 2. Socrates, Sozomenus: Church Histories.* Oxford and London: Parker & Company (1890)

Scheil, V. "Textes égyptiens divers du musée de constantinople." *Recueil de travaux relatifs a la philologie et a l'archéologie Égyptiennes et Assyriennes. Vol. 15.* Paris: Emile Bouillon (1893)

Schmidt, Carl. *Pistis Sophia, Neu Herausgegeben, Mit Einleitung Nebst Grieschischem und Koptischem Wort- Und Namenregister.* Copenhagen: Gyldendalske Boghandel-Nordisk Forlag (1925)

Schmidt, Carl & Violet Macdermot. *Pistis Sophia*, (text ed. Carl Schmidt, trans. and notes by Violet Macdermot). Leiden: E. J.Brill (1978)

Schodde, George H. *The Book of Enoch translated from the Ethiopic*. Andover: Warren F.Draper (1882)

Scholem, Gershom. *Kabbalah*. New York: Quadrangle (1974)

_____. לחקר קבלת ר' יצחק בן יעקב הכהן, '*Le-Ḥeker Kabbalat R. Yitshak ben Ya'akov Ha-Kohen*,' in תרביץ / *Tarbiz* 4:2. Jerusalem: Mandel Institute for Jewish Studies (1933)

_____ *Origins of the Kabbalah*. Princeton: Princeton University Press (1987)

Scholfield, A.F. *Aelian*, Περὶ ζῴων ἰδιότητος, *On the Characteristics of Animals. Vol. 2*. London: William Heinemann (1959)

Schwartz, Eduard. *Eusebius Werke, Vol. 1*. Leipzig: J. C. Hinrichs'sche Buckhandlung (1903)

Scot, Reginald. *The discouerie of witchcraft, Wherein the lewde dealing of witches and witchmongers is notablie detected, the knauerie of coniurors, the impietie of inchantors, the follie of soothsaiers, the impudent falshood of cousenors, the infidelitie of atheists, the pestilent practises of Pythonists, the curiositie of figurecrafters, the vanitie of dreamers, the beggerlie art of Alcumystrie, The abhomination of idolatrie, the horrible art of poisoning, the vertue and power of naturall magike, and all the conueiances of Legierdemaine and iuggling are deciphered: and many other things opened, which haue long lien hidden, howbeit verie necessarie to be knowne. Heervnto is added a treatise vpon the nature and substance of spirits and diuels, &c.* London (1584)

Seaton, *Apollonius Rhodius, The Argonautica*. London: William Heinemann (1919)

*The* SEPTUAGINT *Version of the Old Testament with an English Translation*. Grand Rapids, MI: Zondervan (1978) <Facsimile of 1884 edition by Samuel Bagster and Sons, Limited. London>

Sethe, Kurt. *Die Altaegyptischen Pyramidentexte nach den Papierabdrücken und Photographien des Berliner Museums*. Leipzig: J.C.Hinrich'sche Buckhandlung. (1908 & 1910).

_____. *Untersuchungen Zur Geschichte und Altertumskunde Ägyptens/Band X. Dramatischetexte Zu Altegyptishchen Mysterienspielen*. Leipzig (1928) < includes text and translation of BM 498>

Sharpe, Samuel. *The Alabaster Sarcophagus of Oimeneptah I, King of Egypt*. London: Longman, Green, Longman, Roberts and Green (1864)

Shoemann, George Frideric. *Comparatio Theogoniae Hesiodeae*. Leipzig: Weidmenn (1847)

Sinha, Purnendu Narayana. *A Study of the Bhagavata Purana or Esoteric Hinduism*. Benares: Freeman & Co. (1901)

Skeat, Walter W. *A Concise Etymological Dictionary of the English Language*. London: Oxford University Presss. (1885)

Skinner, Stephen (ed.). *The Magical Diaries of* ΤΟ ΜΕΓΑ ΘΗΡΙΟΝ *The Beast 666 Aleister Crowley* ΛΟΓΟΣ ΑΙΩΝΟΣ ΘΕΛΗΜΑ *93 - 1923*. York Beach, ME: Weiser (1981)

Smith, Marcell N. *Diamonds, Pearls and Precious Stones*. Boston: Smith Patterson Company (1913)

Smith, Mark S. *The Ugaitic Baal Cycle, Vol.1. Introduction with Text, Translation & Commentary of KTU 1.1-1.2*. Leiden: E. J. Brill (1994)

Smith, William. *Dictionary of Greek and Roman Biography and Mythology. 3 Vols*. London: John Murray (1880)

Sonnerat, Pierre. *Voyages aux Indes orientales et a la Chine, Vol.* 1. Paris (1782)

Spiegelberg, Wilhelm. *Koptisches Handwörterbuch*. Heidelberg: Carl Winters Universitätsbuchhandlung. (1921)

Stallbaum, Johann Gottfried. *Eustatii Archiepiscopi Thessalonicensis Commentarii ad Homeri Iliadem. 5 Vols.* Leipzig: J. A. G. Weigel. (1827-1838)

_____. *Platonis Opera Omnia Uno Volumine Comprehensa.* Leipzig: Otto Holtze. (1881)

Steinschneider, E. *Alphabetum Siracidis utrumque, cum expositione antiquâ.* Berlin: A. Friedlaender (1858) < *The Alphabet of Ben Sira* in Hebrew>

Stern, David & Mark Jay Mirsky. *Rabbinic Fantasies: Imaginative Narratives from Classical Hebrew Literature.* Skokie, IL: Varda Books (2001)

Stoltz, Daniel. *Vidarium Chymicum Figuris Cupro Incisis Adorantum, et Poeticis Picturis Illustratum.* Frankfurt (1624)

Stone, Michael E. "Two Unpublished Eschatological Texts," *Journal for the Study of the Pseudoepigrapha, Vol. 18, 4.* Thousand Oaks, CA: Sage Publications (2009)

*Streane, A. W.* חגיגה*, A Translation of the Treatise Chagigah from the Babalonian Talmud. Cambridge: The University Press. (1891)*

Strong, Eugénie Sellers. *Apotheosis and after life.* London: Constable (1915)

Strong, James. *Strong's Exhaustive Concordance.* Vancouver: Praise *Bible* Publishers, Ltd. [no date].

Sylburg, Frederic (Ed.) *Etymologicon Magnum seu Magnum Grammaticae Penu.* Leipzig: Weigel (1816)

Tattam, Henry. *Lexicon Ægyptico-Latinum.* Oxford: E Typographeo Academico (1835)

Te Velde, Herman. *Seth, God of Confusion. A Study of His Role in Egyptian Mythology and Religion.* Leiden: E. J. Brill (1967)

Tennyson, Alfred. *The Complete Poetical Works of Alfred, Lord Tennyson, Poet Laureate.* New York: Harper & Brothers Publishers (1884)

Thomassetti, Luigi & Charles Cocquelines (ed.) *Bullarum Diplomatum et Privilegiorum Sanctorum Romanorum Pontificum Taurinensis Editio, Vol. 5.* Turin: Franco et Henrico Dalmazzo (1860)

Thomson, Alexander. *The Lives of the Twelve Cæsars by C. Suetonius Tranquillus. Vol. 2.* Philadelphia: Gebbie & Co. Publishers (1889)

Trench, Richard Chenevix. *Synonyms of the New Testament*, Grand Rapids, MI: Wm B. Eerdmans Publishing Co. (1978)

Valarsi, Dominic. *Sancti Eusebii Hieronymi Stridonensis Presbyteri Operum, Vol. 2.* Verona (1735) <Chapter 80 contains *De Viris Illustribus* with Jerome's mention of *De Mortibus Persecutorum* in 392-393 CE, prior to its discovery in 1678 CE.>

Valla, Lorenzo. *De Falso Credita & Emenita Constantini M. Imp. Ro. Donatione Declamatio.* Leiden: Jacob Marci (1620)

Valoi, Henri (Henricus Valensus). **ΣΟΚΡΑΤΟΥΣ ΣΧΟΛΑΣΤΙΚΟΥ ΚΑΙ ΕΡΜΕΙΟΥ ΣΟΖΟΜΕΝΟΥ ΕΚΚΛΗΣΙΑΣΤΙΚΗ ΙΣΤΟΡΙΑ ΕΚΛΟΓΑΙ ΑΠΟ ΤΩΝ ΙΣΤΟΡΙΩΝ ΦΙΛΟΣΤΟΡΓΙΟΥ ΚΑΙ ΘΕΟΔΩΡΟΥ**. *Socratis Scholastici et Hermiae Sozumeni Historia Ecclesiastica Item Excerpta ex Historiis Philostorgii et Theodori Lectoris.* Paris (1668)

Vandier, J. *La tombe de nefer-abou.* Cairo: Imprimerie de l'Institut Français. (1935)

Van Vreeswijk, Goosen. *De Cabinet der Mineralen of De Goude Son.* Amsterdam (1675)

_____. *De Groene Leeuw.* Amsterdam (1674)

_____. *De Roode Leeuw.* Amsterdam (1674)

Vasu, Chandra *The Sacred Books of the Hindus*, Vol. 15 *The Yoga Sastra.* Allahabad (1914) < *The Śiva Saṃhitā*, incomplete, and the translation is considered inaccurate.>

Vaughn, Robert. Tracts *& Treatises of John De Wycliffe, D.D.* London: Blackburn & Pardon (1845)

Verman, Mark. *The Books of Contemplation.* Albany: State University of New York Press (1992)

Vivekananda. *Raja Yoga*. London: Kegan Paul, Trench Trübner & Co., Ltd. (1893)

Volten, Aksel. "Zwei altägyptische politische Schriften die Lehre für König Merikarê," *Alanecta Aegyptiaca, Vol. 4*. Copenhagen: Einar Munksgaard (1945)

Vreeswyk, Goosen van. *De Goude Leeuw, of den Asinj der Wysen*. Amsterdam (1671)

Vycichl, Werner. *Dictionnaire Étymologique de la Langue Copte*. Leuven: Peeters (1983)

Waite, Arthur Edward. *The Brotherhood of The Rosy Cross*. Secaucus, NJ: University Books, (1973)

_____. *The Doctrine and Literature of the Kabalah*. London: Theosophical Publishing Society. (1886)

_____. *The Hermetic Museum*. York Beach, ME: Weiser (1990)

_____. *The Holy Kabbalah*. New York: Carol Publishing Group (1990)

_____. *The Pictorial Key to the Tarot*. Harper & Row (1980)

Walch, Christian Wilhelm Franz. *A Compendious History of the Popes, from the Foundation of the See of Rome to the present Time*. London (1759)

Walford, Edward. *The Ecclesiastical History of Sozomen comprising a History of the Church, from A.D. 324 to A.D. 440 also The Ecclesiastical History of Philostorgius, as Epitomized by Photius, Patriarch of Constantinople*. London: Henry G. Bohn (1855)

Walker, Benjamin. *Hindu World: An Encyclopedic Survey of Hinduism*. 2 Vols. London: Routledge, Taylor & Francis Group (2019)

Ward, William A. *Index of Egyptian Administrative and Religious Titles of the Middle Kingdom*. Beirut: American University of Beirut (1982)

Wilcox, Robert & Emma M. Whitham, "The Symbol of Modern Medicine: why one name is more than two." *Annals of Internal Medicine, Vol. 138, 8*. Philadelphia: American College of Physicians (2003)

Wilder, Alexander. *Theurgia or The Egyptian Mysteries by Iamblichos*. New York: Metaphysical Publishing House (1911)

Wilkinson, Richard. *The Complete Gods and Goddesses of Ancient Egypt*. London. Thames & Hudson. (2020)

Wilson, John A. *The Intellectual Adventure of Early Man. An Essay on Speculative Thought in the Ancient Near East*, pp. 55-60. Chicago: University of Chicago Press (1946)

Wilson, Penelope. *A Ptolmemaic Lexikon, A Lexicographical Study of the Texts in the Temple of Edfu*. Leuven: Peeters (1997)

Winkelmann, Friedhelm. *Eusebius Werke, Über Das Leben des Kaisers Konstantin. Vol. 1, Part 1*. Berlin: Akademie Verlag (1975)

Wither, George. *A Collection of Emblemes, Ancient and Moderne: Quickened VVith Metricall Illvstrations, both Morall and Divine: And disposed into Lotteries, That Instruction, and Good Counsell, may bee furthered by an Honest and Pleasant Recreation. Vol. 1*. London (1635)

Woods, David. "On the Death of the Empress Fausta," *Greece & Rome, Vol. xlv, No. 1*. Cambridge: Cambridge University Press (1998)

Wortabet, William Thomson. *Arabic-English Dictionary*. Beirut: Al-Muktataf Press (1893)

Wreszinski, Walter. *Atlas zur altägyptischen Kulturgeschichte, Vol. 1*. Leipzig: J. C. Hinrichs'sche Buckhandlung (1923)

Zeumer, Karl. "Der älteste Text des Constitutum Constantini," *Festgabe for Rudolf von Gneist, pp. 37-60*. Berlin: Julius Springer (1888)

## III. Papyri, Stelae, Coffin Texts and Tomb Inscriptions Utilized


6th Dynasty Pyramid of , *Meryra* (Pepy I)

6th Dynasty Pyramid of , *Neferkara (Pepy II)*

6th Dynasty Pyramid of , *Teti I*

11th Dynasty Coffin of , *Horhotep* (Cairo CG 28023)

11th Dynasty Inner Coffins of , *Djehutynakht* (Boston 21.962-65)

12th Dynasty Inner & Outer Coffin of , *Iha* (Cairo CG 28089-CG 28090)

12th Dynasty Outer Coffin of 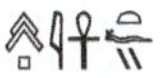, *Hapiankhtyfy* (Met. Mus. of Art 12.183.11a)

12th Dynasty Outer Coffin of , *Neferi* (Cairo CG 28088)

12th Dynasty Outer Coffin of , *Sen* (BM EA308041)

12th Dynasty Coffin of , *Sepi* (Cairo CG 28083)

18th Dynasty Stele of , *Ipuy* (Wien 8390)

18th Dynasty Tomb of , *Khaemhat* (TT 57)

18th Dynasty Papyrus of , *Mesemnether* (Louvre E21324)

18th Dynasty Papyrus of , *Nebseny* (BM EA9900)

18th Dynasty Papyrus of 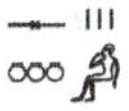, *Nu* (BM EA10477)

18th Dynasty Papyrus, *The Teachings for King* , *Merykara* (Hermitage 116A)

19th Dynasty Papyrus of an unnamed man (Dublin 1661)

19th Dynasty Papyrus of , *Any* (BM EA10470)

19th Dynasty Stele of , *Mutnefert* (Museo Egizio S.6138)

19th Dynasty Papyrus of 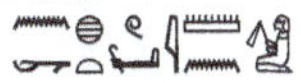, *Nakhtamun* (Berlin 3002)

19th Dynasty Stele of , *Neferabu* (BM EA 589, *verso*)

19th Dynasty Stele of , *Neferabu* (Museo Egizio1593)

19th Dynasty Stele of , *Pay* (Museo Egizio1553)

19th-20th Dynasty Papyrus of , *Ptahmes* (Busca, Milan)

19th Dynasty Papyrus of , *Qenena* (Leiden T2)

19th Dynasty Sarcophagus of 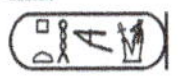, *Sety-Mery-Ptah* (*Sety I*) (Sloan Museum SM M470)

21st Dynasty Papyrus of , *Herweben* (Cairo SR 19325)

26th Dynasty Stele of , *Ankhefenkhonsu I* (Cairo A9422)

26th Dynasty Stele of 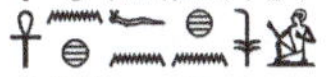, *Ankhefenkhonsu II* (Istanbul 190)

26th Dynasty Stele of , *Ankhefenkhonsu VI* (BM 22914)

26th Dynasty Sarcophagus of , *Hor* (Cairo CG 41017)

26th Dynasty Inner Coffin of , *Neseramun II* (Cairo CG 41044)

26th Dynasty Stele of , *Tairi II* (Cairo SR 9914)

Ptolmaic Period Papyrus of , *Iufankh* (Turin 1791)

# About the Author

J. Daniel Gunther is considered one of the foremost scholar-practitioners of Thelema. He has authored several books that focus on the theology of Thelema while drawing on his extensive knowledge of Egyptology, Jungian Psychology, Qabalah, Alchemy, Gnosticism and Philosophy. He is also the artist and writer of an original work on mystical Alchemy titled: *Opus Alchymicum*. Gunther's overview on the history of academic research in Egyptian religion and philology is published in the 20th Anniversary Edition of the *Egyptian Book of the Dead*, by *Chronicle Books*.

J. Daniel Gunther has lectured extensively worldwide and his works have been translated into multiple languages.

**www.jdanielgunther.com**

Parties interested in contacting the A∴A∴
may address their correspondence to:

Chancellor
BM ANKH
London WC1N 3XX
ENGLAND

www.outercol.org

www.ingramcontent.com/pod-product-compliance
Lightning Source LLC
Chambersburg PA
CBHW080931020526
44118CB00038B/2449
*9780999593684*